Sh[...] Beat

MANGA from the HEART

OTOMEN

STORY AND ART BY
AYA KANNO

VAMPIRE KNIGHT

STORY AND ART BY
MATSURI HINO

Natsume's BOOK of FRIENDS

STORY AND ART BY
YUKI MIDORIKAWA

Want to see more of what you're looking for?

Let your voice be heard!

shojobeat.com/mangasurvey

Help us give you more manga from the heart!

RATED T FOR TEEN ratings.viz.com
RATED T+ FOR OLDER TEEN ratings.viz.com
VIZ media www.viz.com

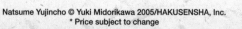

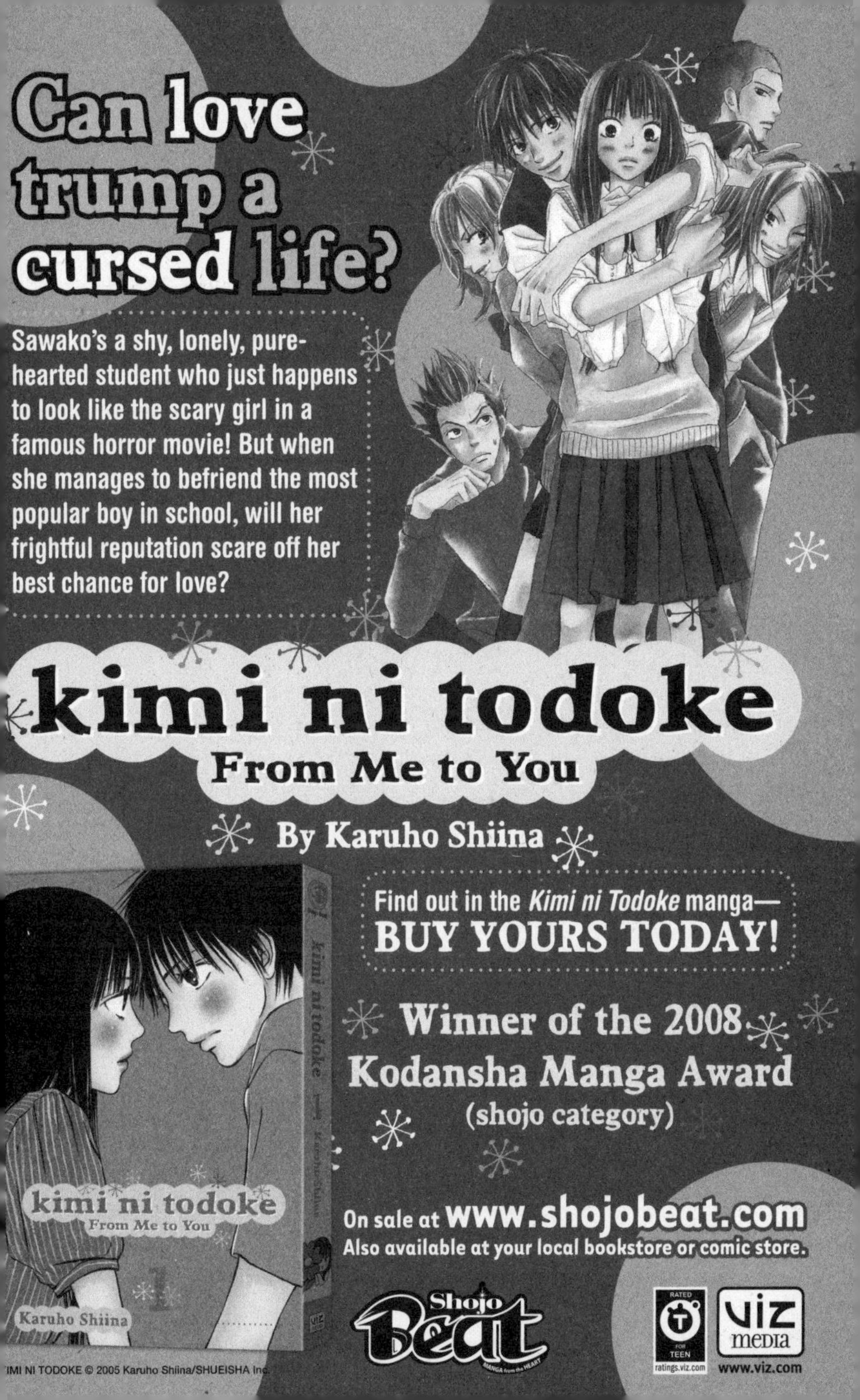
Can love trump a cursed life?
Sawako's a shy, lonely, pure-hearted student who just happens to look like the scary girl in a famous horror movie! But when she manages to befriend the most popular boy in school, will her frightful reputation scare off her best chance for love?
kimi ni todoke
From Me to You
By Karuho Shiina
Find out in the Kimi ni Todoke manga—
BUY YOURS TODAY!
Winner of the 2008
Kodansha Manga Award
(shojo category)
kimi ni todoke
From Me to You
1
Karuho Shiina
On sale at www.shojobeat.com
Also available at your local bookstore or comic store.
Shojo Beat
RATED T FOR TEEN
ratings.viz.com
VIZ media
www.viz.com
KIMI NI TODOKE © 2005 Karuho Shiina/SHUEISHA Inc.

Cactus's Secret

VOL. 3
Shojo Beat Edition

Story and Art by
Nana Haruta

TRANSLATION & ADAPTATION Su Mon Han
TOUCH-UP ART & LETTERING Deron Bennett
DESIGN Courtney Utt
EDITORS Nancy Thistlethwaite, Yuki Murashige

SABOTEN NO HIMITSU © 2003 by Nana Haruta. All rights
reserved. First published in Japan in 2003 by SHUEISHA Inc.,
Tokyo. English translation rights arranged by SHUEISHA Inc.

The rights of the author(s) of the work(s) in this publication to
be so identified have been asserted in accordance with the
Copyright, Designs and Patents Act 1988. A CIP catalogue
record for this book is available from the British Library.

Printed in Canada

Published by VIZ Media, LLC
P.O. Box 77010
San Francisco, CA 94107

10 9 8 7 6 5 4 3 2 1
First printing, September 2010

www.shojobeat.com   www.viz.com

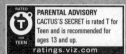

Cactus's Secret

3 Nana Haruta

Contents

CAST OF CHARACTERS

Plain Middle Schooler Miku

Nami Minase
Fujioka's childhood friend. She used to be in love with Fujioka.

Miku Yamada (high schooler, 2nd year)
She's had a one-sided crush on Fujioka since middle school. She's called a "cactus alien" because she's quick-tempered.

Kyohei Fujioka (high schooler, 2nd-year)
Miku's classmate. A former delinquent and completely clueless about love.

Itsuki Natsukawa
The son of the school chairman and the top-ranked student. He's incredibly popular with the girls.

Delinquent (?!) Middle Schooler Fujioka

Cactus's Secret

Miku has had a one-sided crush on Fujioka since middle school. In order to win his affection, Miku strives to improve her appearance and works up the courage to confess her love to him. However, just before she can confess, the oblivious-about-love Fujioka makes fun of her makeup!

Miku struggles over the mixed signals the clueless Fujioka gives her, and at the end of the first year, she accidentally blurts out her love for him! Unfortunately, Fujioka doesn't feel the same way. But despite that, Miku declares to Fujioka that she won't give up on winning him over. When the new school year begins, Miku and Fujioka find themselves in the same class again. Miku is relieved to find that her confession hasn't made their friendship awkward.

However, the school heartthrob, Itsuki Natsukawa, is now showing a lot of interest in Miku! What's worse, he misinterprets Miku's relationship with Fujioka and then frames Fujioka as the thief who stole the answers to the midterm exams. But Miku won't stand for that!! She declares, "It won't change the fact that I love Fujioka," effectively bringing the case to a close.

Thanks to the incident with Natsukawa, Fujioka and Miku become even closer.♥ After spending a fun afternoon together, Fujioka tells Miku to wait just a little longer for him. And with both of them on the Sports Day Planning Committee, Miku's hopes of winning over Fujioka rise!

Into this situation comes the mysterious Kudo, who Miku (literally) bumps into on the street one day. Kudo seems to know intimate details about Fujioka and tells Miku to spend the day with him if she wants to find out Fujioka's "secret." Lured by such a promise, Miku ends up going with him…

•• STORY THUS FAR ••

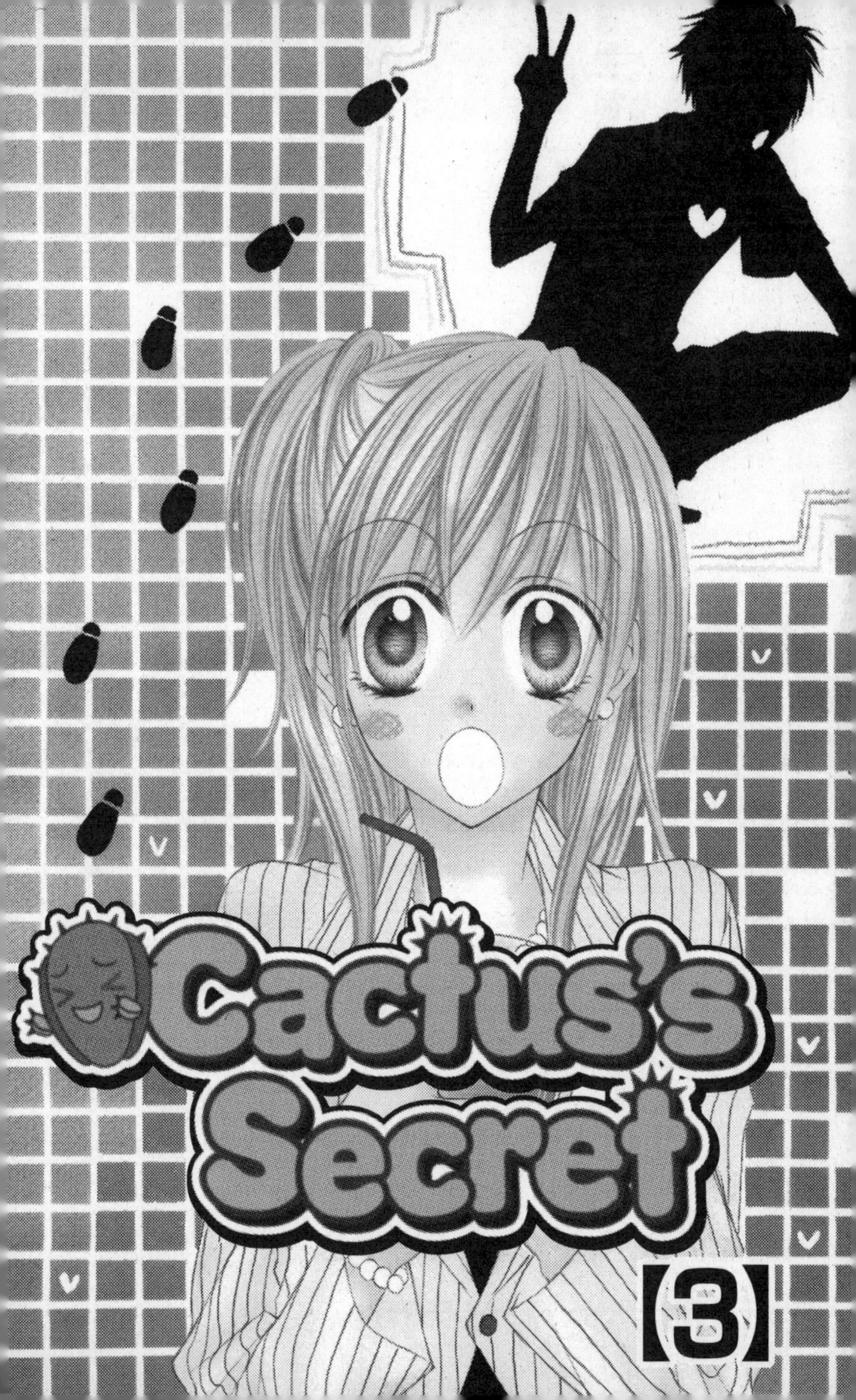
Cactus's Secret
3

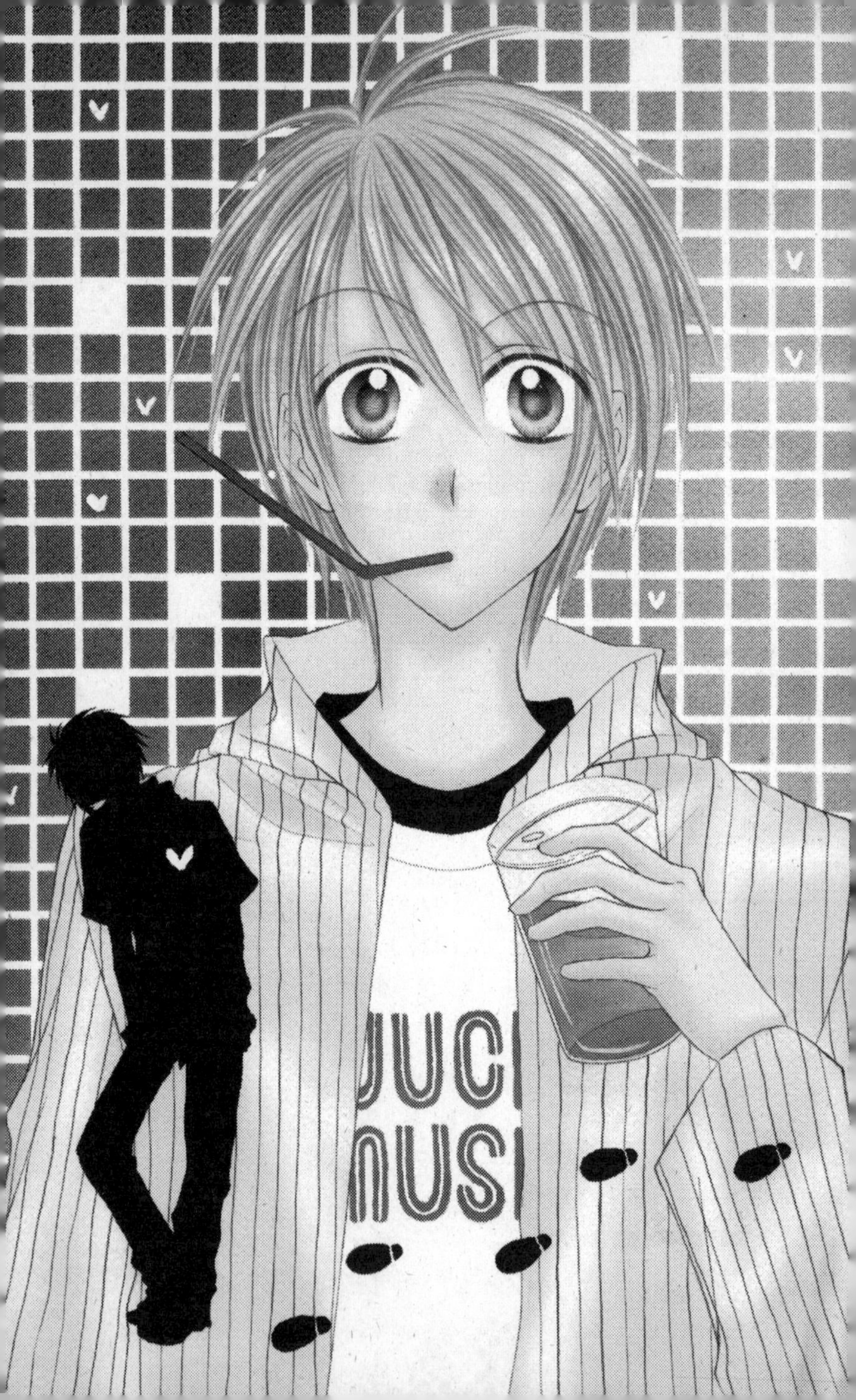

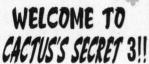

WELCOME TO *CACTUS'S SECRET* 3!!

Hello, this is Haruta! So, uh, in the last volume, I abandoned my author's columns midway through, I didn't do any of the Small Talk blurbs and I had a sparse bonus section... I am so sorry about all that! I feel bad that I couldn't put enough extras in volume 2. (It must have been REALLY disappointing for the readers who follow the story in Ribon magazine since there was hardly any extra incentive to buy the book.)

That's why, this time, I'm back with a vengeance!! I intend to fill every last blank space in this volume! Here I goooooo!!!

Oh, and please read the story too! ☆

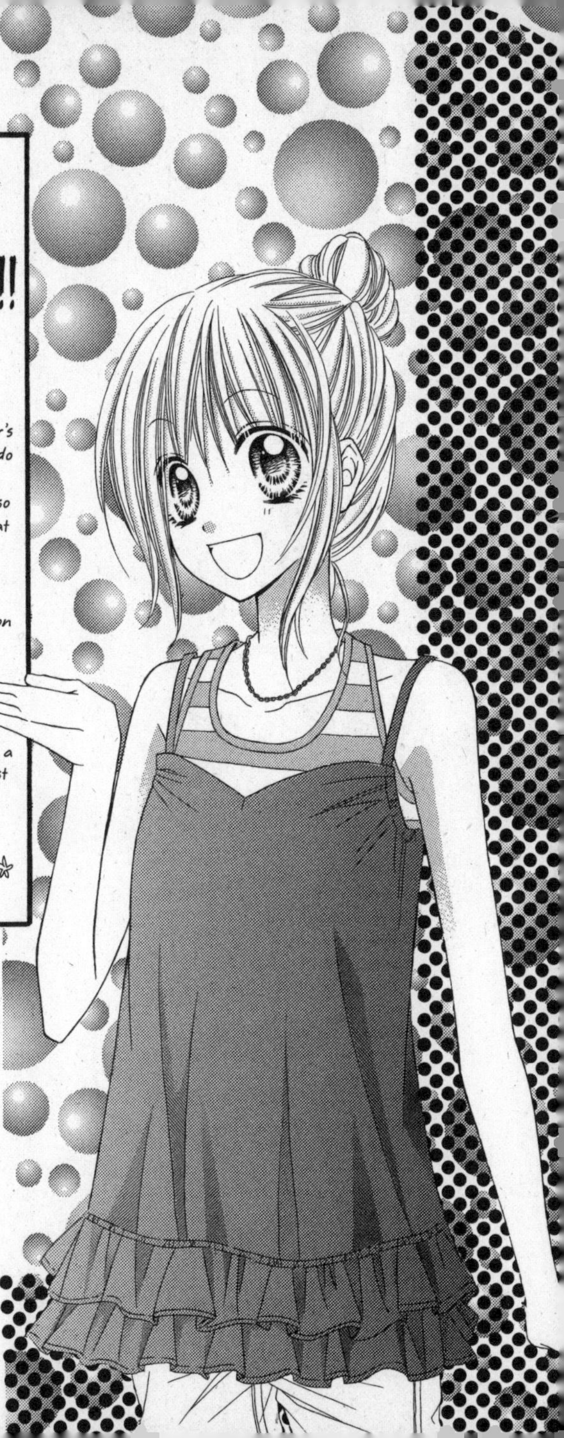

GO!

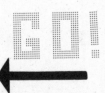

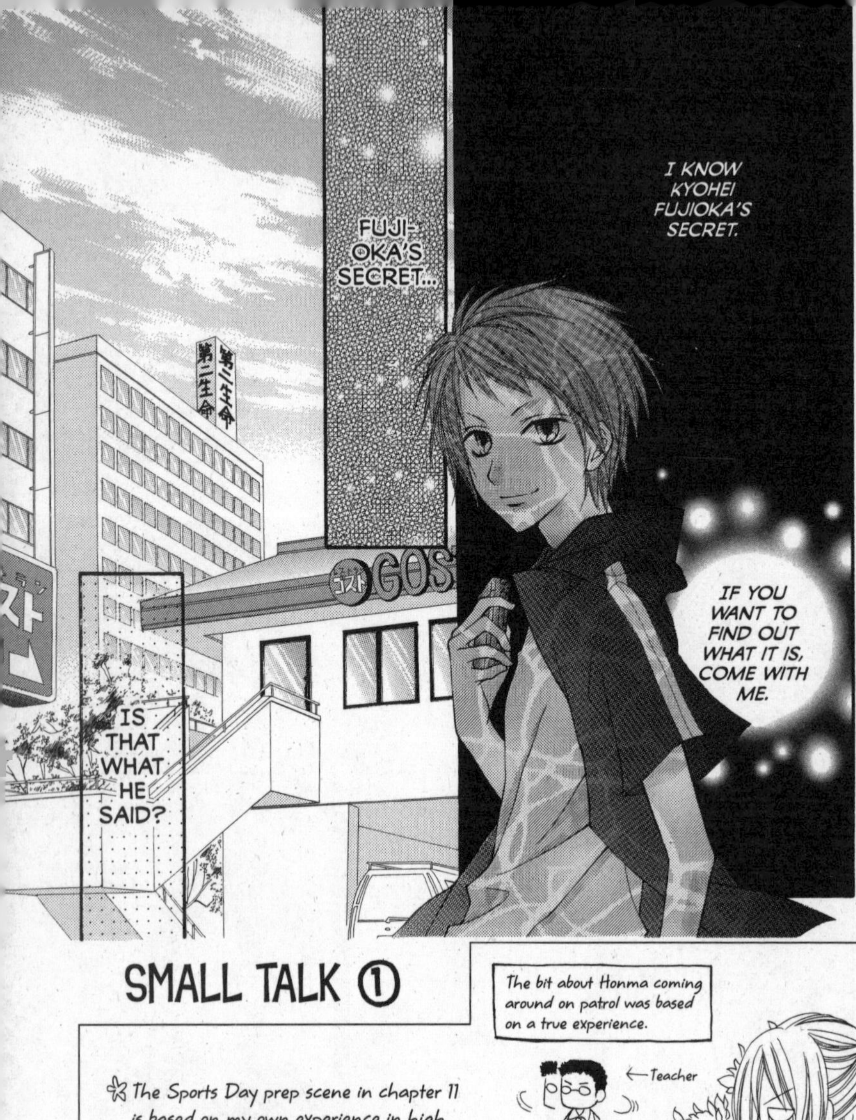
I KNOW KYOHEI FUJIOKA'S SECRET.
FUJI-OKA'S SECRET...
IF YOU WANT TO FIND OUT WHAT IT IS, COME WITH ME.
第二生命
IS THAT WHAT HE SAID?

SMALL TALK ①

✿ The Sports Day prep scene in chapter 11 is based on my own experience in high school. I was on the Sports Day Planning Committee during my first year. The upperclassmen were all so nice. Well, not all of them—some were scary... (laugh) It was so much fun. Ahh, adolescence—it's so bright!

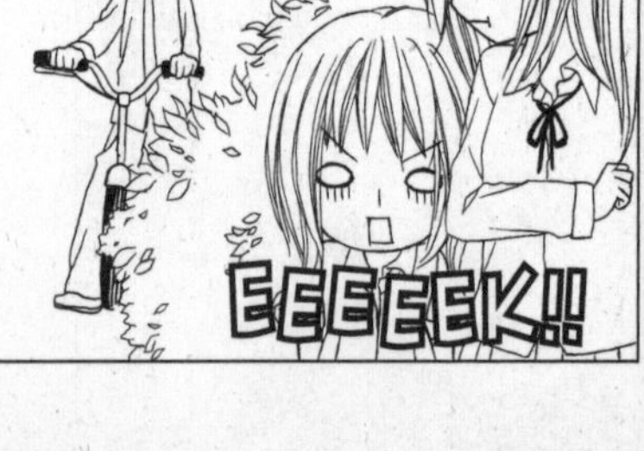
The bit about Honma coming around on patrol was based on a true experience.
←Teacher
EEEEEK!!

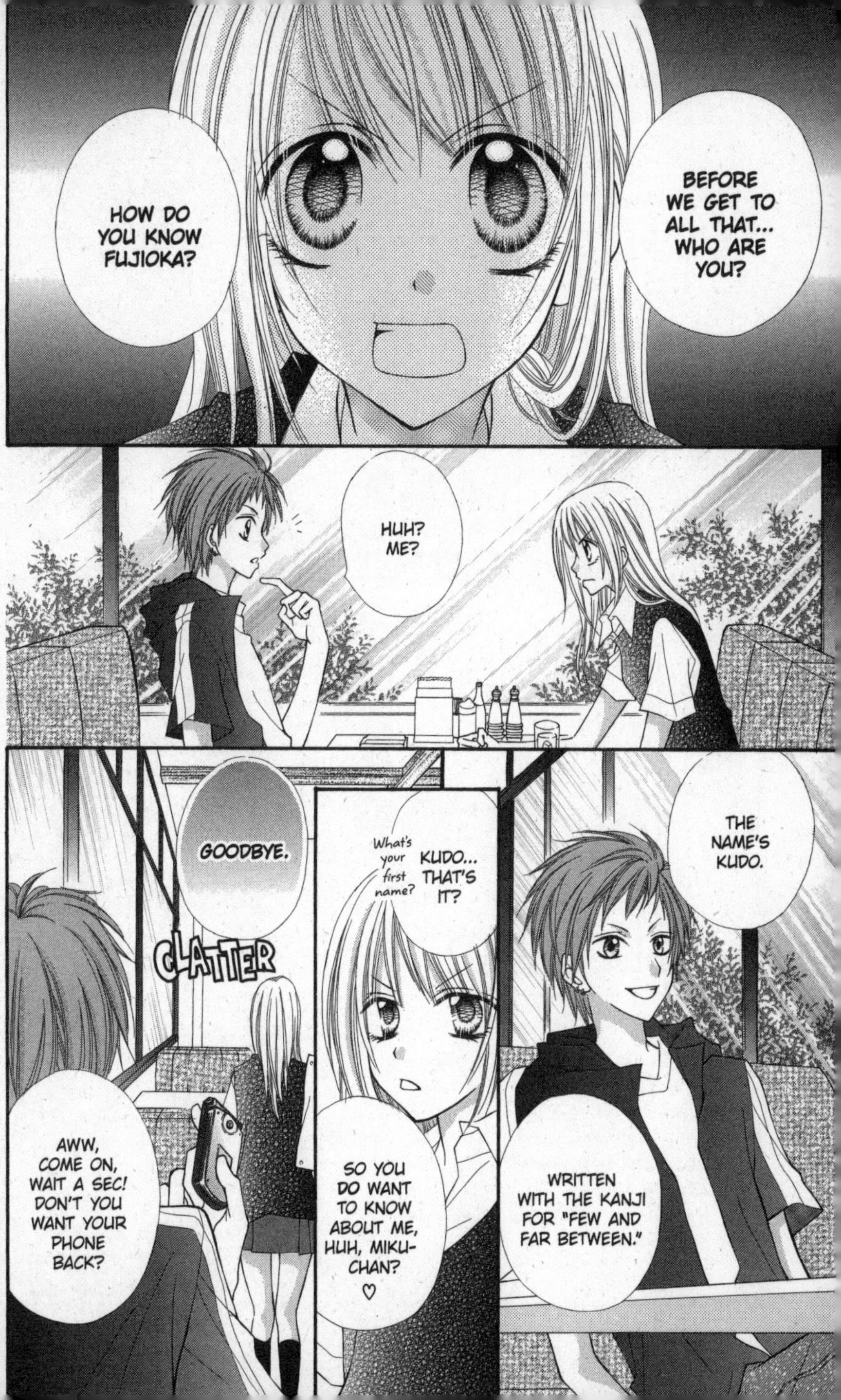
BEFORE WE GET TO ALL THAT... WHO ARE YOU?
HOW DO YOU KNOW FUJIOKA?
HUH? ME?
THE NAME'S KUDO.
WRITTEN WITH THE KANJI FOR "FEW AND FAR BETWEEN."
KUDO... THAT'S IT?
What's your first name?
SO YOU DO WANT TO KNOW ABOUT ME, HUH, MIKU-CHAN? ♡
GOODBYE.
CLATTER
AWW, COME ON, WAIT A SEC! DON'T YOU WANT YOUR PHONE BACK?

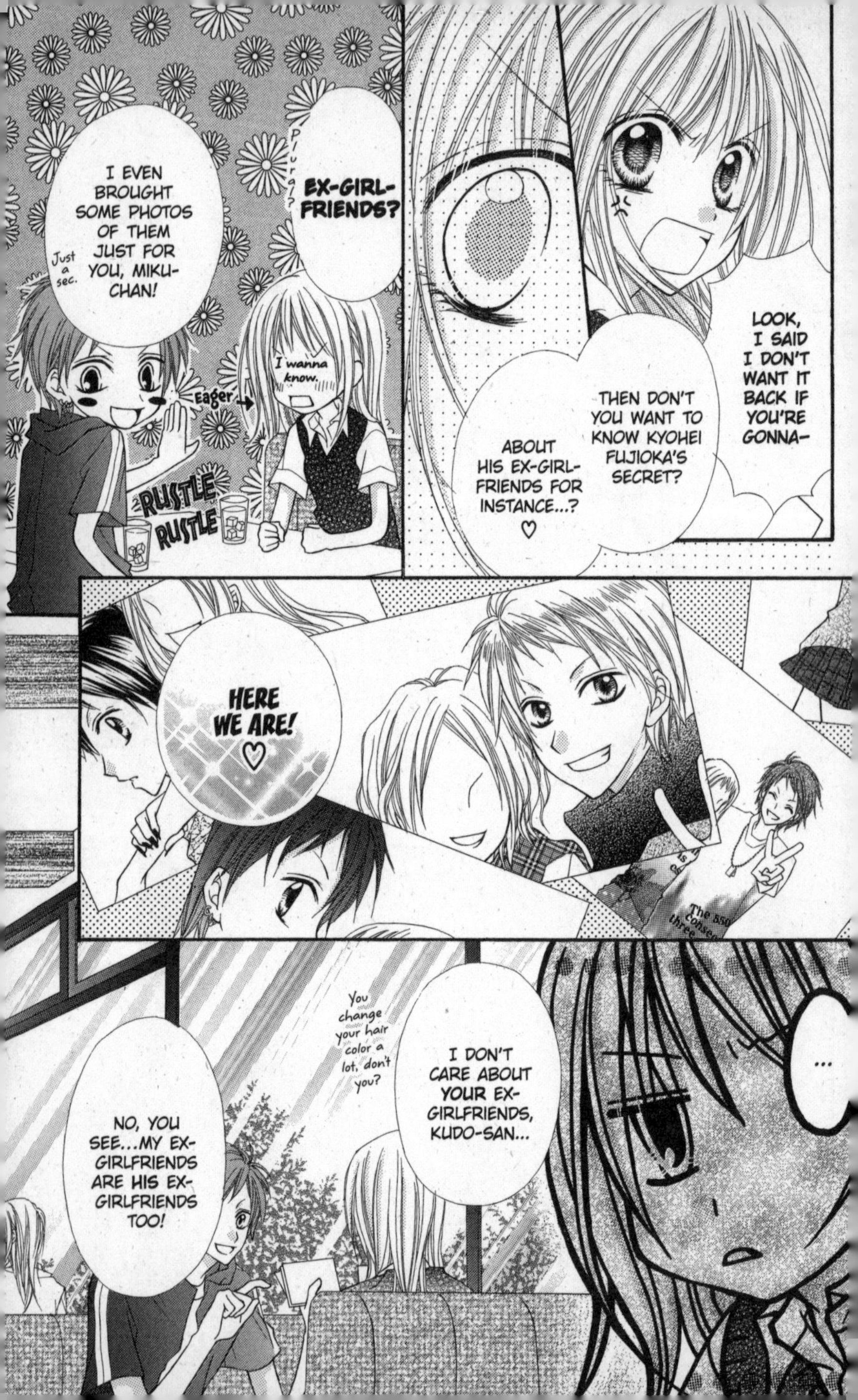
LOOK, I SAID I DON'T WANT IT BACK IF YOU'RE GONNA-
THEN DON'T YOU WANT TO KNOW KYOHEI FUJIOKA'S SECRET?
ABOUT HIS EX-GIRL-FRIENDS FOR INSTANCE...? ♡
EX-GIRL-FRIENDS?
Plural?
I wanna know.
Eager
I EVEN BROUGHT SOME PHOTOS OF THEM JUST FOR YOU, MIKU-CHAN!
Just a sec.
RUSTLE RUSTLE
HERE WE ARE! ♡
...
I DON'T CARE ABOUT YOUR EX-GIRLFRIENDS, KUDO-SAN...
You change your hair color a lot, don't you?
NO, YOU SEE...MY EX-GIRLFRIENDS ARE HIS EX-GIRLFRIENDS TOO!

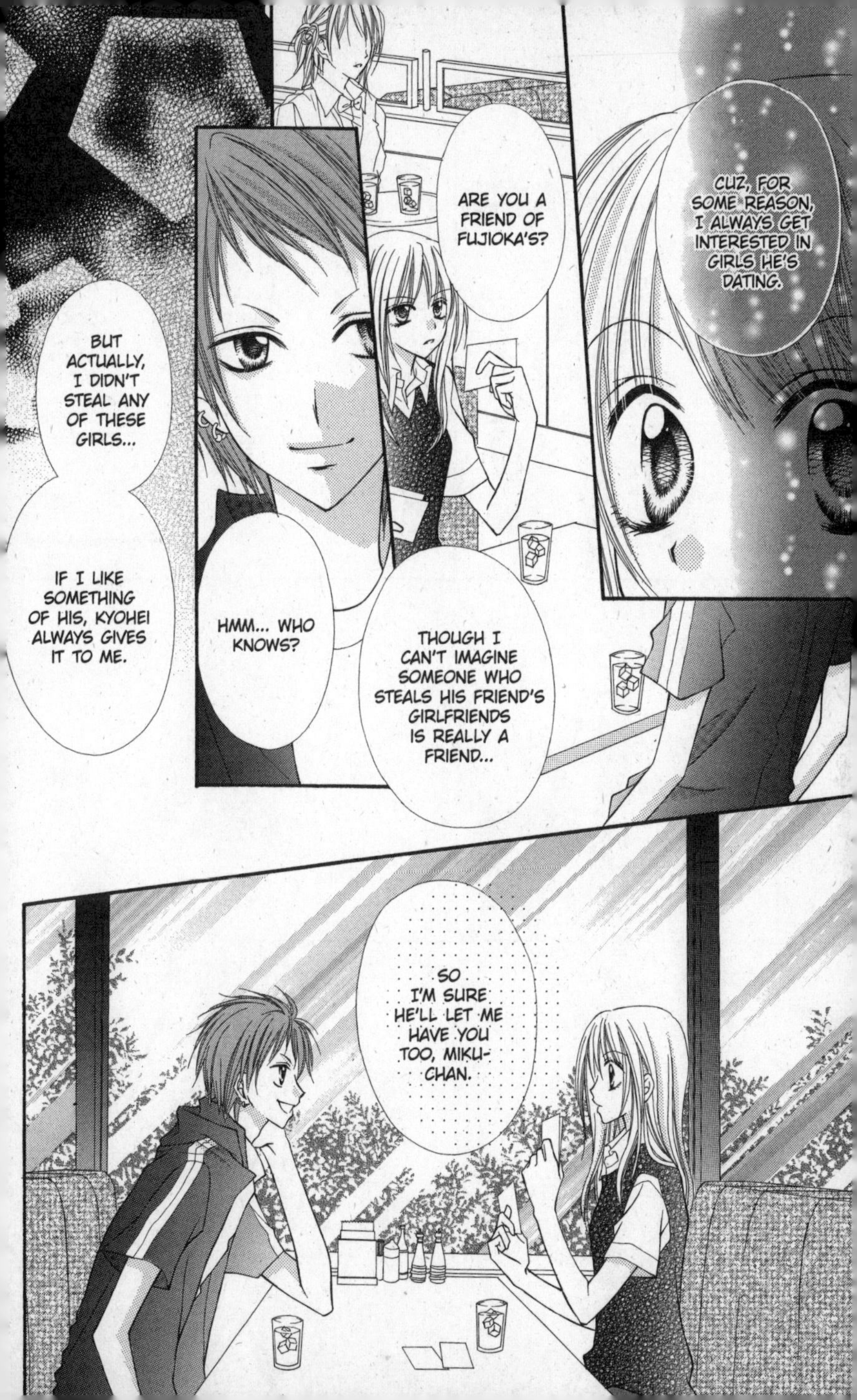
ARE YOU A FRIEND OF FUJIOKA'S?
THOUGH I CAN'T IMAGINE SOMEONE WHO STEALS HIS FRIEND'S GIRLFRIENDS IS REALLY A FRIEND...
HMM... WHO KNOWS?
CUZ, FOR SOME REASON, I ALWAYS GET INTERESTED IN GIRLS HE'S DATING.
BUT ACTUALLY, I DIDN'T STEAL ANY OF THESE GIRLS...
IF I LIKE SOMETHING OF HIS, KYOHEI ALWAYS GIVES IT TO ME.
SO I'M SURE HE'LL LET ME HAVE YOU TOO, MIKU-CHAN.

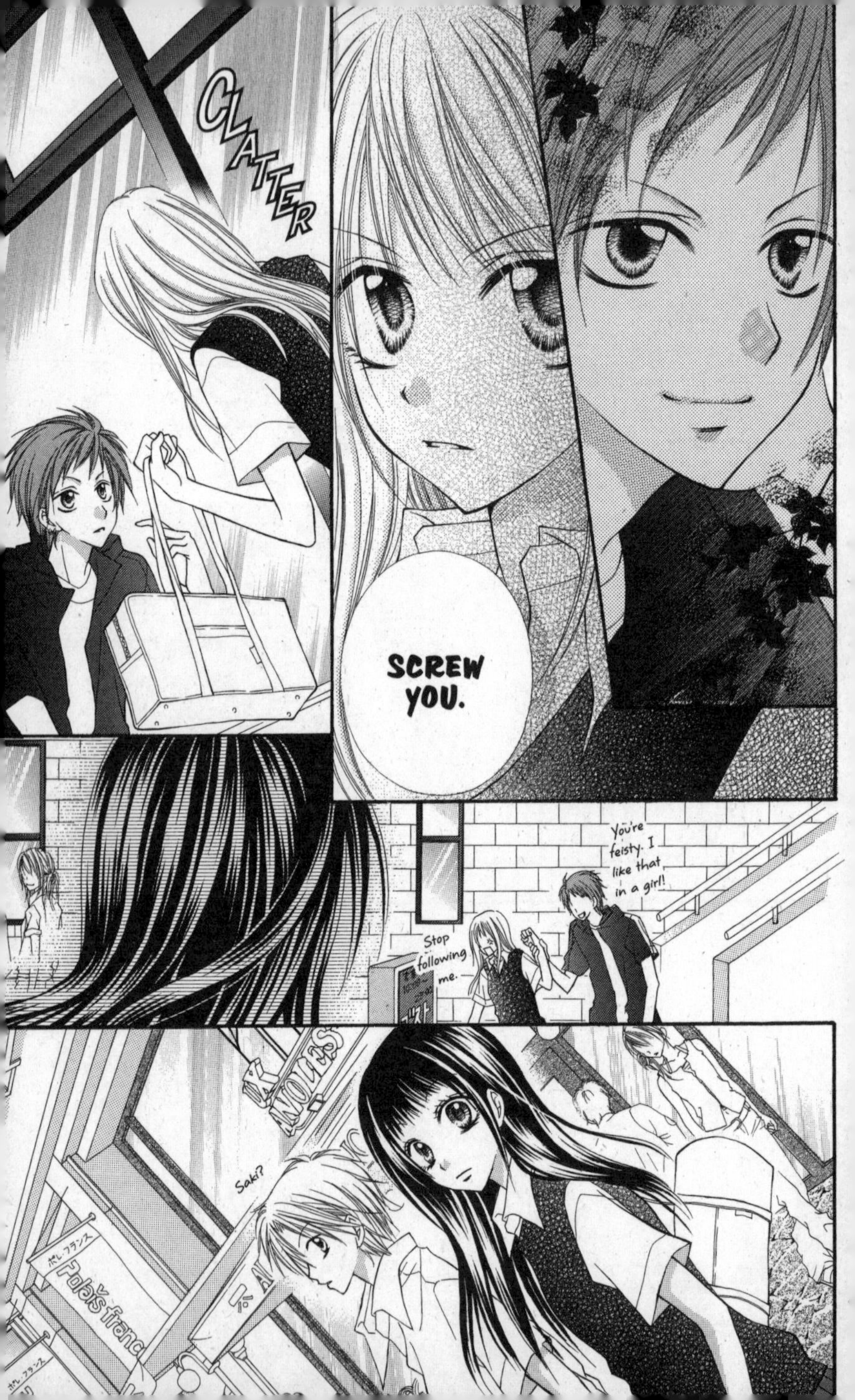
SCREW YOU.
CLATTER
You're feisty. I like that in a girl!
Stop following me.
Saki?

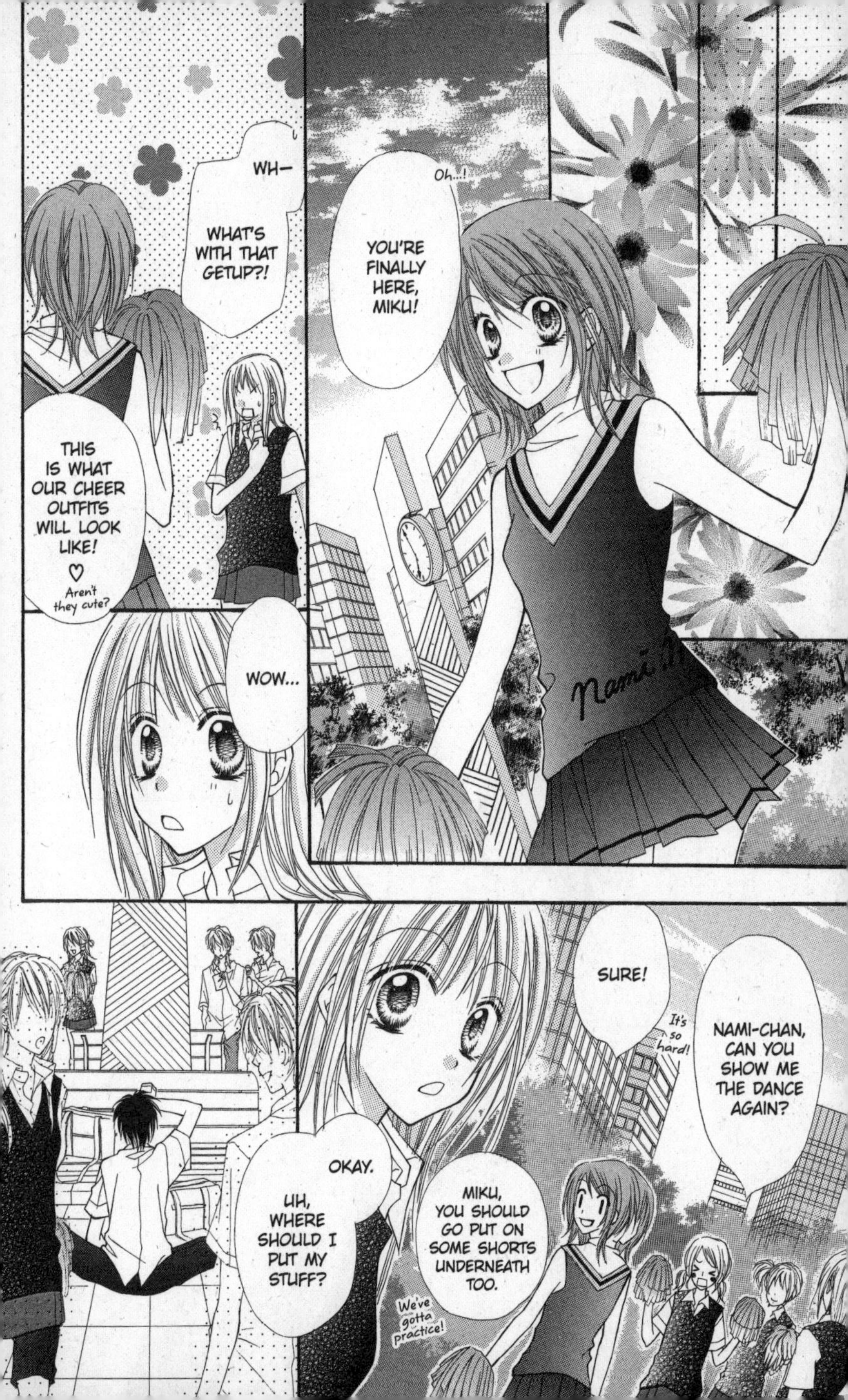
Oh...!
YOU'RE FINALLY HERE, MIKU!
WH—
WHAT'S WITH THAT GETUP?!
THIS IS WHAT OUR CHEER OUTFITS WILL LOOK LIKE! ♡
Aren't they cute?
WOW...
NAMI-CHAN, CAN YOU SHOW ME THE DANCE AGAIN?
It's so hard!
SURE!
MIKU, YOU SHOULD GO PUT ON SOME SHORTS UNDERNEATH TOO.
We've gotta practice!
OKAY.
UH, WHERE SHOULD I PUT MY STUFF?

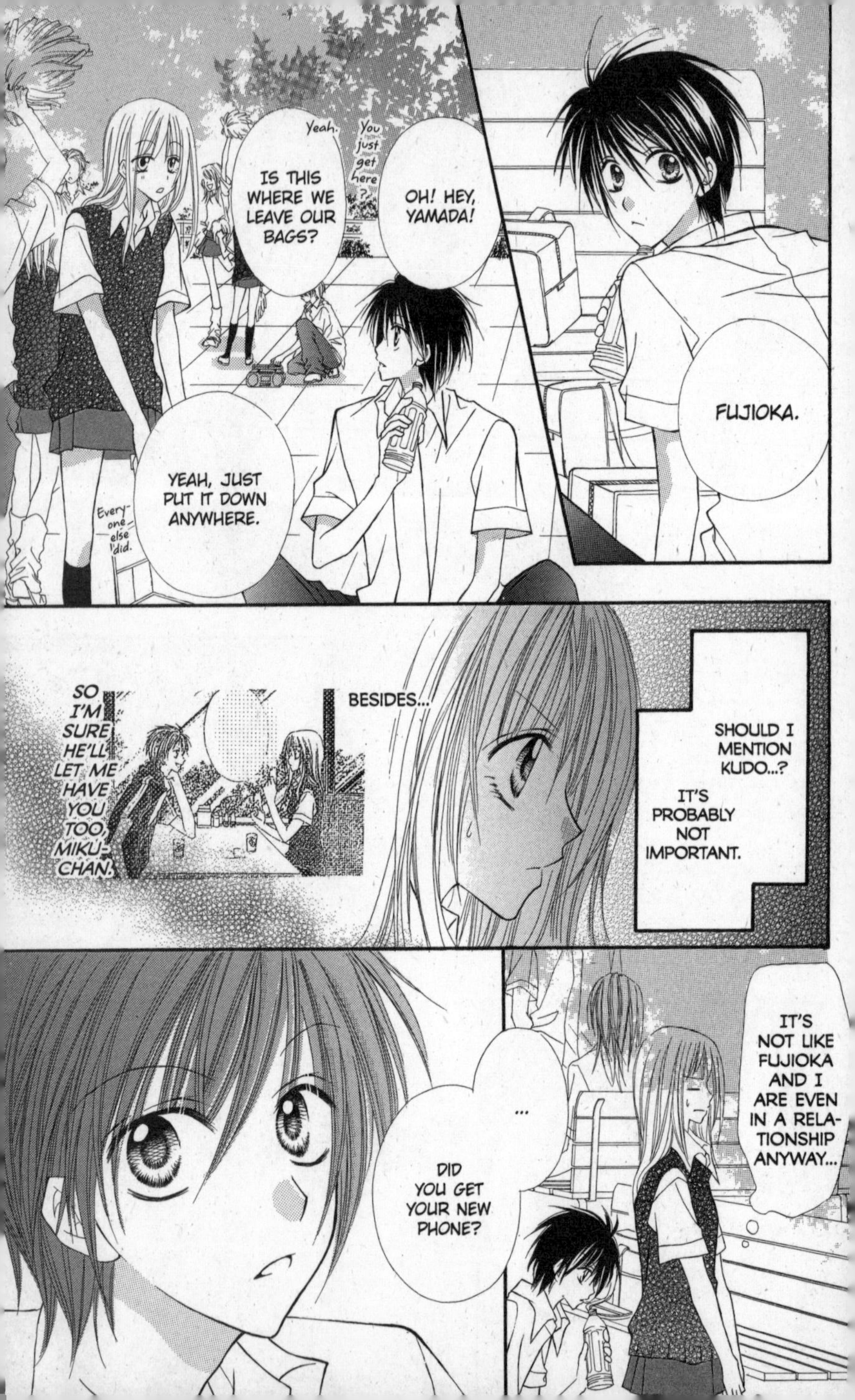
FUJIOKA.
OH! HEY, YAMADA!
You just get here?
Yeah.
IS THIS WHERE WE LEAVE OUR BAGS?
YEAH, JUST PUT IT DOWN ANYWHERE.
Everyone else did.
SHOULD I MENTION KUDO...?
IT'S PROBABLY NOT IMPORTANT.
BESIDES...
SO I'M SURE HE'LL LET ME HAVE YOU TOO, MIKU-CHAN.
IT'S NOT LIKE FUJIOKA AND I ARE EVEN IN A RELATIONSHIP ANYWAY...
...
DID YOU GET YOUR NEW PHONE?

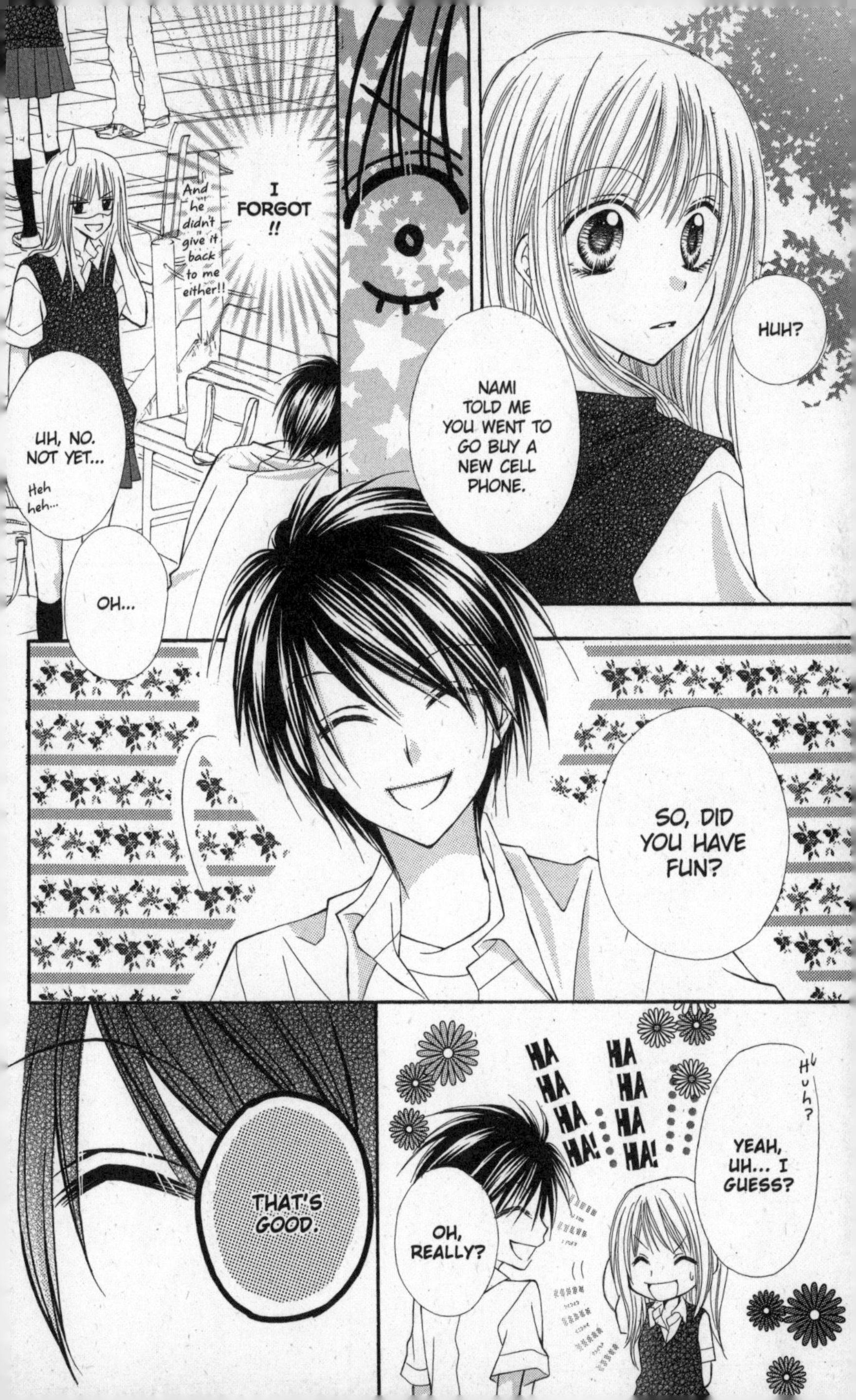
NAMI TOLD ME YOU WENT TO GO BUY A NEW CELL PHONE.
HUH?
I FORGOT!!
And he didn't give it back to me either!!
UH, NO. NOT YET...
Heh heh...
OH...
SO, DID YOU HAVE FUN?
Huh?
YEAH, UH... I GUESS?
HA HA HA HA!
HA HA HA HA!
OH, REALLY?
THAT'S GOOD.

1

THIS IS CACTUS'S SECRET VOLUME 3!!

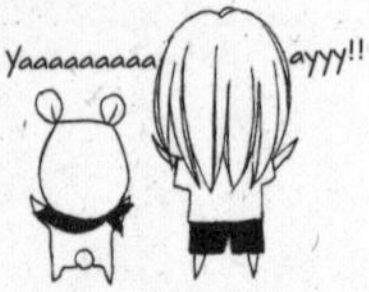
Yaaaaaaaaa ayyy!!

Hello! I am Nana Haruta. Somehow we've made it to volume 3. By the time this volume hits stores, the series will have ended. The final chapter came out in the June 2005 issue of Ribon, meaning the next volume will be the last for Cactus—four volumes in all. I'd be so happy if you'd stick with me to the end! Oh, but we're still on volume 3, so please enjoy it!

Please read on at your leisure!

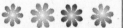

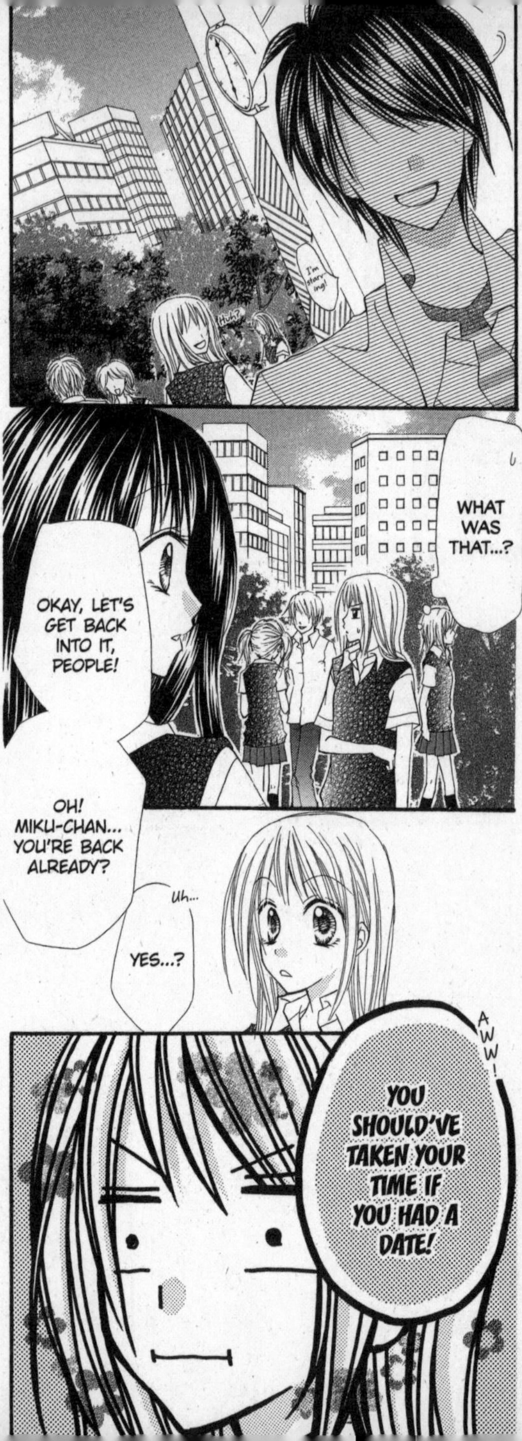
I'm starving!
Huh?
WHAT WAS THAT...?
OKAY, LET'S GET BACK INTO IT, PEOPLE!
OH! MIKU-CHAN... YOU'RE BACK ALREADY?
Uh...
YES...?
AWW!
YOU SHOULD'VE TAKEN YOUR TIME IF YOU HAD A DATE!

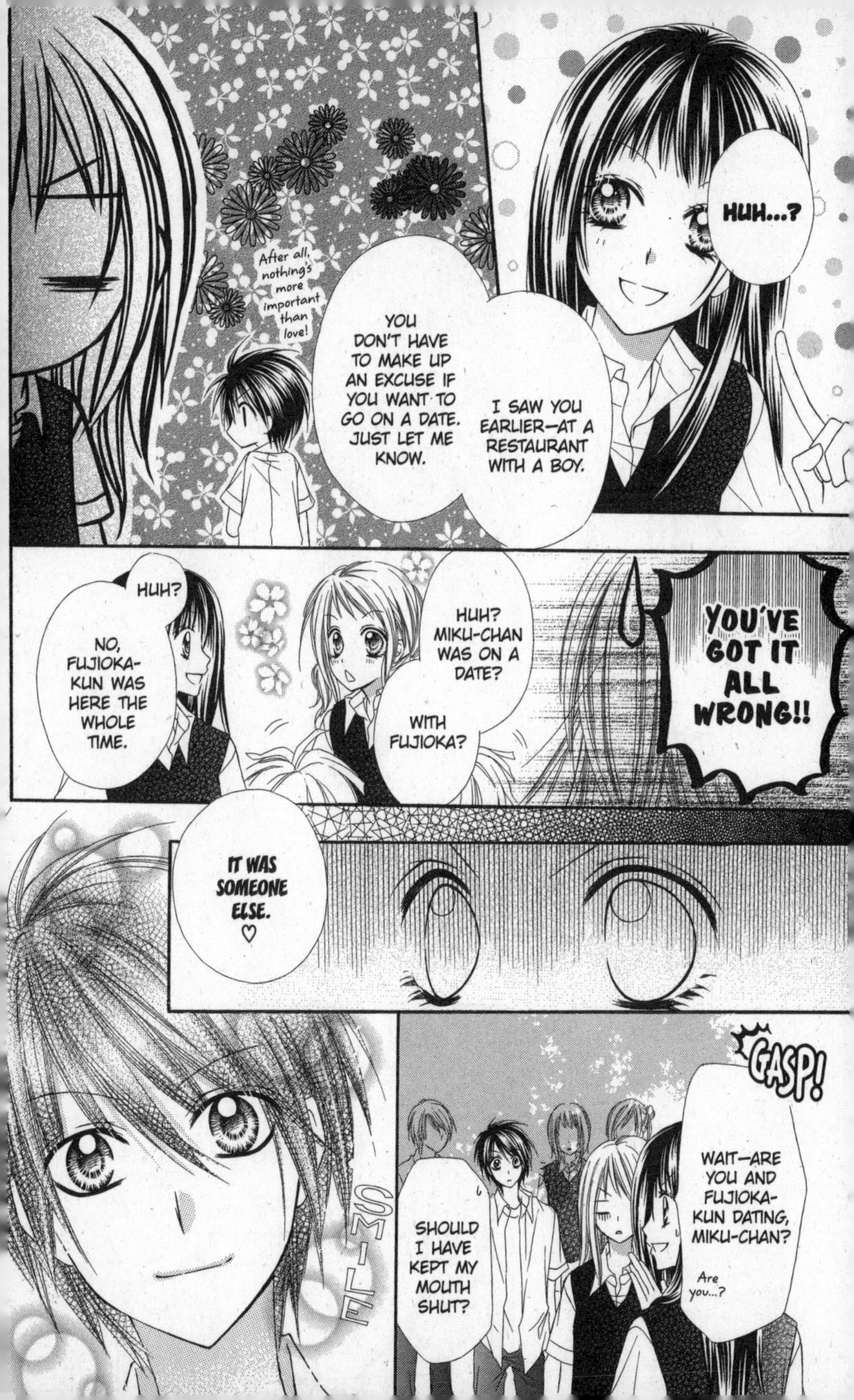
HUH...?
I SAW YOU EARLIER—AT A RESTAURANT WITH A BOY.
YOU DON'T HAVE TO MAKE UP AN EXCUSE IF YOU WANT TO GO ON A DATE. JUST LET ME KNOW.
After all, nothing's more important than love!
YOU'VE GOT IT ALL WRONG!!
HUH? MIKU-CHAN WAS ON A DATE?
WITH FUJIOKA?
HUH?
NO, FUJIOKA-KUN WAS HERE THE WHOLE TIME.
IT WAS SOMEONE ELSE. ♡
GASP!
WAIT—ARE YOU AND FUJIOKA-KUN DATING, MIKU-CHAN?
Are you...?
SHOULD I HAVE KEPT MY MOUTH SHUT?
SMILE

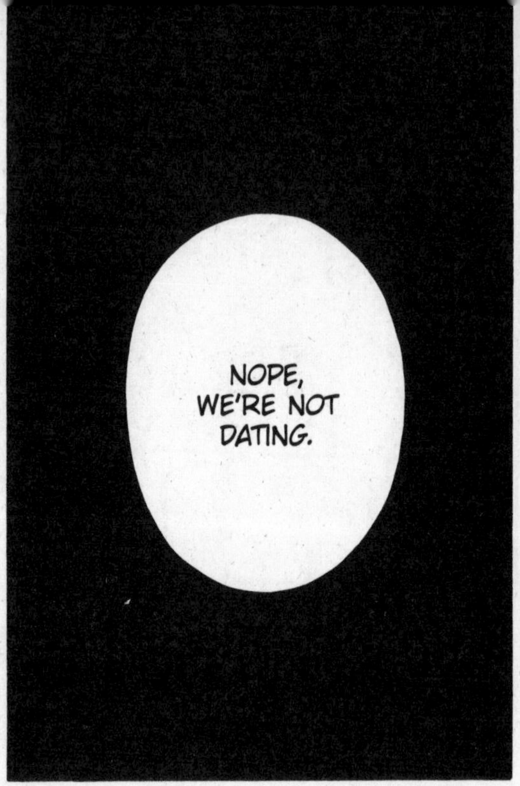
NOPE, WE'RE NOT DATING.

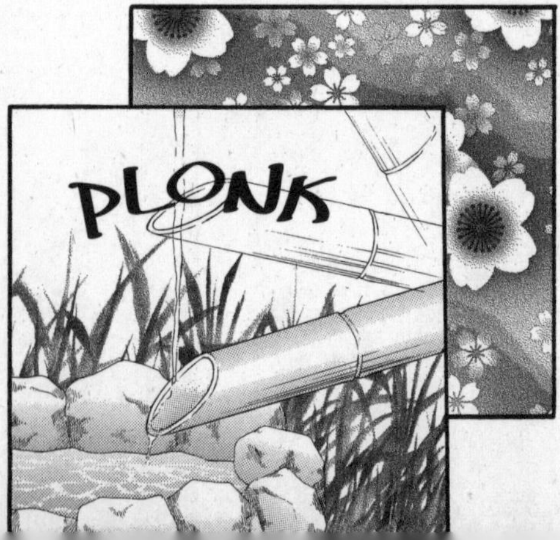
PLONK

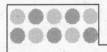

2

Do you all believe in fortune telling? I'm a big believer because I've had experiences where fortunes have been so dead-on accurate that it was pretty scary. I still remember something from when I was in middle school. No matter which magazine I checked, my horoscope was really good! My grades went up without me studying at all, my manga submission got accepted for publication, plus I was super lucky in love (laugh). But after that, my good luck suddenly plummeted in one fell swoop. But that was foretold in my horoscope too! Scary!! Or something like that. There are times when it's completely off too. But fortunes and horoscopes sure are fun!

The other day when I was in Yokohama's Chinatown with my older sister, we saw this street lined with fortunetellers. I really wanted to get my fortune read but I didn't. I mean, what if they told me something bad was going to happen? I'd agonize over it so much!! Unlike the general horoscopes you see in magazines or on TV, it'd be a fortune tailored just for me... Yeah, I'm a big chicken.

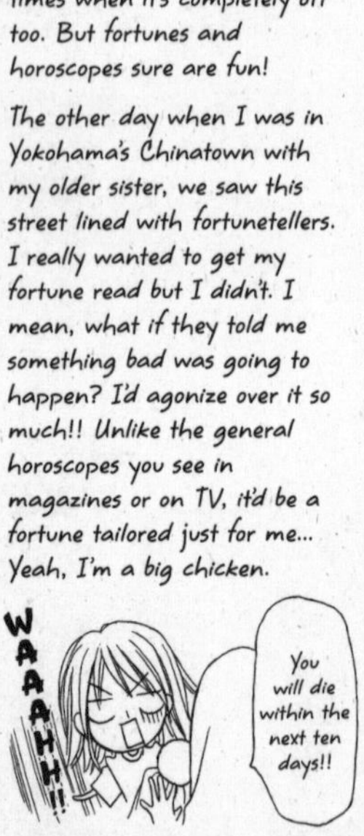
WAAAHH!!
You will die within the next ten days!!

Or something like that. Don't you think?

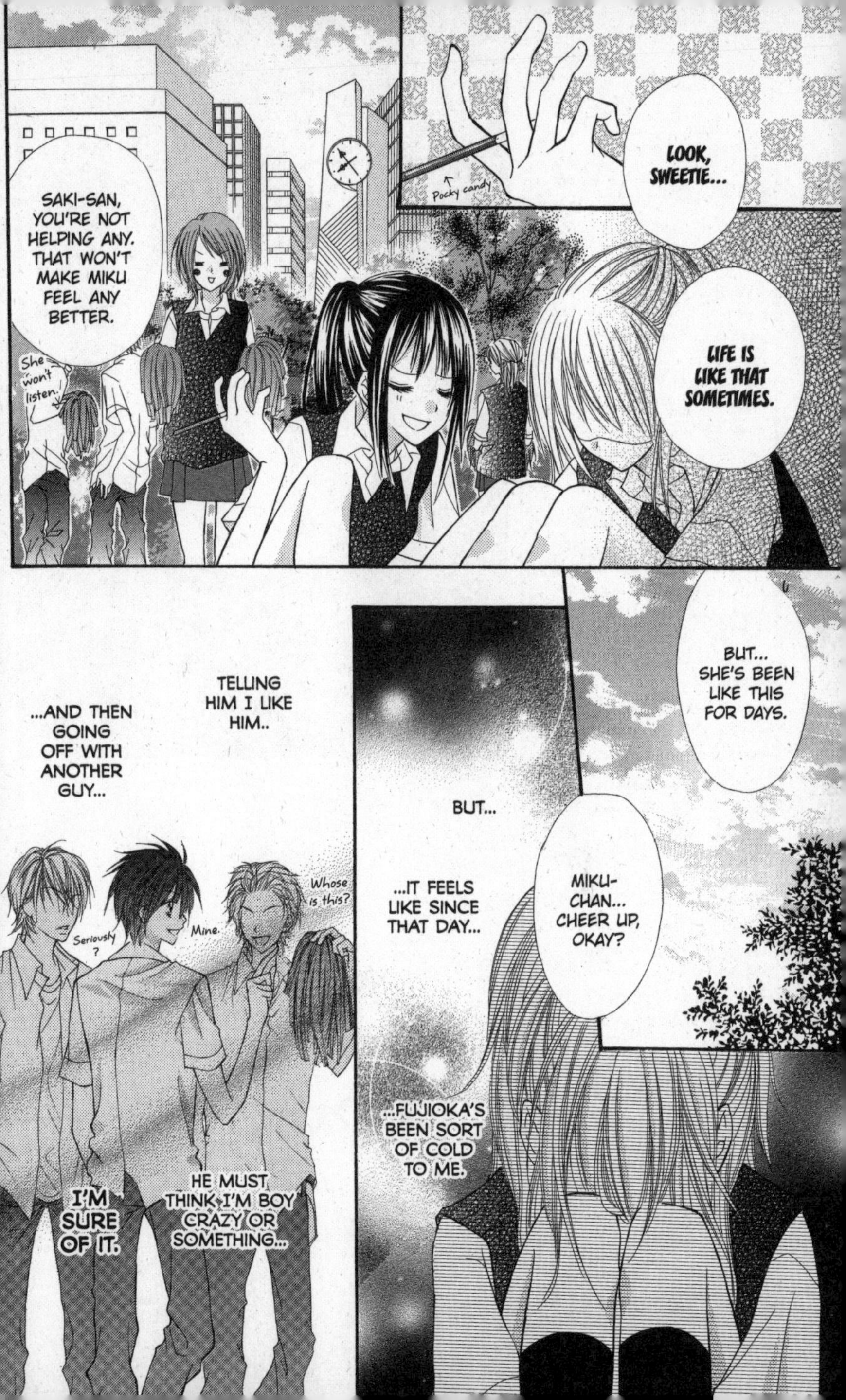
LOOK, SWEETIE...
Pocky candy
LIFE IS LIKE THAT SOMETIMES.
SAKI-SAN, YOU'RE NOT HELPING ANY. THAT WON'T MAKE MIKU FEEL ANY BETTER.
She won't listen.
BUT... SHE'S BEEN LIKE THIS FOR DAYS.
MIKU-CHAN... CHEER UP, OKAY?
BUT...
...IT FEELS LIKE SINCE THAT DAY...
...FUJIOKA'S BEEN SORT OF COLD TO ME.
TELLING HIM I LIKE HIM..
...AND THEN GOING OFF WITH ANOTHER GUY...
Whose is this?
Mine.
Seriously?
HE MUST THINK I'M BOY CRAZY OR SOMETHING...
I'M SURE OF IT.

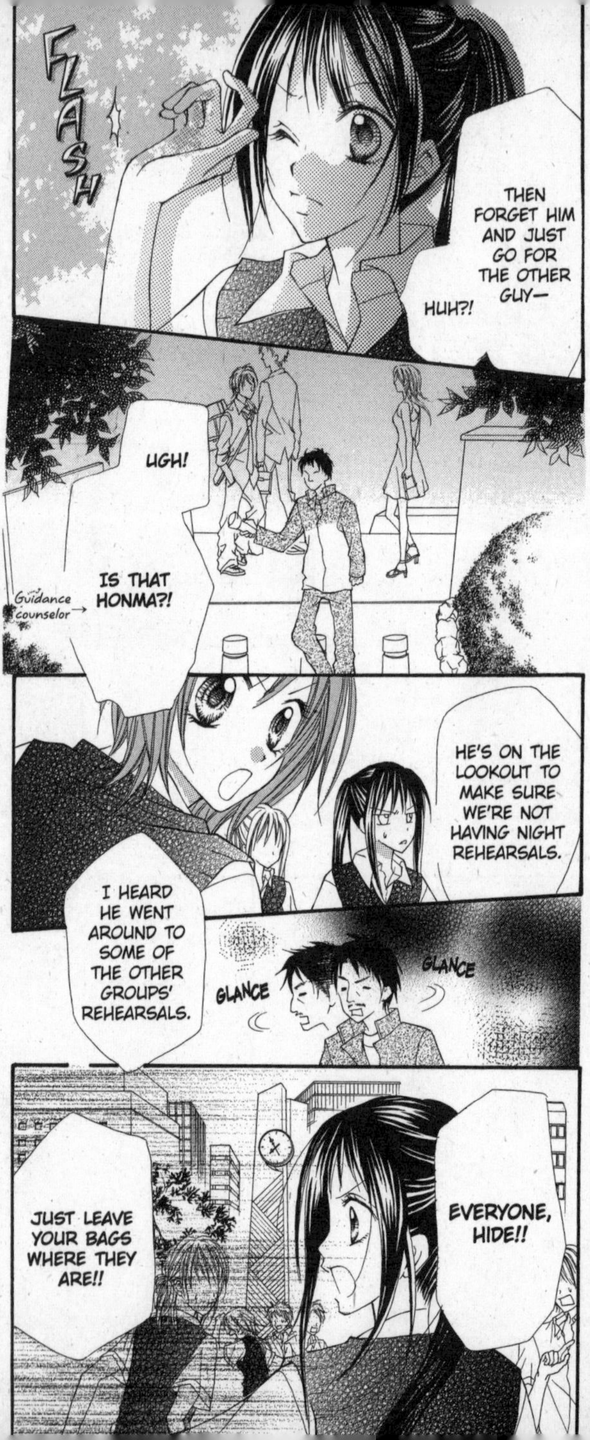
FLASH
THEN FORGET HIM AND JUST GO FOR THE OTHER GUY—
HUH?!
UGH!
IS THAT HONMA?!
Guidance counselor
HE'S ON THE LOOKOUT TO MAKE SURE WE'RE NOT HAVING NIGHT REHEARSALS.
I HEARD HE WENT AROUND TO SOME OF THE OTHER GROUPS' REHEARSALS.
GLANCE
GLANCE
EVERYONE, HIDE!!
JUST LEAVE YOUR BAGS WHERE THEY ARE!!

3

Speaking of fortune telling, lately blood-type horoscopes are all the rage. Those are really accurate too! Incidentally, my blood type is O. O's are said to not sweat the small stuff and don't pay attention to details. That is totally me! However... There's one trait that doesn't match! According to the blood type horoscopes, Type O's are supposed to be very sociable.

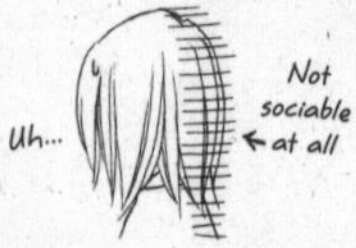
Uh...
Not sociable at all

Even I can tell I'm really anti-social. I never, ever text anyone first. I know I can't go on like this.♭

If you were to ask the people around me, they'd probably say that even if they text me, the odds are low that I'll send a reply. No, that's not entirely true! I do send replies! Although a friend recently sent me a text in which she wrote "You better reply to this!!" in the subject line... Just what is she implying?

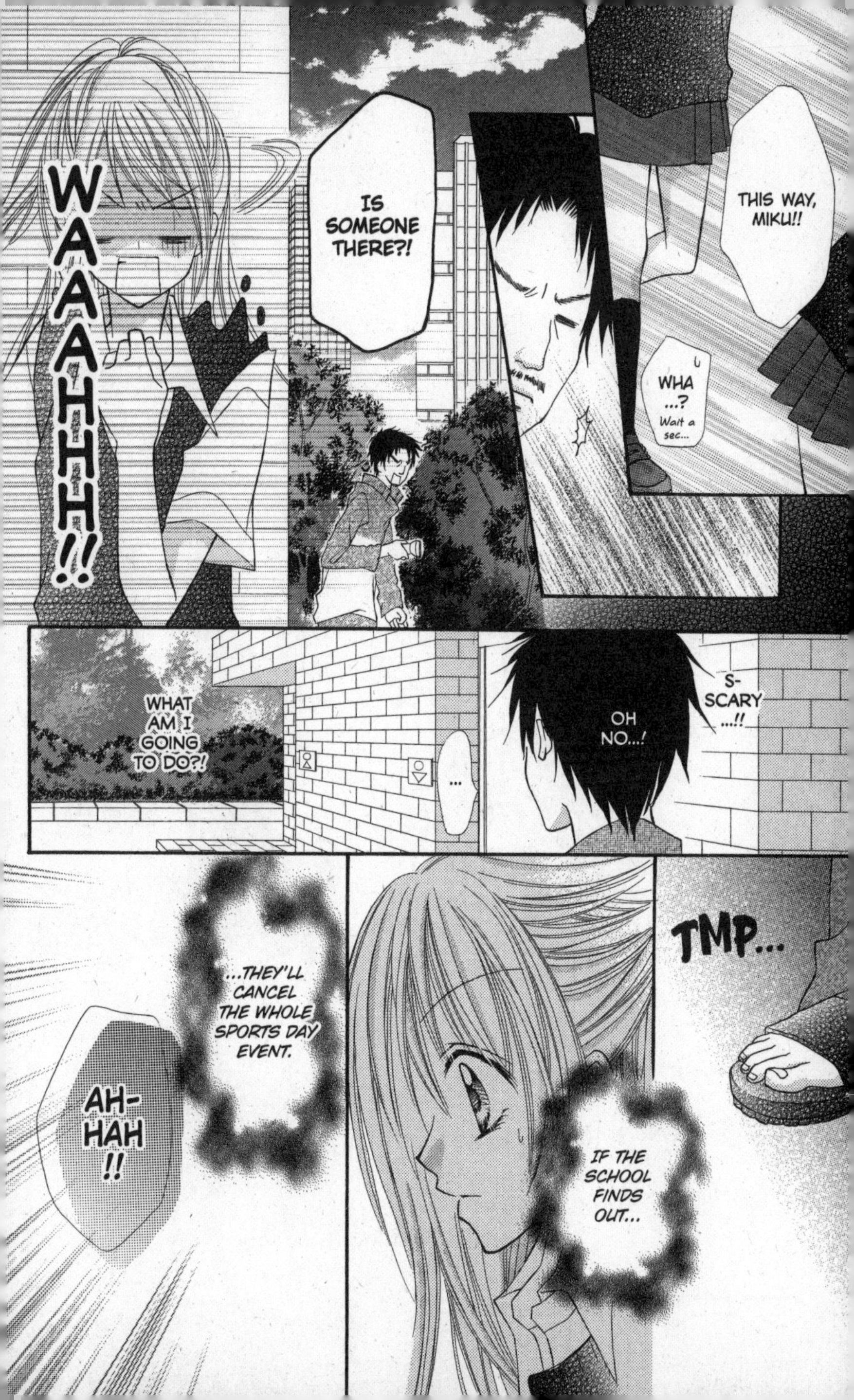
THIS WAY, MIKU!!
WHA ...? Wait a sec...
IS SOMEONE THERE?!
WAAAAHHHH!!
S-SCARY ...!!
OH NO...!
...
WHAT AM I GOING TO DO?!
TMP...
IF THE SCHOOL FINDS OUT...
...THEY'LL CANCEL THE WHOLE SPORTS DAY EVENT.
AH-HAH!!

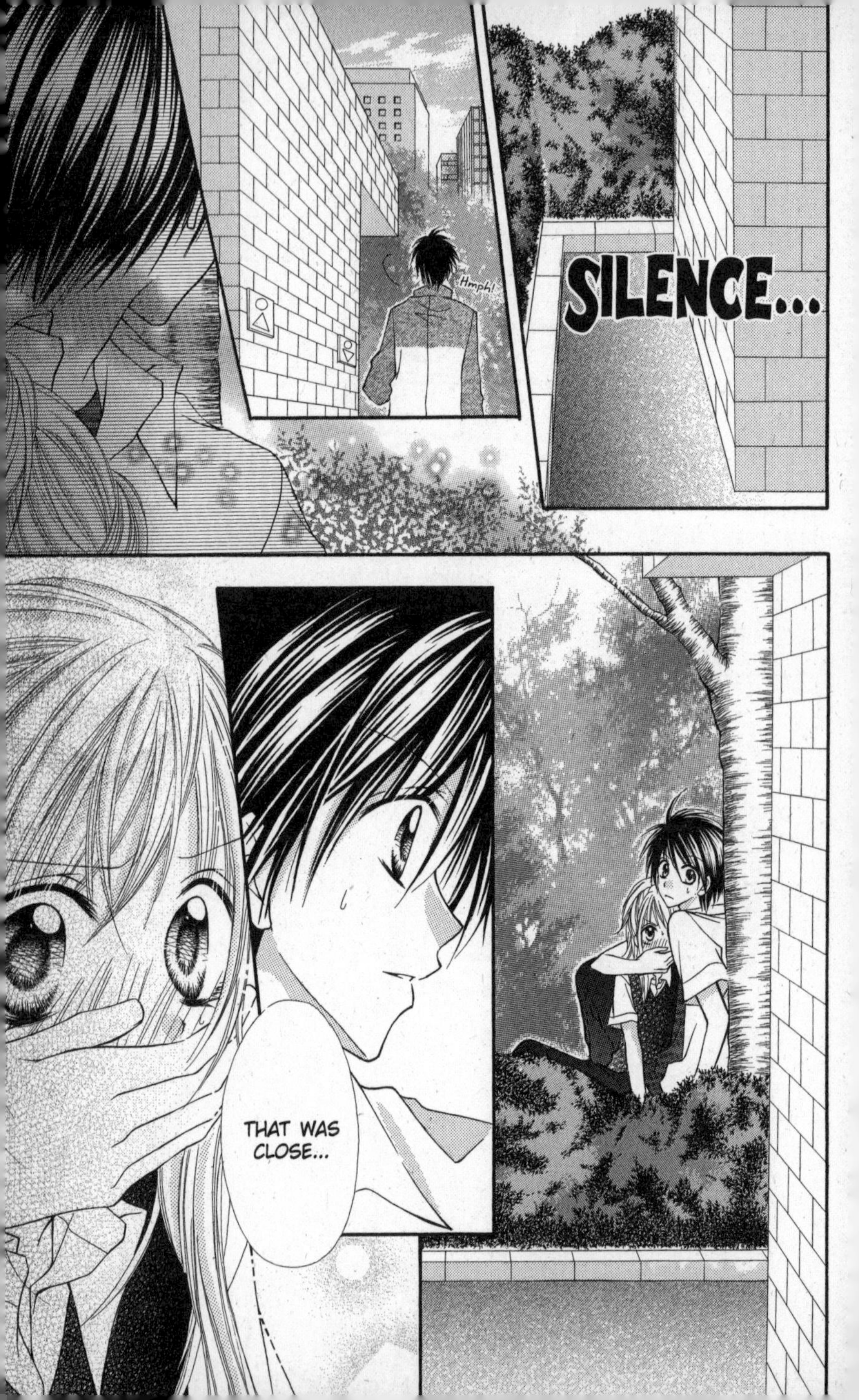

SILENCE...
Hmph!
THAT WAS CLOSE...

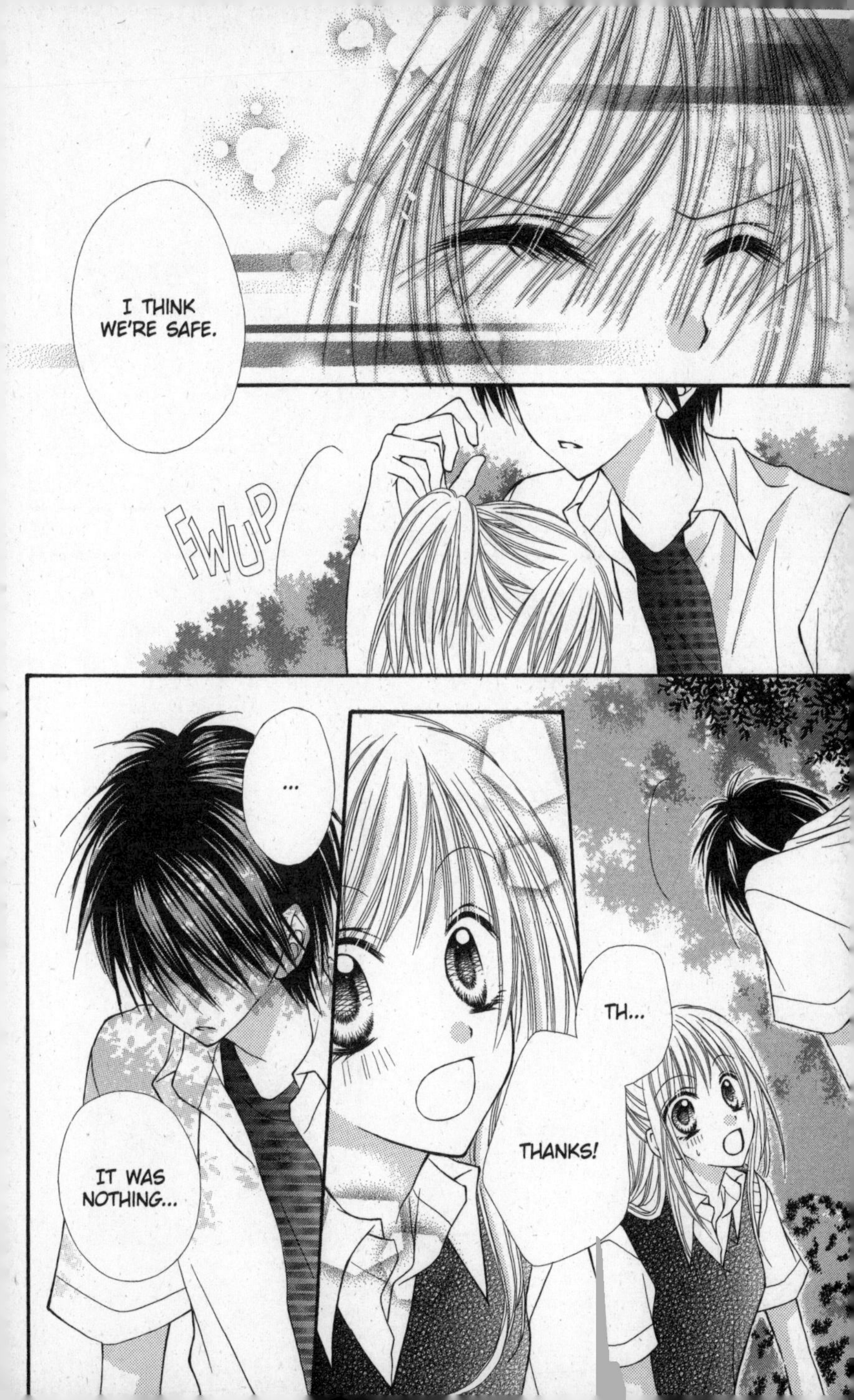
I THINK WE'RE SAFE.
FWUP
TH...
THANKS!
...
IT WAS NOTHING...

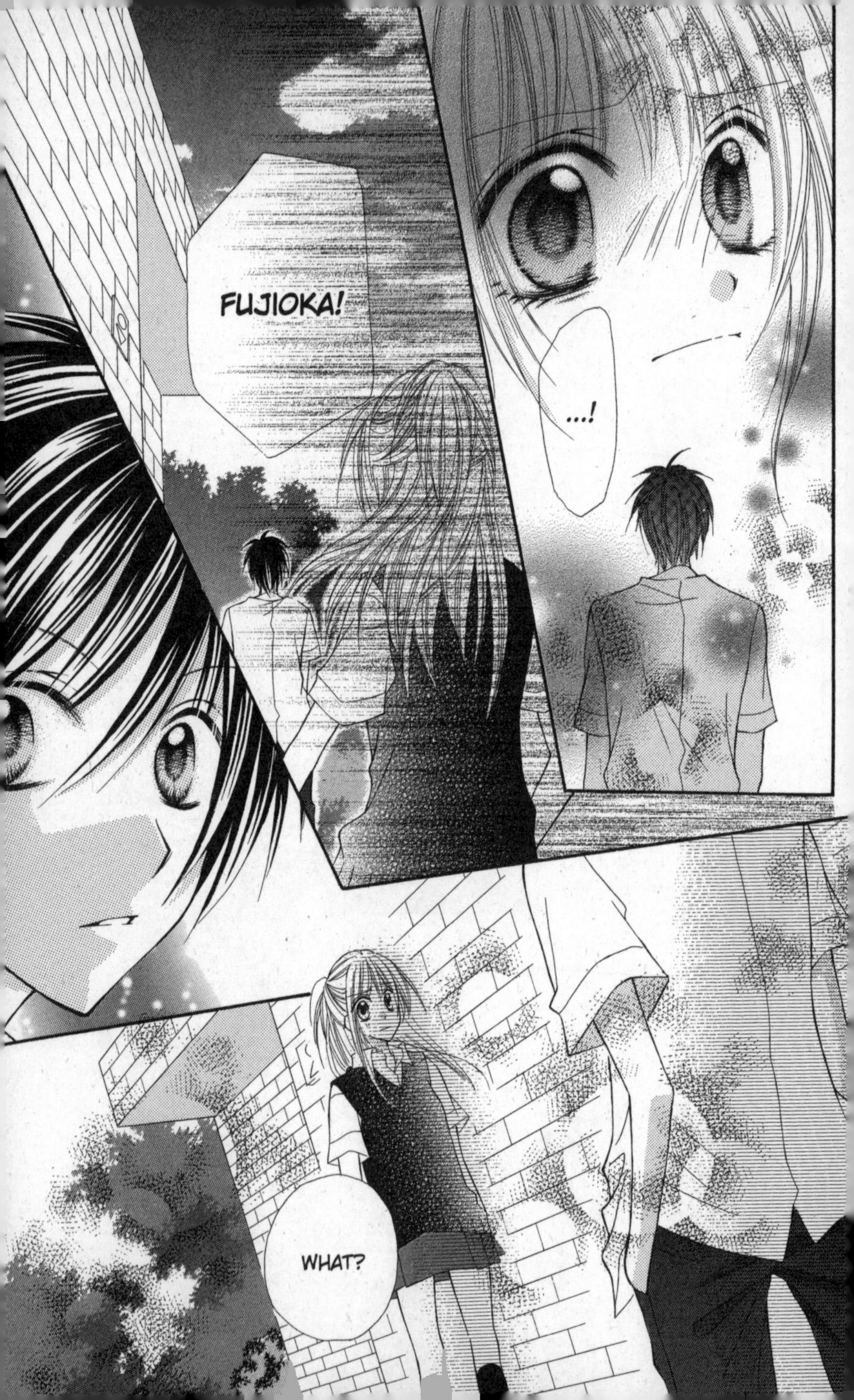
...!
FUJIOKA!
WHAT?

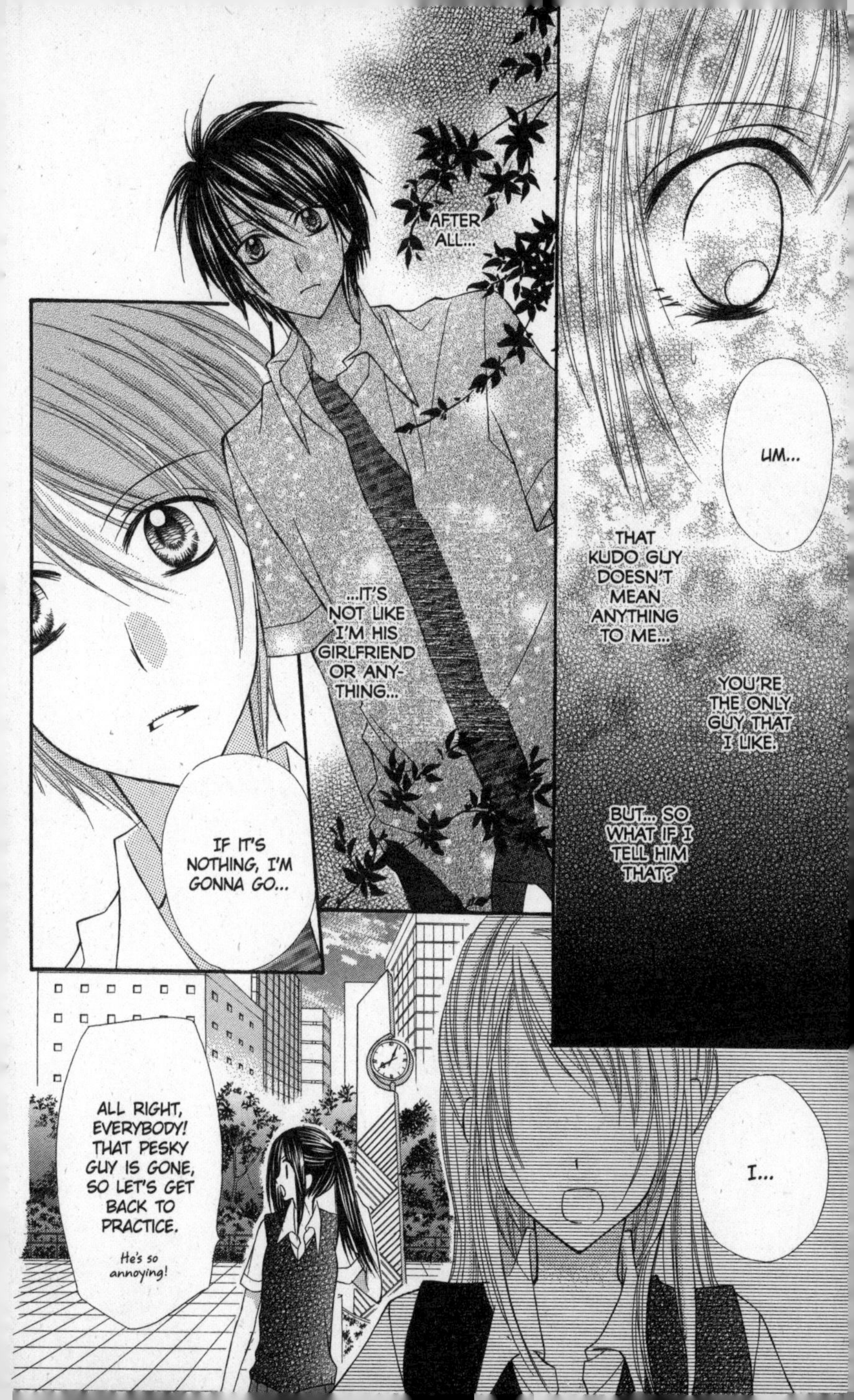
UM...
THAT KUDO GUY DOESN'T MEAN ANYTHING TO ME...
YOU'RE THE ONLY GUY THAT I LIKE.
BUT... SO WHAT IF I TELL HIM THAT?
AFTER ALL...
...IT'S NOT LIKE I'M HIS GIRLFRIEND OR ANY-THING...
IF IT'S NOTHING, I'M GONNA GO...
I...
ALL RIGHT, EVERYBODY! THAT PESKY GUY IS GONE, SO LET'S GET BACK TO PRACTICE.
He's so annoying!

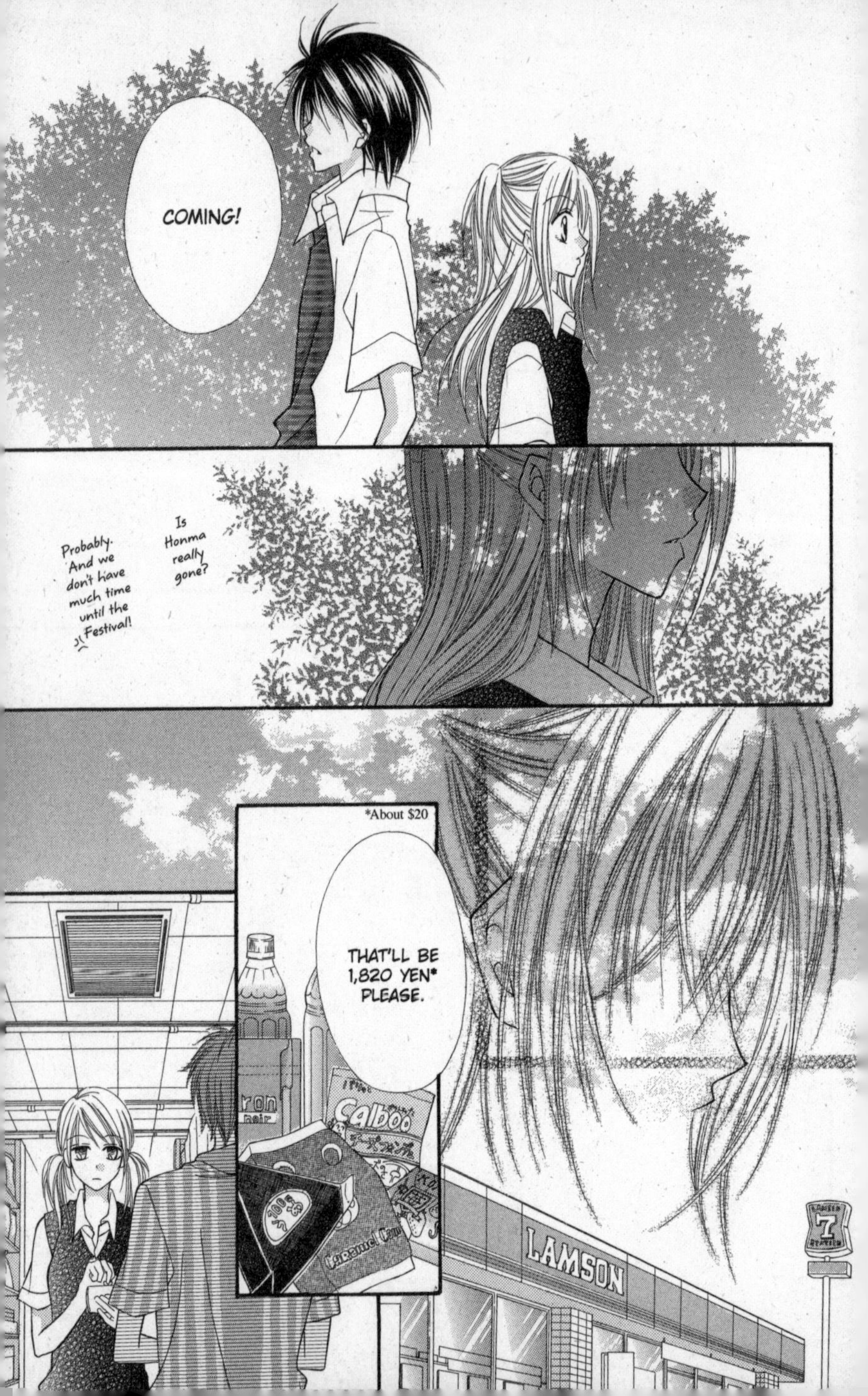
COMING!
Is Honma really gone?
Probably. And we don't have much time until the Festival!
THAT'LL BE 1,820 YEN* PLEASE.
*About $20
LAMSON

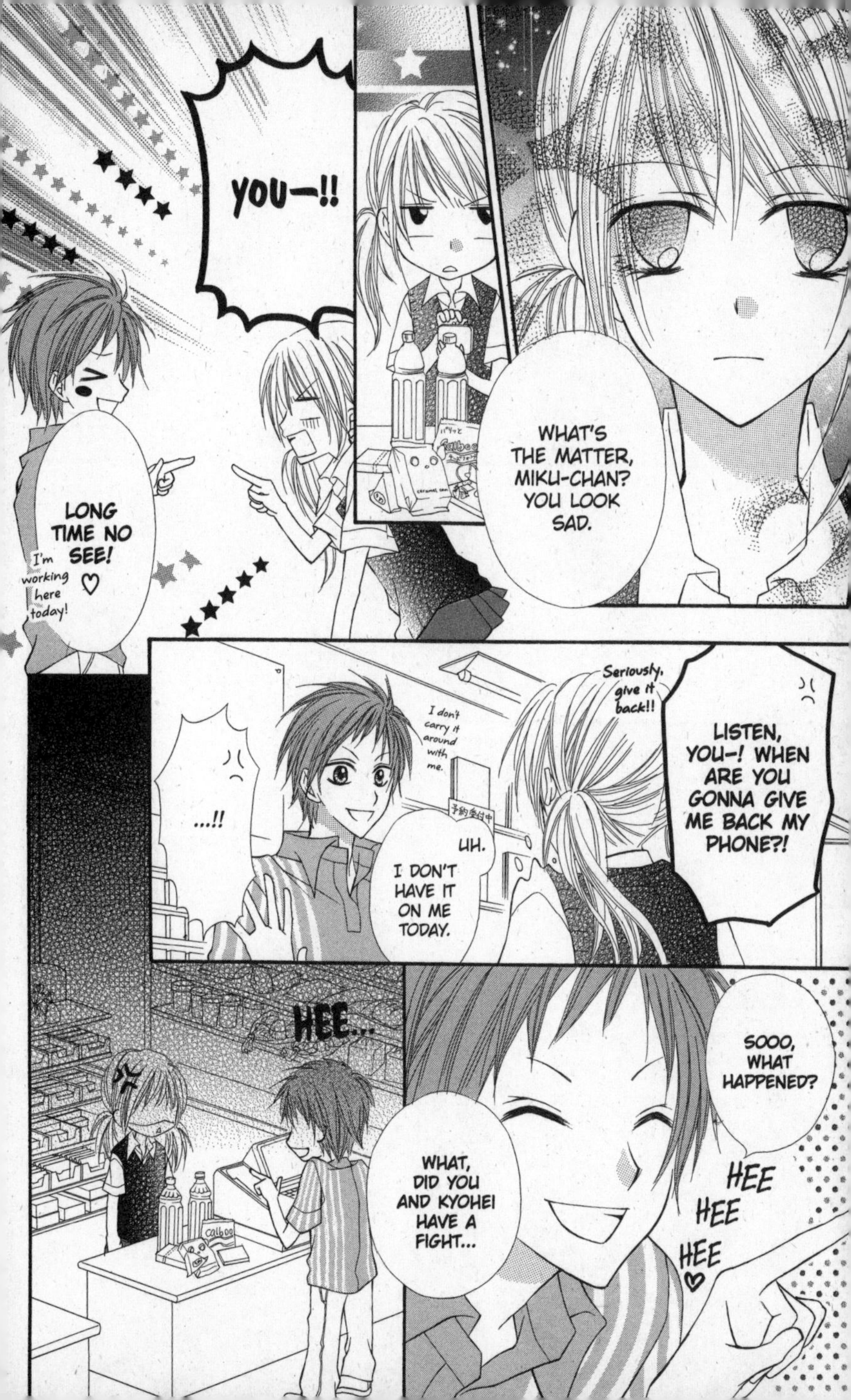
WHAT'S THE MATTER, MIKU-CHAN? YOU LOOK SAD.
YOU—!!
LONG TIME NO SEE! ♡
I'm working here today!
Seriously, give it back!!
LISTEN, YOU—! WHEN ARE YOU GONNA GIVE ME BACK MY PHONE?!
UH.
I DON'T HAVE IT ON ME TODAY.
I don't carry it around with me.
...!!
SOOO, WHAT HAPPENED?
HEE HEE HEE ♡
WHAT, DID YOU AND KYOHEI HAVE A FIGHT...
HEE...

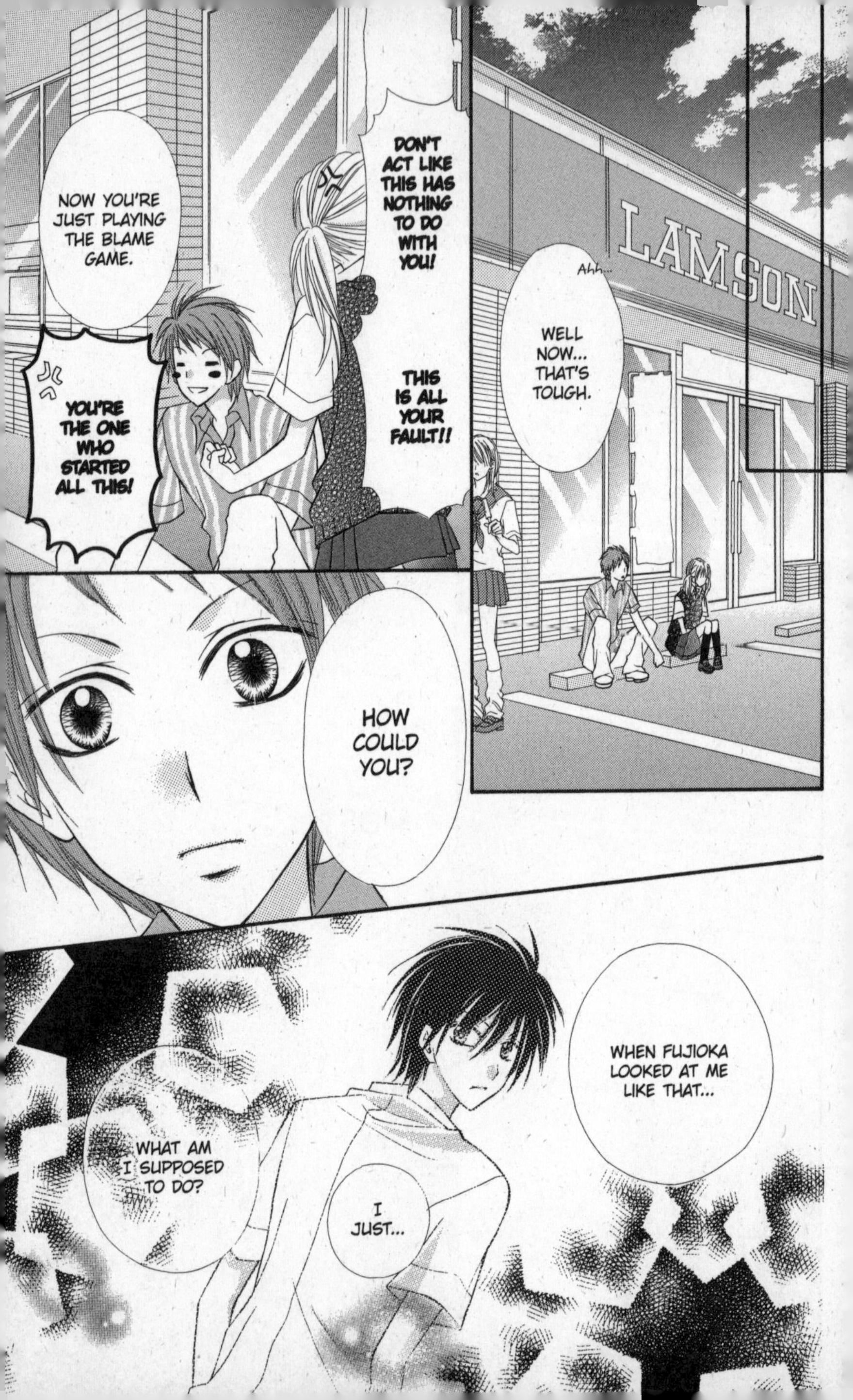
LAMSON
Ahh...
WELL NOW... THAT'S TOUGH.
DON'T ACT LIKE THIS HAS NOTHING TO DO WITH YOU!
NOW YOU'RE JUST PLAYING THE BLAME GAME.
THIS IS ALL YOUR FAULT!!
YOU'RE THE ONE WHO STARTED ALL THIS!
HOW COULD YOU?
WHEN FUJIOKA LOOKED AT ME LIKE THAT...
I JUST...
WHAT AM I SUPPOSED TO DO?

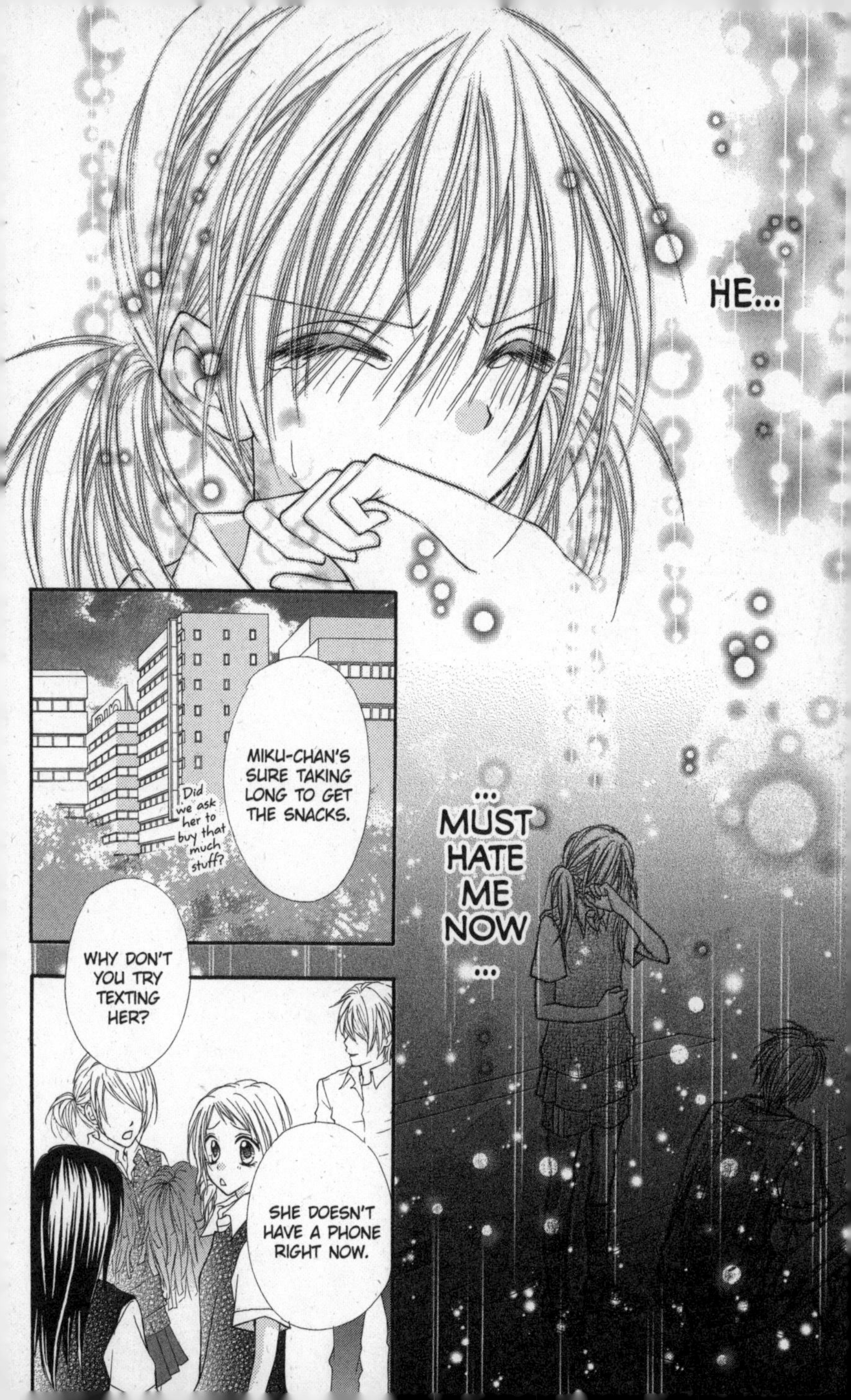
HE...
...MUST HATE ME NOW...
MIKU-CHAN'S SURE TAKING LONG TO GET THE SNACKS.
Did we ask her to buy that much stuff?
WHY DON'T YOU TRY TEXTING HER?
SHE DOESN'T HAVE A PHONE RIGHT NOW.

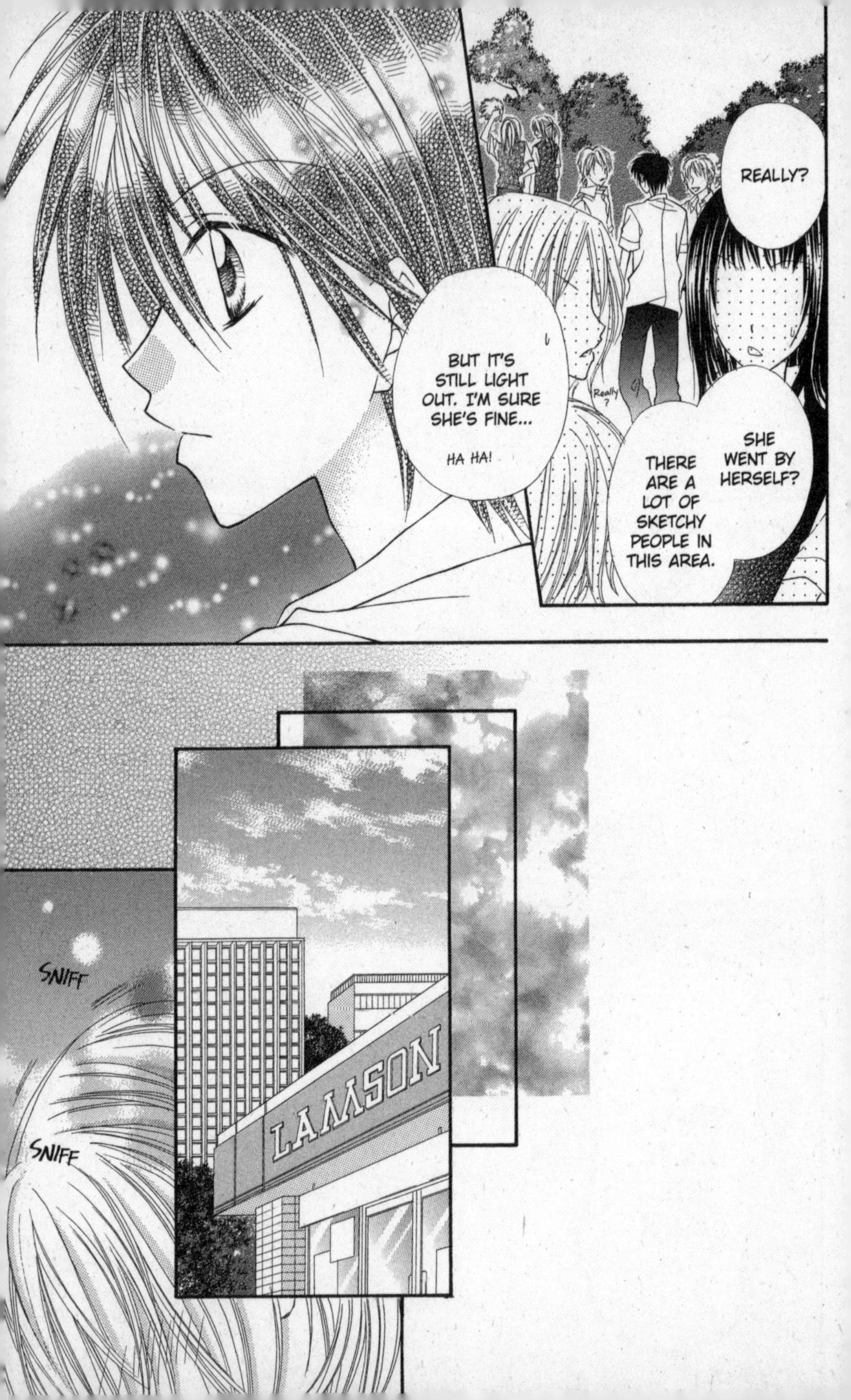
REALLY?
SHE WENT BY HERSELF?
THERE ARE A LOT OF SKETCHY PEOPLE IN THIS AREA.
Really?
BUT IT'S STILL LIGHT OUT. I'M SURE SHE'S FINE...
HA HA!
LAAASON
SNIFF
SNIFF

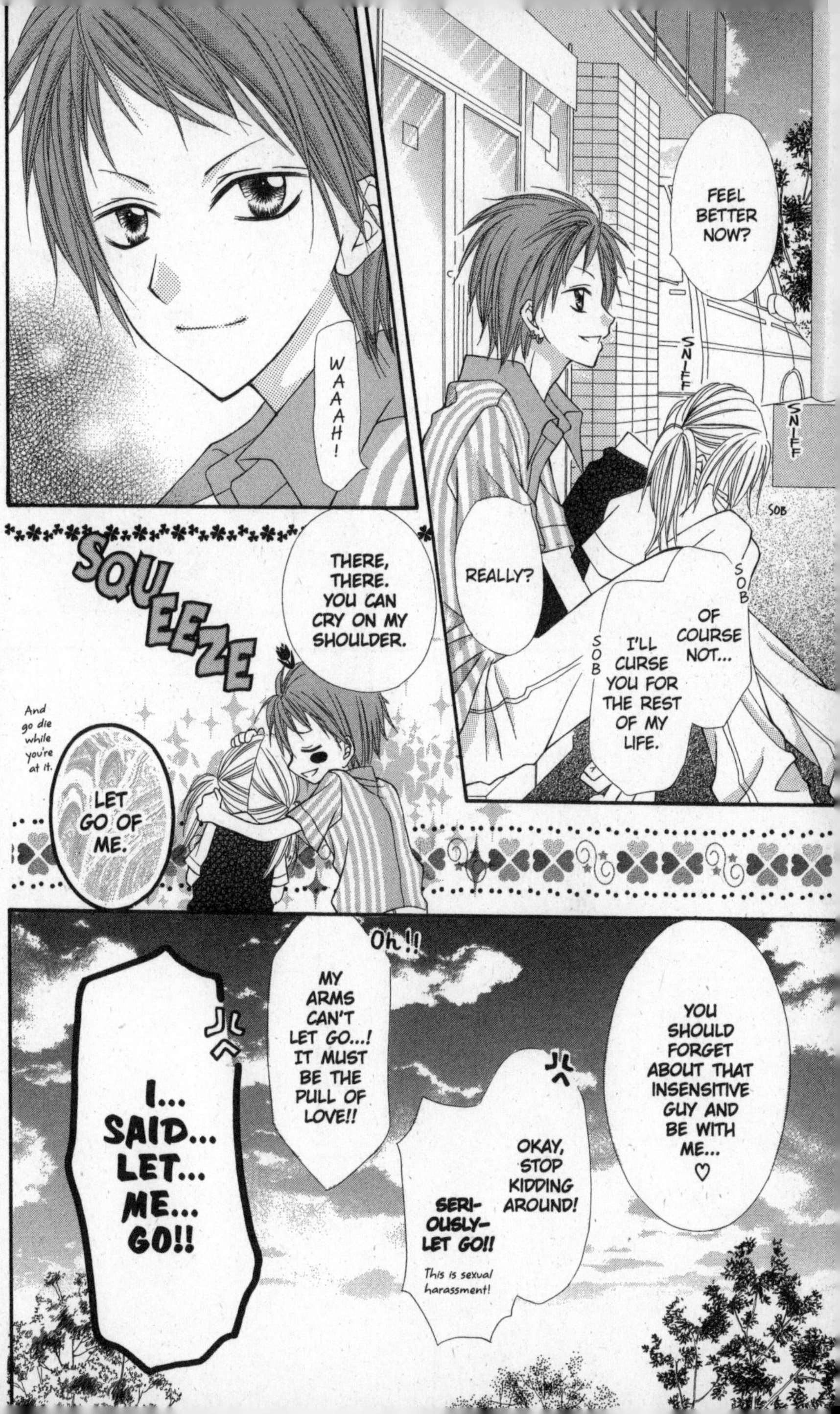

FEEL BETTER NOW?
SNIFF
SNIFF
SOB
REALLY?
SOB
OF COURSE NOT...
SOB
I'LL CURSE YOU FOR THE REST OF MY LIFE.
WAAAAH!
THERE, THERE. YOU CAN CRY ON MY SHOULDER.
SQUEEZE
LET GO OF ME.
And go die while you're at it.
YOU SHOULD FORGET ABOUT THAT INSENSITIVE GUY AND BE WITH ME... ♡
Oh!!
MY ARMS CAN'T LET GO...! IT MUST BE THE PULL OF LOVE!!
OKAY, STOP KIDDING AROUND!
SERI-OUSLY-LET GO!!
This is sexual harassment!
I... SAID... LET... ME... GO!!

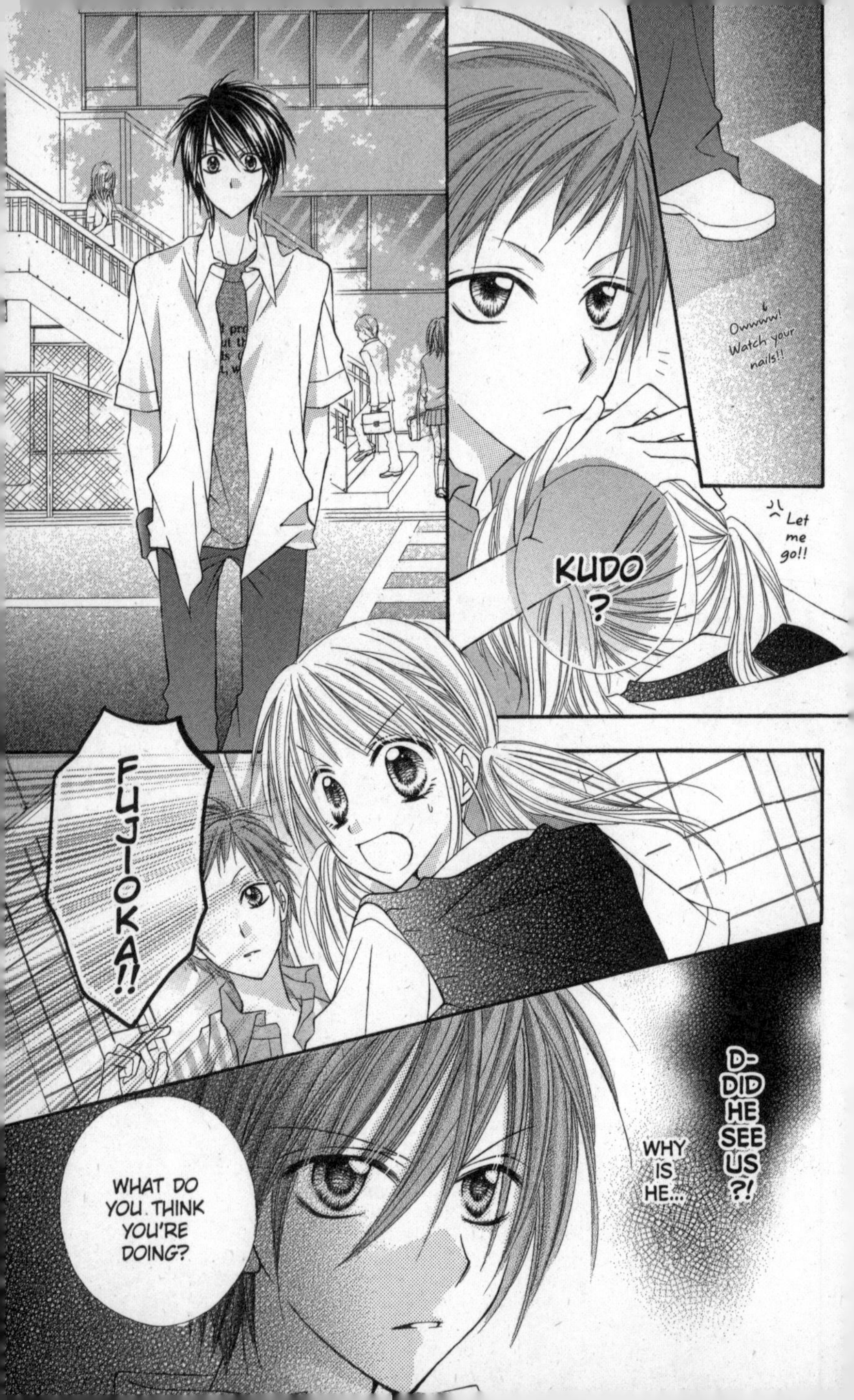
Owwww! Watch your nails!!
Let me go!!
KUDO?
FUJIOKA!!
D-DID HE SEE US?!
WHY IS HE...
WHAT DO YOU THINK YOU'RE DOING?

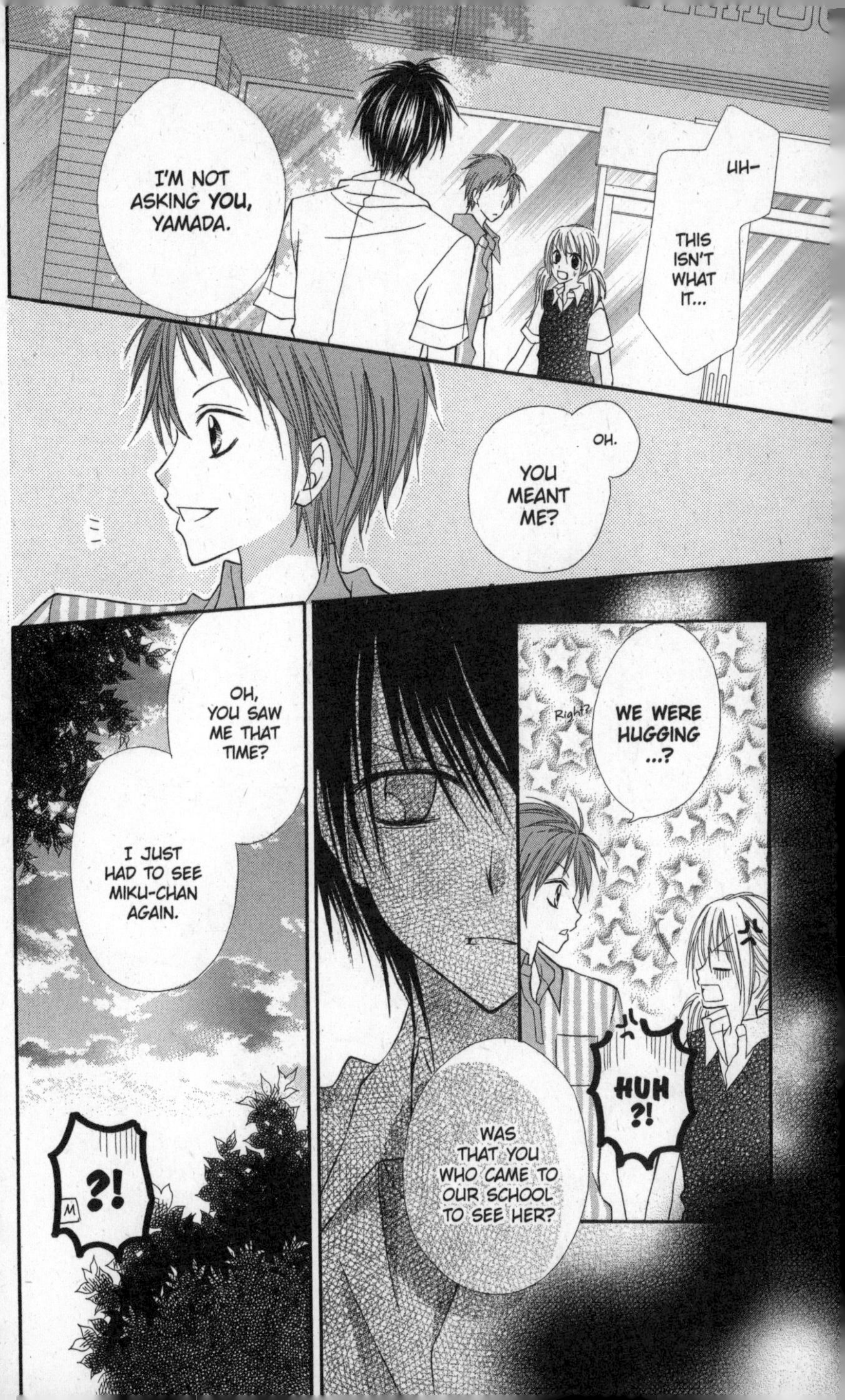
UH-
THIS ISN'T WHAT IT...
I'M NOT ASKING YOU, YAMADA.
OH.
YOU MEANT ME?
WE WERE HUGGING ...?
Right?
HUH ?!
WAS THAT YOU WHO CAME TO OUR SCHOOL TO SEE HER?
OH, YOU SAW ME THAT TIME?
I JUST HAD TO SEE MIKU-CHAN AGAIN.
?!

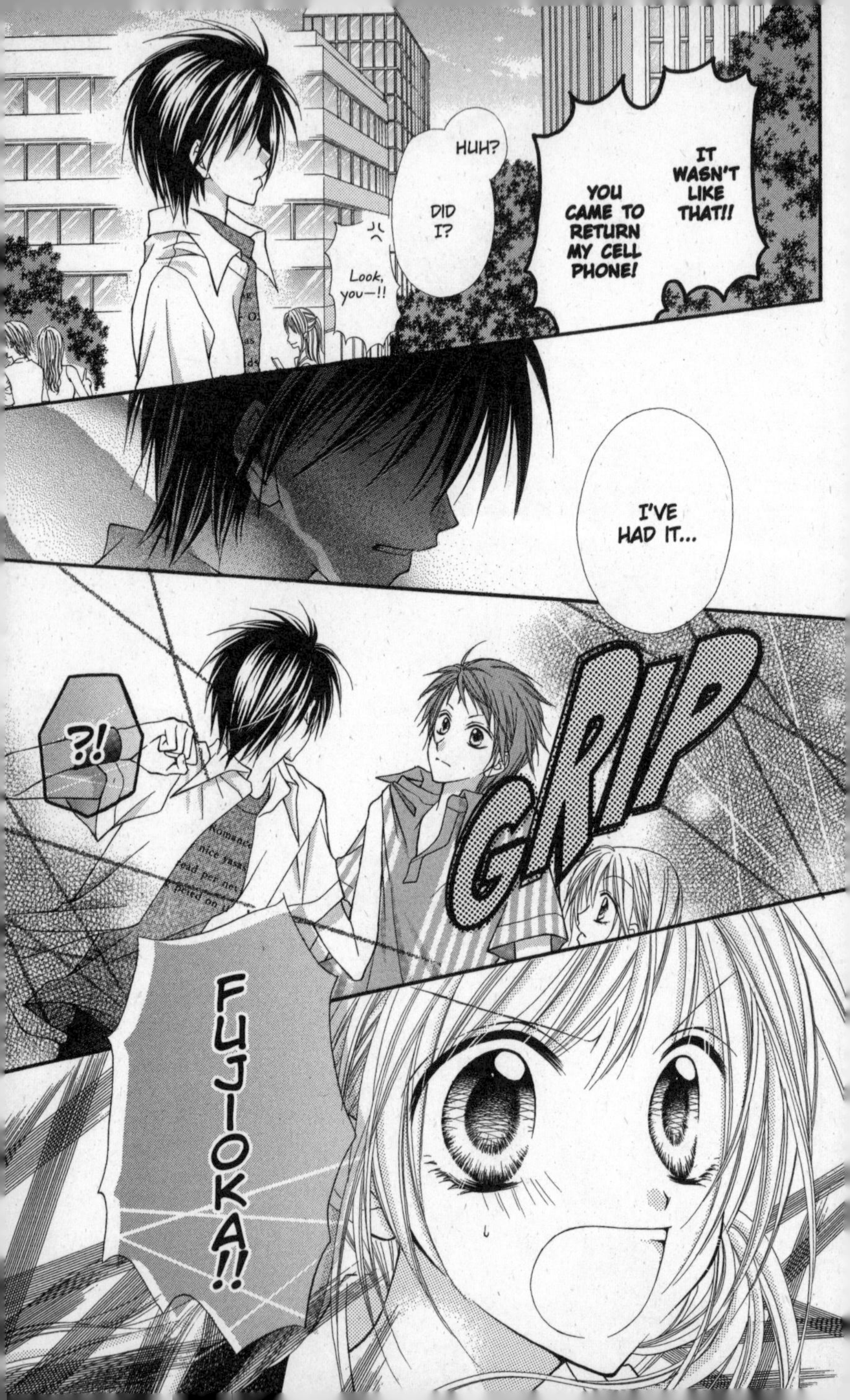
IT WASN'T LIKE THAT!!
YOU CAME TO RETURN MY CELL PHONE!
HUH?
DID I?
Look, you—!!
I'VE HAD IT...
GRIP
?!
FUJIOKA!!

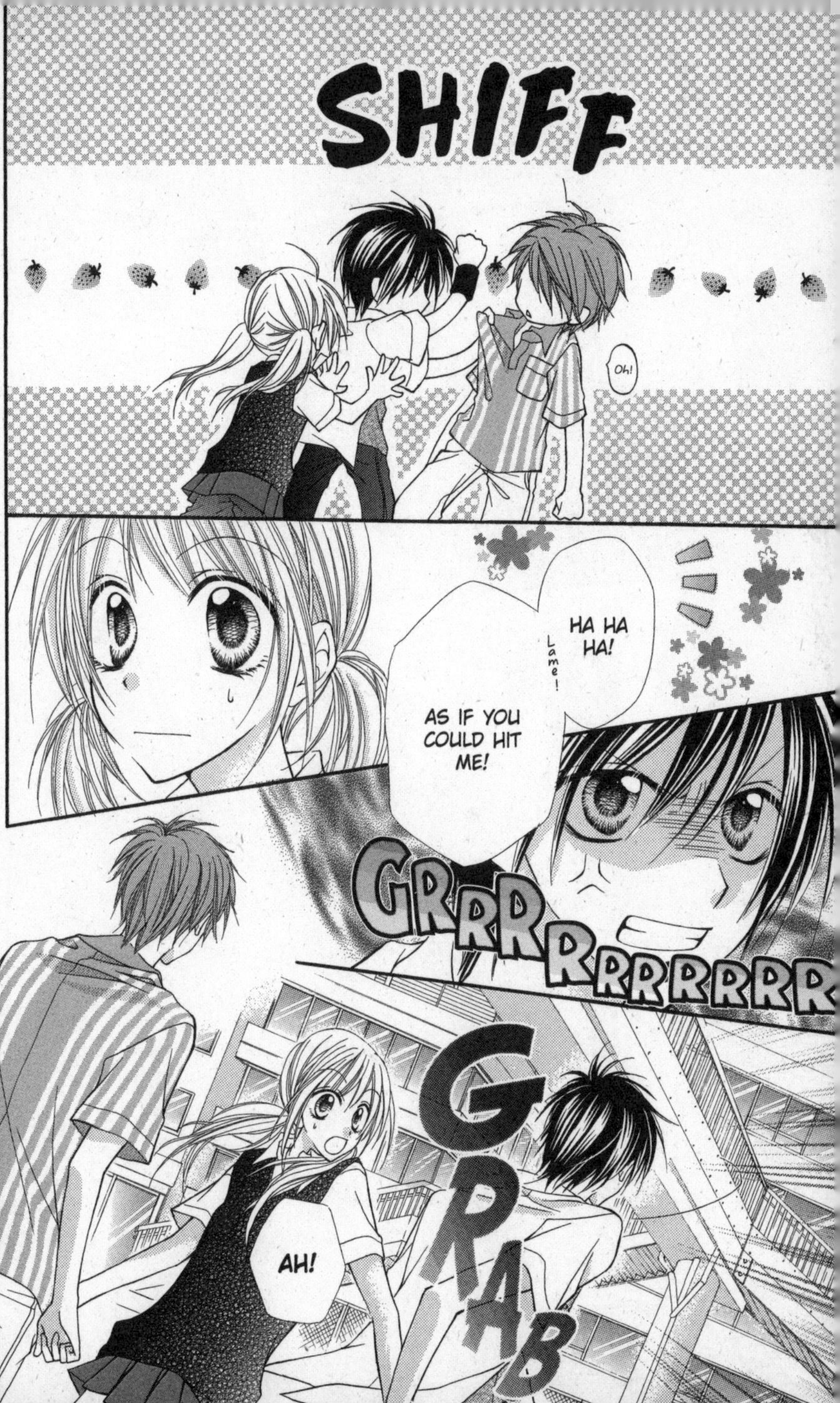
SHIFF
Oh!
HA HA HA!
Lame!
AS IF YOU COULD HIT ME!
GRRRRRRRRRRRR
GRAB
AH!

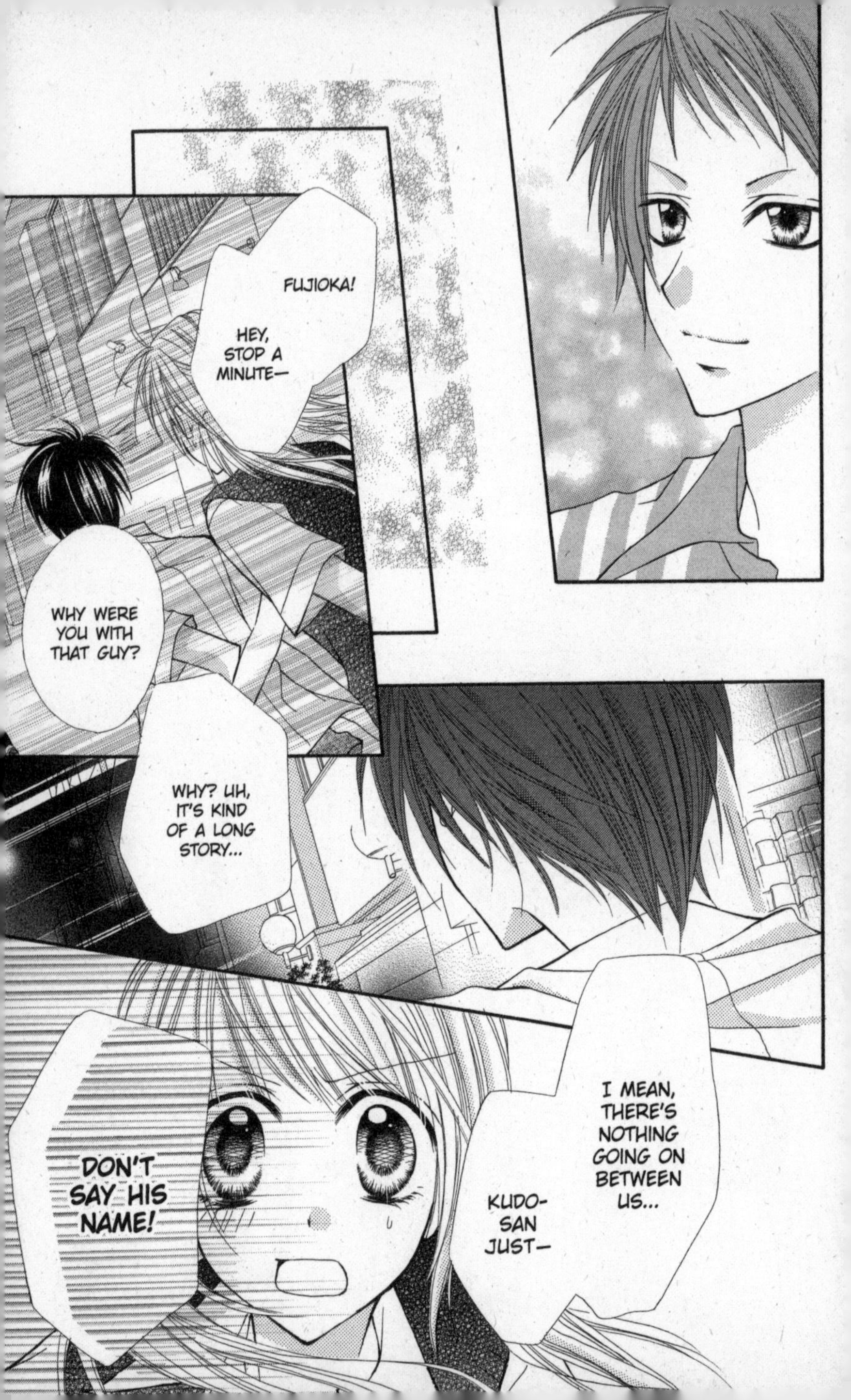
FUJIOKA!
HEY, STOP A MINUTE—
WHY WERE YOU WITH THAT GUY?
WHY? UH, IT'S KIND OF A LONG STORY...
I MEAN, THERE'S NOTHING GOING ON BETWEEN US...
KUDO-SAN JUST—
DON'T SAY HIS NAME!

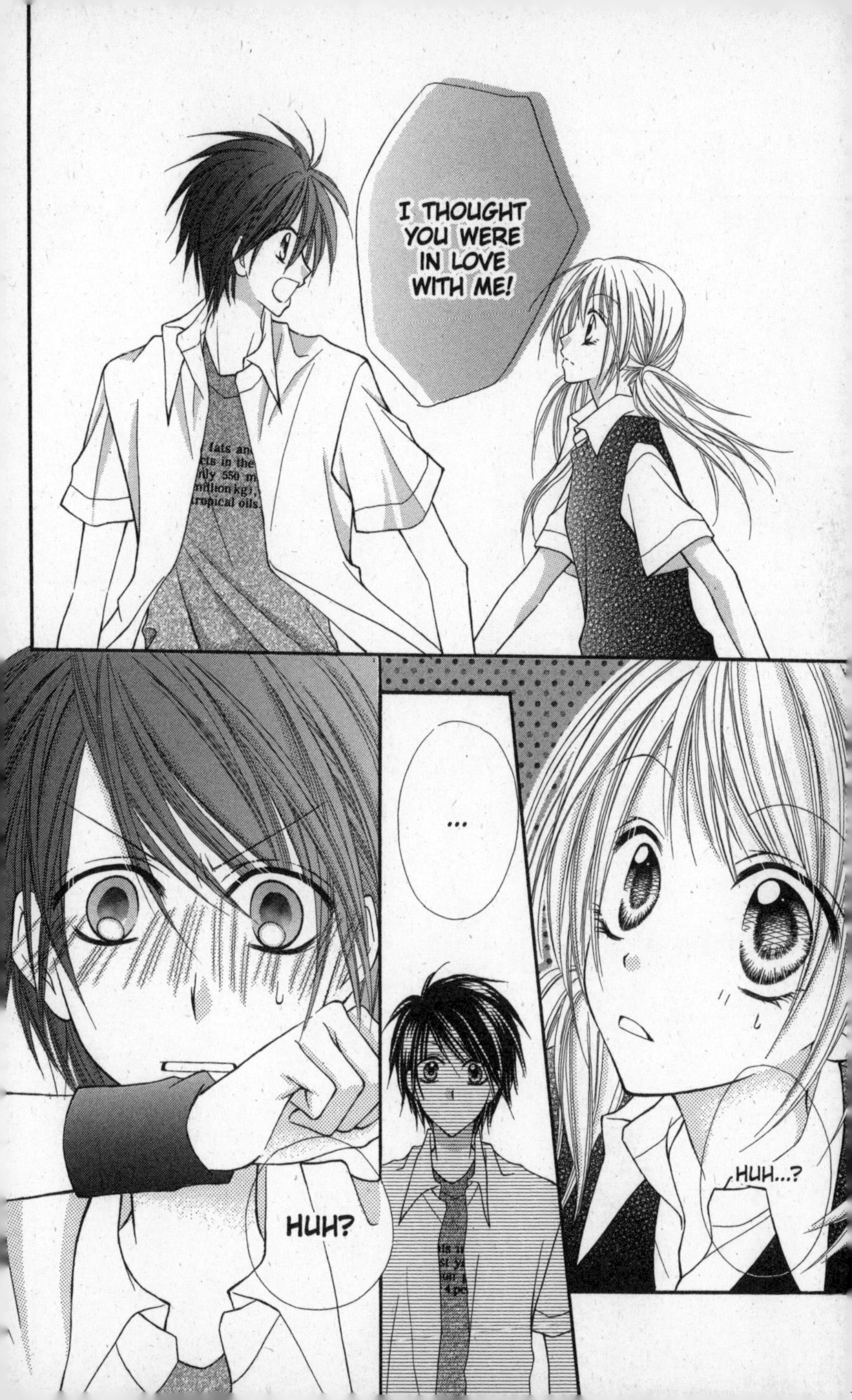
I THOUGHT YOU WERE IN LOVE WITH ME!
HUH...?
...
HUH?

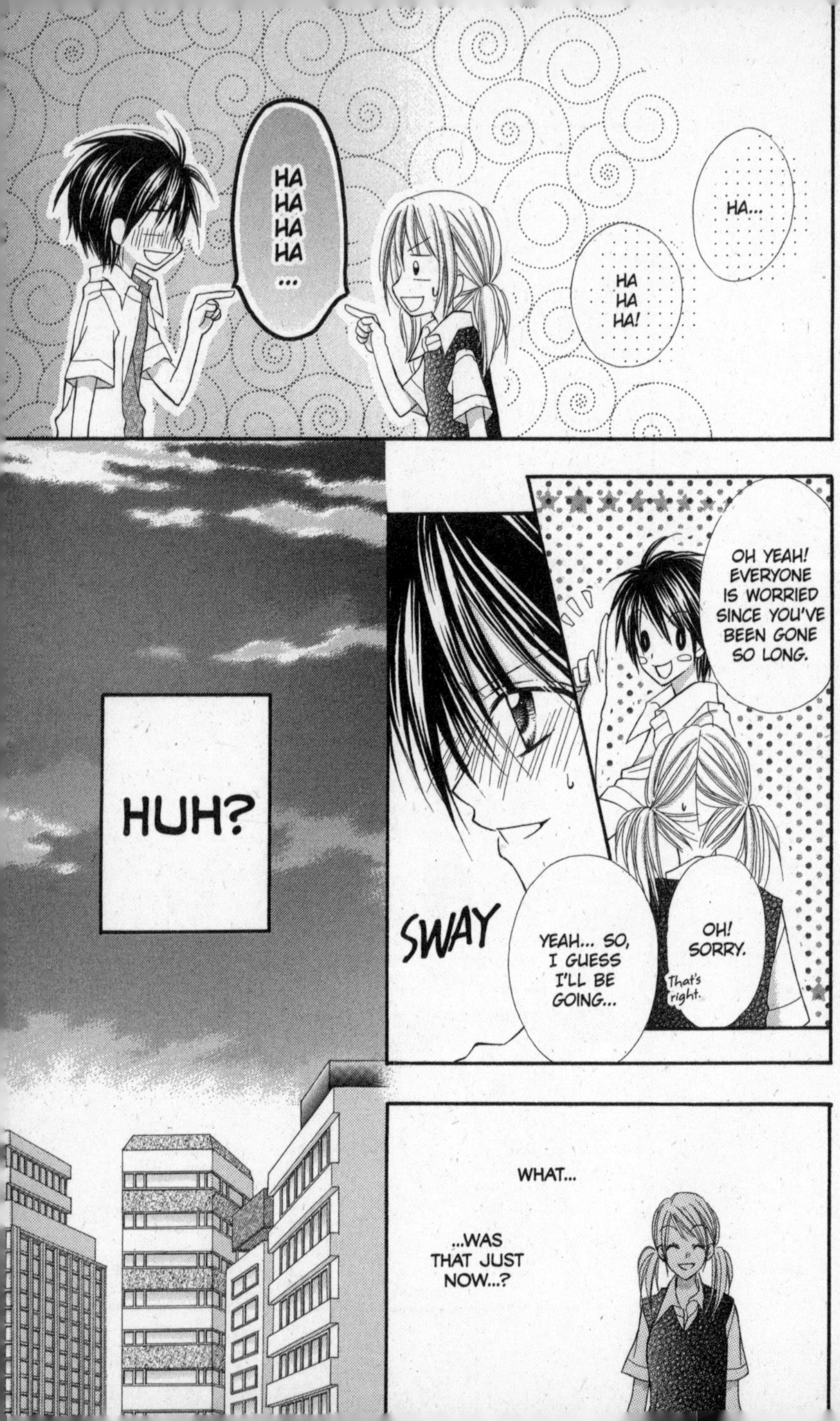
HA...
HA HA HA!
HA HA HA HA ...
OH YEAH! EVERYONE IS WORRIED SINCE YOU'VE BEEN GONE SO LONG.
OH! SORRY.
That's right.
YEAH... SO, I GUESS I'LL BE GOING...
SWAY
WHAT...
...WAS THAT JUST NOW...?
HUH?

Haruta's Diary

"This is getting really scary..."

Part ①

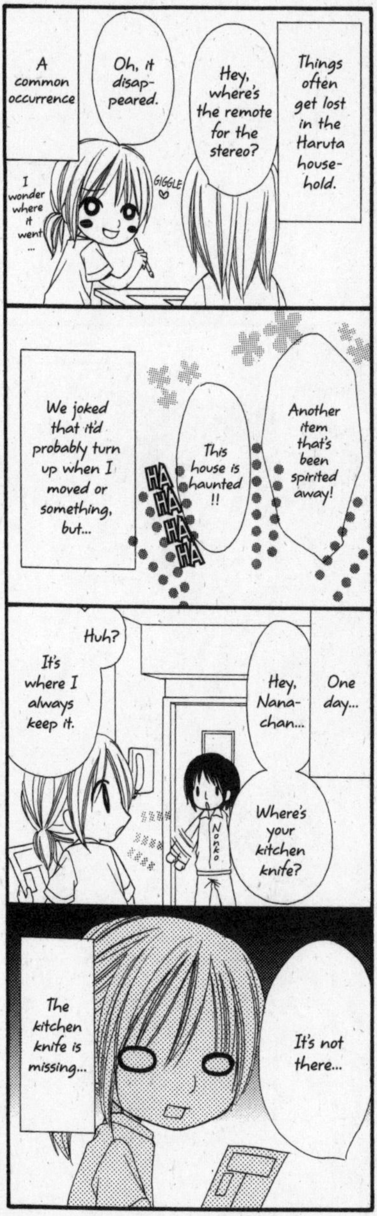
Things often get lost in the Haruta household.
Hey, where's the remote for the stereo?
Oh, it disappeared.
A common occurrence
GIGGLE
I wonder where it went...
Another item that's been spirited away!
This house is haunted!!
HA HA HA HA
We joked that it'd probably turn up when I moved or something, but...
One day...
Hey, Nana-chan...
Where's your kitchen knife?
Nonko
Huh?
It's where I always keep it.
It's not there...
The kitchen knife is missing...

Continued in part ②

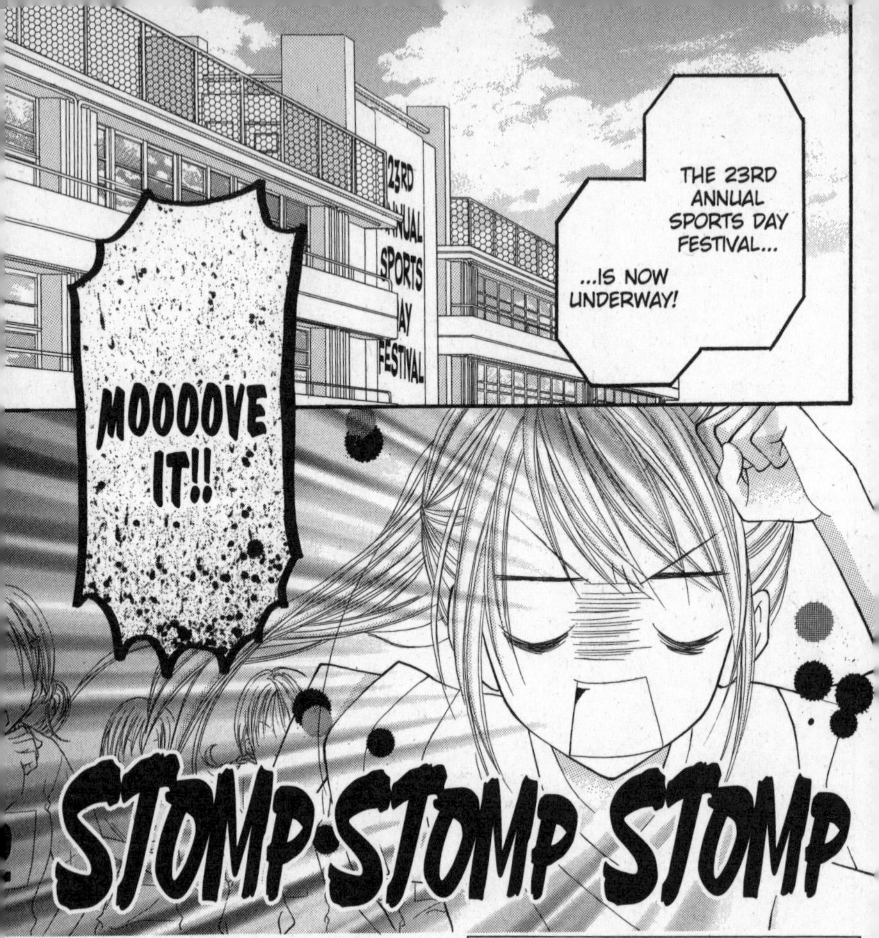
THE 23RD ANNUAL SPORTS DAY FESTIVAL...
...IS NOW UNDERWAY!
MOOOOVE IT!!
STOMP STOMP STOMP

SMALL TALK ②

✿ The one-shot story "The Sweetness After" was originally published in the February issue of Ribon magazine (along with chapter 13 of Cactus, but I had actually finished it before I had drawn chapter 12. I've come to the conclusion that I shouldn't draw extra stories when I'm working on a serialized series.

I really, really, really love drawing one-shots, but I physically can't handle the extra work! (laugh)

I nearly died after drinking three energy drinks in a single day.

*After the energy high wears off, the exhaustion hits you all at once.

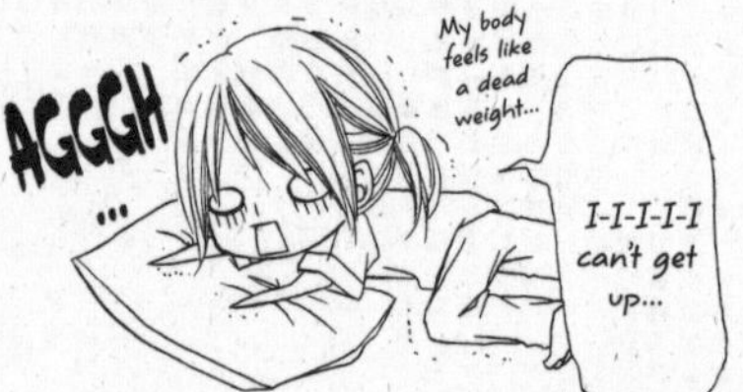
AGGGH
...
My body feels like a dead weight...
I-I-I-I-I can't get up...

I learned the value of following recommended dosages that day.

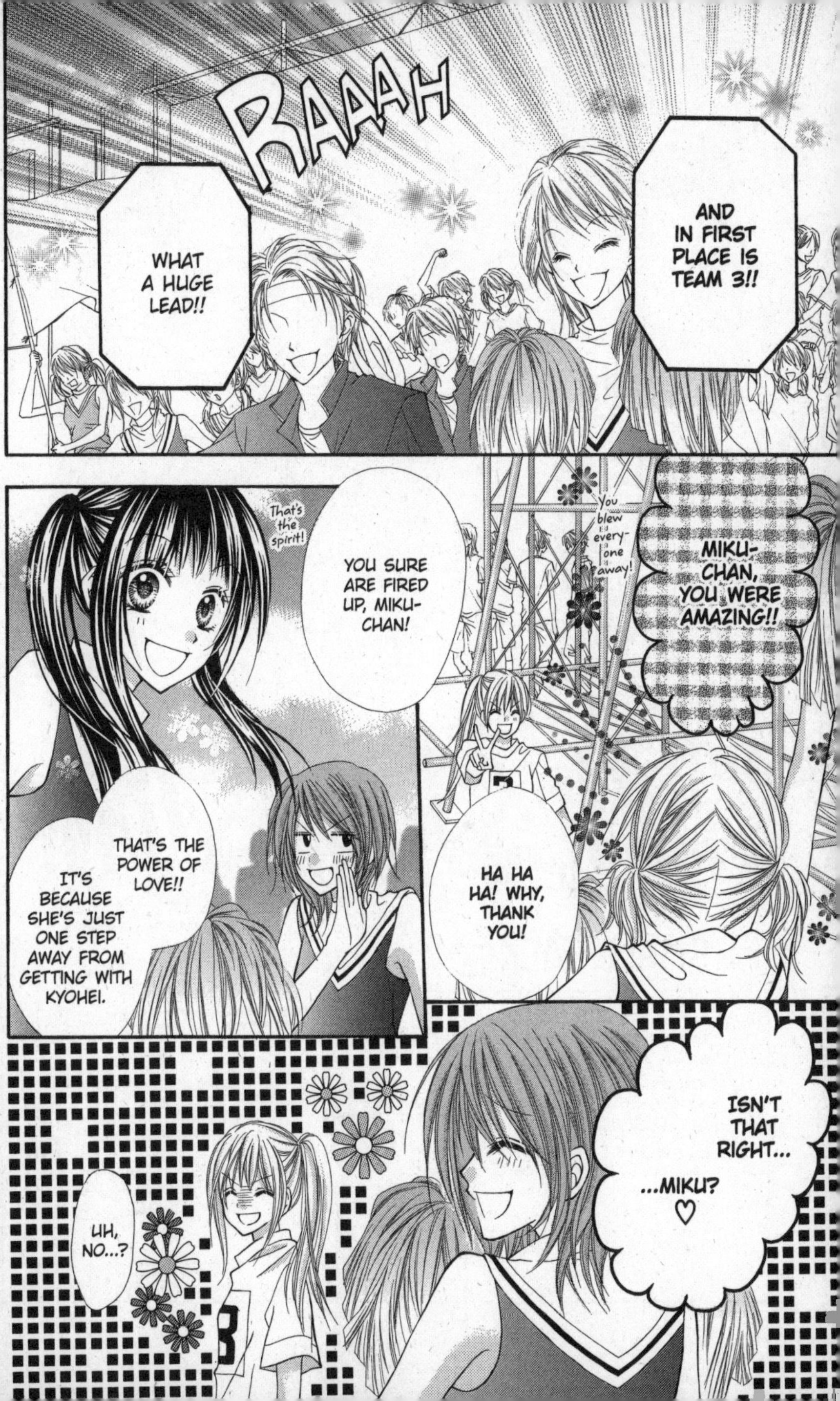
RAAAH
AND IN FIRST PLACE IS TEAM 3!!
WHAT A HUGE LEAD!!
MIKU-CHAN, YOU WERE AMAZING!!
You blew every-one away!
HA HA HA! WHY, THANK YOU!
YOU SURE ARE FIRED UP, MIKU-CHAN!
That's the spirit!
THAT'S THE POWER OF LOVE!!
IT'S BECAUSE SHE'S JUST ONE STEP AWAY FROM GETTING WITH KYOHEI.
ISN'T THAT RIGHT...
...MIKU? ♡
UH, NO...?

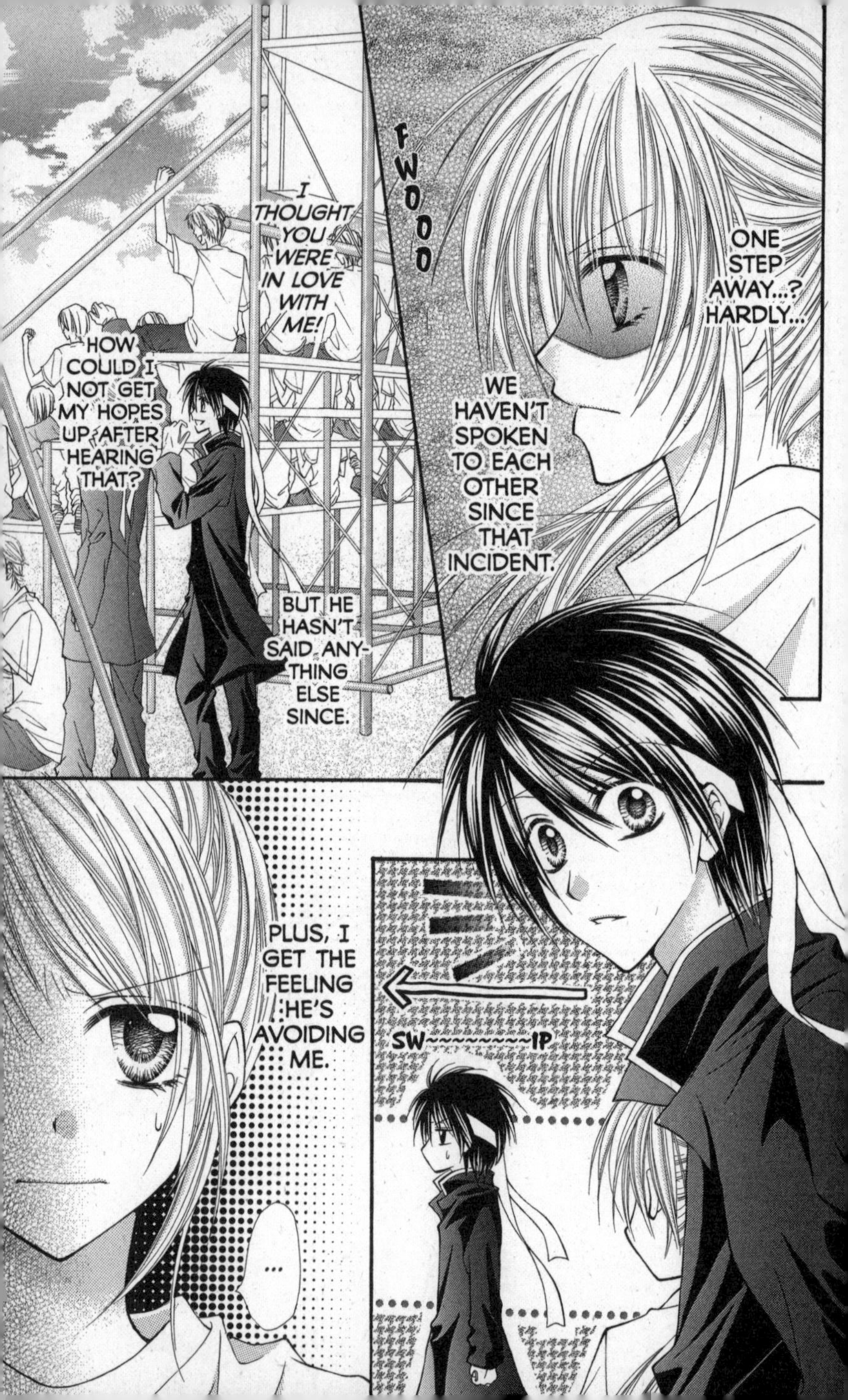
FWOOO
ONE STEP AWAY...? HARDLY...
WE HAVEN'T SPOKEN TO EACH OTHER SINCE THAT INCIDENT.
I THOUGHT YOU WERE IN LOVE WITH ME!
HOW COULD I NOT GET MY HOPES UP AFTER HEARING THAT?
BUT HE HASN'T SAID ANYTHING ELSE SINCE.
SW~~~~~~~~~IP
PLUS, I GET THE FEELING HE'S AVOIDING ME.
...

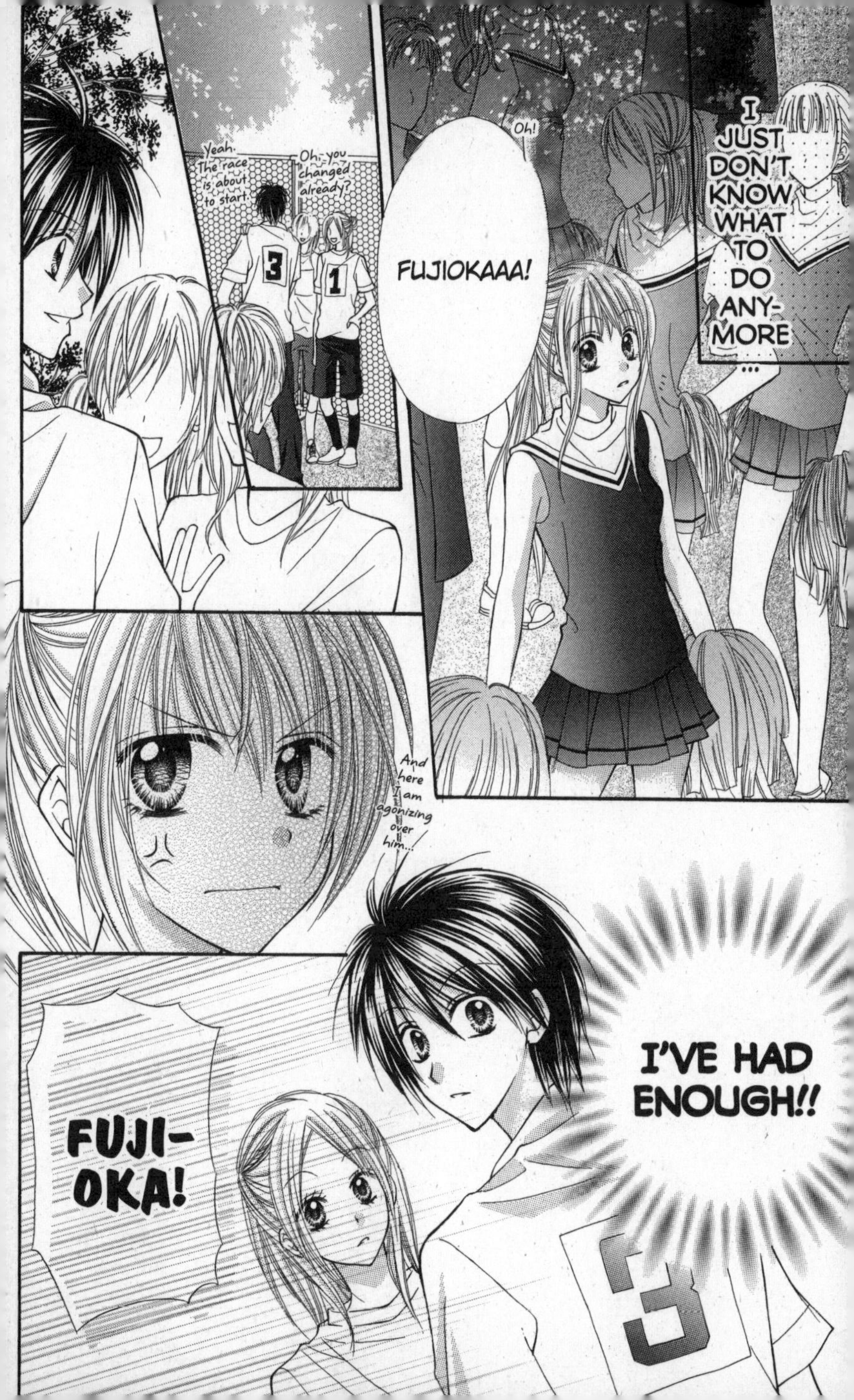
I JUST DON'T KNOW WHAT TO DO ANYMORE...
Oh!
FUJIOKAAA!
Oh, you changed already?
Yeah. The race is about to start.
And here I am agonizing over him...
I'VE HAD ENOUGH!!
FUJI-OKA!

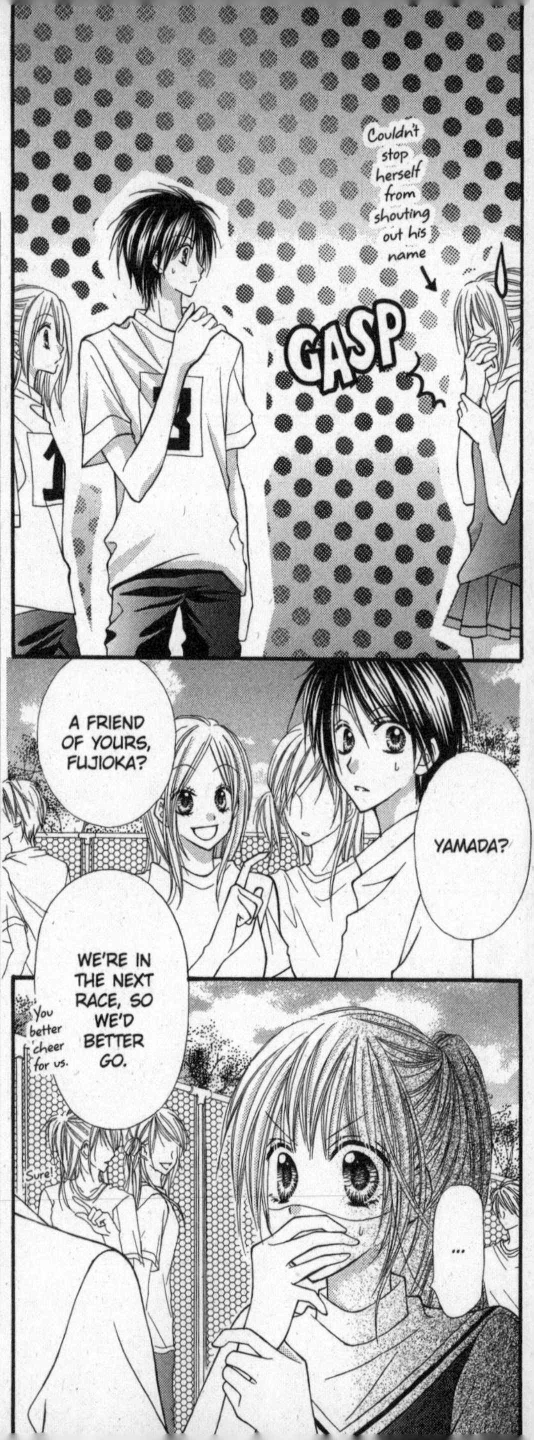
Couldn't stop herself from shouting out his name
GASP
YAMADA?
A FRIEND OF YOURS, FUJIOKA?
WE'RE IN THE NEXT RACE, SO WE'D BETTER GO.
You better cheer for us.
Sure!
...

4

That's right, a while back (okay, a long while back) I took this fortune-telling quiz on the Internet that said I am a Blood Type O who has similar personality traits to a Blood Type A.

My family said that was totally off but my assistants agreed with it. Hmm, why is there such a difference of opinions here?? When one of my assistants found out I was Type O, she was surprised and said, "I thought you were a Type A!"

Meaning, as a Type A, that I'm highly strung and detail-oriented? The only thing I agonize over is my manga (but I'm sure I don't think it over as other mangaka do.♭)

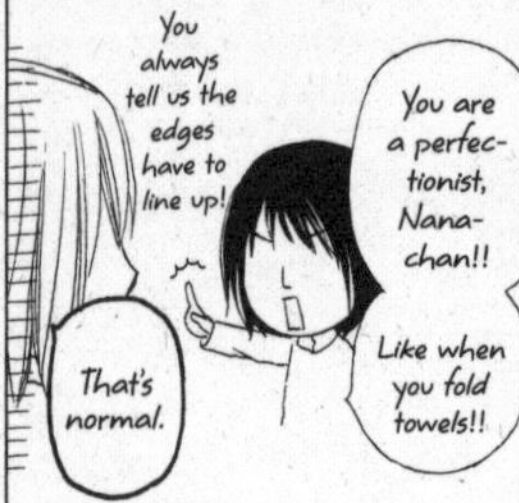
You are a perfectionist, Nana-chan!!
You always tell us the edges have to line up!
Like when you fold towels!!
That's normal.

Wait, isn't it...?

Speaking of which, no one who works with me has Type A blood! Even though studies show that the biggest percentage of Japanese are Type A! There are mostly AB's here—a flock of individualistic personalities! I'm the most average one here—how boring.

No, really. I am.

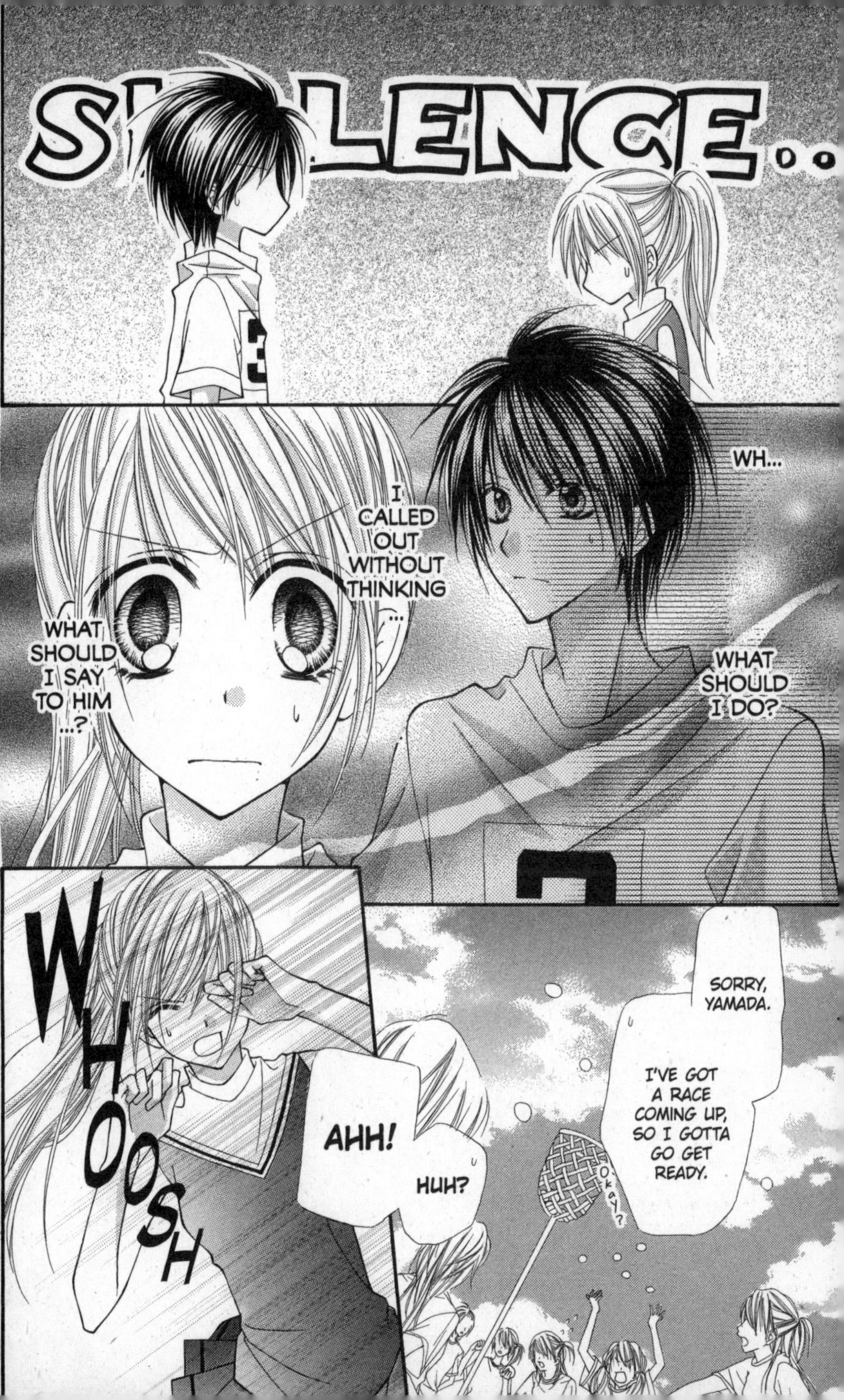
SILENCE...
WH...
WHAT SHOULD I DO?
I CALLED OUT WITHOUT THINKING...
WHAT SHOULD I SAY TO HIM...?
SORRY, YAMADA.
I'VE GOT A RACE COMING UP, SO I GOTTA GO GET READY.
Okay?
HUH?
AHH!
WHOOSH

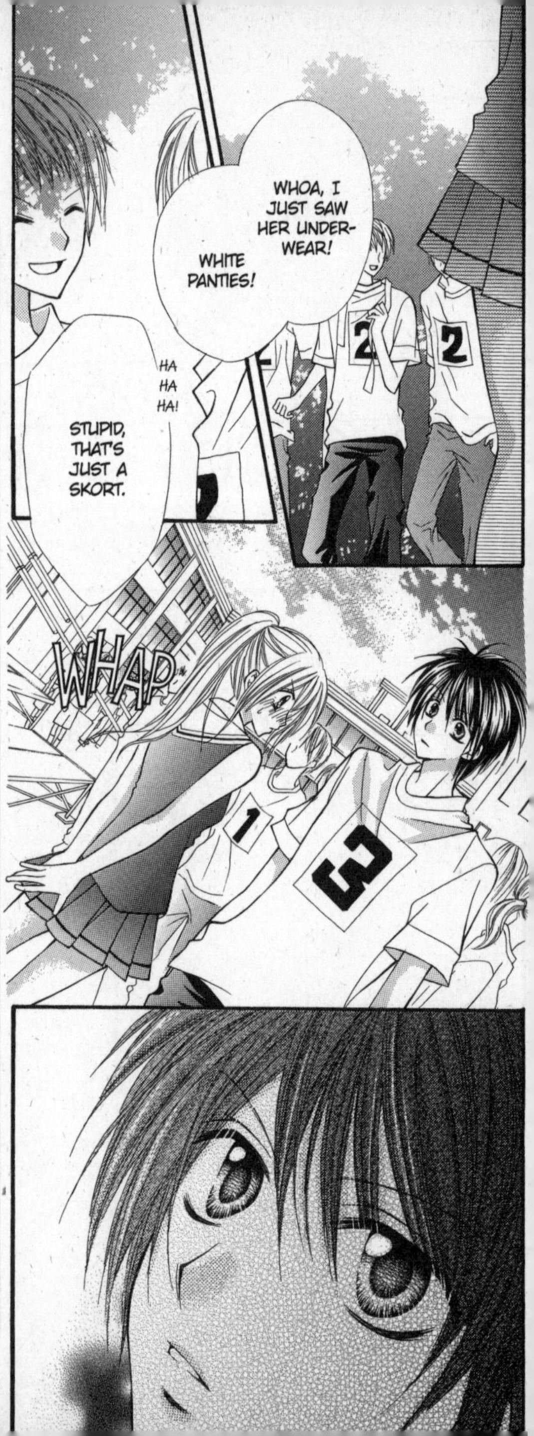
WHOA, I JUST SAW HER UNDER-WEAR!
WHITE PANTIES!
HA HA HA!
STUPID, THAT'S JUST A SKORT.
WHAP

5

So anyway, in this volume (in chapter 12), it finally comes to light that Kudo is Fujioka's older brother. I've been wanting to use a big brother character for a while now. The two don't look alike, but their voices are exactly the same—a pretty convenient set-up in a manga, isn't it? I alluded to that a little in Miku's internal monologue when Kudo first makes an appearance. Some people were able to guess the connection between the two boys just from that. Was it too obvious? I was trying to make it harder to figure out...

Kudo's name was thought up by me and one of my assistants. In order to keep people from guessing the sibling connection between Kudo and Fujioka, I needed a name that could be misconstrued as a last name. Thank you so much, Marinakko! Even though it was a difficult request, you were so nice in helping me. Kudo ended up having a really cool-sounding name despite being such a minor character. The typesetters put the furigana spelling of the name as "Kudoh," but personally, I read his name as "Kudo"... Hm, I guess it doesn't really matter. After all, the kanji for "遠" is normally read as "toh" (or "doh"). But when I enter the letters "kudo" into my cell phone, the kanji for Kudo's name comes up!

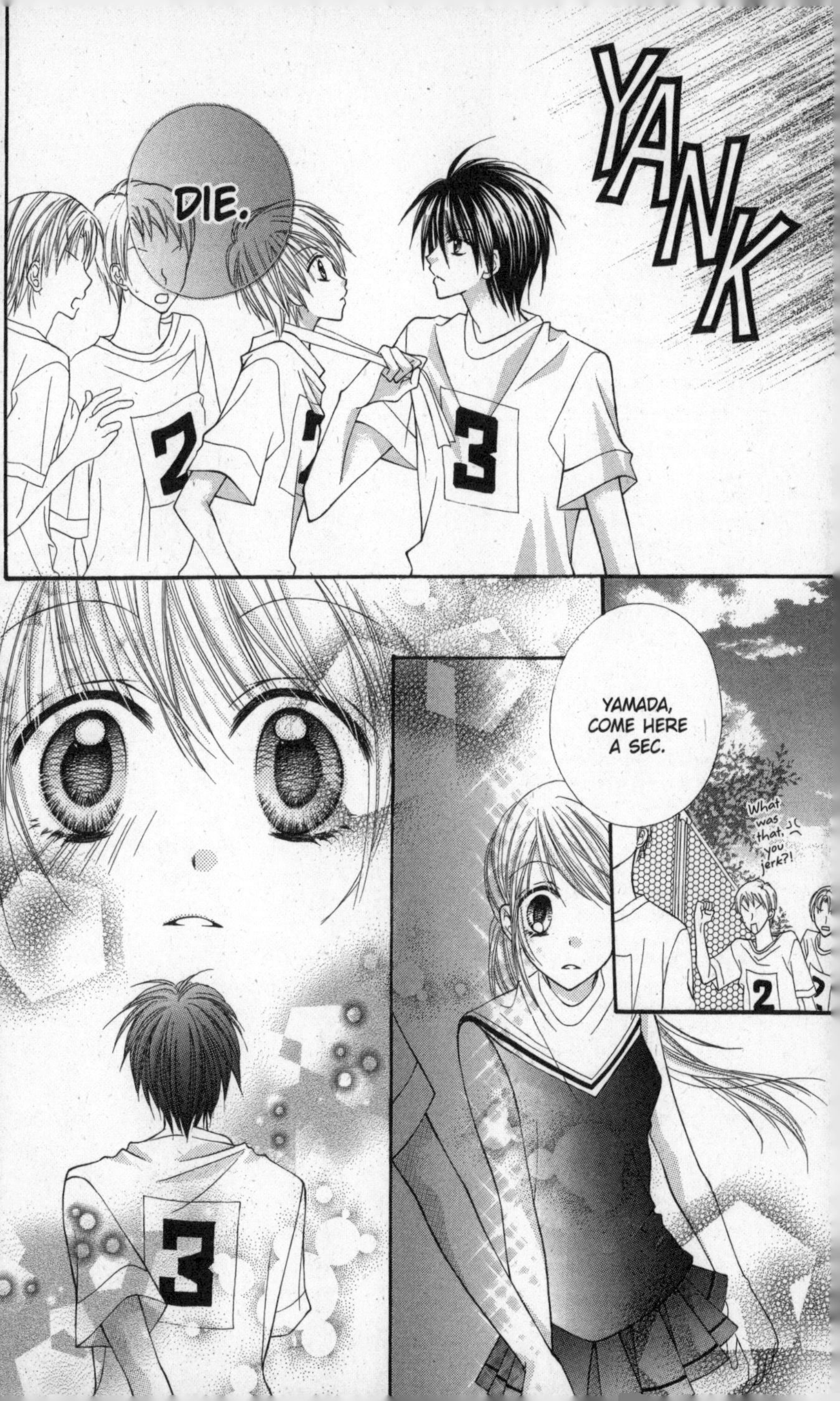
YANK
DIE.
YAMADA, COME HERE A SEC.
What was that, you jerk?!

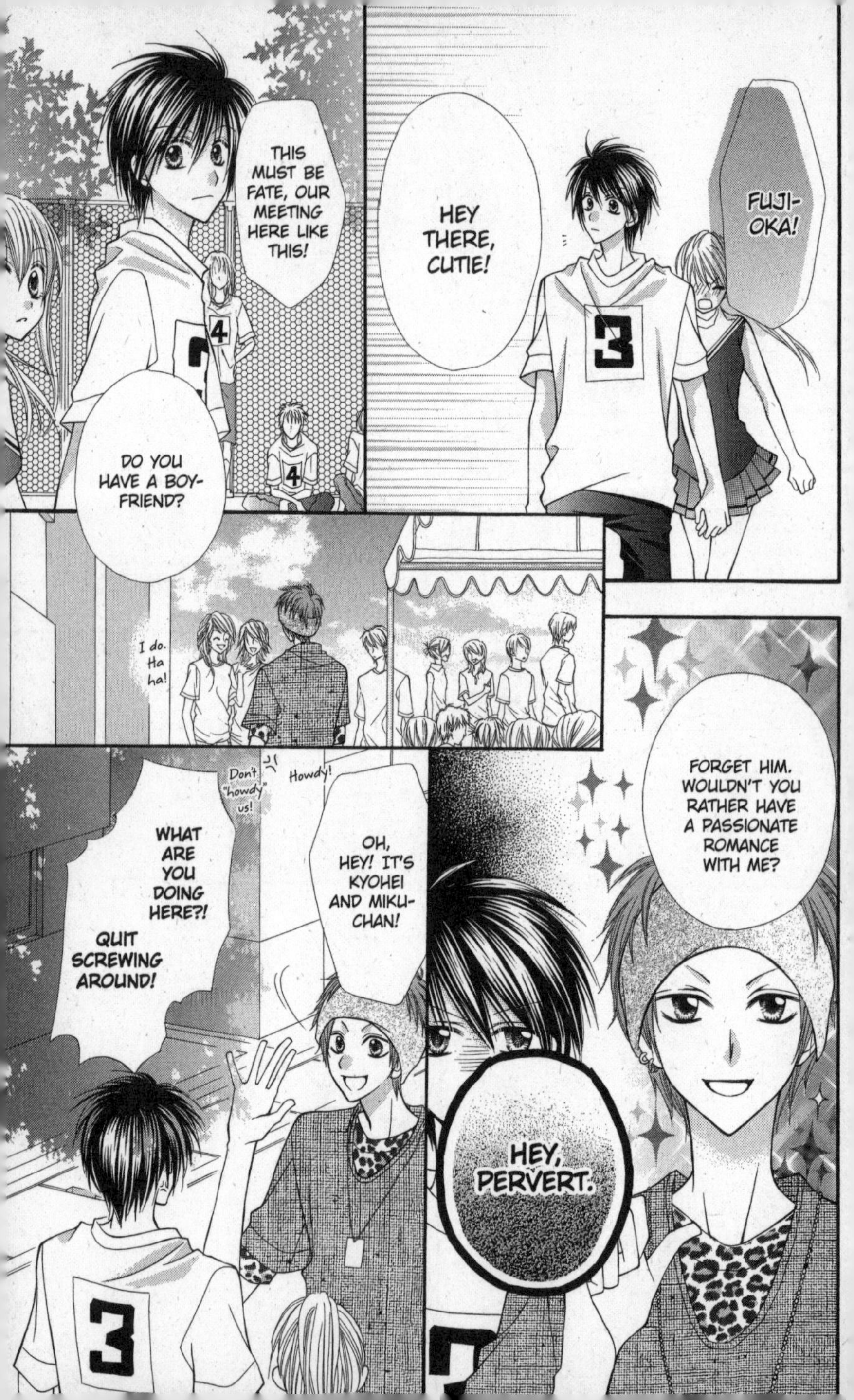
FUJI-OKA!
HEY THERE, CUTIE!
THIS MUST BE FATE, OUR MEETING HERE LIKE THIS!
DO YOU HAVE A BOY-FRIEND?
I do. Ha ha!
FORGET HIM. WOULDN'T YOU RATHER HAVE A PASSIONATE ROMANCE WITH ME?
HEY, PERVERT.
OH, HEY! IT'S KYOHEI AND MIKU-CHAN!
Howdy!
Don't "howdy" us!
WHAT ARE YOU DOING HERE?!
QUIT SCREWING AROUND!

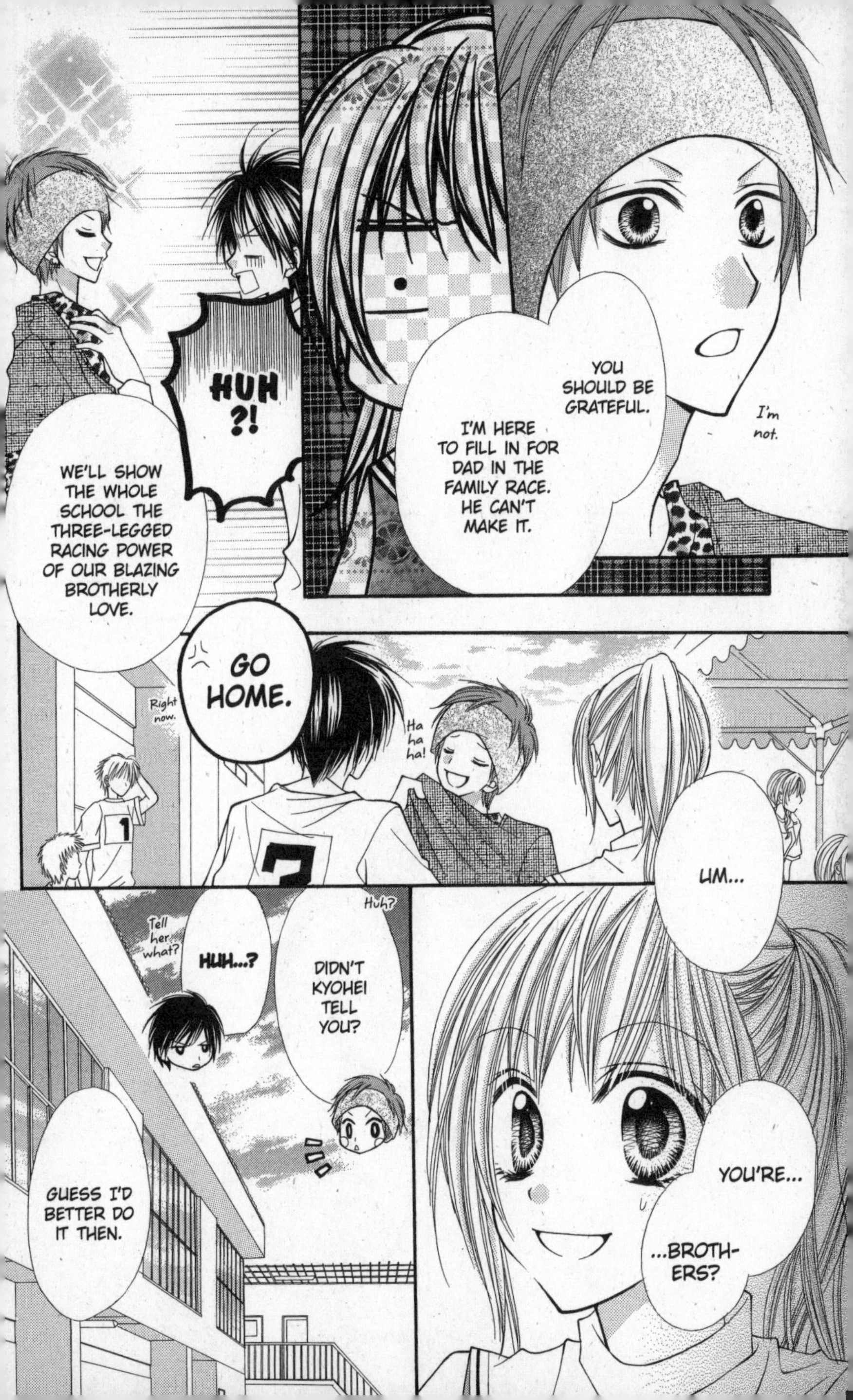
YOU SHOULD BE GRATEFUL.
I'M HERE TO FILL IN FOR DAD IN THE FAMILY RACE. HE CAN'T MAKE IT.
I'm not.
WE'LL SHOW THE WHOLE SCHOOL THE THREE-LEGGED RACING POWER OF OUR BLAZING BROTHERLY LOVE.
HUH ?!
GO HOME.
Right now.
Ha ha ha!
UM...
YOU'RE...
...BROTH-ERS?
DIDN'T KYOHEI TELL YOU?
Huh?
HUH...?
Tell her what?
GUESS I'D BETTER DO IT THEN.

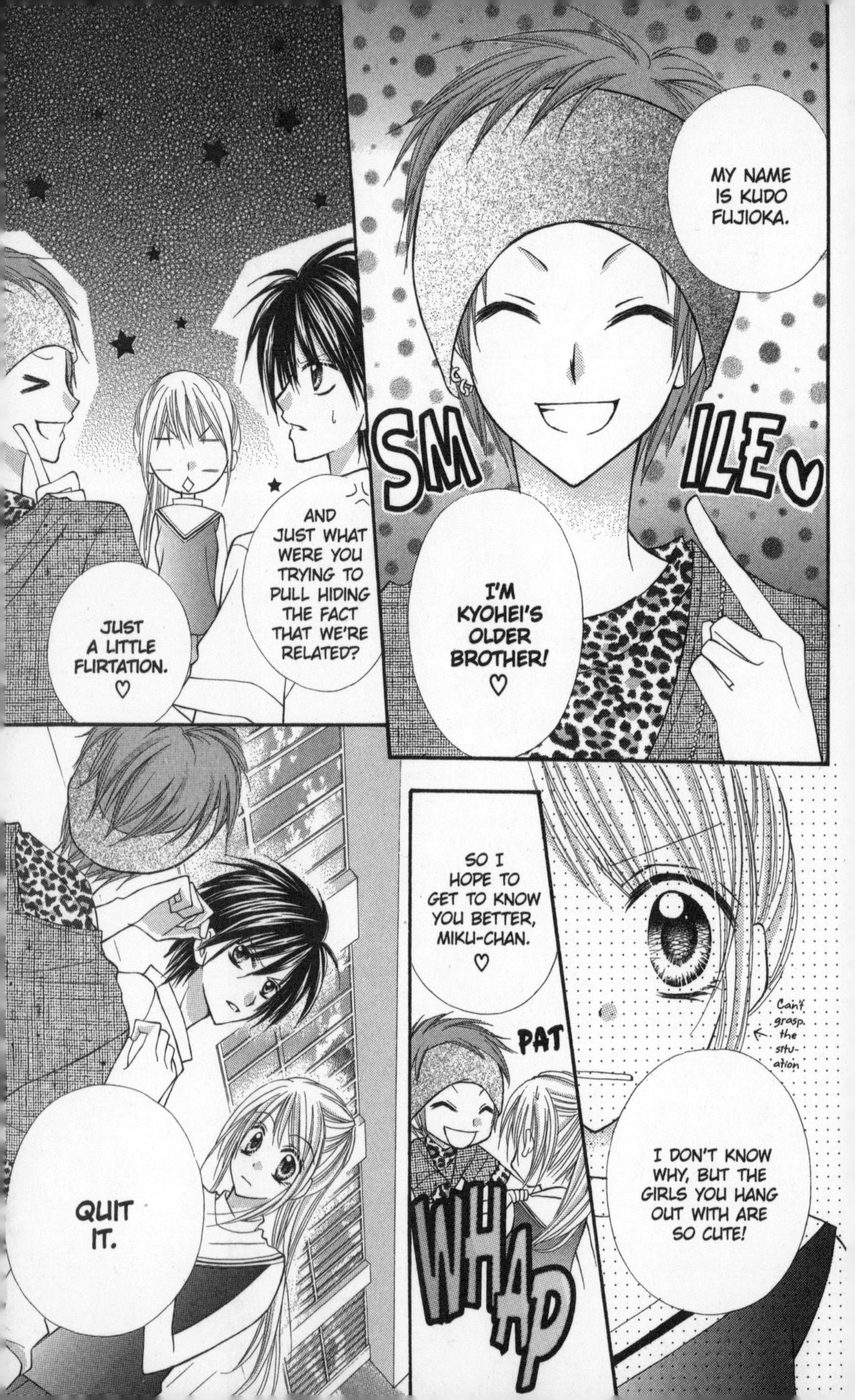
MY NAME IS KUDO FUJIOKA.
SMILE♡
I'M KYOHEI'S OLDER BROTHER! ♡
AND JUST WHAT WERE YOU TRYING TO PULL HIDING THE FACT THAT WE'RE RELATED?
JUST A LITTLE FLIRTATION. ♡
SO I HOPE TO GET TO KNOW YOU BETTER, MIKU-CHAN. ♡
Can't grasp. the situation
PAT
I DON'T KNOW WHY, BUT THE GIRLS YOU HANG OUT WITH ARE SO CUTE!
WHAP
QUIT IT.

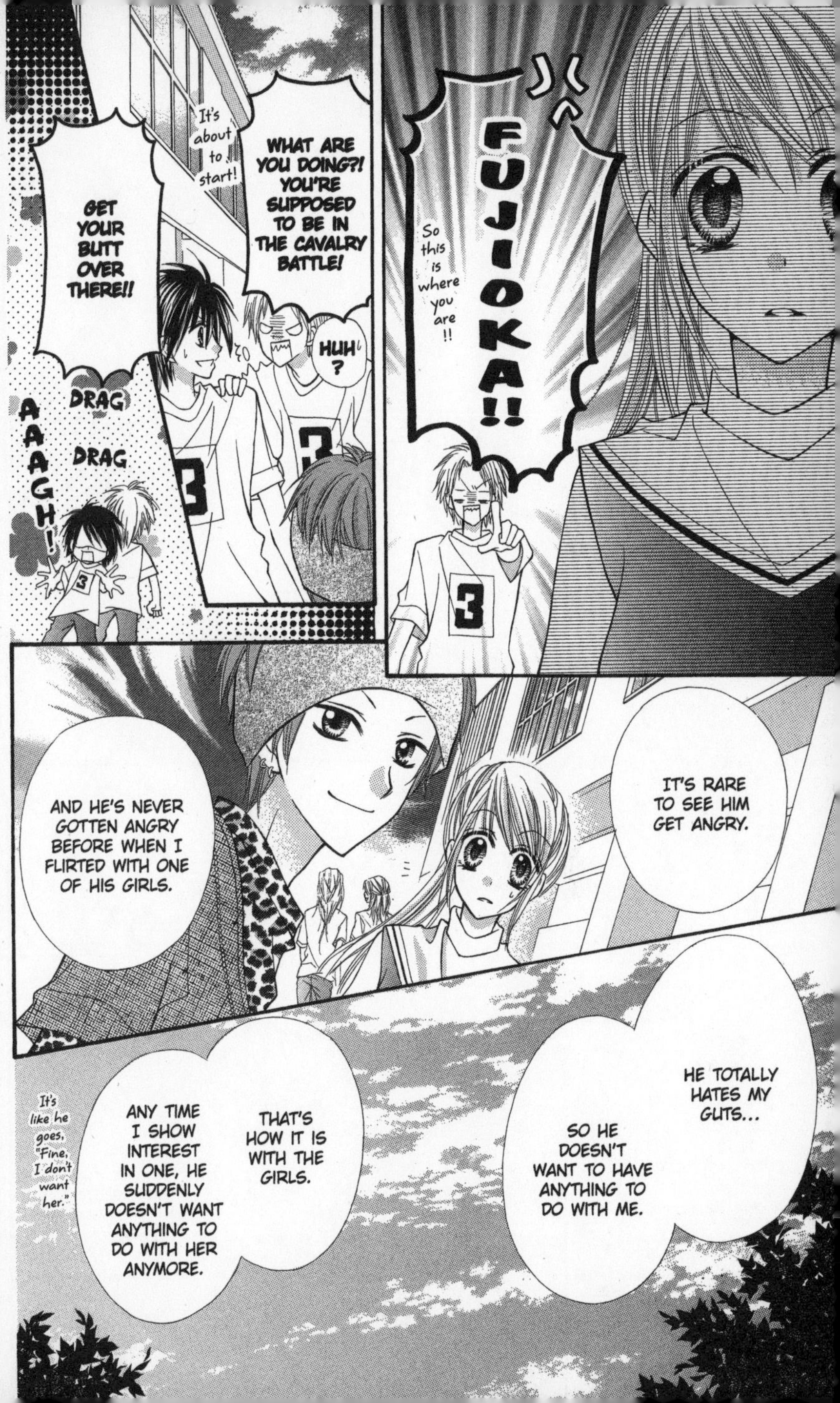
FUJIOKA!!
So this is where you are !!
WHAT ARE YOU DOING?! YOU'RE SUPPOSED TO BE IN THE CAVALRY BATTLE!
It's about to start!
HUH?
GET YOUR BUTT OVER THERE!!
DRAG
DRAG
AAAGH!
IT'S RARE TO SEE HIM GET ANGRY.
AND HE'S NEVER GOTTEN ANGRY BEFORE WHEN I FLIRTED WITH ONE OF HIS GIRLS.
HE TOTALLY HATES MY GUTS...
SO HE DOESN'T WANT TO HAVE ANYTHING TO DO WITH ME.
THAT'S HOW IT IS WITH THE GIRLS.
ANY TIME I SHOW INTEREST IN ONE, HE SUDDENLY DOESN'T WANT ANYTHING TO DO WITH HER ANYMORE.
It's like he goes, "Fine, I don't want her."

6

Oh, that's right, that's right! Volume 3 is coming out right at the same time the July issue of *Ribon* magazine comes out, right?

In that case, I've got another real-time announcement to make! (I'm not gonna worry how this will be totally irrelevant for anyone reading this later.)

Even though *Cactus* finished its serialization in June 2005, there will be a one-shot story by me included in the July issue of *Ribon*!

On top of the one-shot, there's also an essay manga and an announcement about my new series... It'll be (about) 50 pages total!! Please do read the story "The Bratty Kid," when it comes out! That goes for those of you who read *Cactus* books too! The cherry blossoms were just in bloom when I was drawing that one-shot story. The next time I saw the blossoms, they had all fallen and the new, green leaves of spring had sprouted. I was a little sad about that, but I'm not gonna let it bug me!

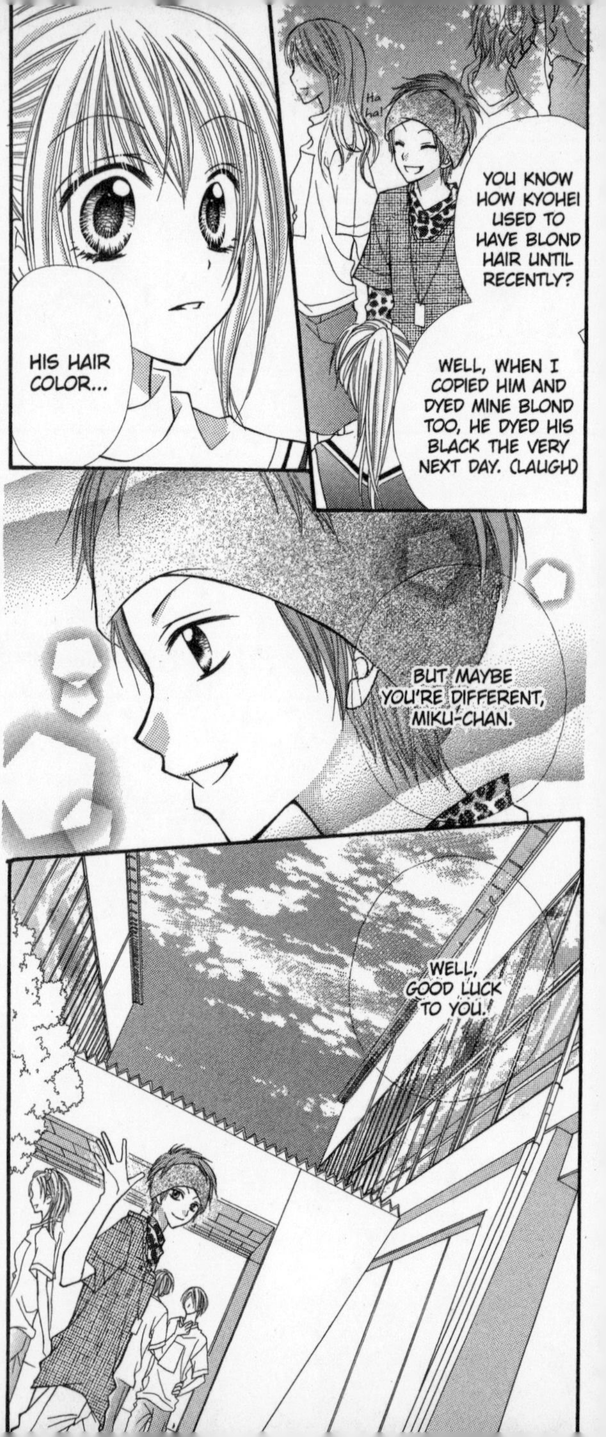
Ha ha!
YOU KNOW HOW KYOHEI USED TO HAVE BLOND HAIR UNTIL RECENTLY?
WELL, WHEN I COPIED HIM AND DYED MINE BLOND TOO, HE DYED HIS BLACK THE VERY NEXT DAY. (LAUGH)
HIS HAIR COLOR...
BUT MAYBE YOU'RE DIFFERENT, MIKU-CHAN.
WELL, GOOD LUCK TO YOU.

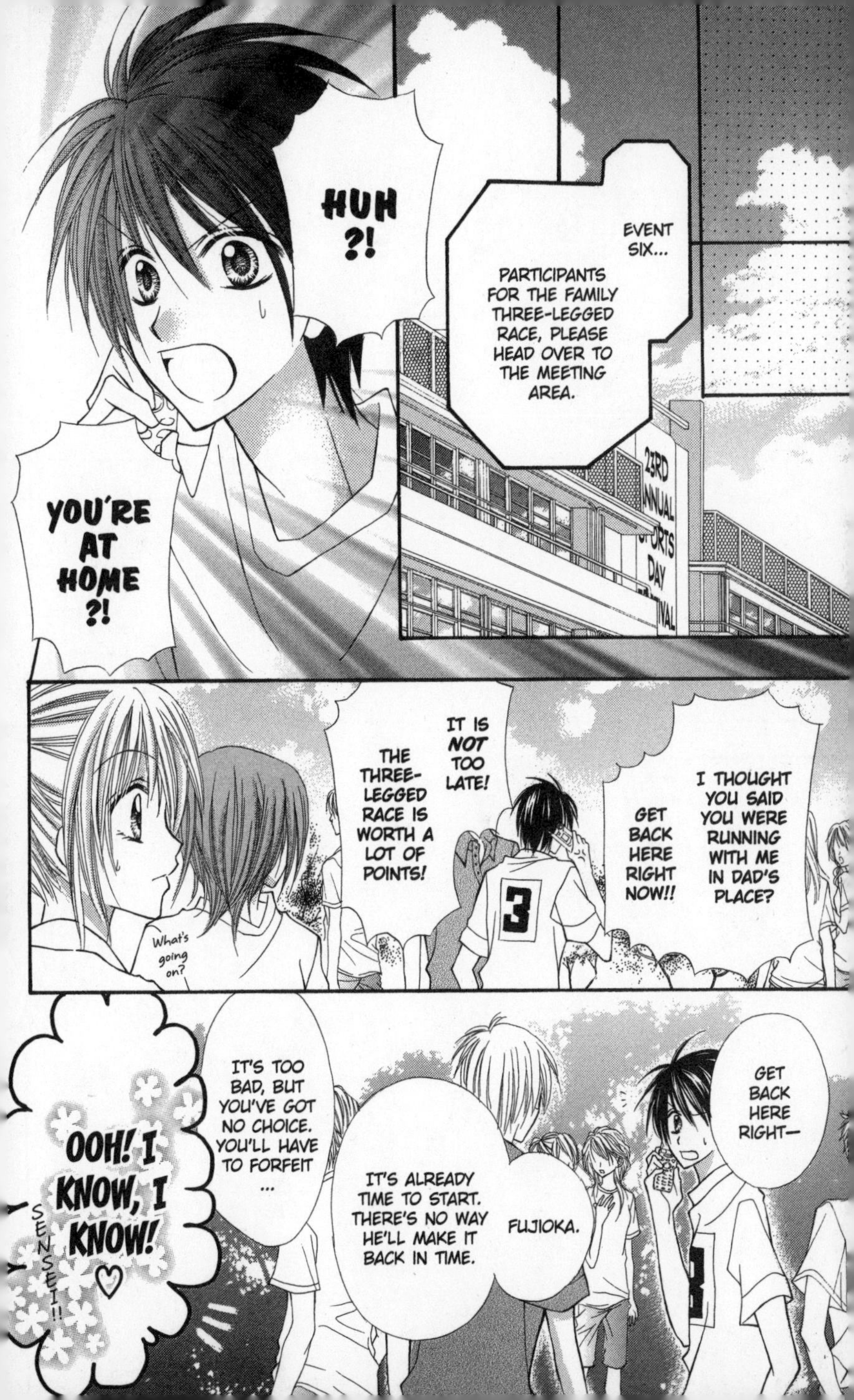
EVENT SIX...
PARTICIPANTS FOR THE FAMILY THREE-LEGGED RACE, PLEASE HEAD OVER TO THE MEETING AREA.
HUH ?!
YOU'RE AT HOME ?!
I THOUGHT YOU SAID YOU WERE RUNNING WITH ME IN DAD'S PLACE?
GET BACK HERE RIGHT NOW!!
IT IS *NOT* TOO LATE!
THE THREE-LEGGED RACE IS WORTH A LOT OF POINTS!
What's going on?
GET BACK HERE RIGHT—
FUJIOKA.
IT'S ALREADY TIME TO START. THERE'S NO WAY HE'LL MAKE IT BACK IN TIME.
IT'S TOO BAD, BUT YOU'VE GOT NO CHOICE. YOU'LL HAVE TO FORFEIT ...
OOH! I KNOW, I KNOW! ♡
SENSEI!!

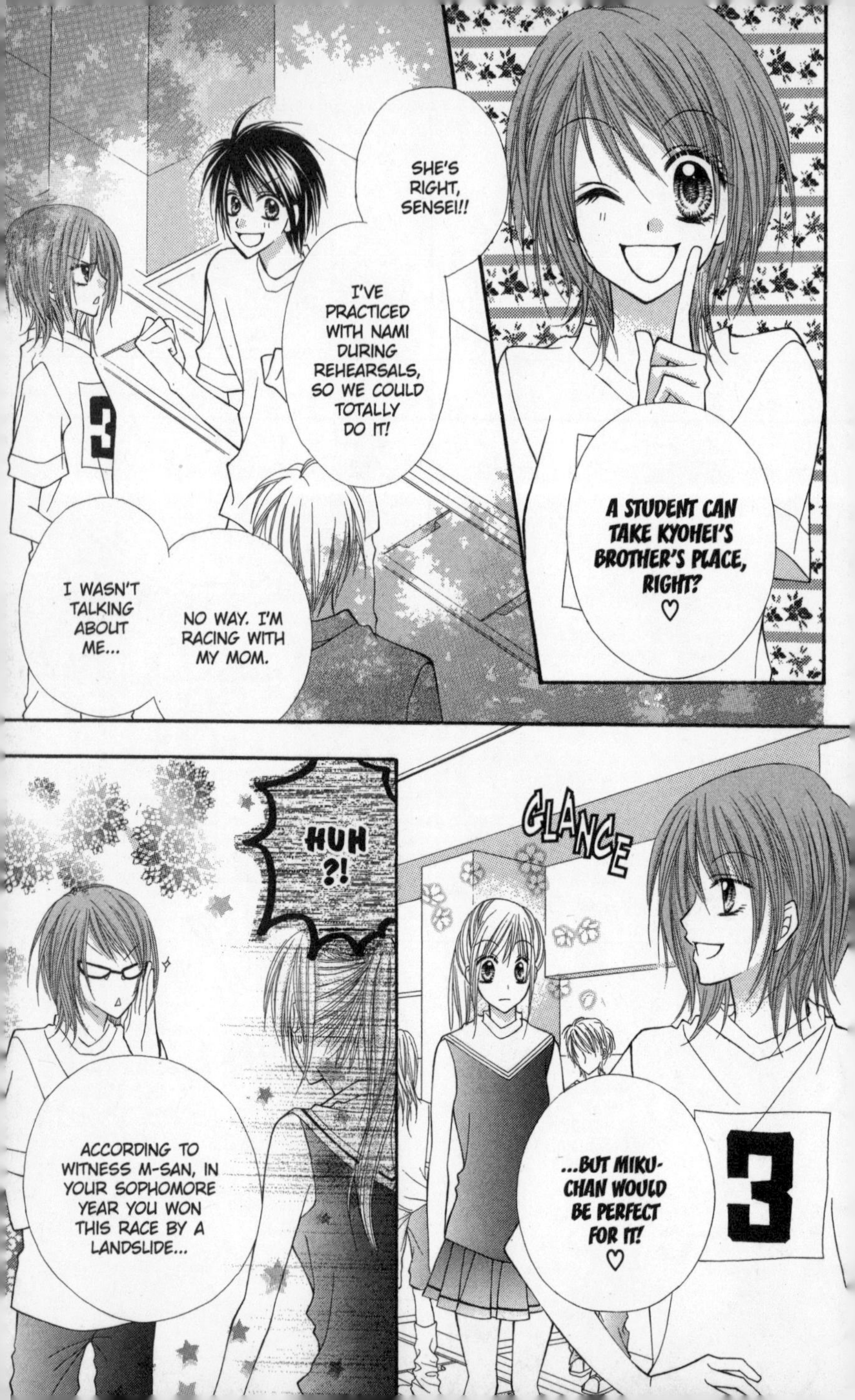
A STUDENT CAN TAKE KYOHEI'S BROTHER'S PLACE, RIGHT? ♡
SHE'S RIGHT, SENSEI!!
I'VE PRACTICED WITH NAMI DURING REHEARSALS, SO WE COULD TOTALLY DO IT!
NO WAY. I'M RACING WITH MY MOM.
I WASN'T TALKING ABOUT ME...
GLANCE
...BUT MIKU-CHAN WOULD BE PERFECT FOR IT! ♡
HUH ?!
ACCORDING TO WITNESS M-SAN, IN YOUR SOPHOMORE YEAR YOU WON THIS RACE BY A LANDSLIDE...

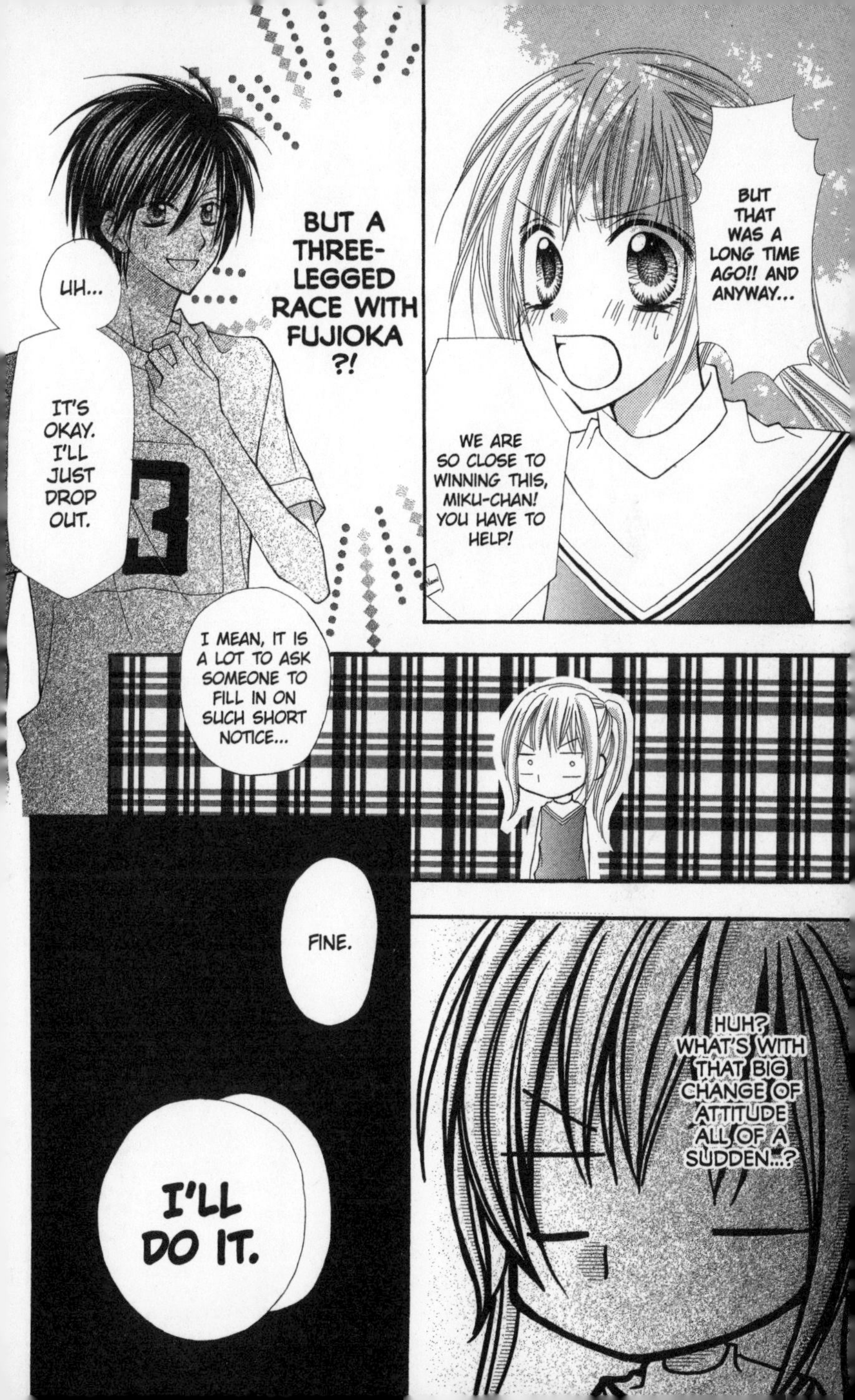
BUT THAT WAS A LONG TIME AGO!! AND ANYWAY...
WE ARE SO CLOSE TO WINNING THIS, MIKU-CHAN! YOU HAVE TO HELP!
BUT A THREE-LEGGED RACE WITH FUJIOKA?!
UH...
IT'S OKAY. I'LL JUST DROP OUT.
I MEAN, IT IS A LOT TO ASK SOMEONE TO FILL IN ON SUCH SHORT NOTICE...
HUH? WHAT'S WITH THAT BIG CHANGE OF ATTITUDE ALL OF A SUDDEN...?
FINE.
I'LL DO IT.

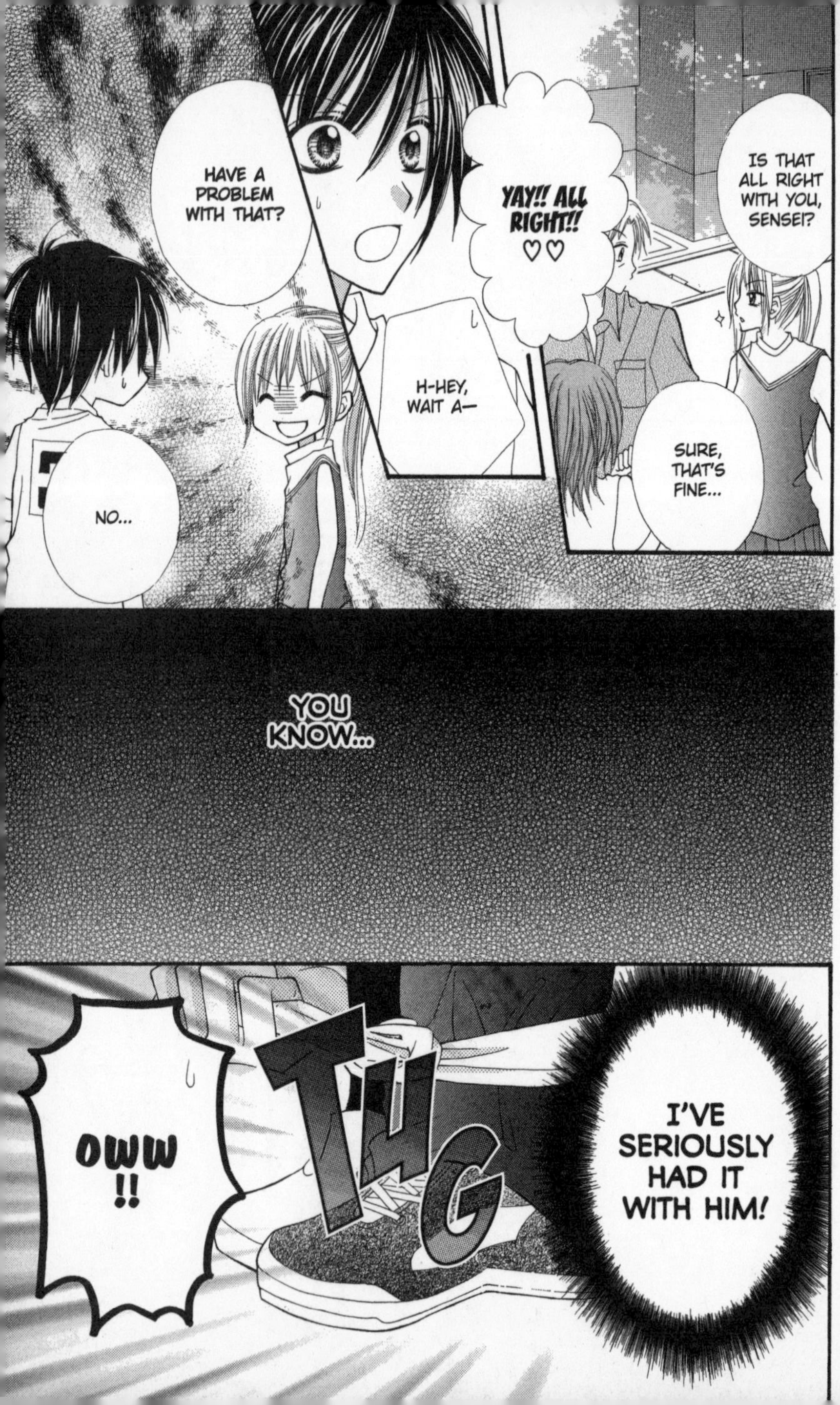
IS THAT ALL RIGHT WITH YOU, SENSEI?
SURE, THAT'S FINE...
YAY!! ALL RIGHT!! ♡♡
H-HEY, WAIT A—
HAVE A PROBLEM WITH THAT?
NO...
YOU KNOW...
I'VE SERIOUSLY HAD IT WITH HIM!
THG
OWW !!

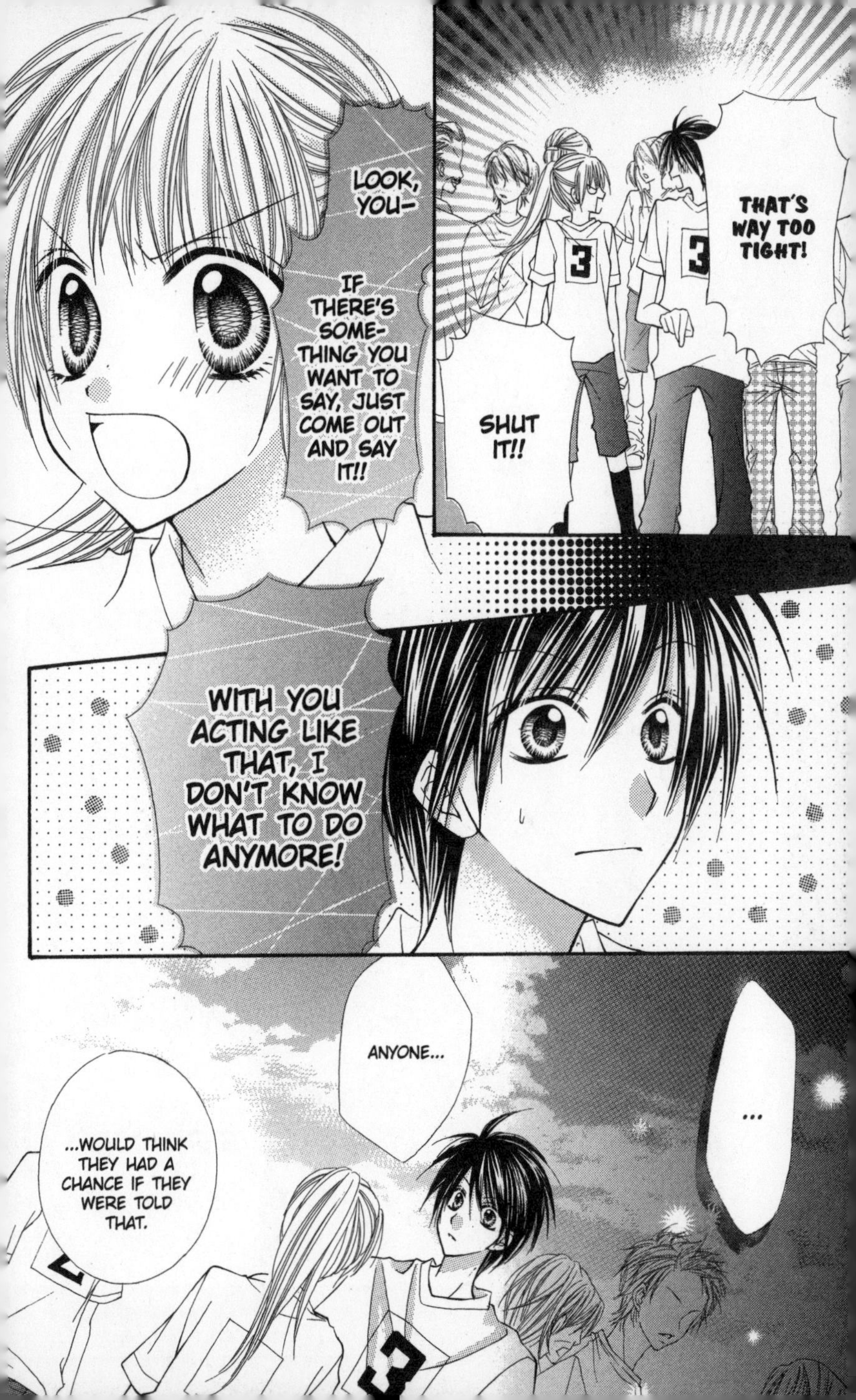
THAT'S WAY TOO TIGHT!
SHUT IT!!
LOOK, YOU–
IF THERE'S SOME-THING YOU WANT TO SAY, JUST COME OUT AND SAY IT!!
WITH YOU ACTING LIKE THAT, I DON'T KNOW WHAT TO DO ANYMORE!
...
ANYONE...
...WOULD THINK THEY HAD A CHANCE IF THEY WERE TOLD THAT.

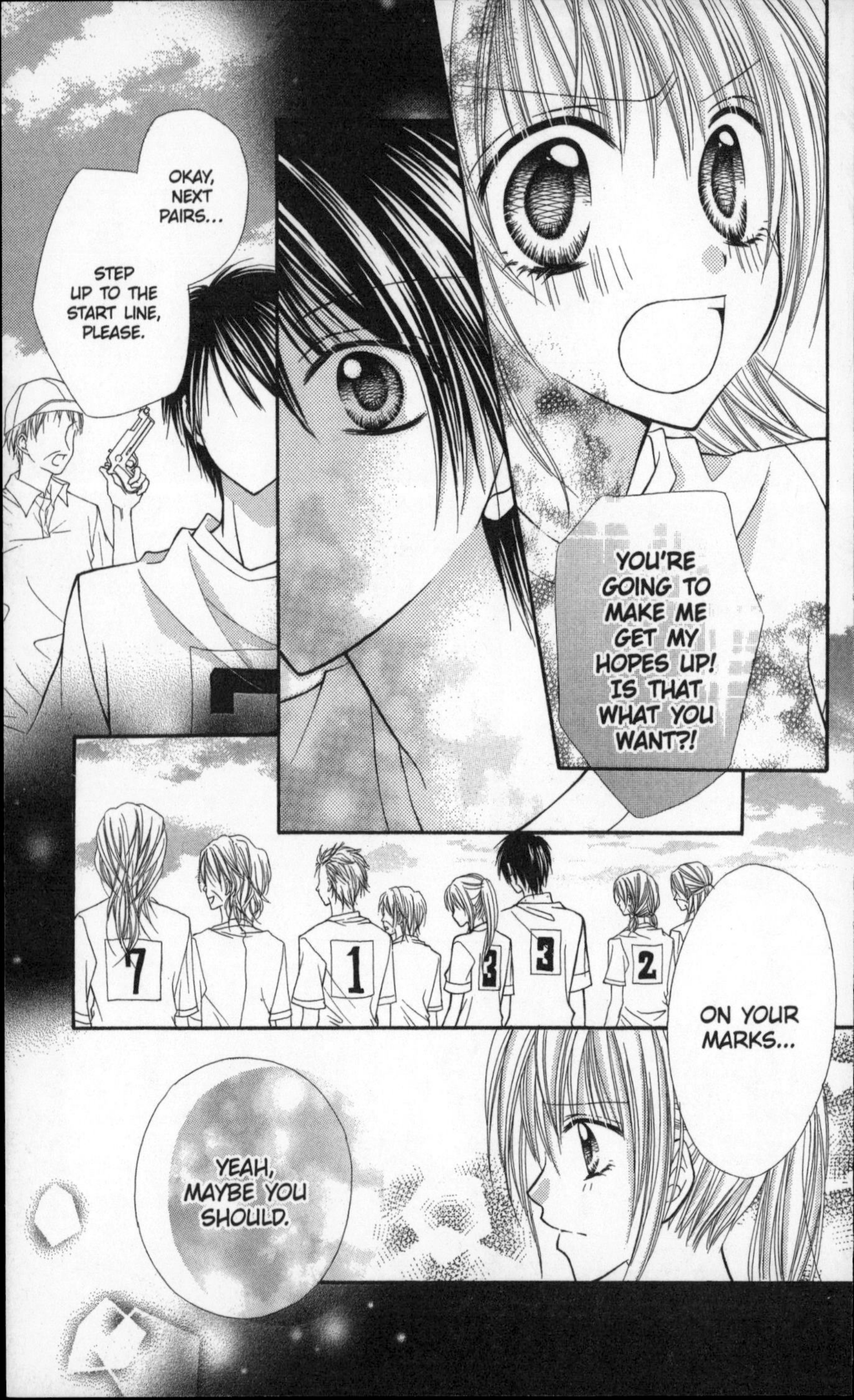
YOU'RE GOING TO MAKE ME GET MY HOPES UP! IS THAT WHAT YOU WANT?!
OKAY, NEXT PAIRS...
STEP UP TO THE START LINE, PLEASE.
ON YOUR MARKS...
YEAH, MAYBE YOU SHOULD.

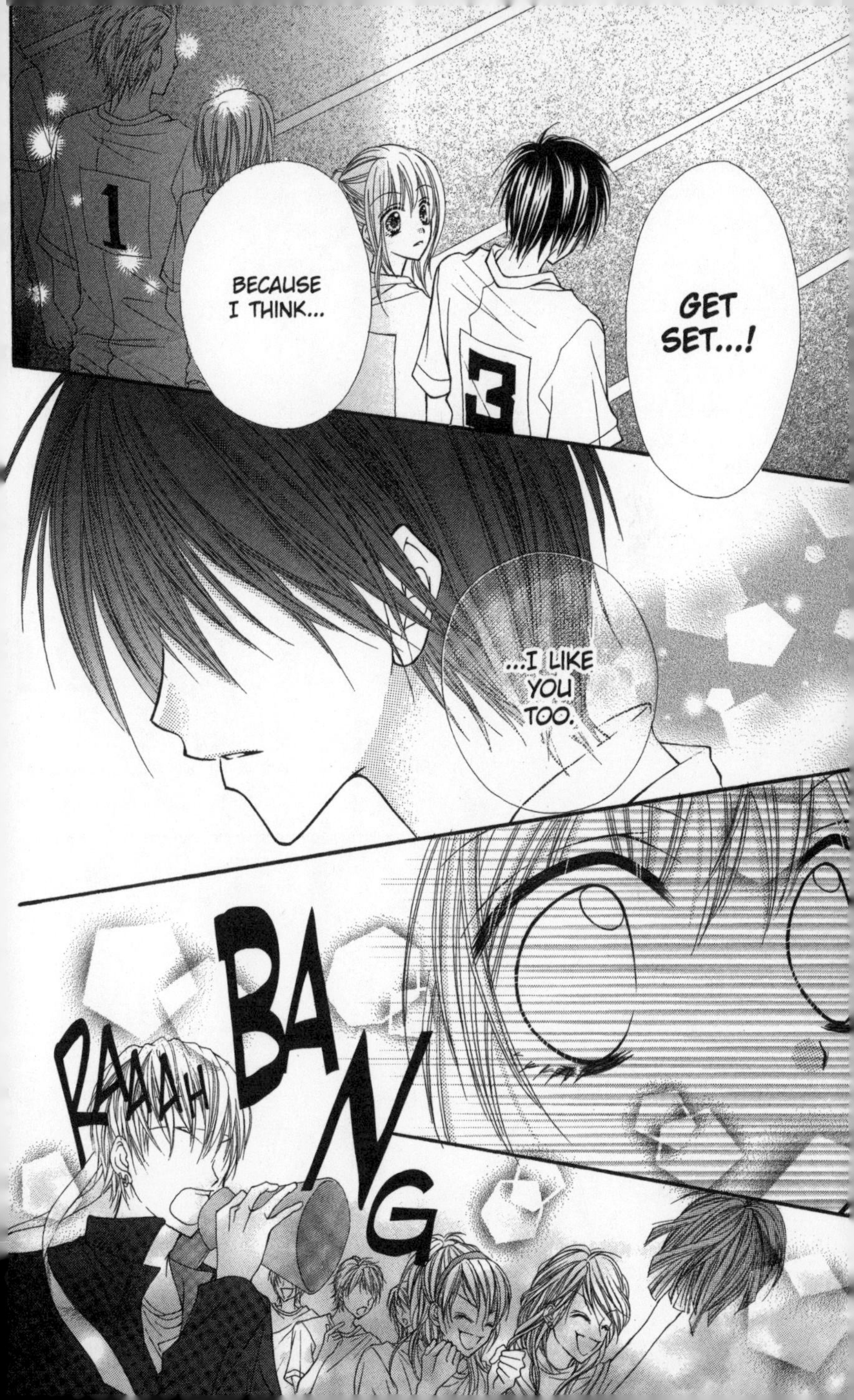
GET SET...!
BECAUSE I THINK...
...I LIKE YOU TOO.
BANG
RAAAH

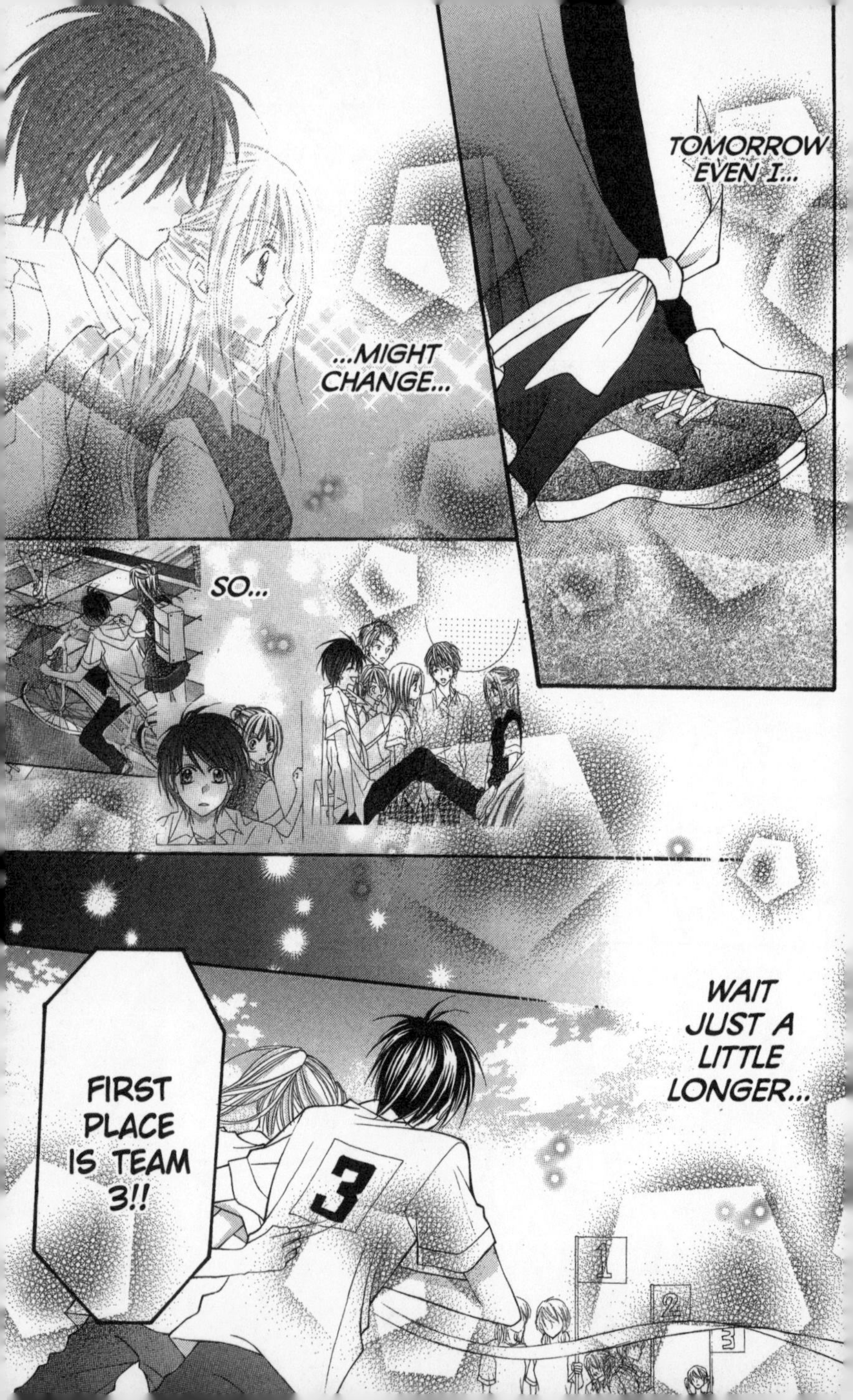
TOMORROW EVEN I...
...MIGHT CHANGE...
SO...
WAIT JUST A LITTLE LONGER...
FIRST PLACE IS TEAM 3!!
3
1
2
3

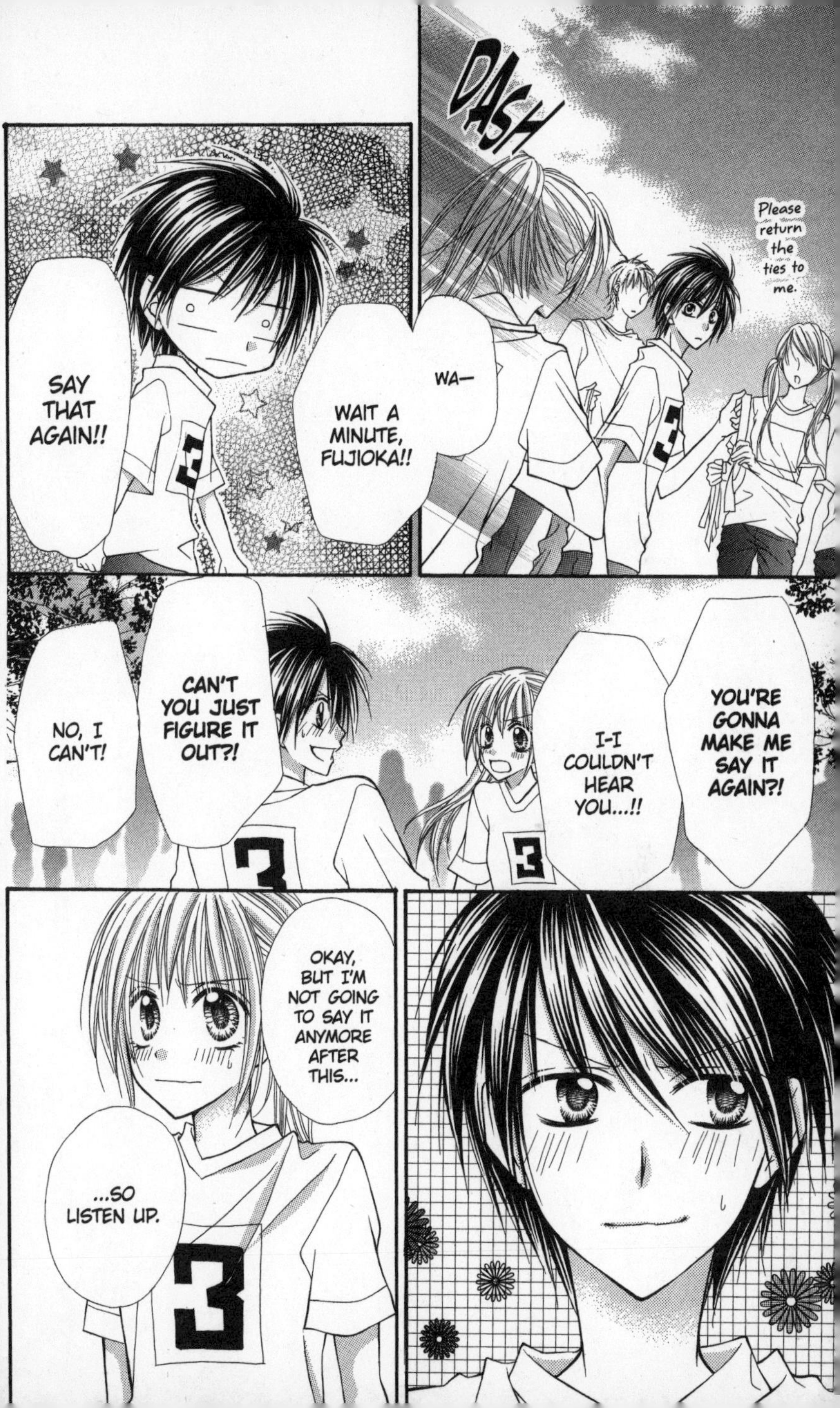
DASH
Please return the ties to me.
WA—
WAIT A MINUTE, FUJIOKA!!
SAY THAT AGAIN!!
YOU'RE GONNA MAKE ME SAY IT AGAIN?!
I-I COULDN'T HEAR YOU...!!
CAN'T YOU JUST FIGURE IT OUT?!
NO, I CAN'T!
OKAY, BUT I'M NOT GOING TO SAY IT ANYMORE AFTER THIS...
...SO LISTEN UP.

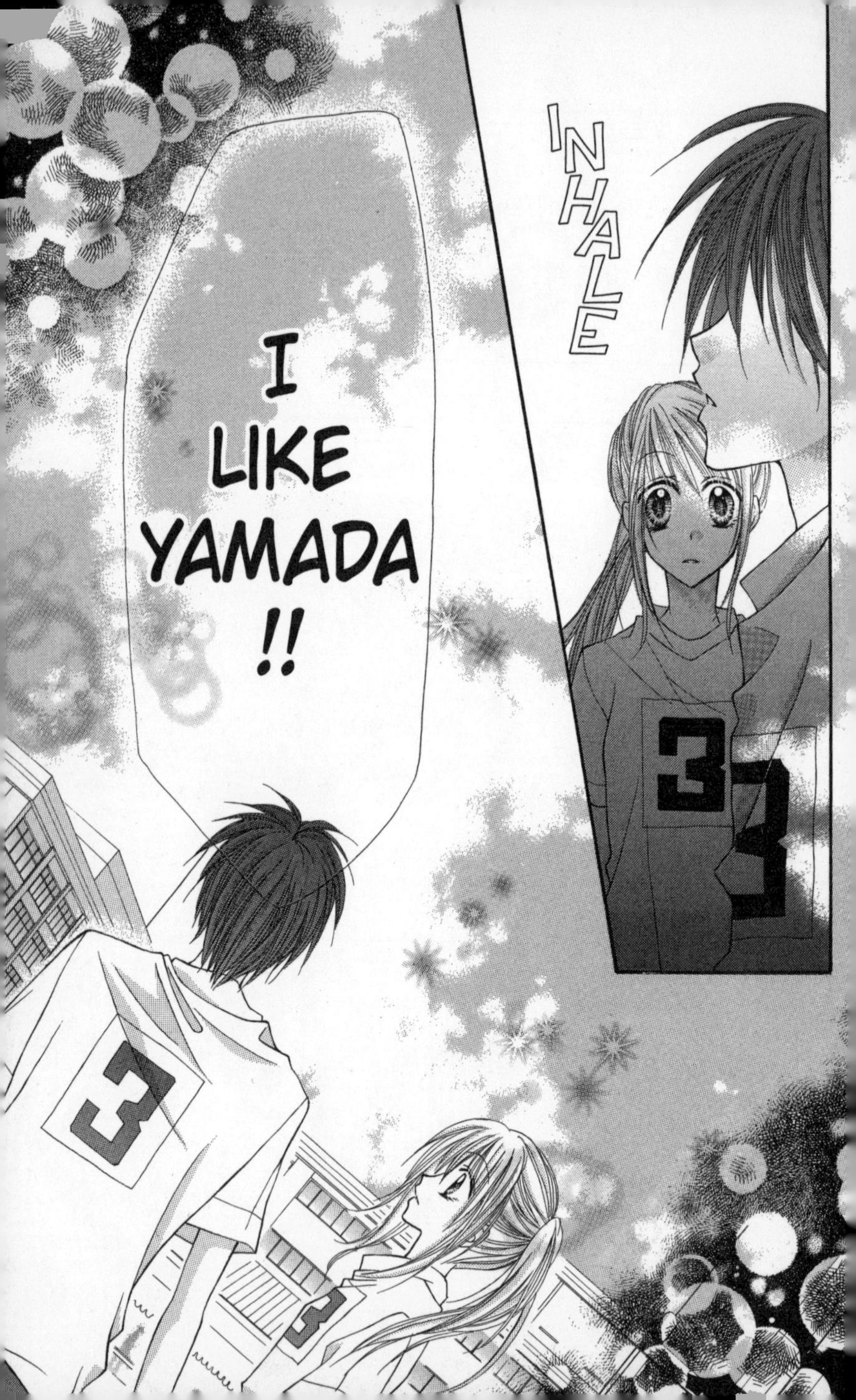
INHALE
I LIKE YAMADA!!

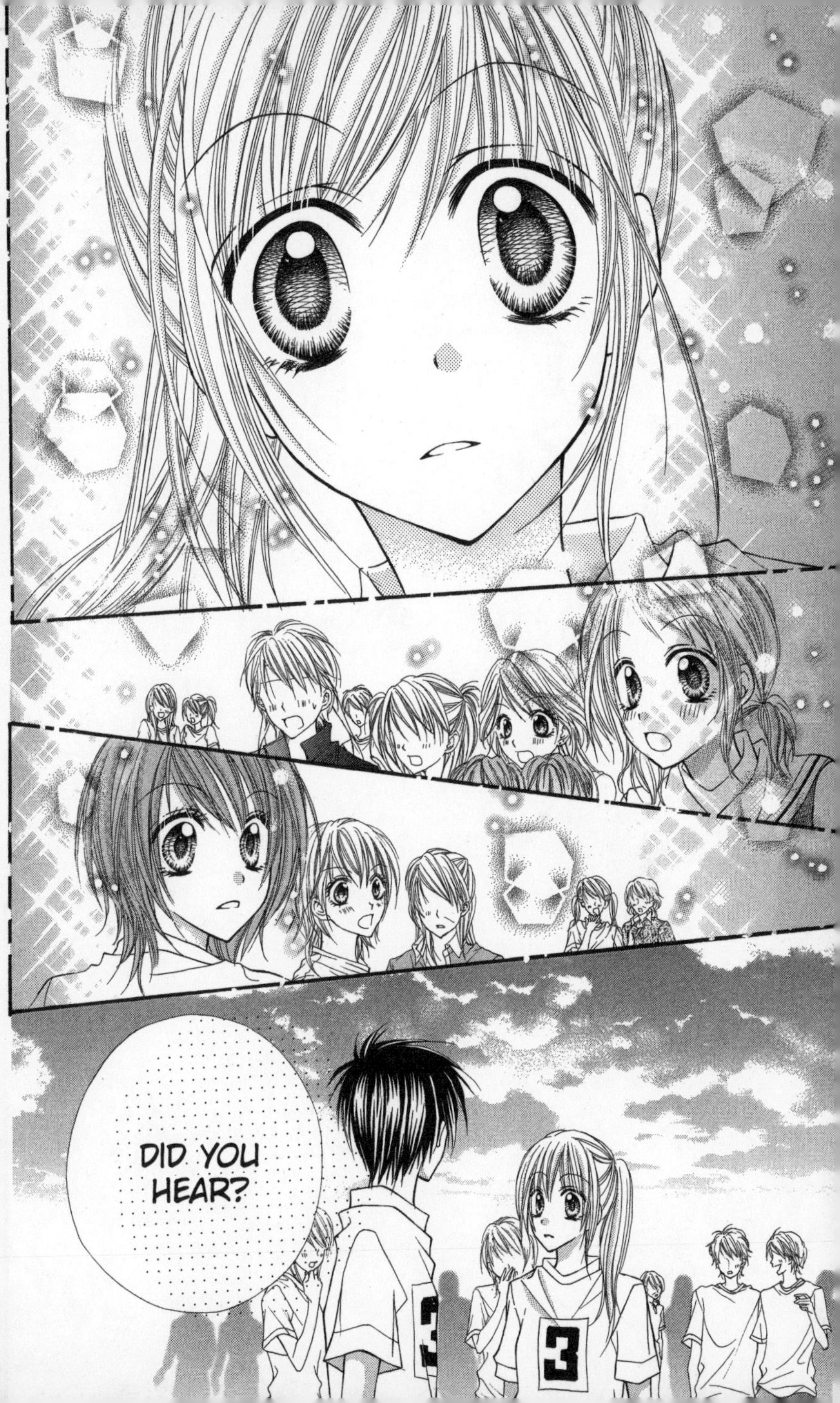
DID YOU HEAR?

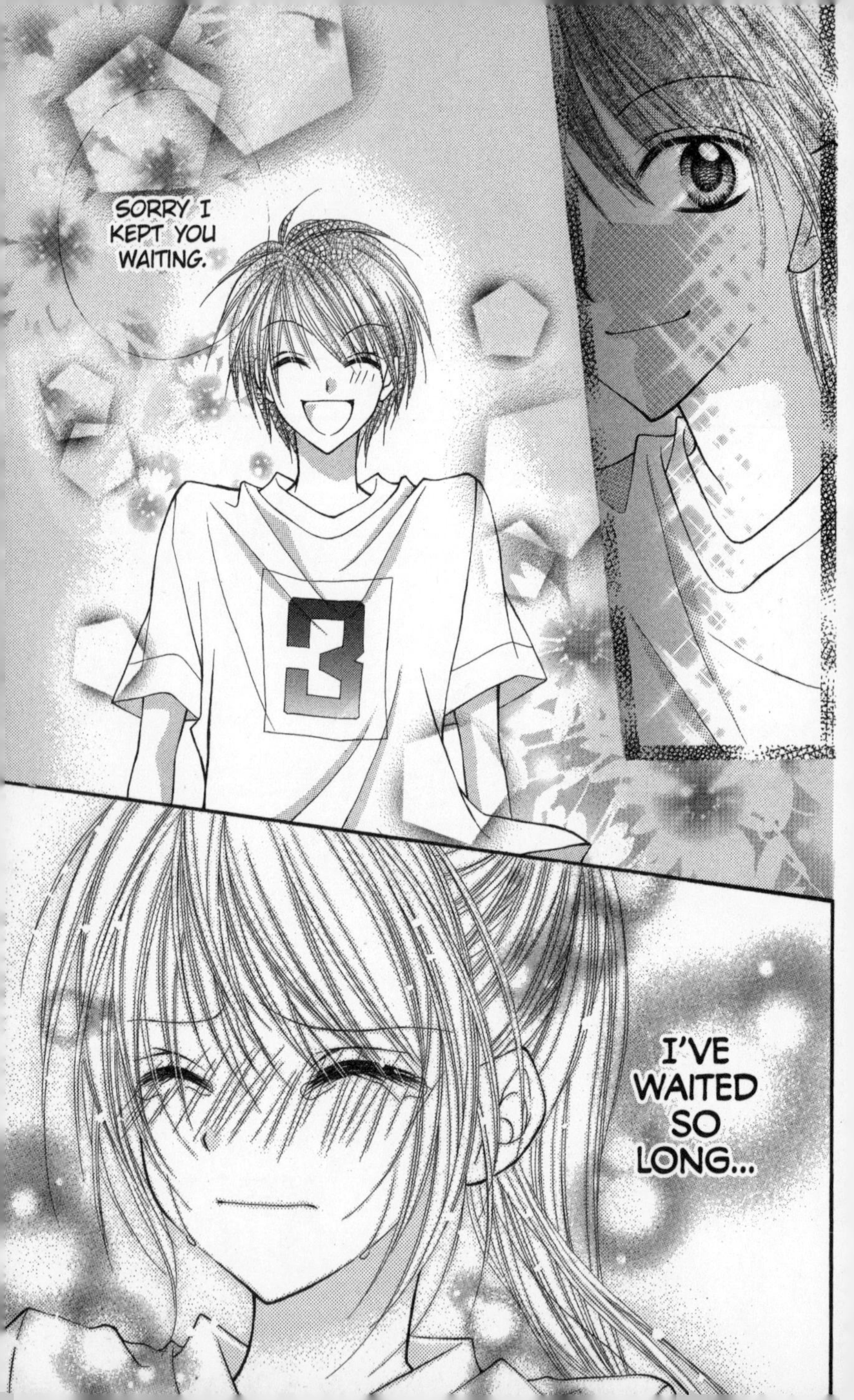
SORRY I KEPT YOU WAITING.
I'VE WAITED SO LONG...

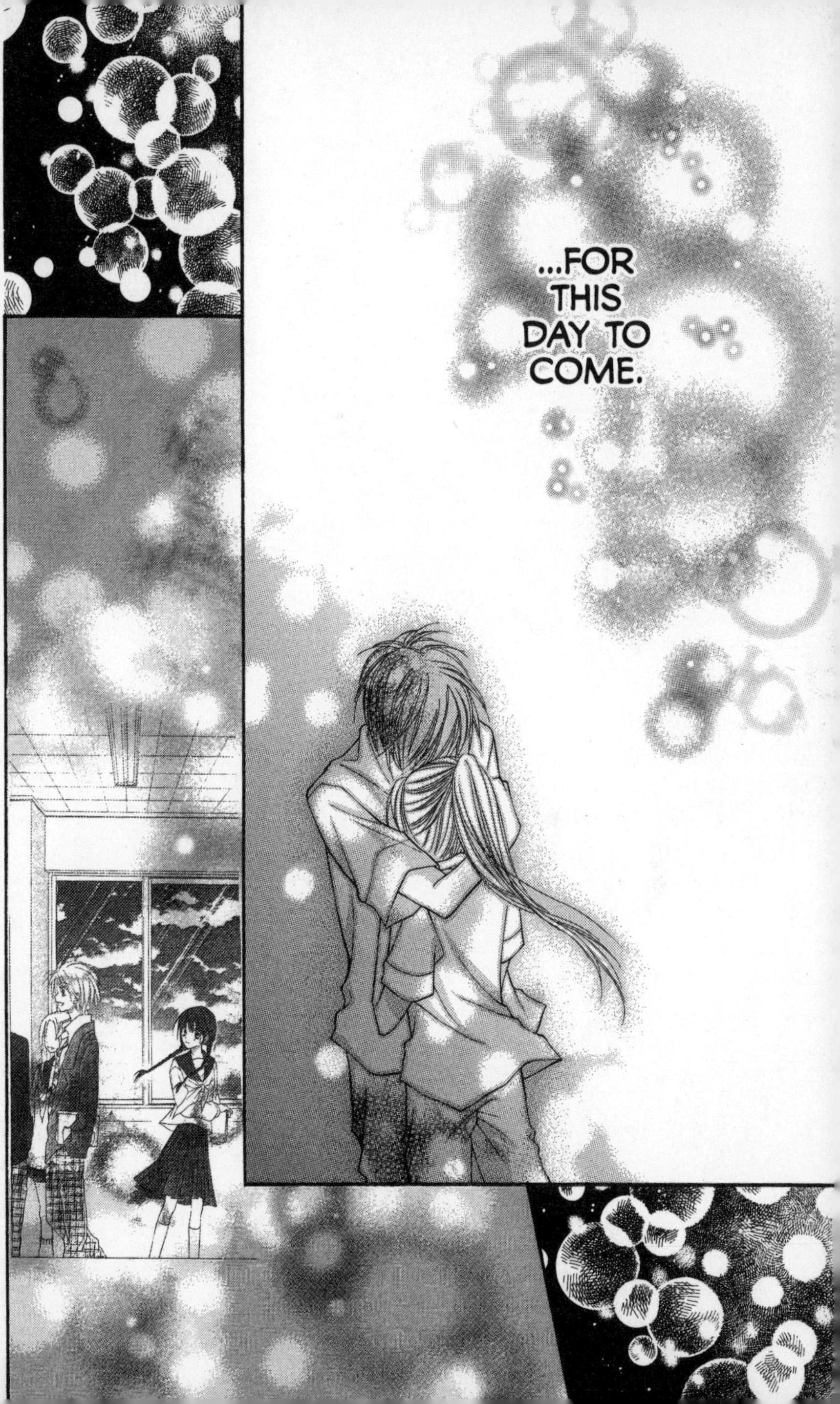
...FOR
THIS
DAY TO
COME.

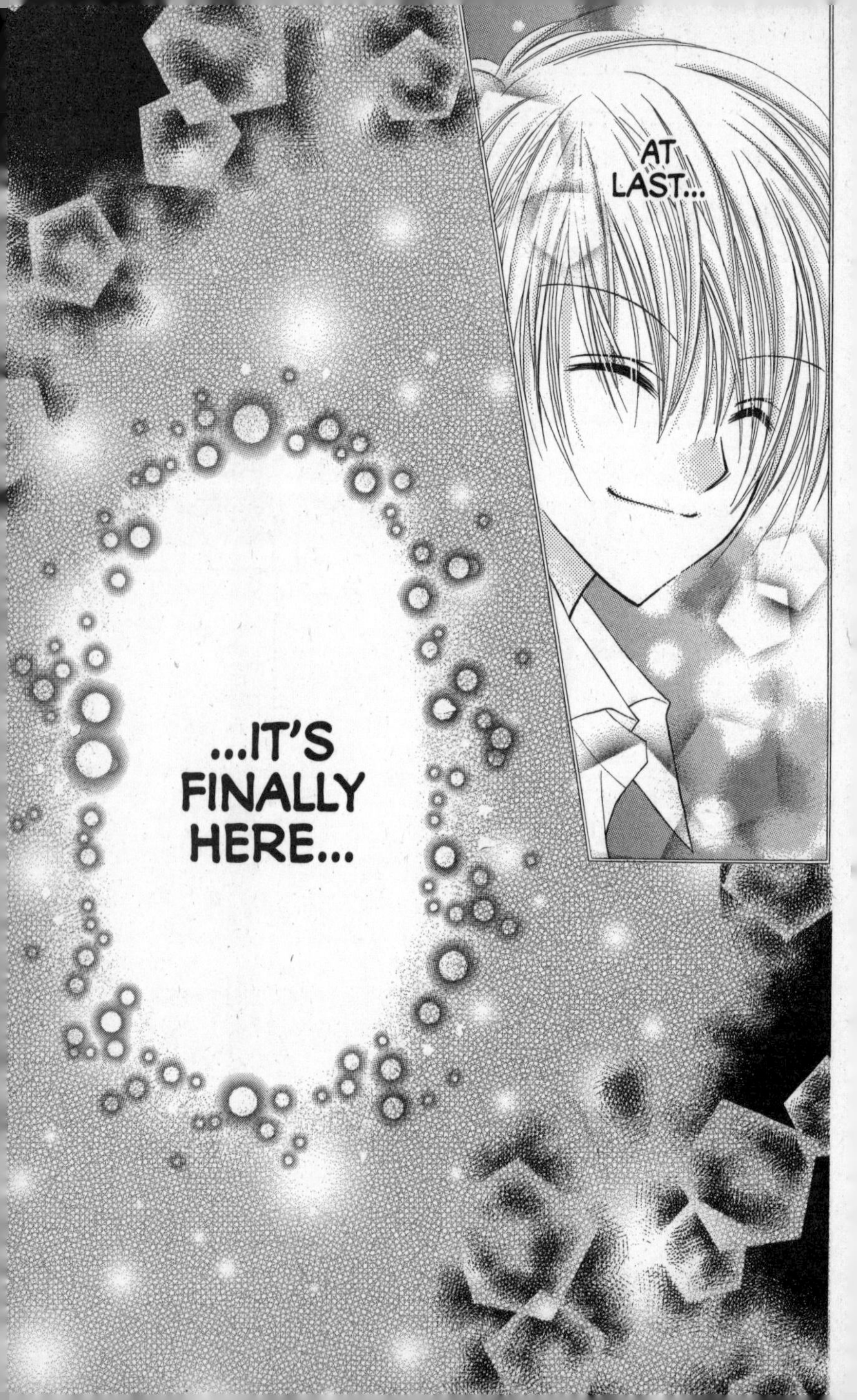
AT LAST...
...IT'S FINALLY HERE...

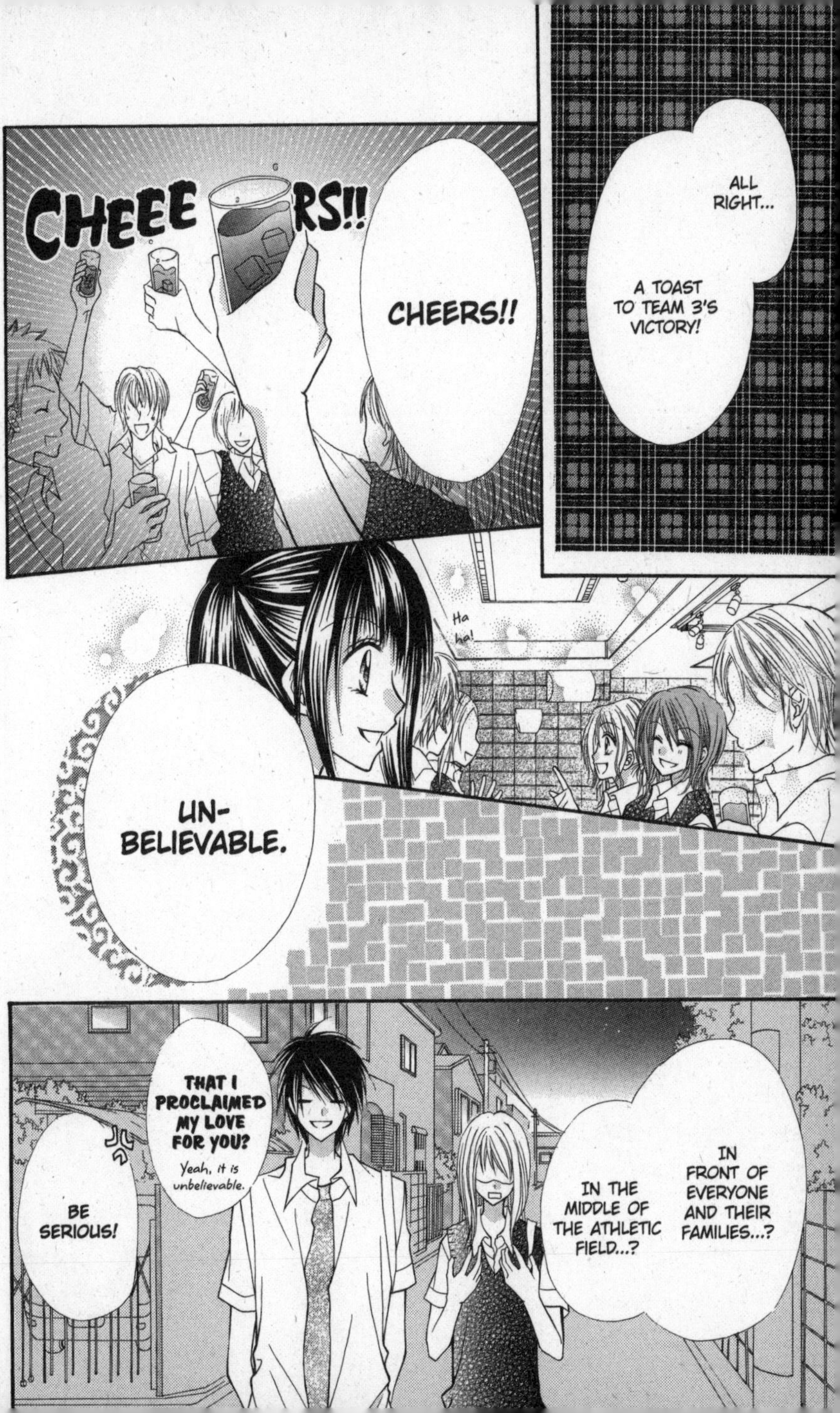
ALL RIGHT...
A TOAST TO TEAM 3'S VICTORY!
CHEEE RS!!
CHEERS!!
Ha ha!
UN-BELIEVABLE.
IN FRONT OF EVERYONE AND THEIR FAMILIES...?
IN THE MIDDLE OF THE ATHLETIC FIELD...?
THAT I PROCLAIMED MY LOVE FOR YOU?
Yeah, it is unbelievable.
BE SERIOUS!

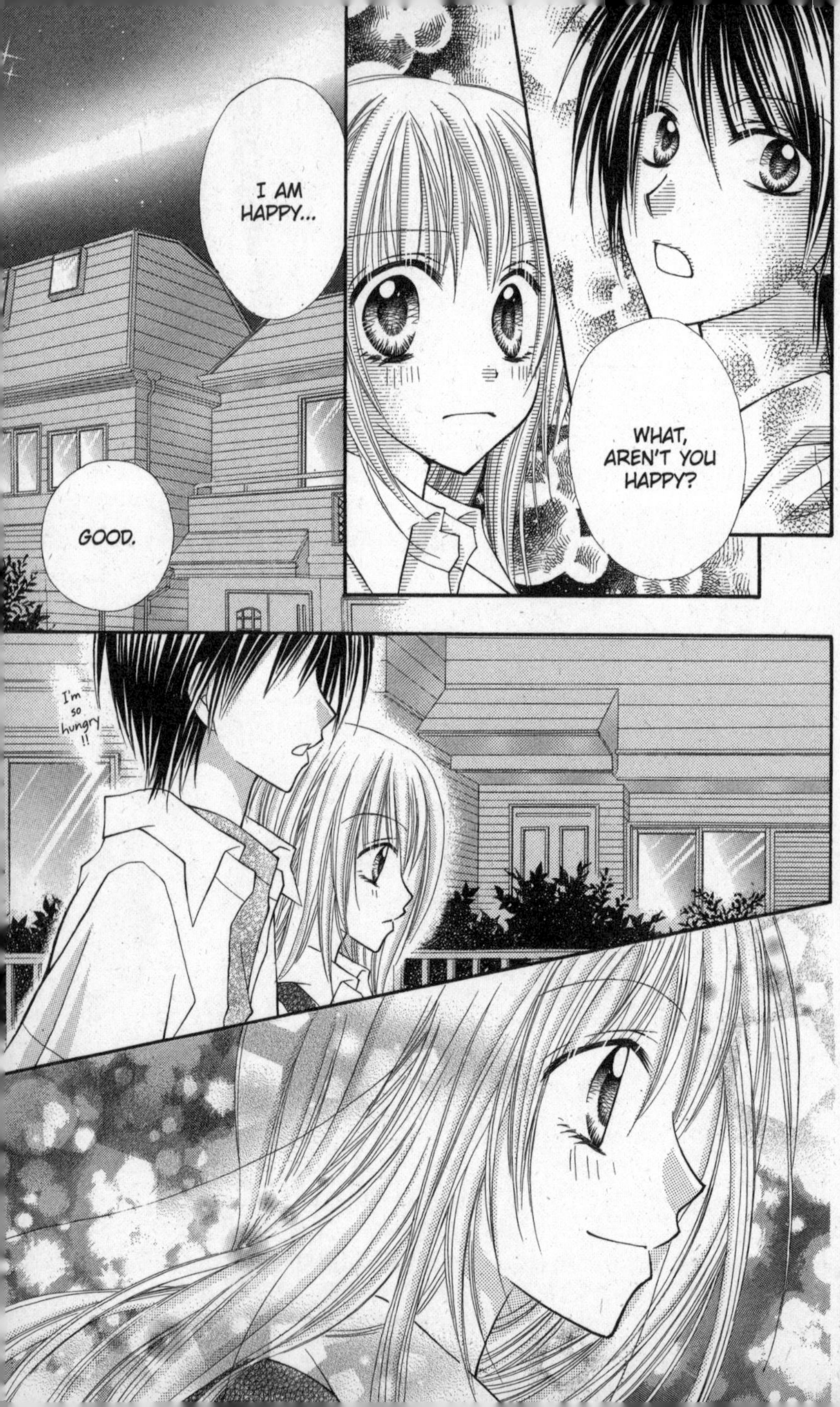
WHAT, AREN'T YOU HAPPY?
I AM HAPPY...
GOOD.
I'm so hungry!!

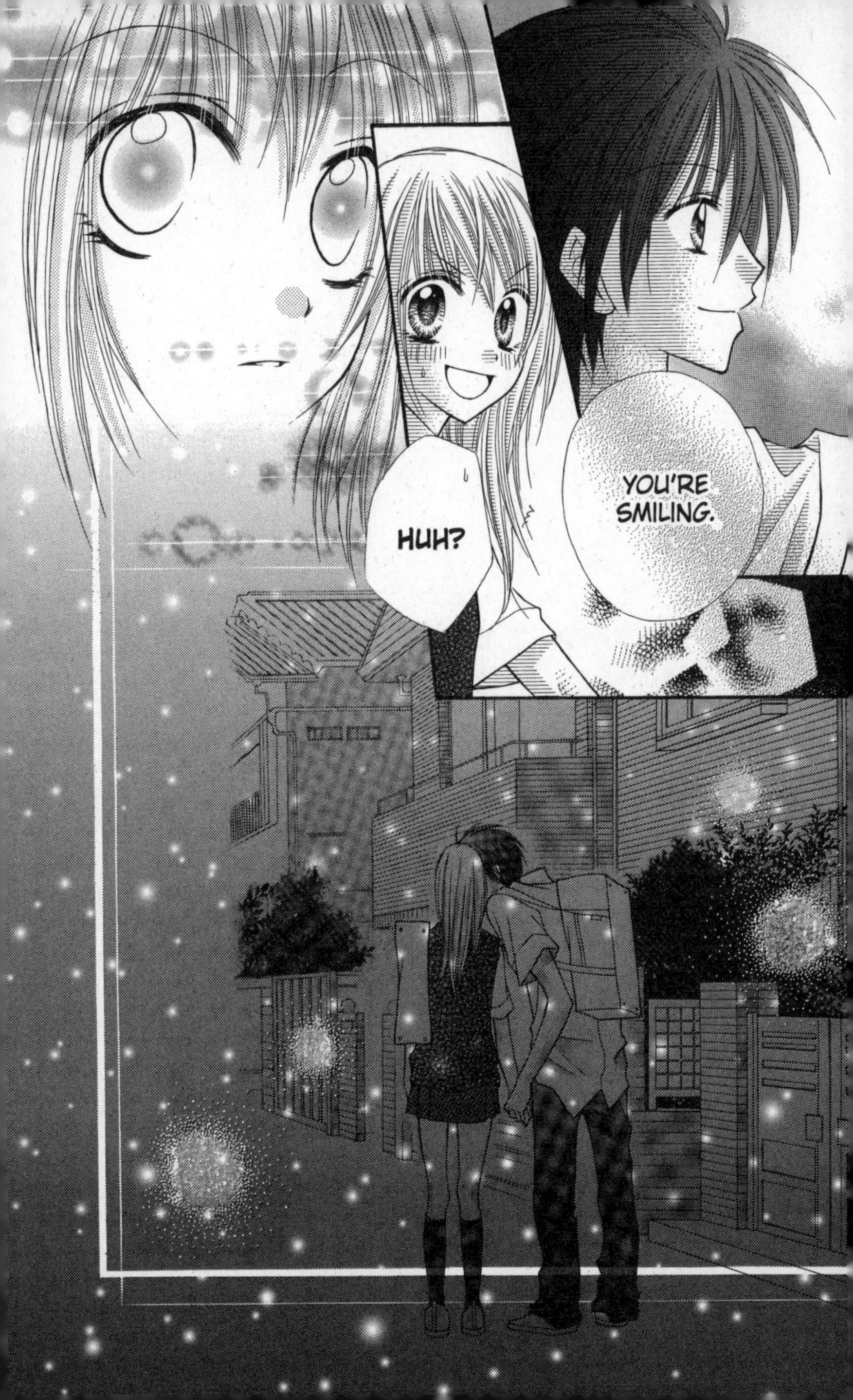
YOU'RE SMILING.
HUH?

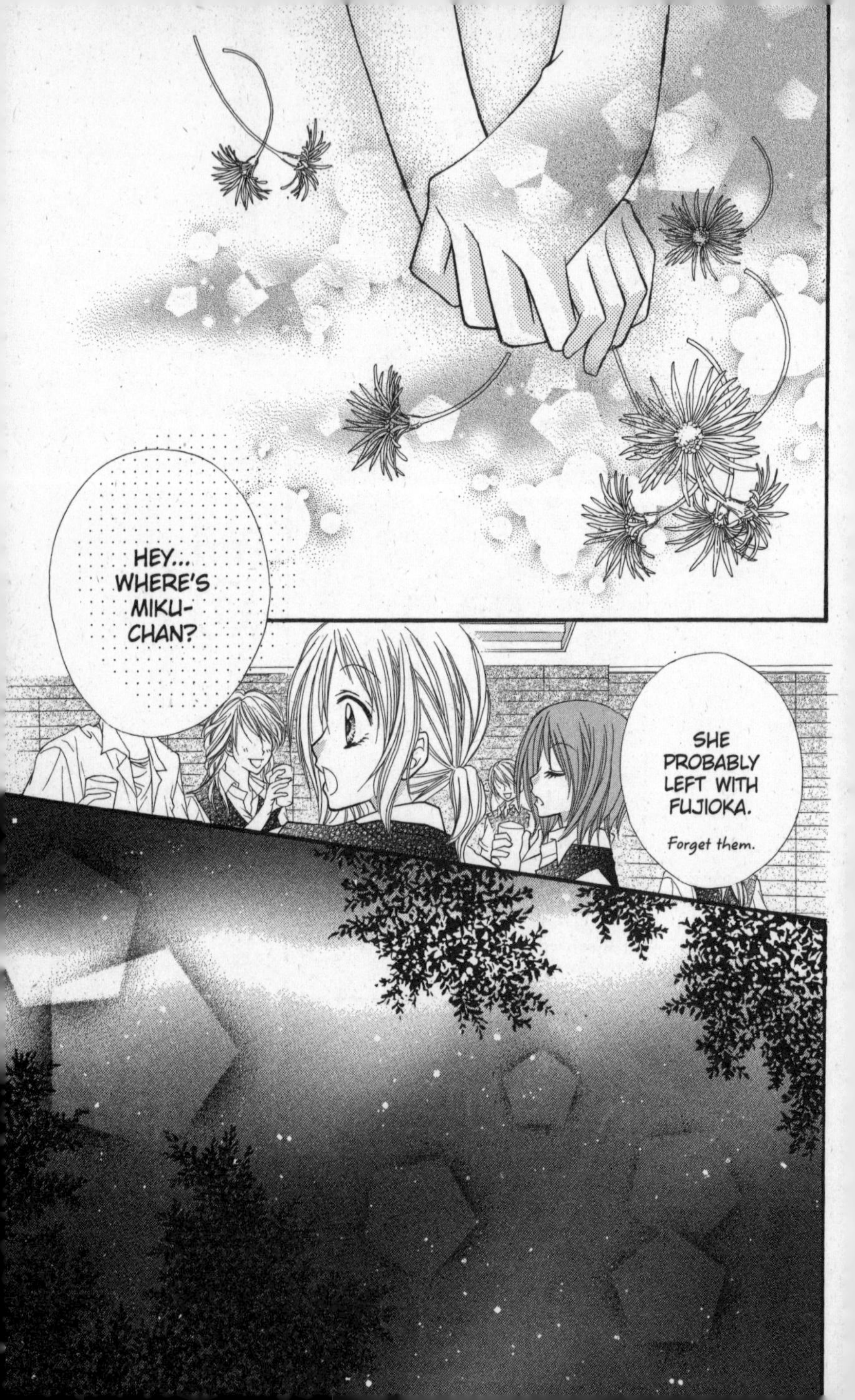
HEY... WHERE'S MIKU-CHAN?
SHE PROBABLY LEFT WITH FUJIOKA.
Forget them.

Haruta's Diary

"This is getting really scary..." Part ②

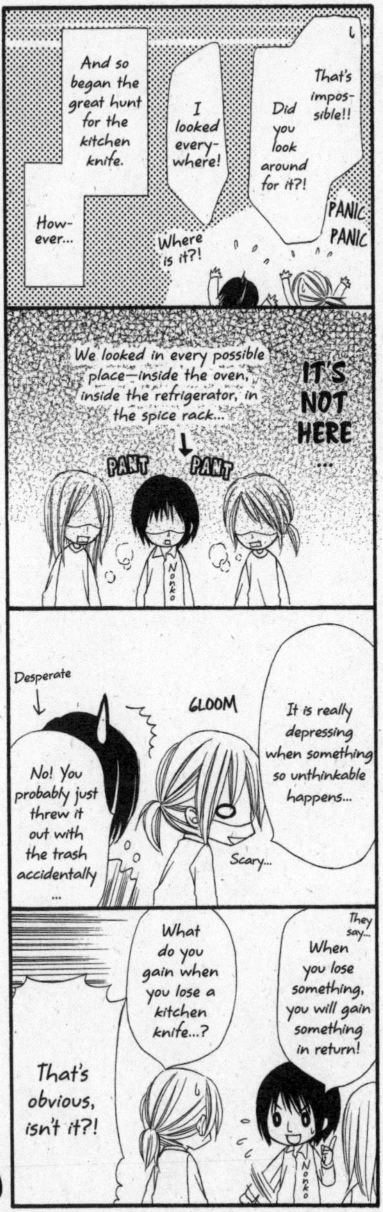
That's impossible!!
Did you look around for it?!
PANIC PANIC
I looked everywhere!
And so began the great hunt for the kitchen knife.
Where is it?!
However...
IT'S NOT HERE ...
We looked in every possible place—inside the oven, inside the refrigerator, in the spice rack...
PANT PANT
It is really depressing when something so unthinkable happens...
GLOOM
Scary...
Desperate
No! You probably just threw it out with the trash accidentally...
They say...
When you lose something, you will gain something in return!
What do you gain when you lose a kitchen knife...?
That's obvious, isn't it?!

Continued in part ③

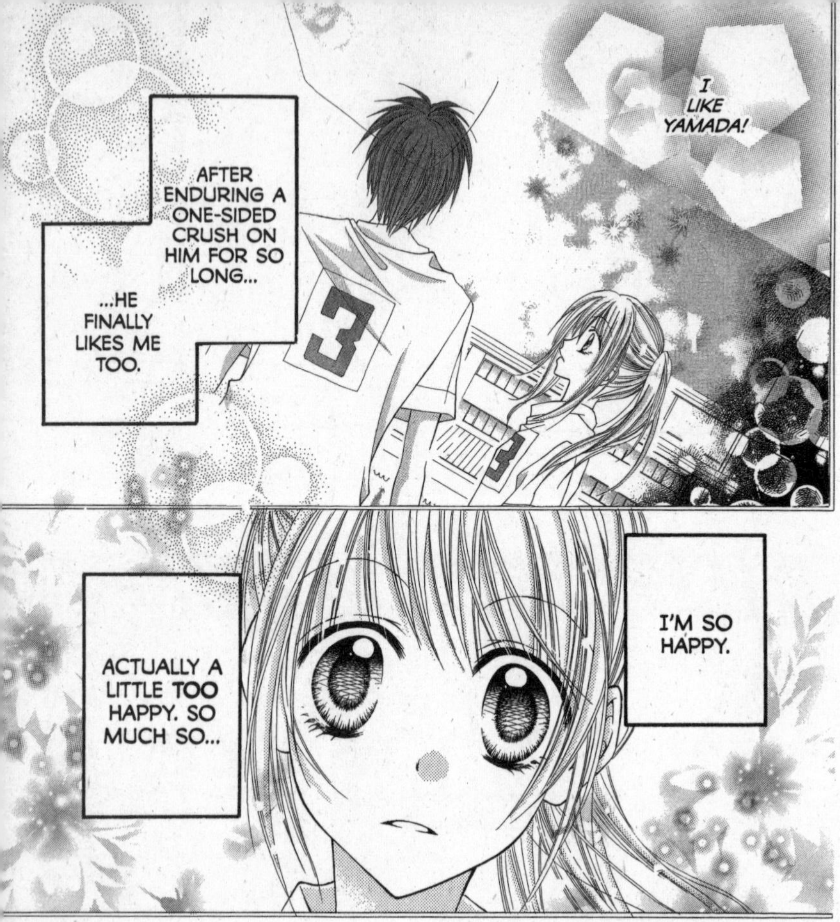
I LIKE YAMADA!
AFTER ENDURING A ONE-SIDED CRUSH ON HIM FOR SO LONG...
...HE FINALLY LIKES ME TOO.
I'M SO HAPPY.
ACTUALLY A LITTLE TOO HAPPY. SO MUCH SO...

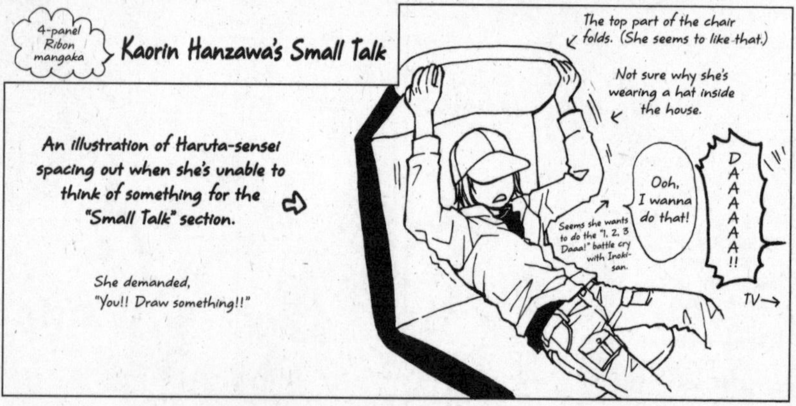
4-panel Ribon mangaka
Kaorin Hanzawa's Small Talk
An illustration of Haruta-sensei spacing out when she's unable to think of something for the "Small Talk" section.
She demanded, "You!! Draw something!!"
The top part of the chair folds. (She seems to like that.)
Not sure why she's wearing a hat inside the house.
Ooh, I wanna do that!
DAAAAAA!!
Seems she wants to do the "1, 2, 3 Daaa!" battle cry with Inoki-san.
TV→

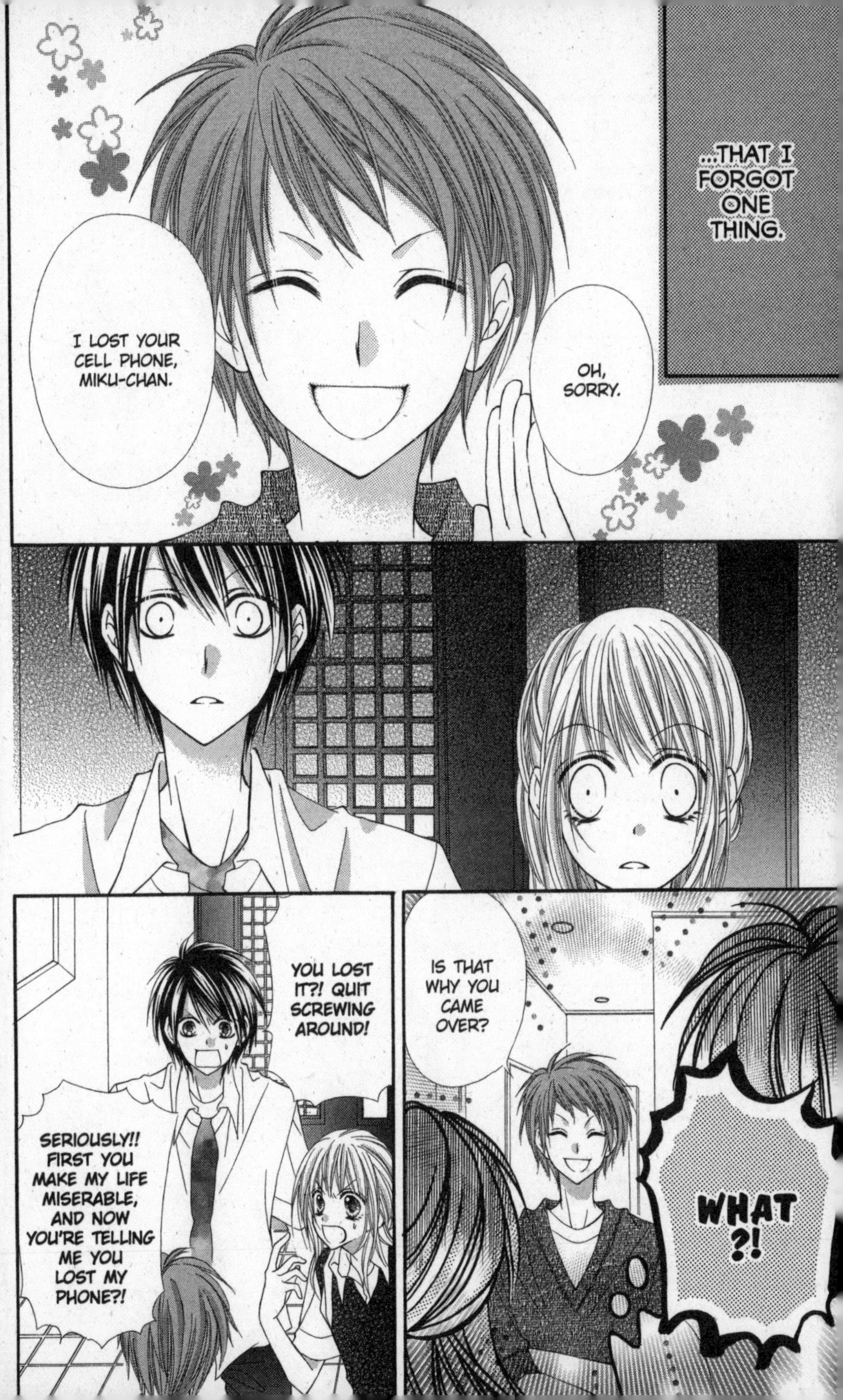
...THAT I FORGOT ONE THING.
I LOST YOUR CELL PHONE, MIKU-CHAN.
OH, SORRY.
IS THAT WHY YOU CAME OVER?
WHAT?!
YOU LOST IT?! QUIT SCREWING AROUND!
SERIOUSLY!! FIRST YOU MAKE MY LIFE MISERABLE, AND NOW YOU'RE TELLING ME YOU LOST MY PHONE?!

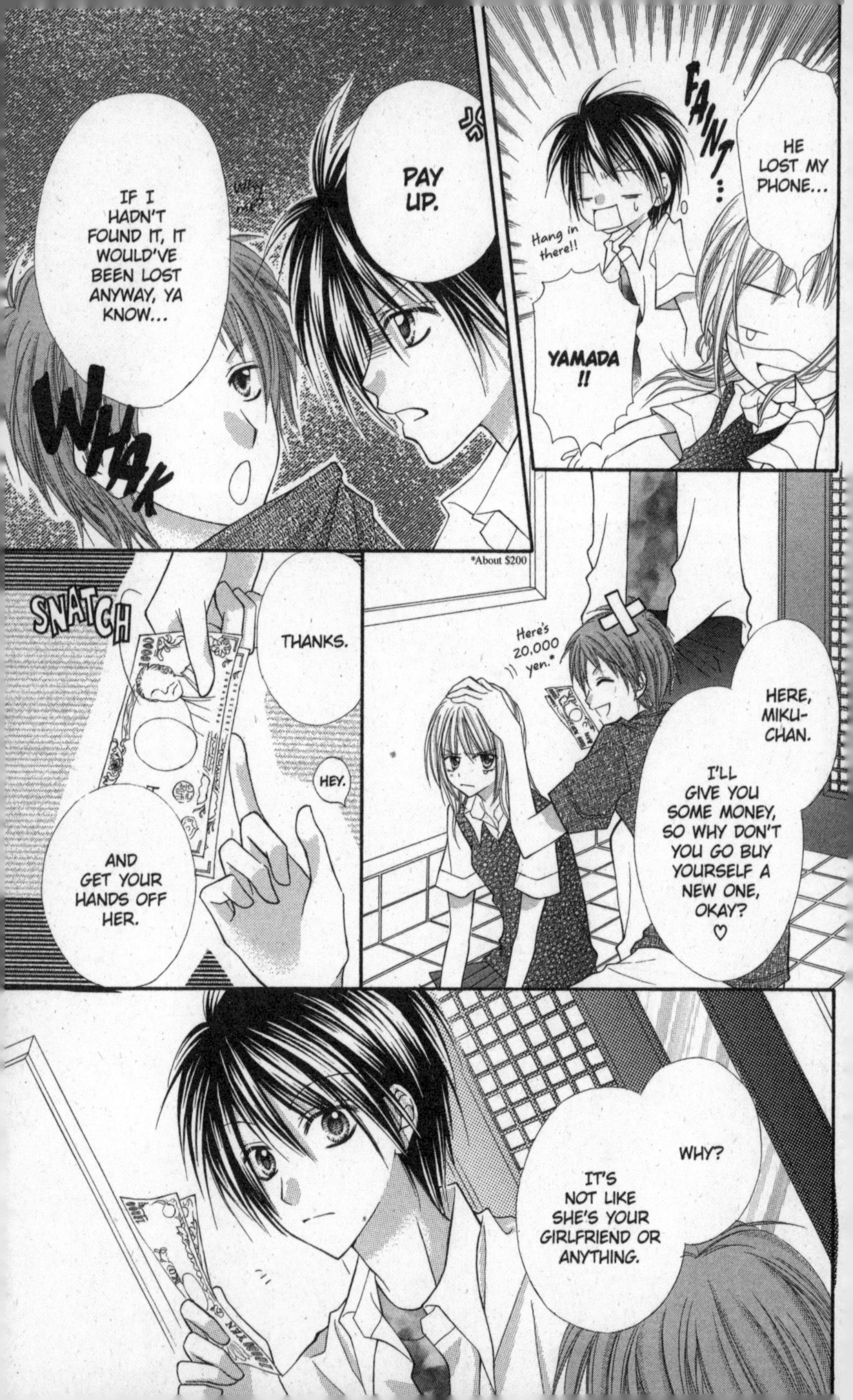

HE LOST MY PHONE...
FAINT...
Hang in there!!
YAMADA!!
PAY UP.
Why me??
IF I HADN'T FOUND IT, IT WOULD'VE BEEN LOST ANYWAY, YA KNOW...
WHAK
HERE, MIKU-CHAN.
I'LL GIVE YOU SOME MONEY, SO WHY DON'T YOU GO BUY YOURSELF A NEW ONE, OKAY? ♡
Here's 20,000 yen.*
*About $200
THANKS.
SNATCH
HEY.
AND GET YOUR HANDS OFF HER.
WHY?
IT'S NOT LIKE SHE'S YOUR GIRLFRIEND OR ANYTHING.

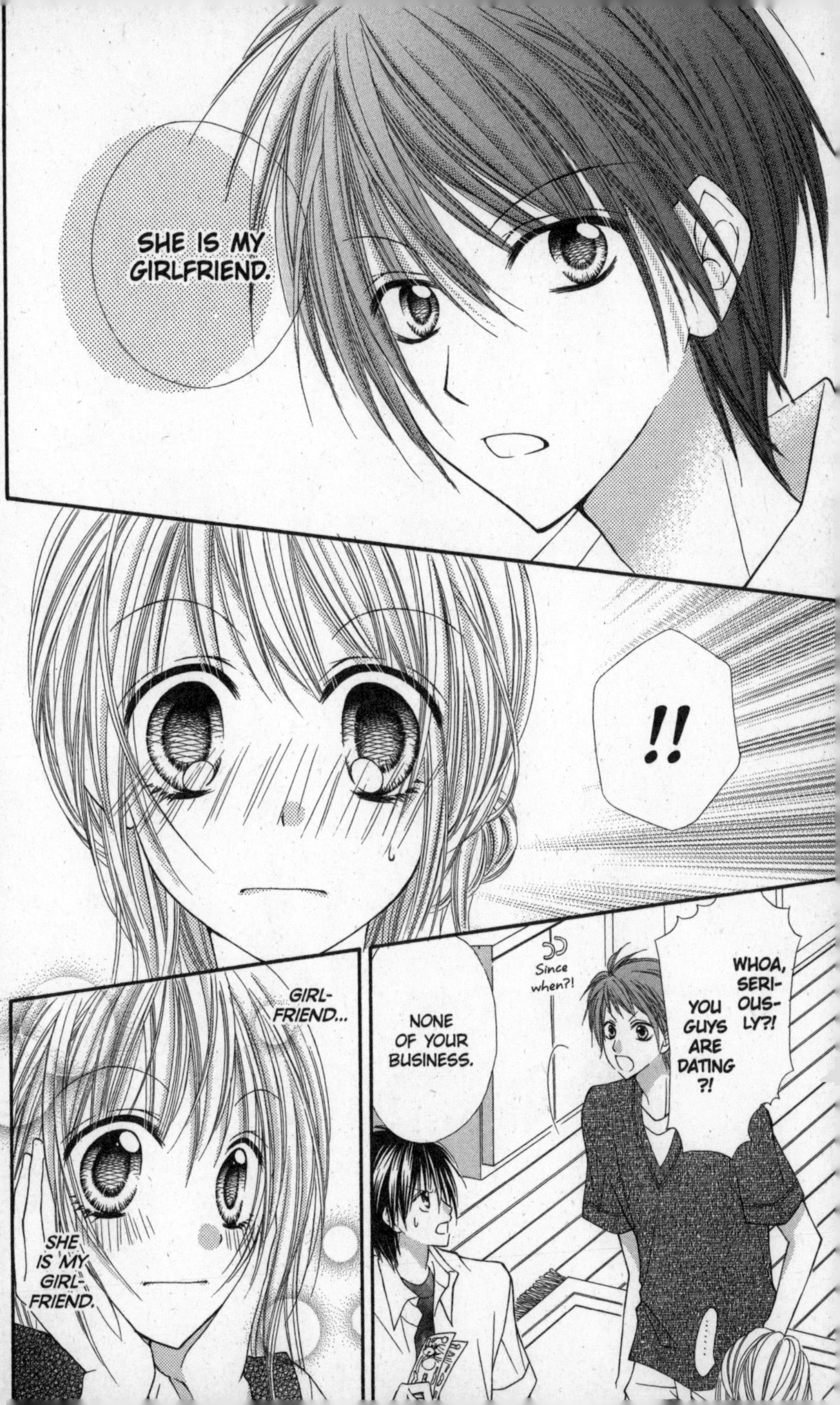
SHE IS MY GIRLFRIEND.
!!
WHOA, SERI-OUS-LY?!
YOU GUYS ARE DATING?!
Since when?!
NONE OF YOUR BUSINESS.
GIRL-FRIEND...
SHE IS MY GIRL-FRIEND.

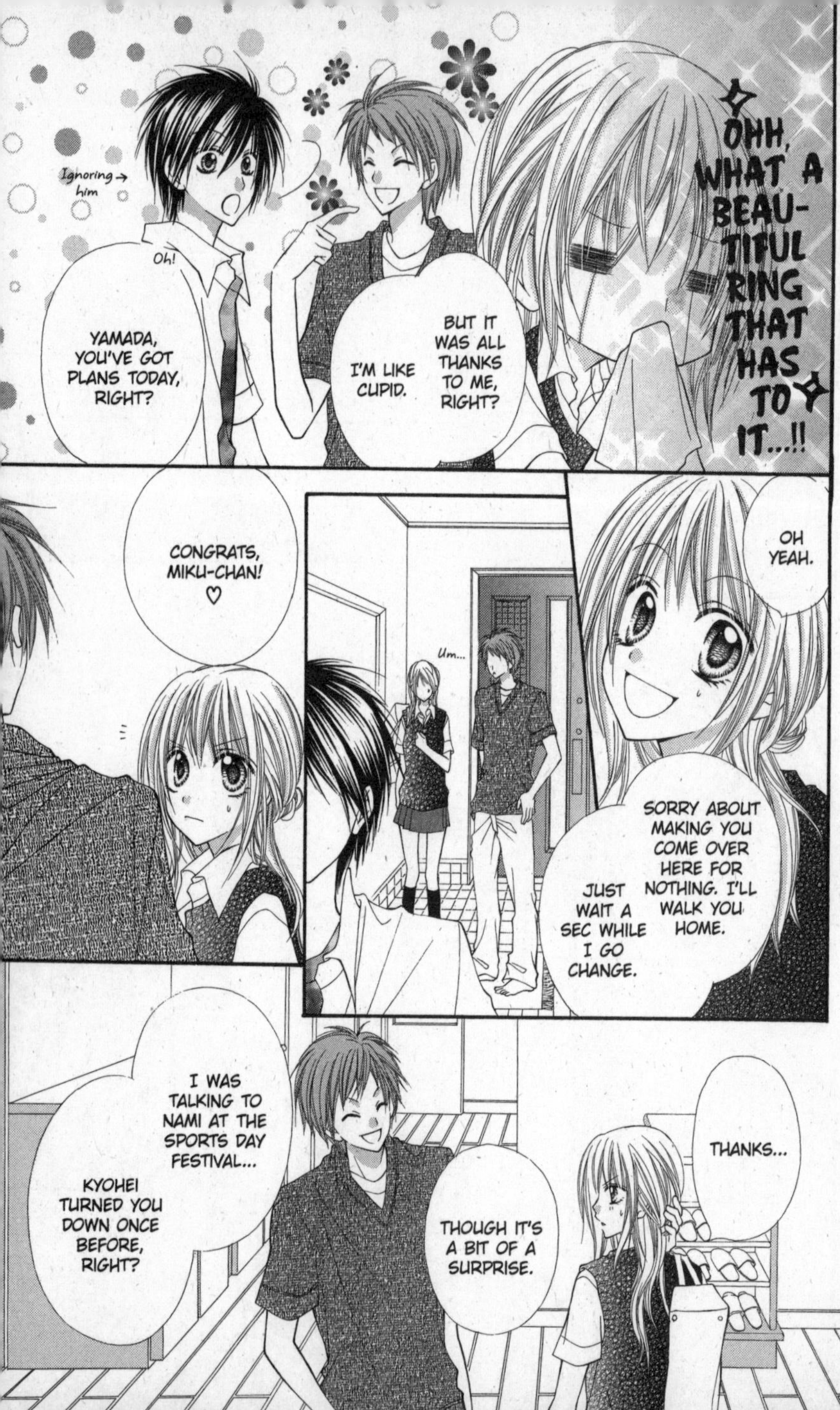

OHH, WHAT A BEAU-TIFUL RING THAT HAS TO IT...!!
BUT IT WAS ALL THANKS TO ME, RIGHT?
I'M LIKE CUPID.
Ignoring him
Oh!
YAMADA, YOU'VE GOT PLANS TODAY, RIGHT?
OH YEAH.
SORRY ABOUT MAKING YOU COME OVER HERE FOR NOTHING. I'LL WALK YOU HOME.
JUST WAIT A SEC WHILE I GO CHANGE.
Um...
CONGRATS, MIKU-CHAN! ♡
THANKS...
THOUGH IT'S A BIT OF A SURPRISE.
I WAS TALKING TO NAMI AT THE SPORTS DAY FESTIVAL...
KYOHEI TURNED YOU DOWN ONCE BEFORE, RIGHT?

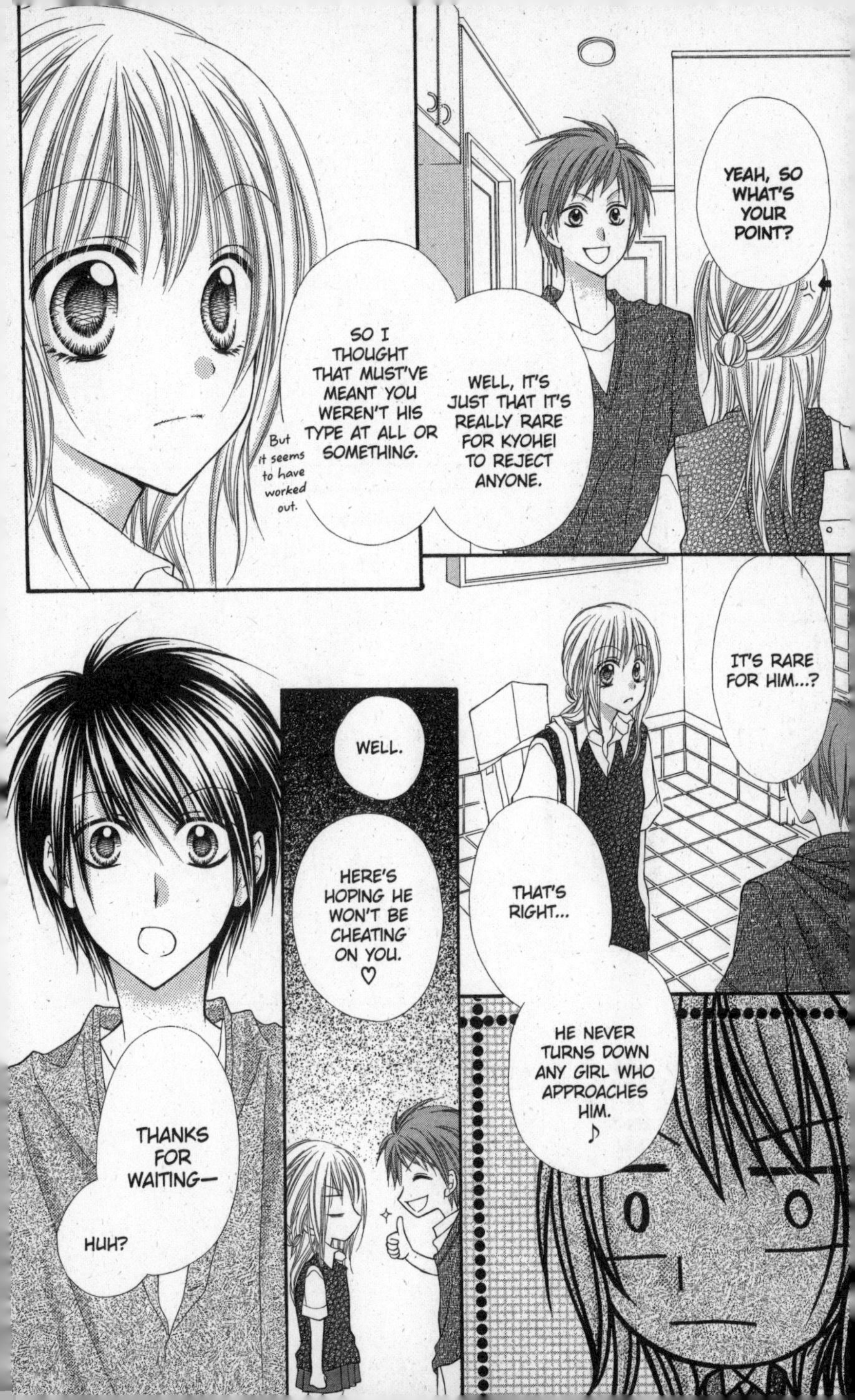
YEAH, SO WHAT'S YOUR POINT?
WELL, IT'S JUST THAT IT'S REALLY RARE FOR KYOHEI TO REJECT ANYONE.
SO I THOUGHT THAT MUST'VE MEANT YOU WEREN'T HIS TYPE AT ALL OR SOMETHING.
But it seems to have worked out.
IT'S RARE FOR HIM...?
THAT'S RIGHT...
HE NEVER TURNS DOWN ANY GIRL WHO APPROACHES HIM. ♪
WELL.
HERE'S HOPING HE WON'T BE CHEATING ON YOU. ♡
THANKS FOR WAITING—
HUH?

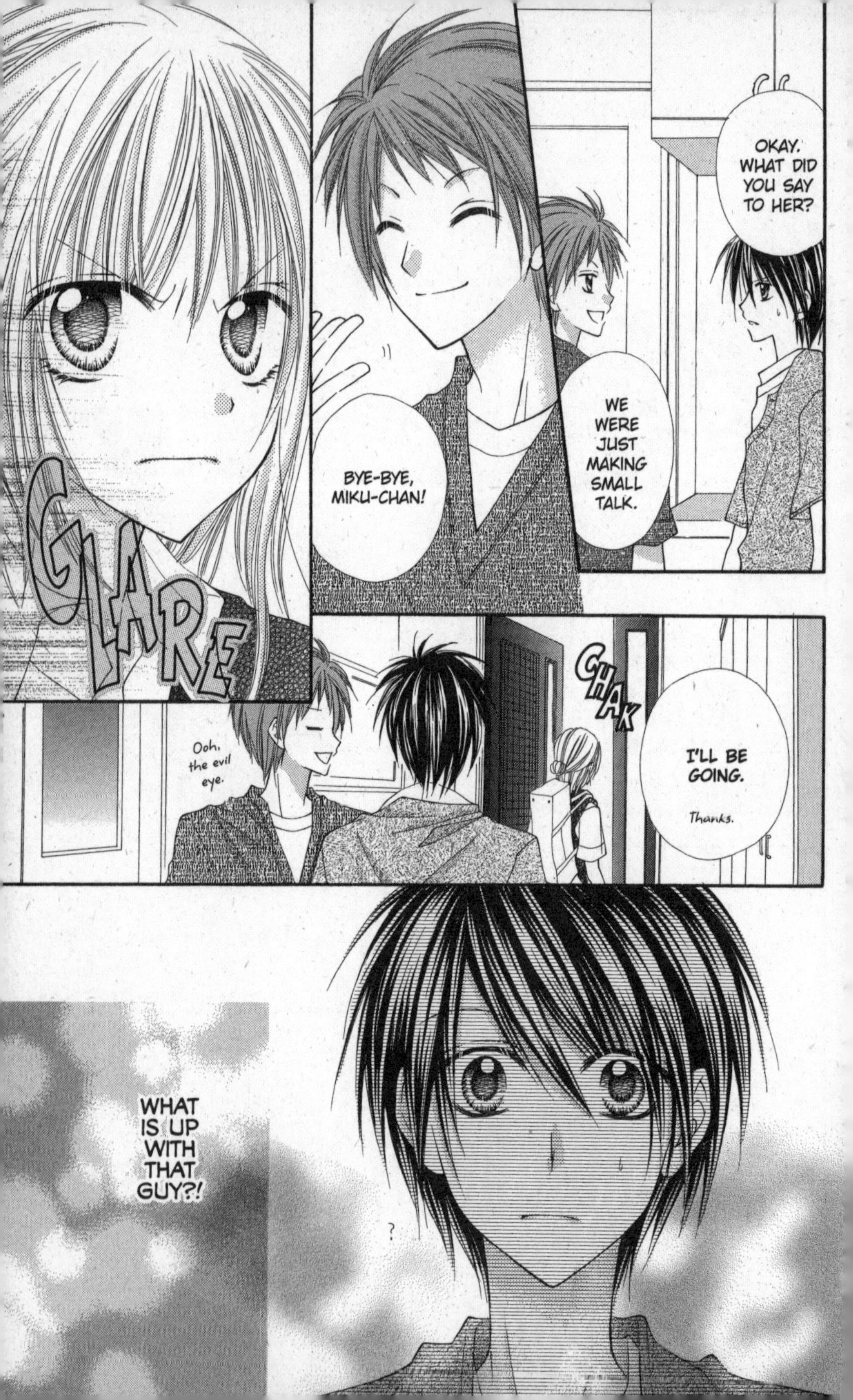
OKAY. WHAT DID YOU SAY TO HER?
WE WERE JUST MAKING SMALL TALK.
BYE-BYE, MIKU-CHAN!
GLARE
CHAK
I'LL BE GOING.
Thanks.
Ooh, the evil eye.
?
WHAT IS UP WITH THAT GUY?!

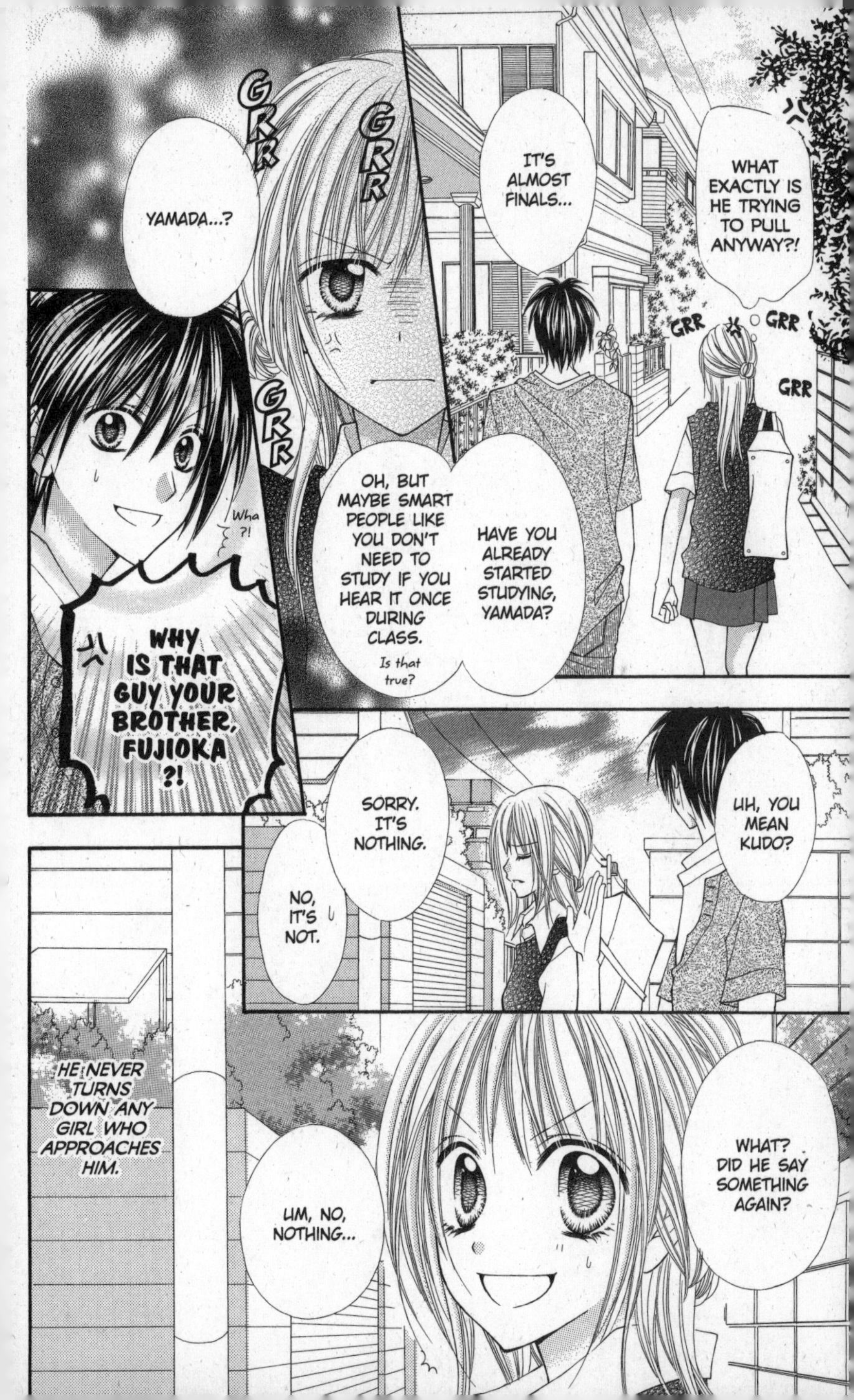
WHAT EXACTLY IS HE TRYING TO PULL ANYWAY?!
IT'S ALMOST FINALS...
GRR
GRR
GRR
HAVE YOU ALREADY STARTED STUDYING, YAMADA?
OH, BUT MAYBE SMART PEOPLE LIKE YOU DON'T NEED TO STUDY IF YOU HEAR IT ONCE DURING CLASS.
Is that true?
GRR
GRR
YAMADA...?
GRR
Wha ?!
WHY IS THAT GUY YOUR BROTHER, FUJIOKA ?!
UH, YOU MEAN KUDO?
SORRY. IT'S NOTHING.
NO, IT'S NOT.
WHAT? DID HE SAY SOMETHING AGAIN?
UM, NO, NOTHING...
HE NEVER TURNS DOWN ANY GIRL WHO APPROACHES HIM.

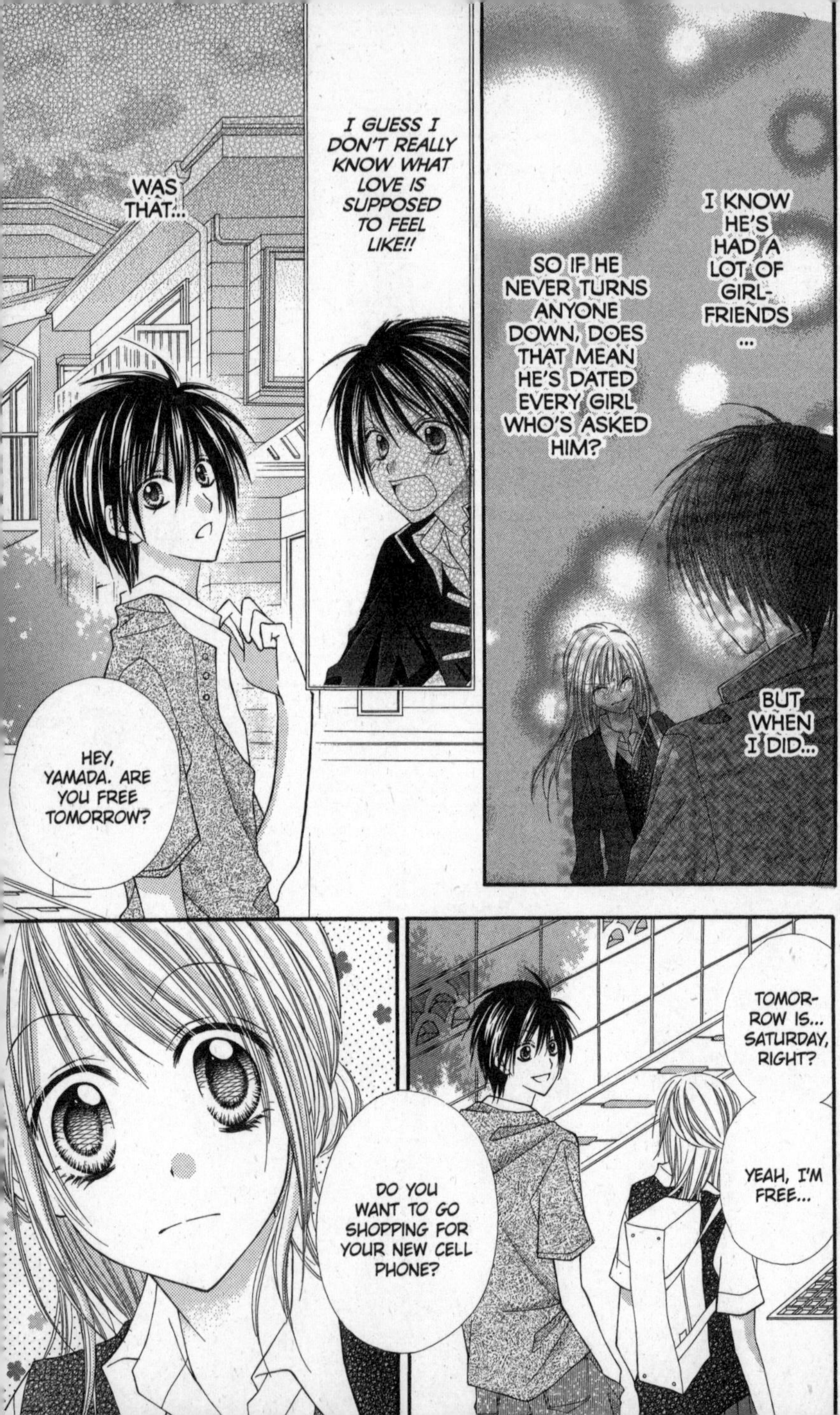
I KNOW HE'S HAD A LOT OF GIRL-FRIENDS...
SO IF HE NEVER TURNS ANYONE DOWN, DOES THAT MEAN HE'S DATED EVERY GIRL WHO'S ASKED HIM?
BUT WHEN I DID...
I GUESS I DON'T REALLY KNOW WHAT LOVE IS SUPPOSED TO FEEL LIKE!!
WAS THAT...
HEY, YAMADA. ARE YOU FREE TOMORROW?
TOMOR-ROW IS... SATURDAY, RIGHT?
YEAH, I'M FREE...
DO YOU WANT TO GO SHOPPING FOR YOUR NEW CELL PHONE?

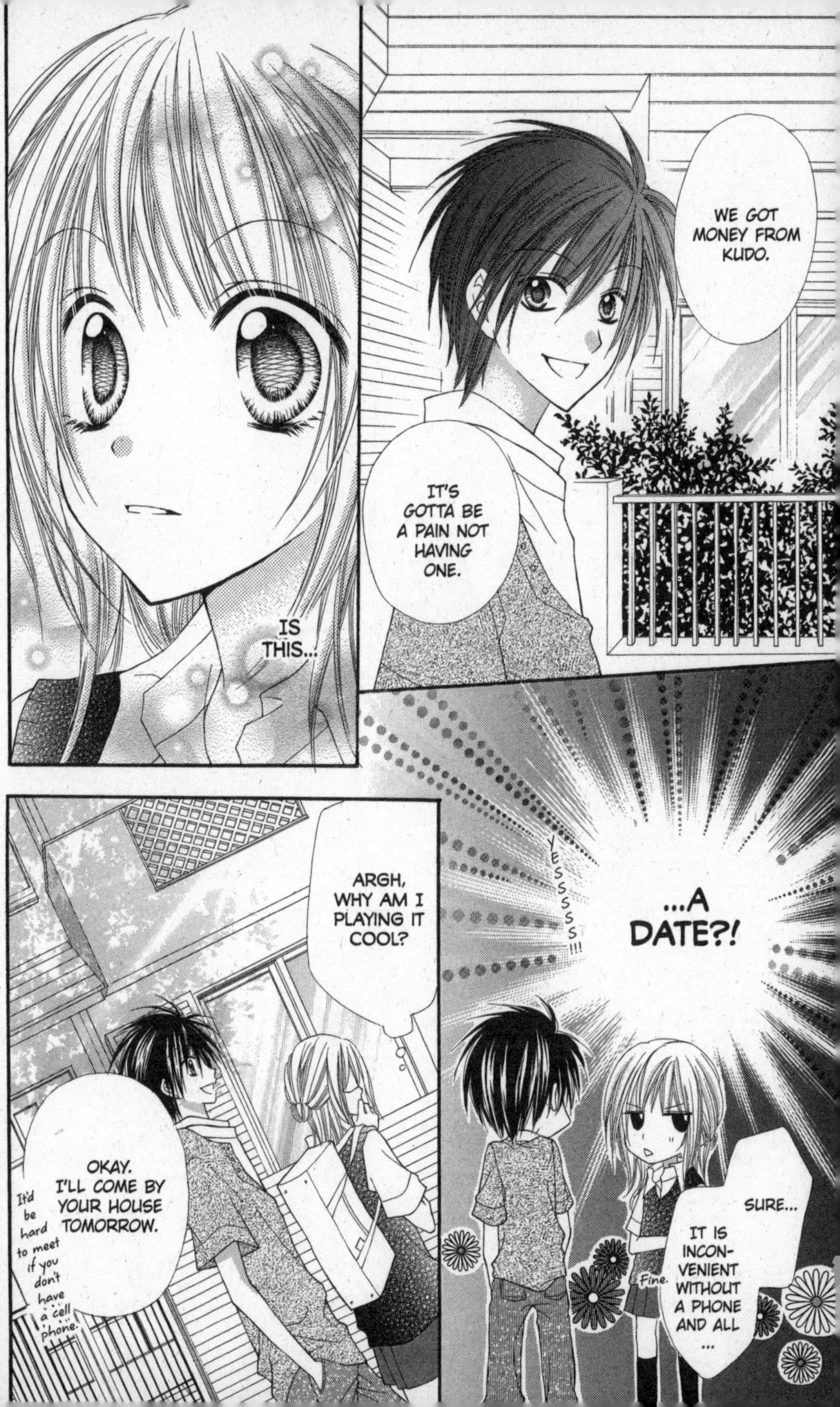

WE GOT MONEY FROM KUDO.
IT'S GOTTA BE A PAIN NOT HAVING ONE.
IS THIS...
...A DATE?!
YESSSSS!!!
SURE... IT IS INCONVENIENT WITHOUT A PHONE AND ALL ...
Fine.
ARGH, WHY AM I PLAYING IT COOL?
OKAY. I'LL COME BY YOUR HOUSE TOMORROW.
It'd be hard to meet if you don't have a cell phone.

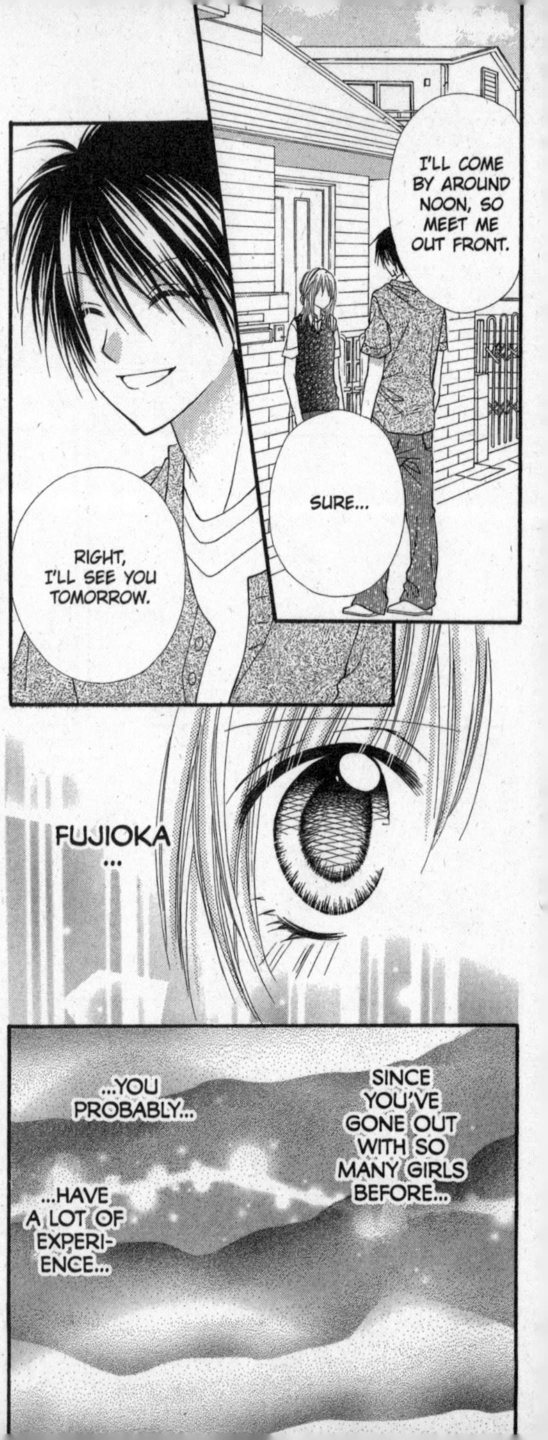
I'LL COME BY AROUND NOON, SO MEET ME OUT FRONT.
SURE...
RIGHT, I'LL SEE YOU TOMORROW.
FUJIOKA ...
SINCE YOU'VE GONE OUT WITH SO MANY GIRLS BEFORE...
...YOU PROBABLY...
...HAVE A LOT OF EXPERIENCE...

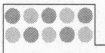

7

Recently I experienced a moment of extreme culture shock. Readers, do you use the phrase "sorotto"??

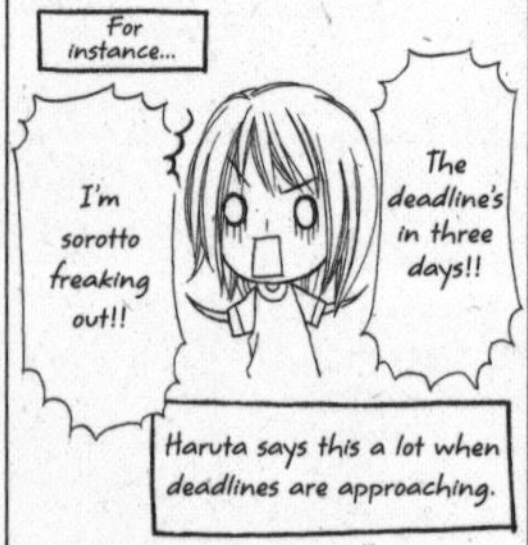
For instance...
I'm sorotto freaking out!!
The deadline's in three days!!
Haruta says this a lot when deadlines are approaching.

It means the same as "soro soro" (starting to/gradually) and I always thought it was standard Japanese. But my assistants from the Kanto region always point out that it's country jargon. It was even pointed out to me when I went to the *Ribon* New Year's party too. When we were talking about colloquial dialects, they said, "Nana-chan, you say 'sorotto' a lot." (It feels weird calling myself "Nana.") That was when I first realized it was a regional phrase. It never even occurred to me that it wasn't mainstream Japanese— I've even used it in my manga!! How embarrassing... I don't normally use my regional dialect because I don't really like it. Though I do love Niigata. I wish there was a *Ribon* editorial office in Niigata. Though I doubt that'll ever happen.

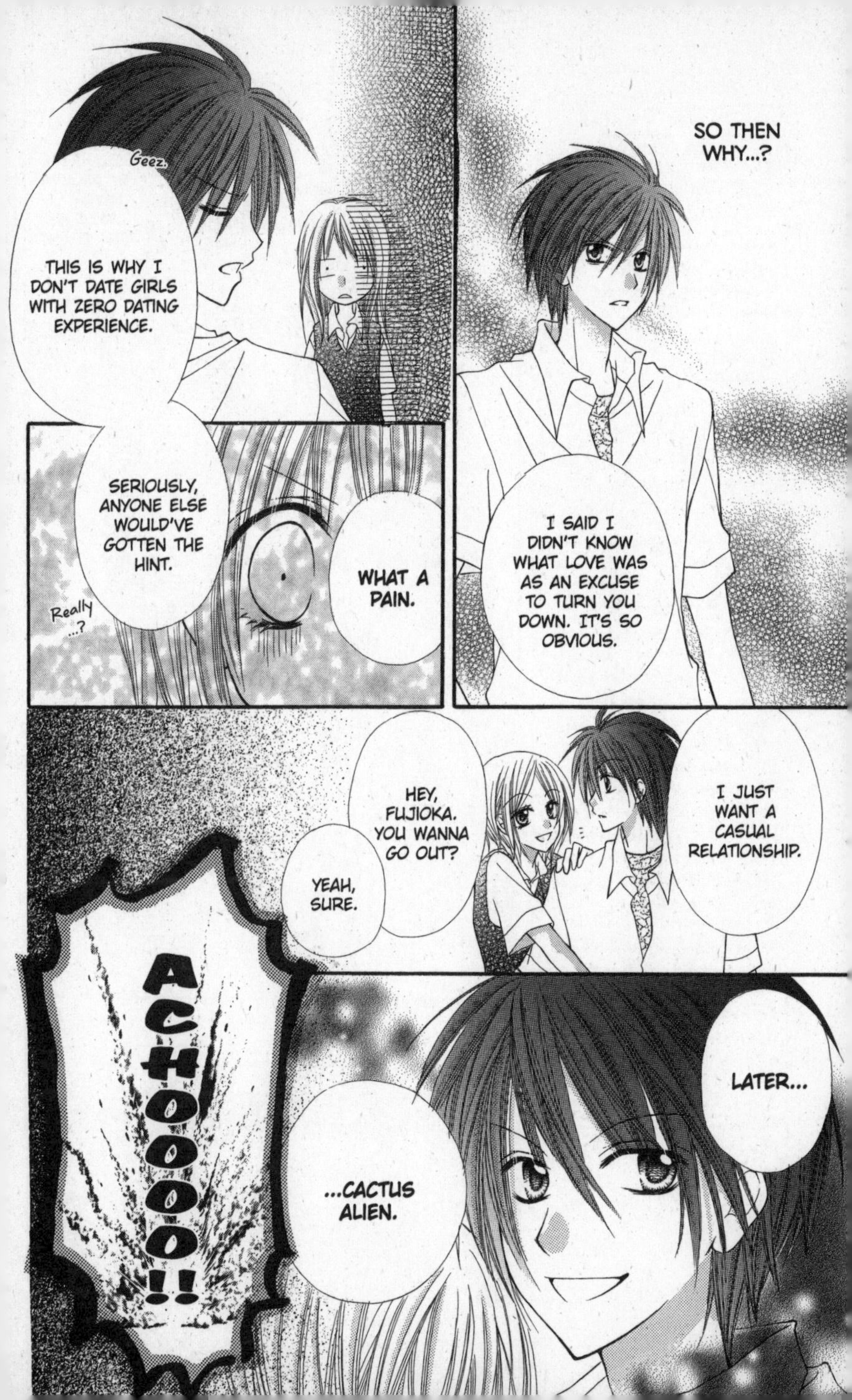
SO THEN WHY...?
I SAID I DIDN'T KNOW WHAT LOVE WAS AS AN EXCUSE TO TURN YOU DOWN. IT'S SO OBVIOUS.
Geez.
THIS IS WHY I DON'T DATE GIRLS WITH ZERO DATING EXPERIENCE.
SERIOUSLY, ANYONE ELSE WOULD'VE GOTTEN THE HINT.
WHAT A PAIN.
Really ...?
I JUST WANT A CASUAL RELATIONSHIP.
HEY, FUJIOKA. YOU WANNA GO OUT?
YEAH, SURE.
LATER...
...CACTUS ALIEN.
ACHOOOOO!!

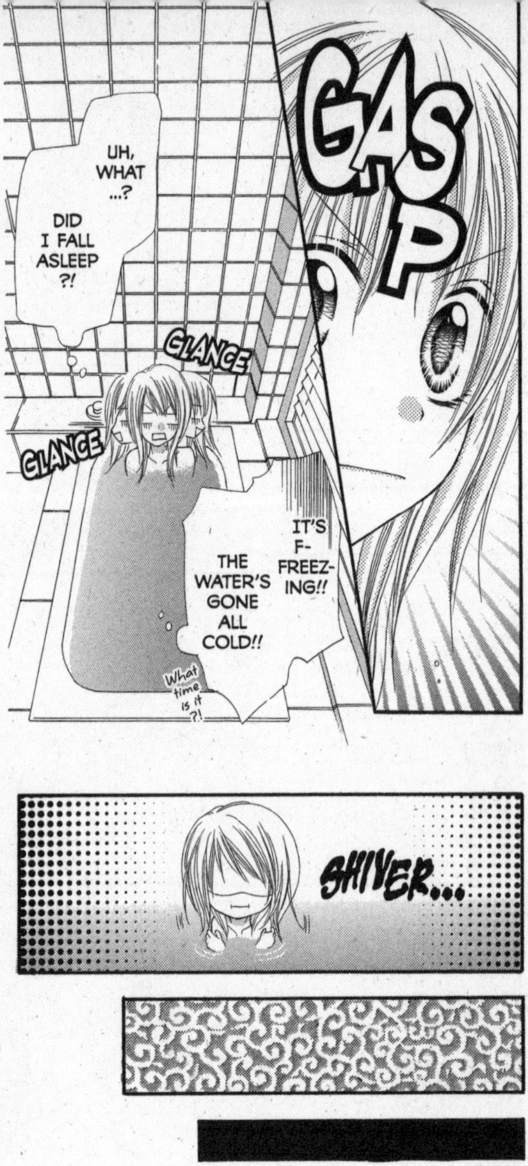
GASP
UH, WHAT ...?
DID I FALL ASLEEP ?!
GLANCE
GLANCE
IT'S F-FREEZING!!
THE WATER'S GONE ALL COLD!!
What time is it ?!
SHIVER...

8

So in this volume, Fujioka and Miku finally get together. A lot of readers wrote in and said, "I'm so happy for Miku!" It made me realize you guys had really been rooting for her—I'm so happy! To think that readers could really take a character I created to heart like that—to be happy for her or sympathize with her like she was a friend...! To me, that is the greatest thing about being a mangaka.

However, their getting together was not a popular decision with my assistants.

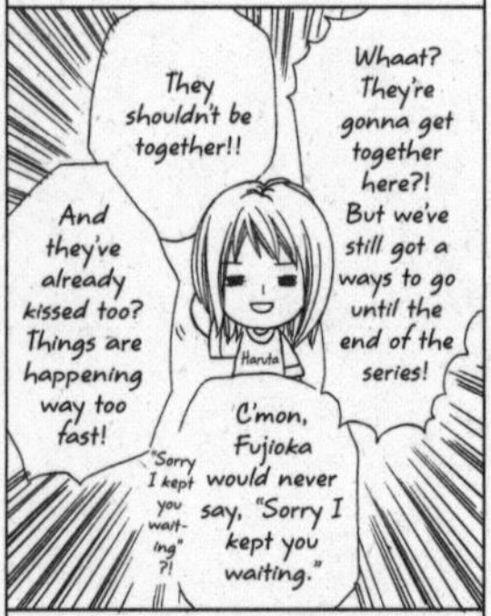
Whaat? They're gonna get together here?! But we've still got a ways to go until the end of the series!
They shouldn't be together!!
And they've already kissed too? Things are happening way too fast!
C'mon, Fujioka would never say, "Sorry I kept you waiting."
"Sorry I kept you wait-ing" ?!
Haruta

At this point we already knew when the series would end. To be honest, I think that the two of them shouldn't have gotten together either. (Hey...) I just couldn't imagine the two of them all lovey-dovey, so it felt kinda weird to draw this at first. I still feel that way. Wait—still?! Seriously?

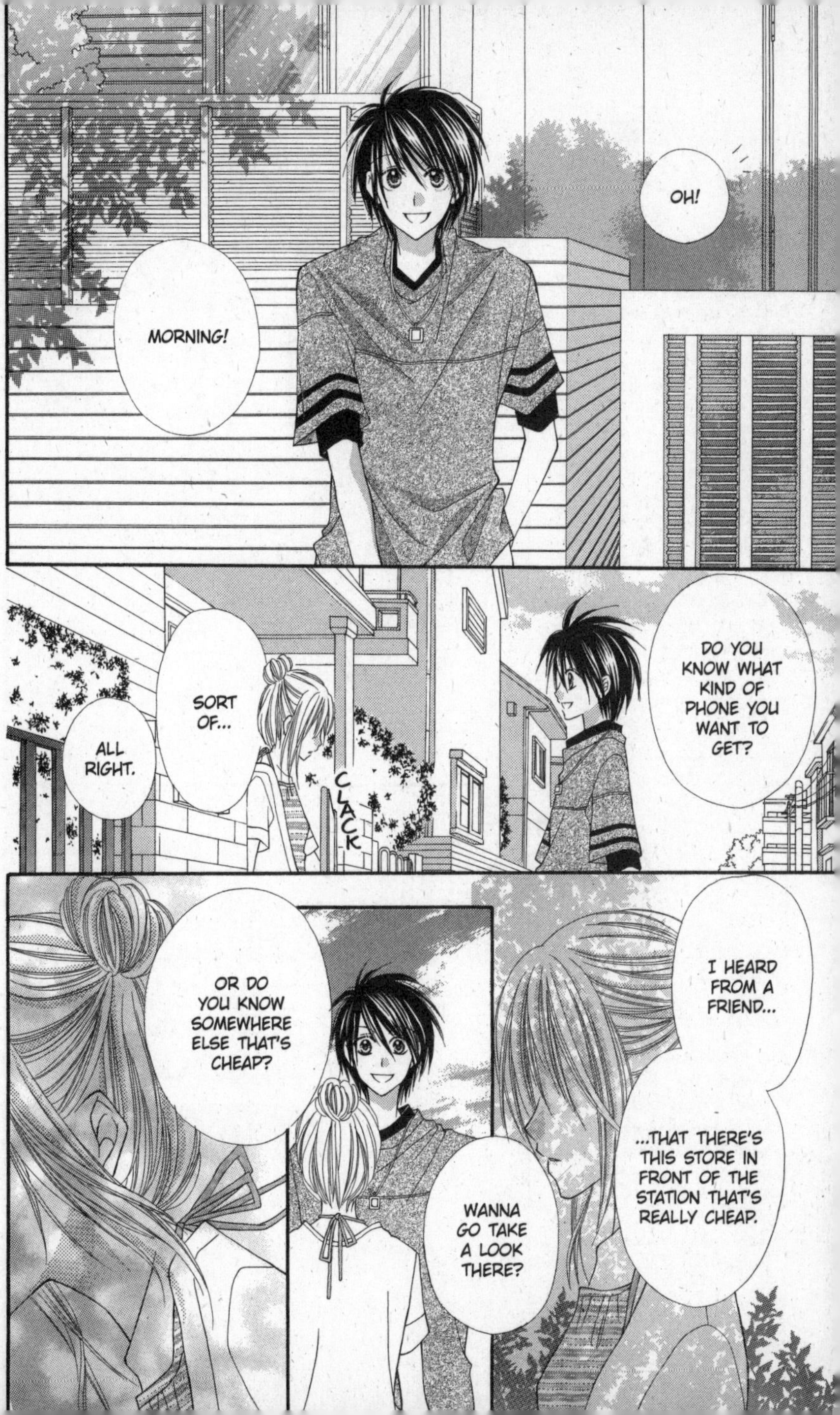
OH!
MORNING!
DO YOU KNOW WHAT KIND OF PHONE YOU WANT TO GET?
CLACK
SORT OF...
ALL RIGHT.
I HEARD FROM A FRIEND...
...THAT THERE'S THIS STORE IN FRONT OF THE STATION THAT'S REALLY CHEAP.
WANNA GO TAKE A LOOK THERE?
OR DO YOU KNOW SOMEWHERE ELSE THAT'S CHEAP?

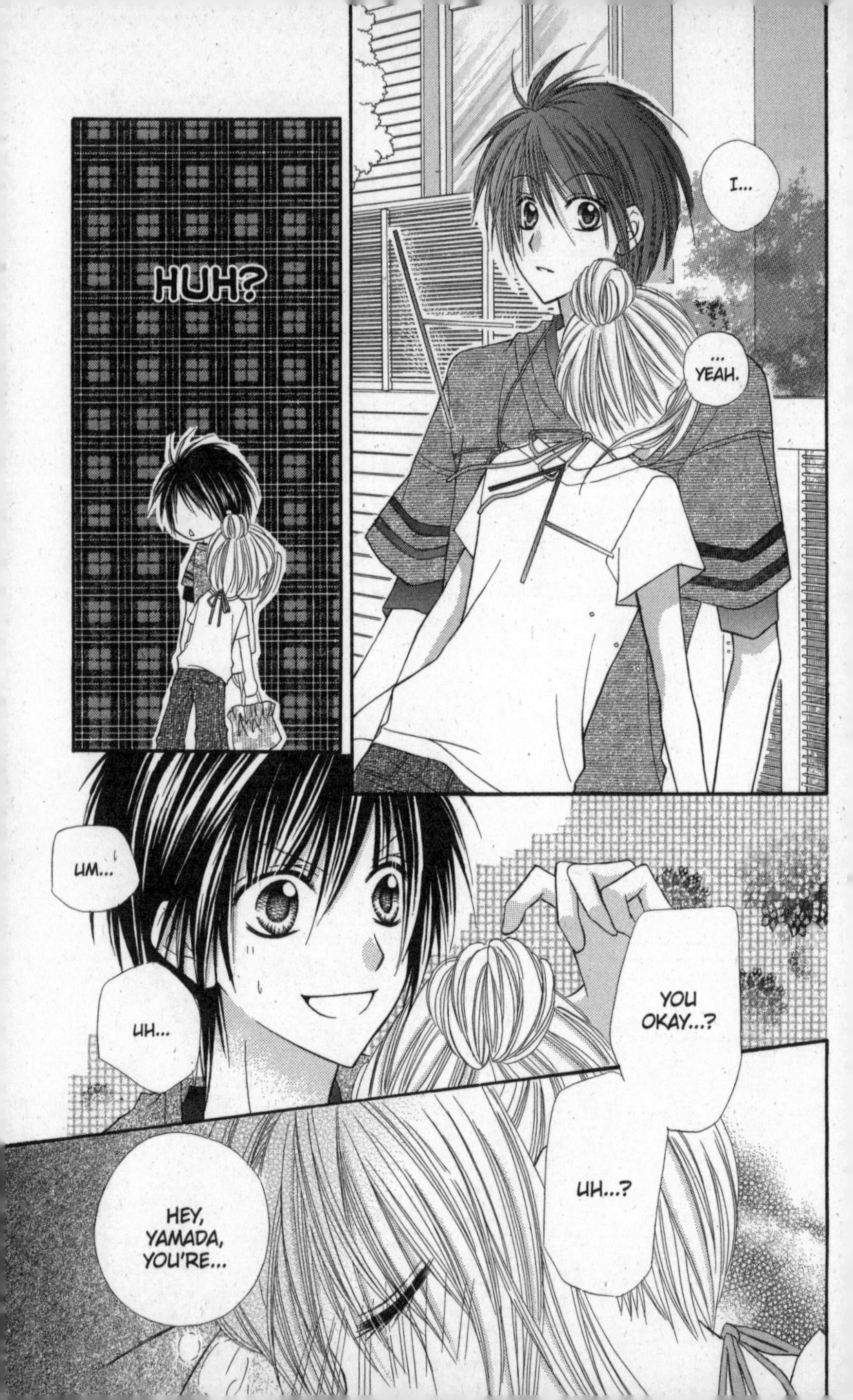
I...
... YEAH.
HUH?
YOU OKAY...?
UM...
UH...
UH...?
HEY, YAMADA, YOU'RE...

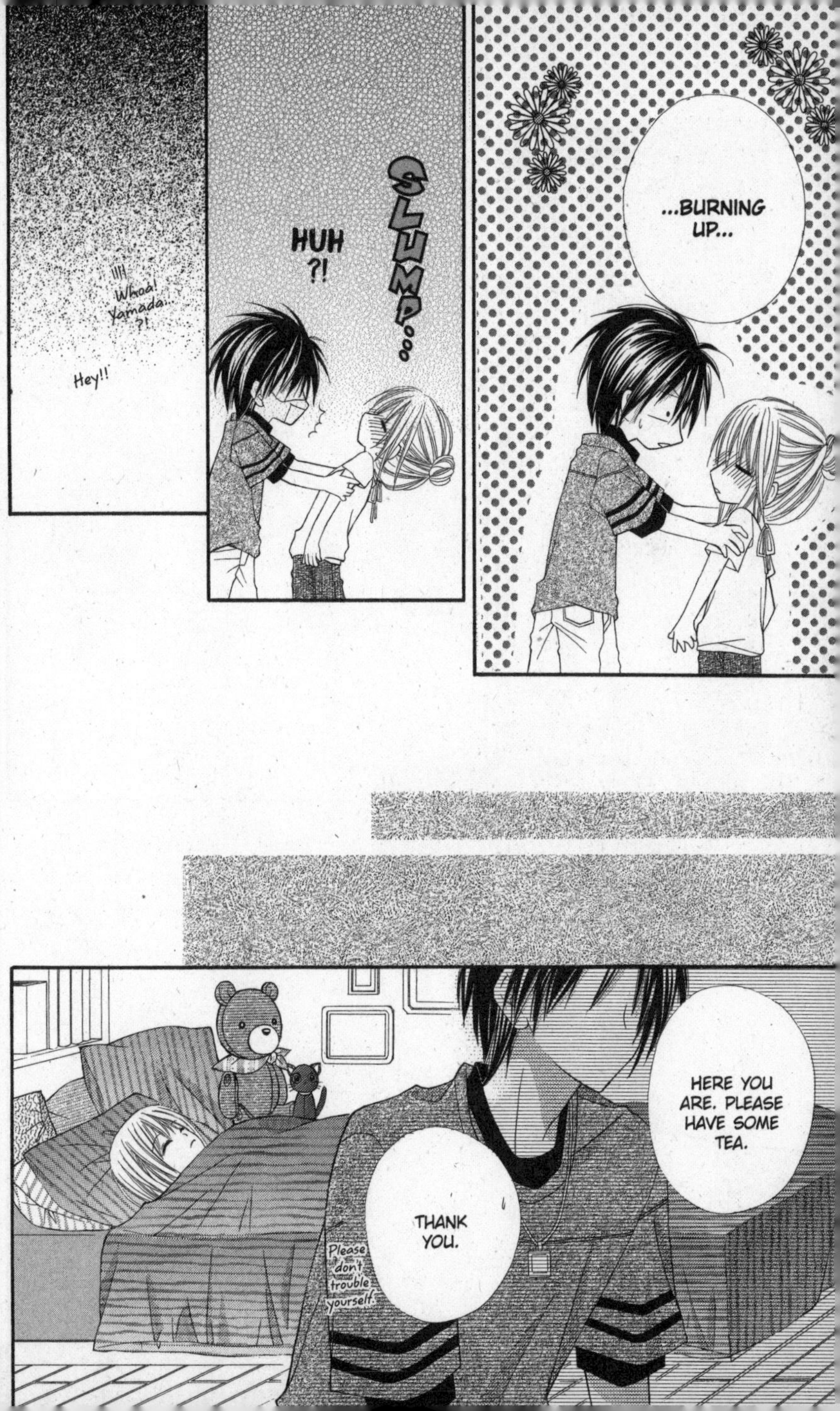
...BURNING UP...
HUH ?!
SLUMP...
Whoa! Yamada...?!
Hey!!
HERE YOU ARE. PLEASE HAVE SOME TEA.
THANK YOU.
Please don't trouble yourself.

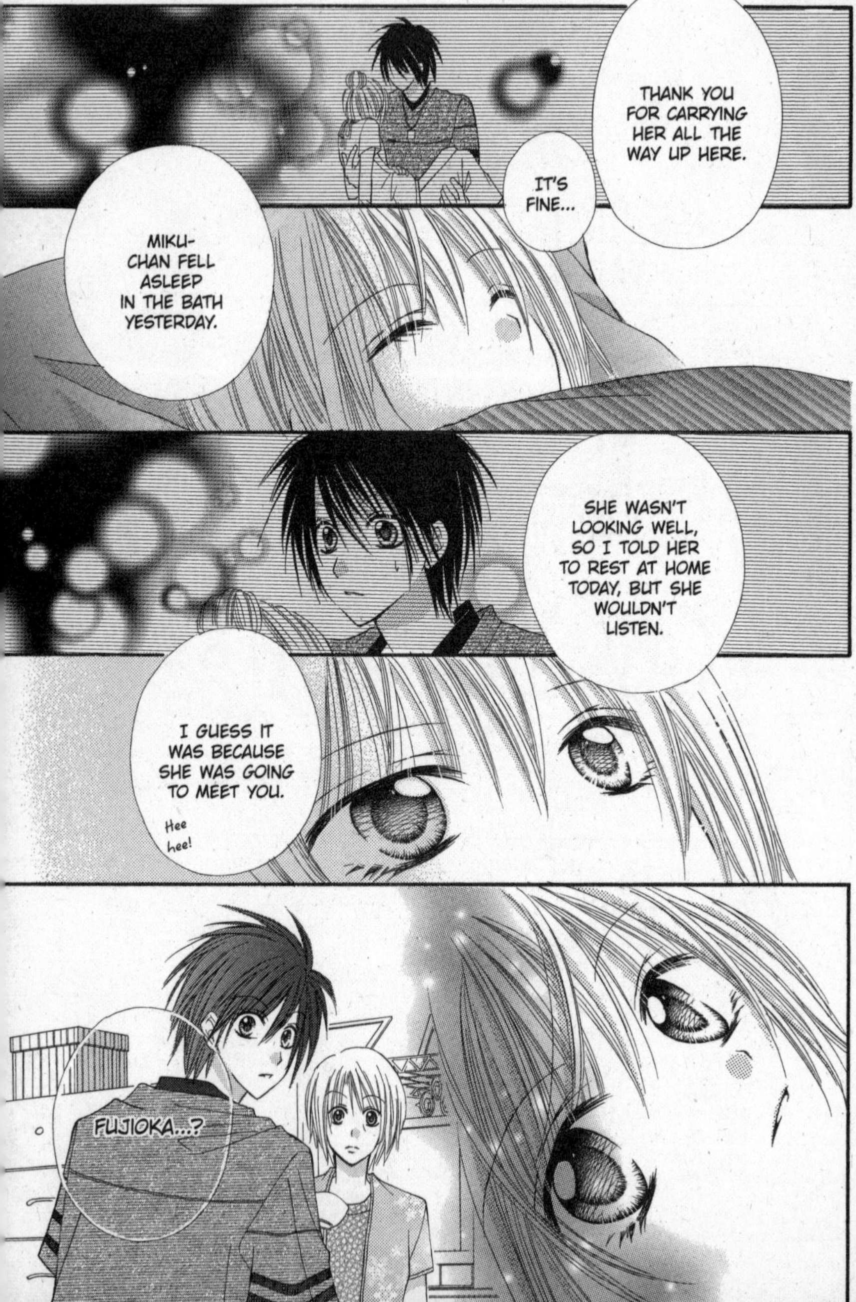
THANK YOU FOR CARRYING HER ALL THE WAY UP HERE.
IT'S FINE...
MIKU-CHAN FELL ASLEEP IN THE BATH YESTERDAY.
SHE WASN'T LOOKING WELL, SO I TOLD HER TO REST AT HOME TODAY, BUT SHE WOULDN'T LISTEN.
I GUESS IT WAS BECAUSE SHE WAS GOING TO MEET YOU.
Hee hee!
FUJIOKA...?

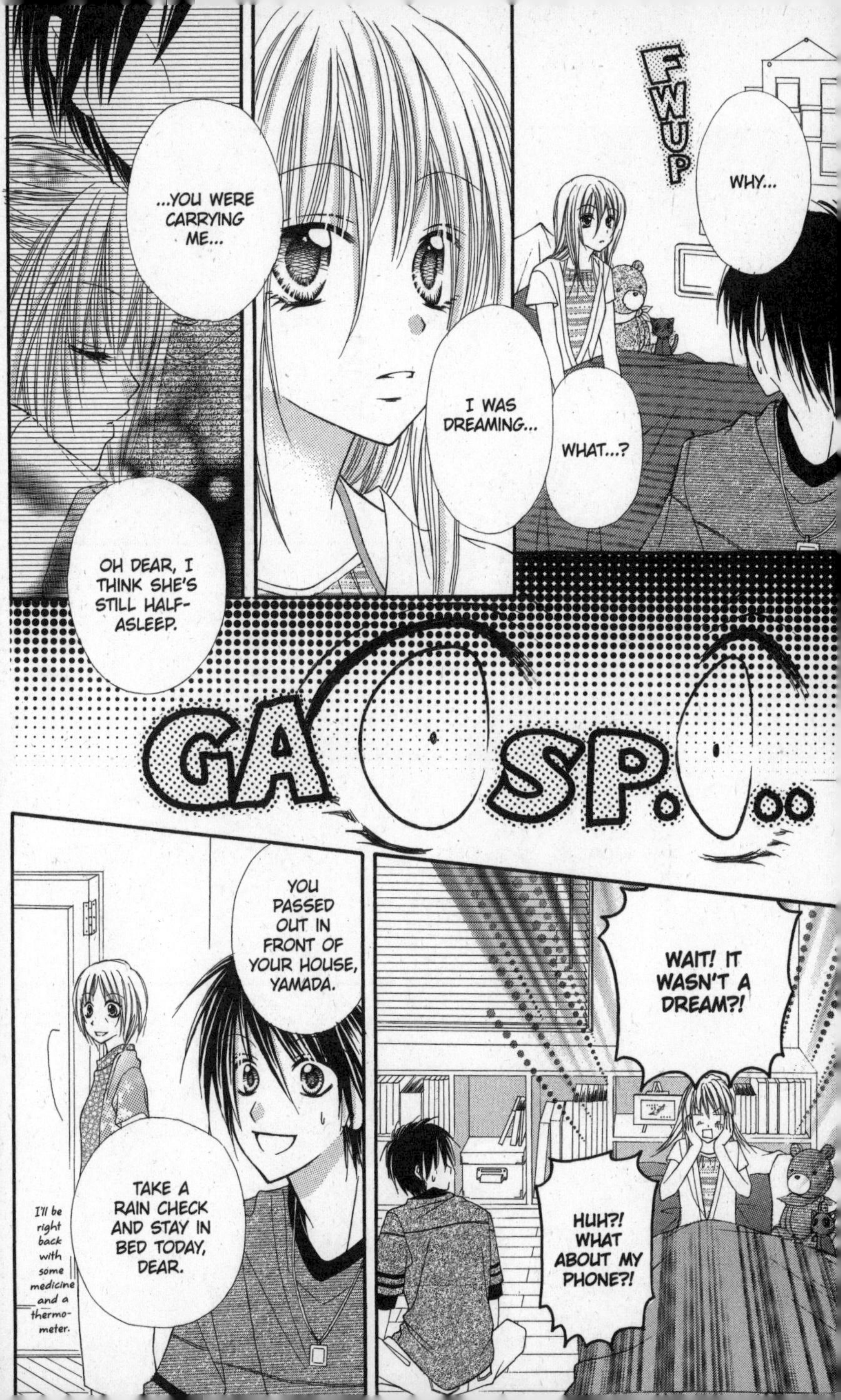
FWUP
WHY...
WHAT...?
I WAS DREAMING...
...YOU WERE CARRYING ME...
OH DEAR, I THINK SHE'S STILL HALF-ASLEEP.
GASP...
WAIT! IT WASN'T A DREAM?!
HUH?! WHAT ABOUT MY PHONE?!
YOU PASSED OUT IN FRONT OF YOUR HOUSE, YAMADA.
TAKE A RAIN CHECK AND STAY IN BED TODAY, DEAR.
I'll be right back with some medicine and a thermometer.

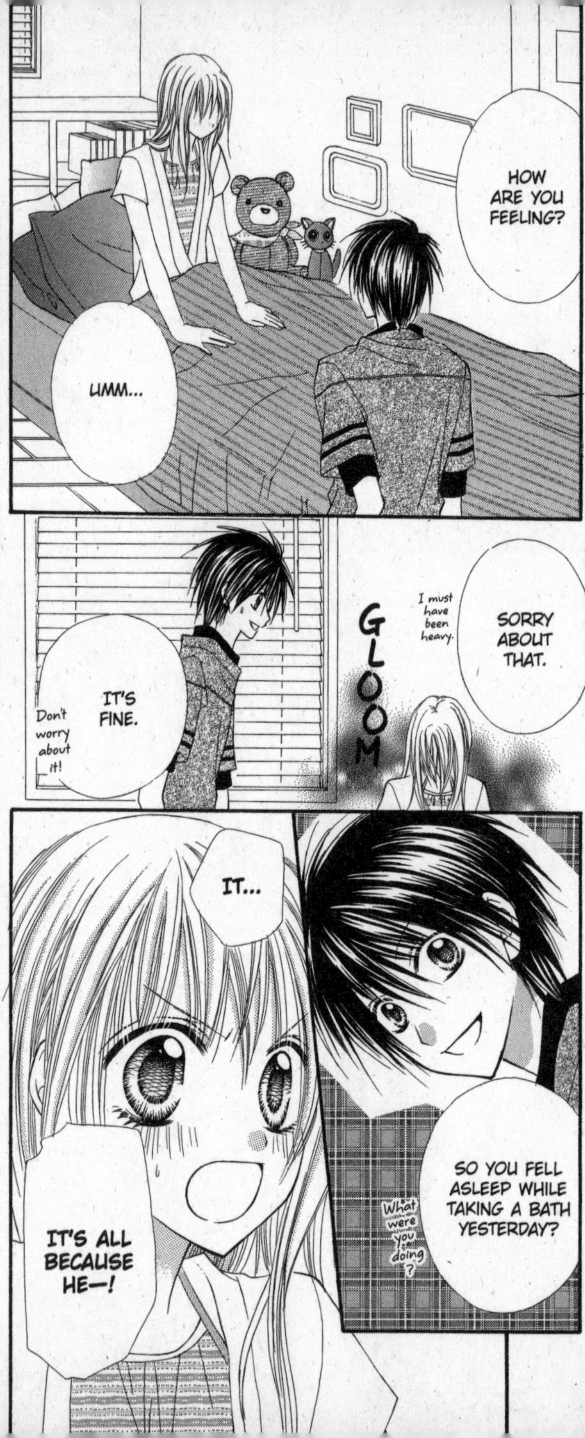
HOW ARE YOU FEELING?
UMM...
I must have been heavy.
SORRY ABOUT THAT.
GLOOM
IT'S FINE.
Don't worry about it!
SO YOU FELL ASLEEP WHILE TAKING A BATH YESTERDAY?
What were you doing?
IT...
IT'S ALL BECAUSE HE—!

9

And what caused an even bigger problem than the Sports Day chapter was the following chapter in which Miku and Fujioka are going to go cell phone shopping. There was a lot of grumbling from my assistants.

What is this?! A bedroom scene?!

Whoa, wait a sec! What is Fujioka doing—he's on top of her!

Wow, this is out of character for Fujioka.

Uh, can we print this sort of thing in Ribon?

I'm so disappointed in Fujioka...

Oh, did he put his **** in? Right?

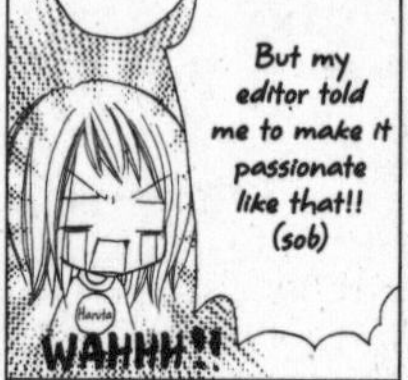
But my editor told me to make it passionate like that!! (sob)
WAHHH!!

They didn't like the scene in Miku's bedroom, so I was afraid of how the readers would react. But it turned out that everyone didn't think it was too much, thank goodness. Ha ha!

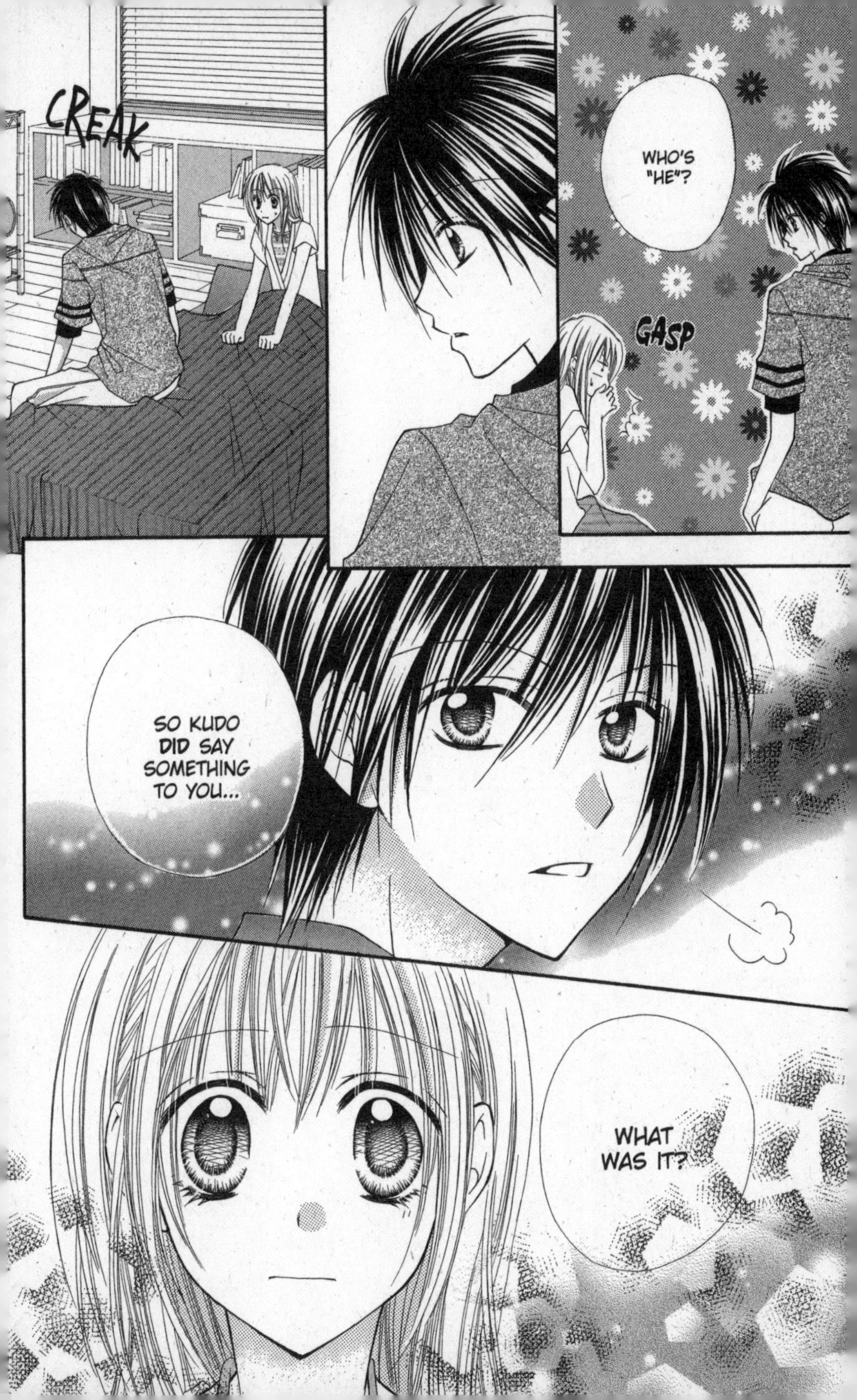
WHO'S "HE"?
GASP
CREAK
SO KUDO DID SAY SOMETHING TO YOU...
WHAT WAS IT?

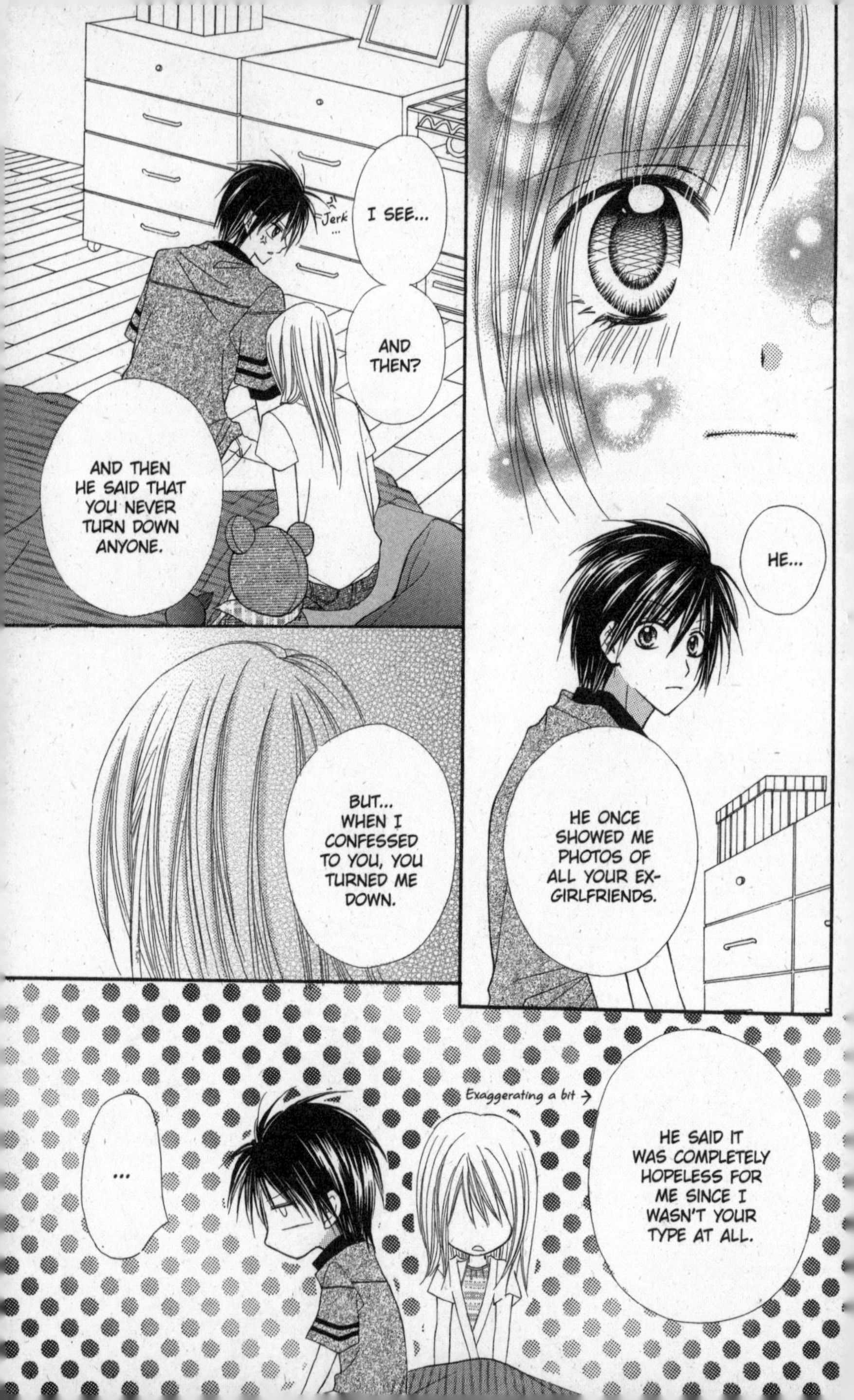
HE...
HE ONCE SHOWED ME PHOTOS OF ALL YOUR EX-GIRLFRIENDS.
I SEE...
Jerk ...
AND THEN?
AND THEN HE SAID THAT YOU NEVER TURN DOWN ANYONE.
BUT... WHEN I CONFESSED TO YOU, YOU TURNED ME DOWN.
HE SAID IT WAS COMPLETELY HOPELESS FOR ME SINCE I WASN'T YOUR TYPE AT ALL.
Exaggerating a bit →
...

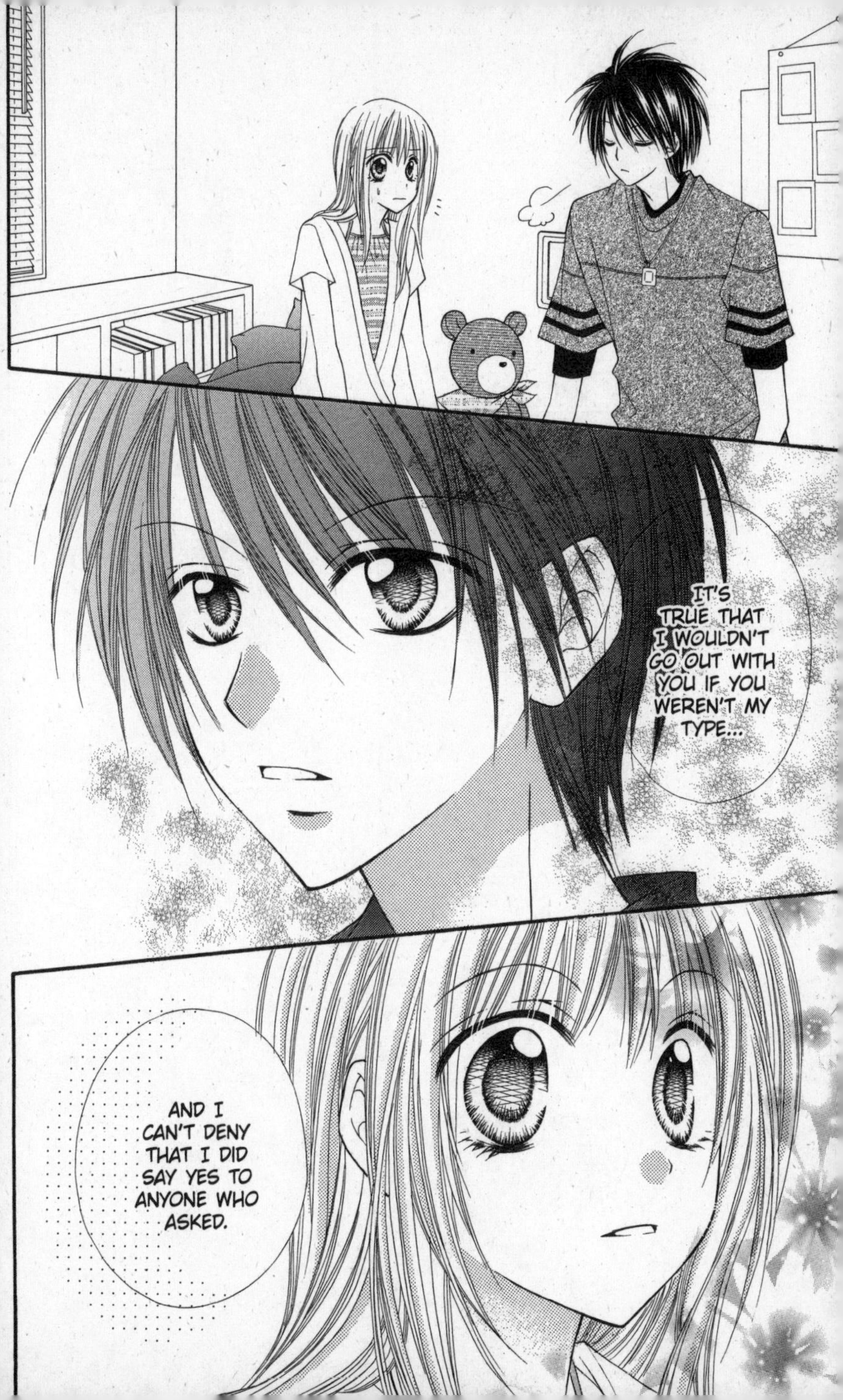
IT'S TRUE THAT I WOULDN'T GO OUT WITH YOU IF YOU WEREN'T MY TYPE...
AND I CAN'T DENY THAT I DID SAY YES TO ANYONE WHO ASKED.

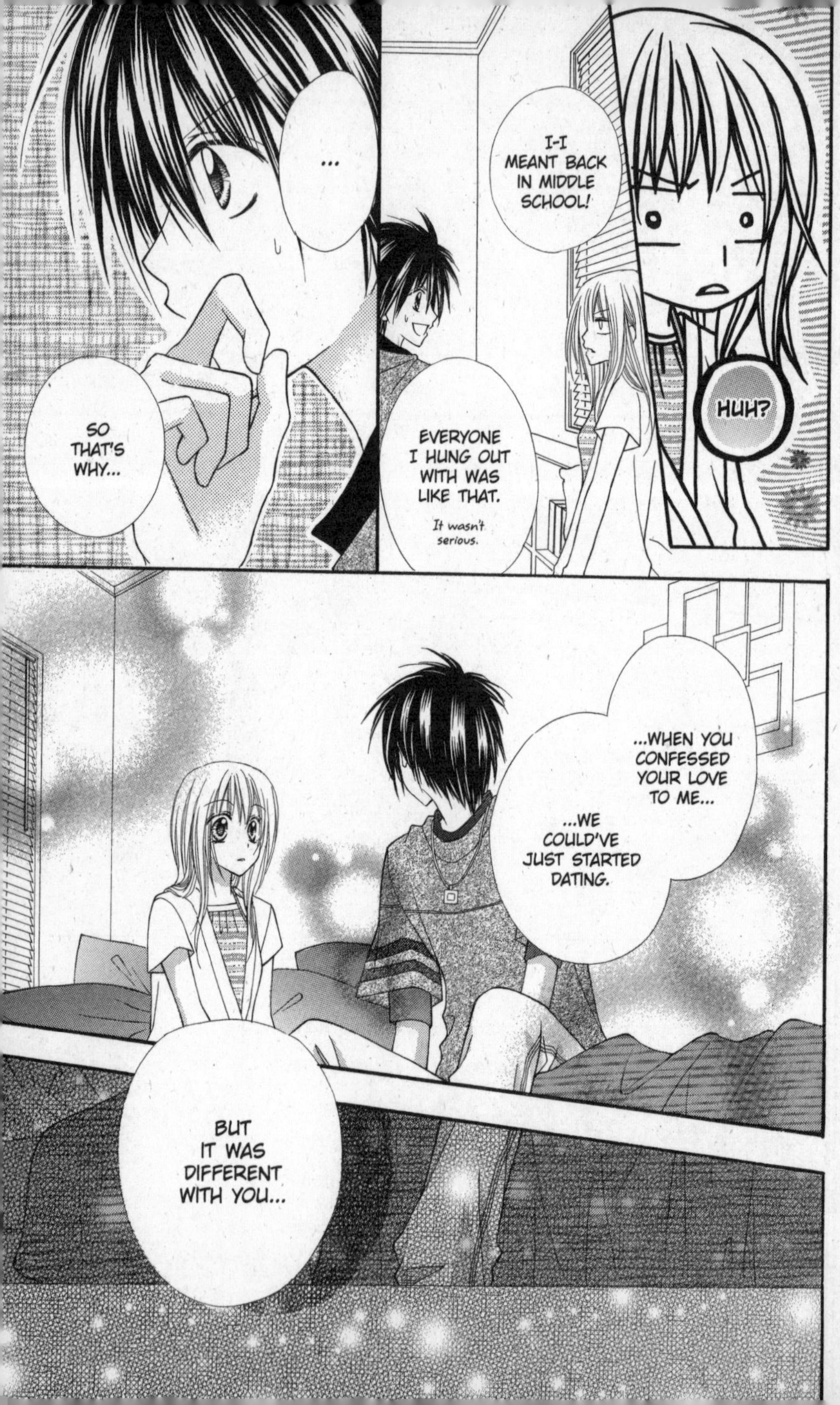
HUH?
I-I MEANT BACK IN MIDDLE SCHOOL!
EVERYONE I HUNG OUT WITH WAS LIKE THAT.
It wasn't serious.
...
SO THAT'S WHY...
...WHEN YOU CONFESSED YOUR LOVE TO ME...
...WE COULD'VE JUST STARTED DATING.
BUT IT WAS DIFFERENT WITH YOU...

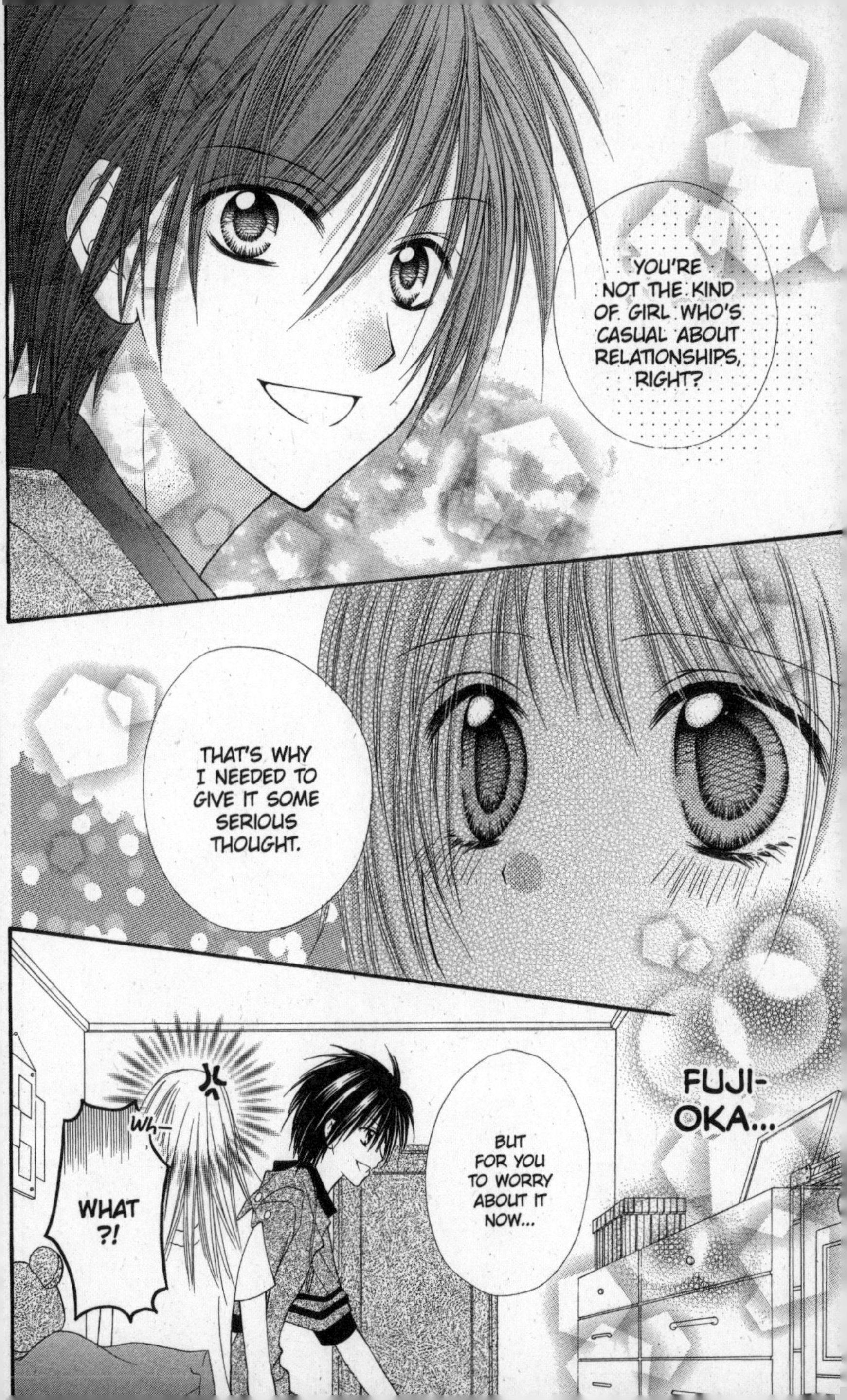
YOU'RE NOT THE KIND OF GIRL WHO'S CASUAL ABOUT RELATIONSHIPS, RIGHT?
THAT'S WHY I NEEDED TO GIVE IT SOME SERIOUS THOUGHT.
FUJI-OKA...
BUT FOR YOU TO WORRY ABOUT IT NOW...
Wh-
WHAT ?!

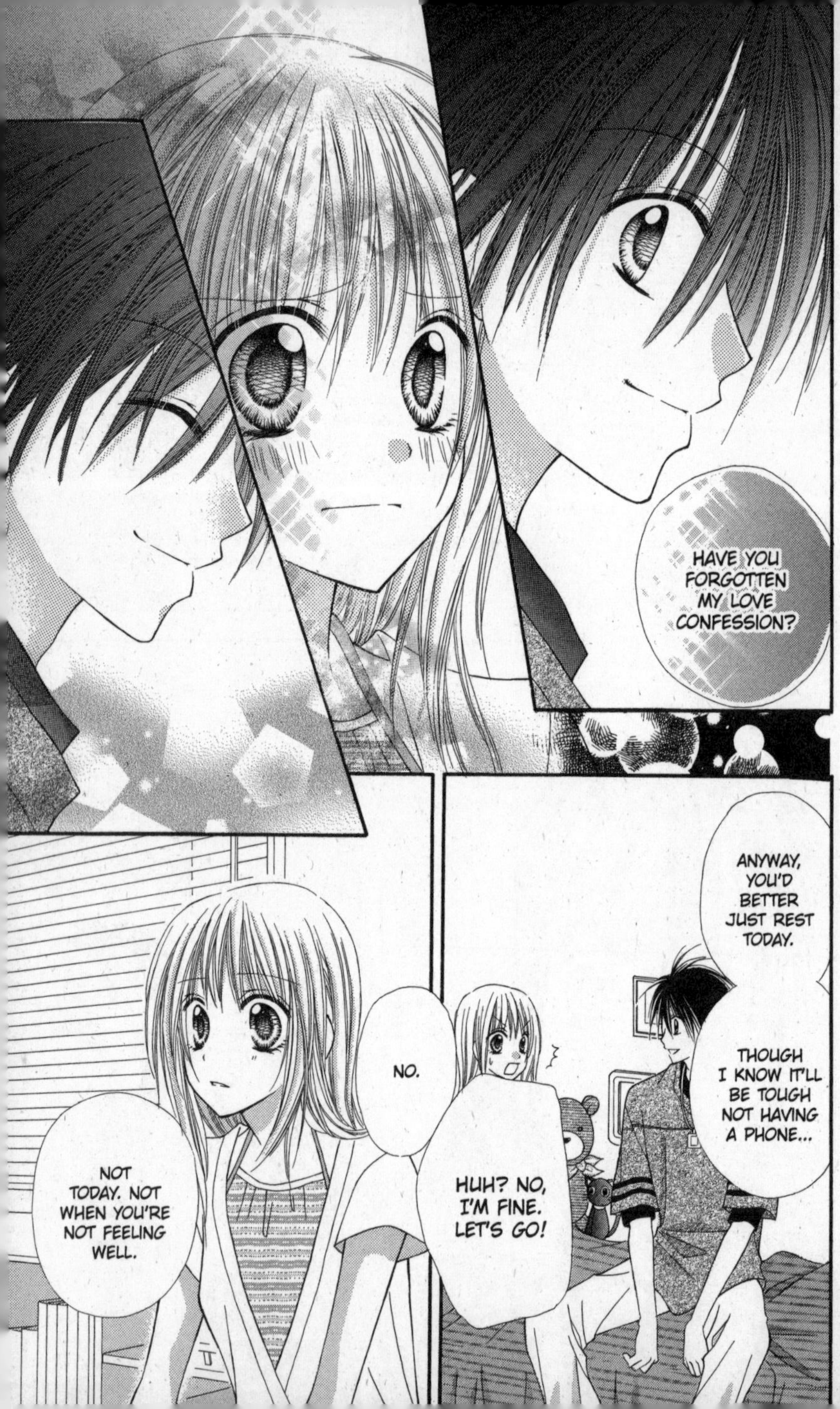
HAVE YOU FORGOTTEN MY LOVE CONFESSION?
ANYWAY, YOU'D BETTER JUST REST TODAY.
THOUGH I KNOW IT'LL BE TOUGH NOT HAVING A PHONE...
HUH? NO, I'M FINE. LET'S GO!
NO.
NOT TODAY. NOT WHEN YOU'RE NOT FEELING WELL.

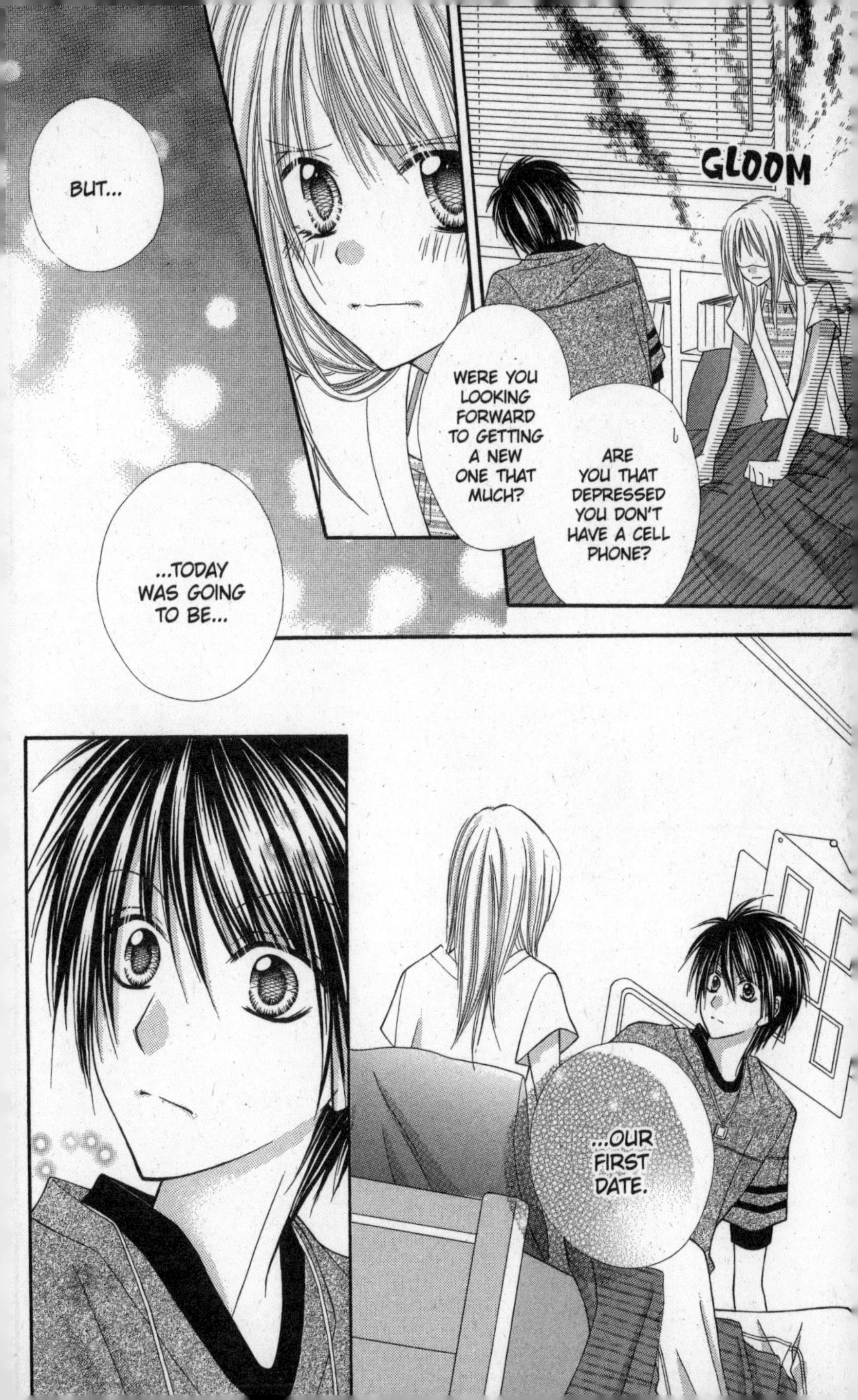
GLOOM
ARE YOU THAT DEPRESSED YOU DON'T HAVE A CELL PHONE?
WERE YOU LOOKING FORWARD TO GETTING A NEW ONE THAT MUCH?
BUT...
...TODAY WAS GOING TO BE...
...OUR FIRST DATE.

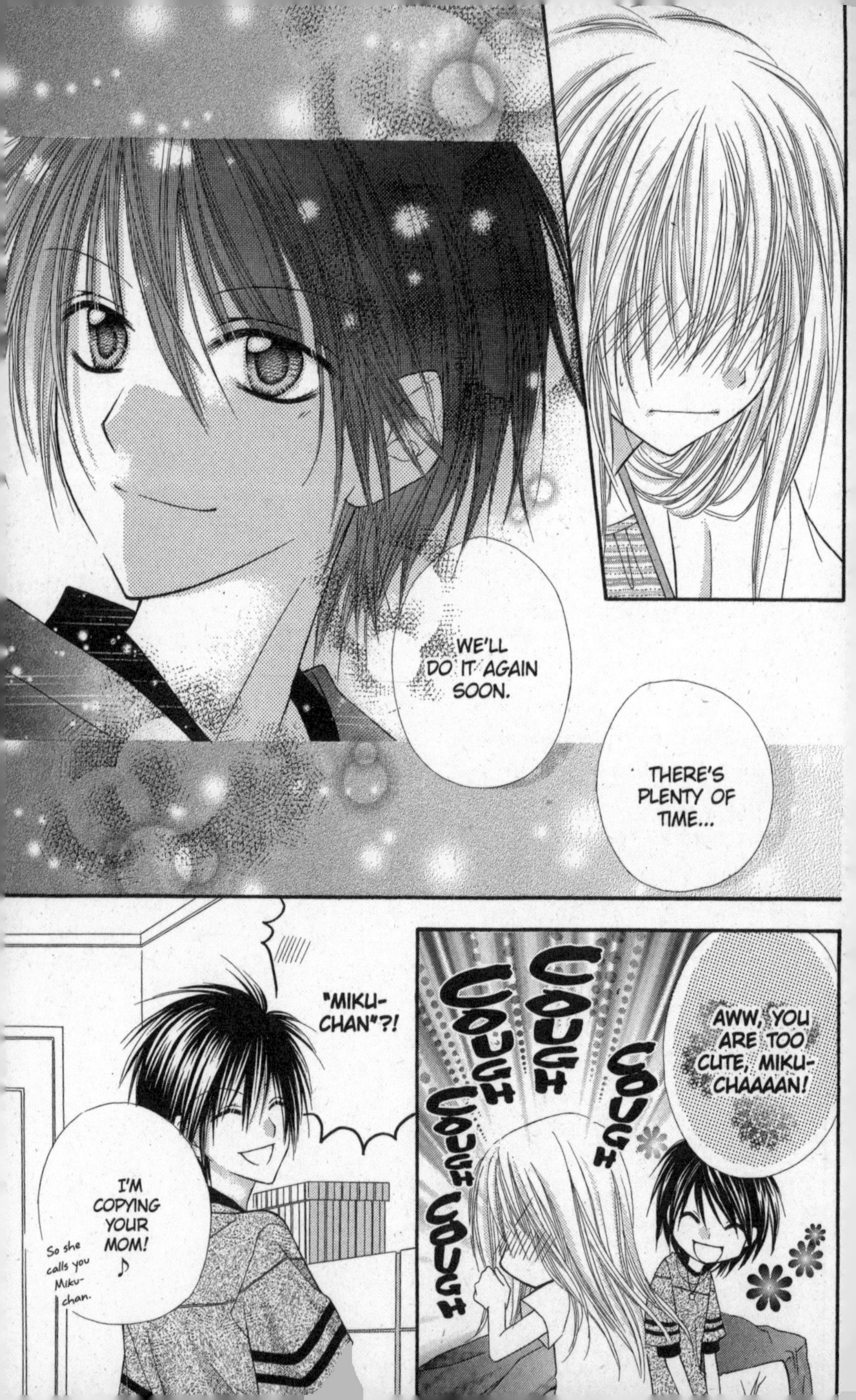
WE'LL DO IT AGAIN SOON.
THERE'S PLENTY OF TIME...
AWW, YOU ARE TOO CUTE, MIKU-CHAAAAN!
COUGH COUGH COUGH COUGH COUGH
"MIKU-CHAN"?!
I'M COPYING YOUR MOM! ♪
So she calls you Miku-chan.

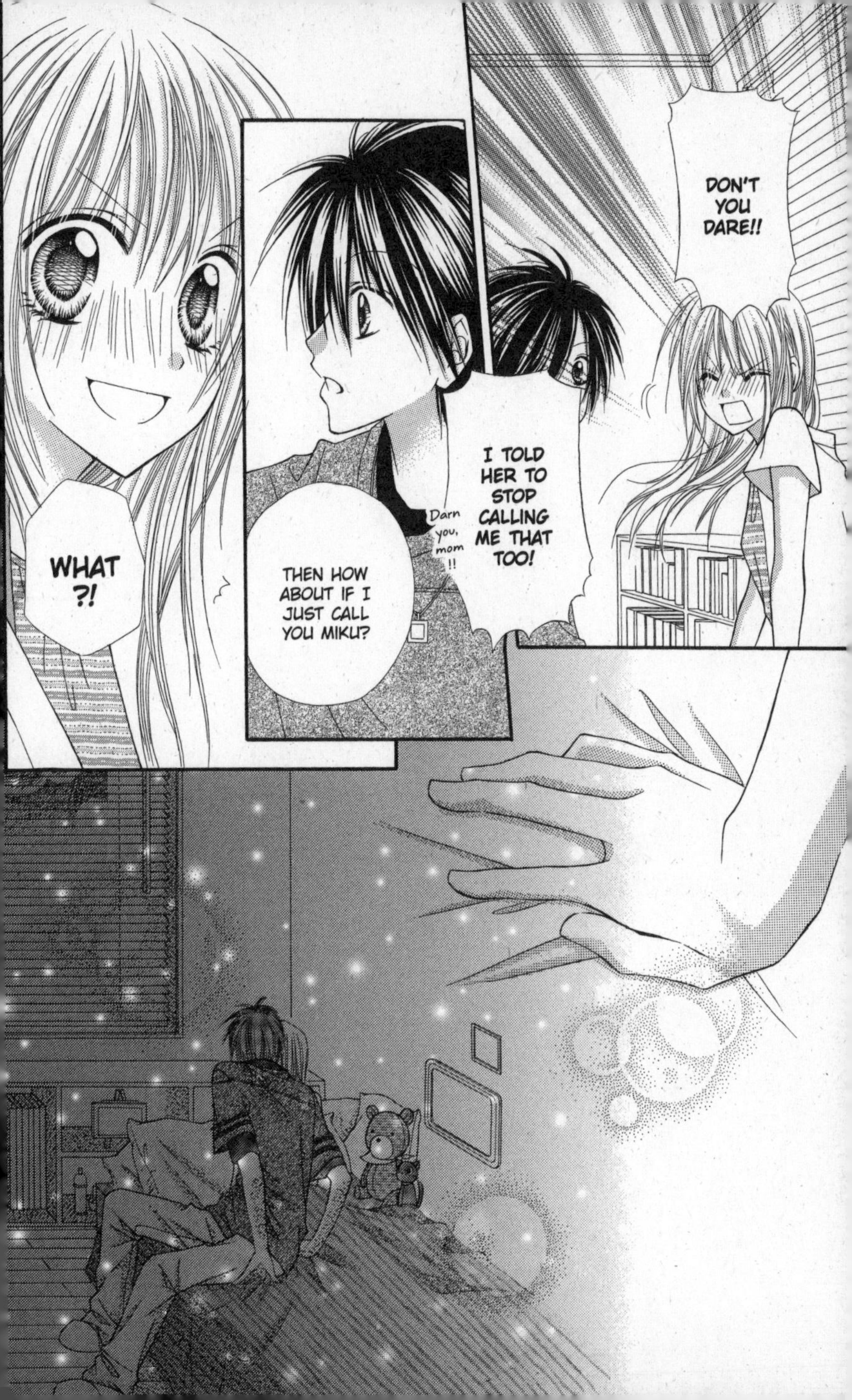
DON'T YOU DARE!!
I TOLD HER TO STOP CALLING ME THAT TOO!
Darn you, mom!!
THEN HOW ABOUT IF I JUST CALL YOU MIKU?
WHAT?!

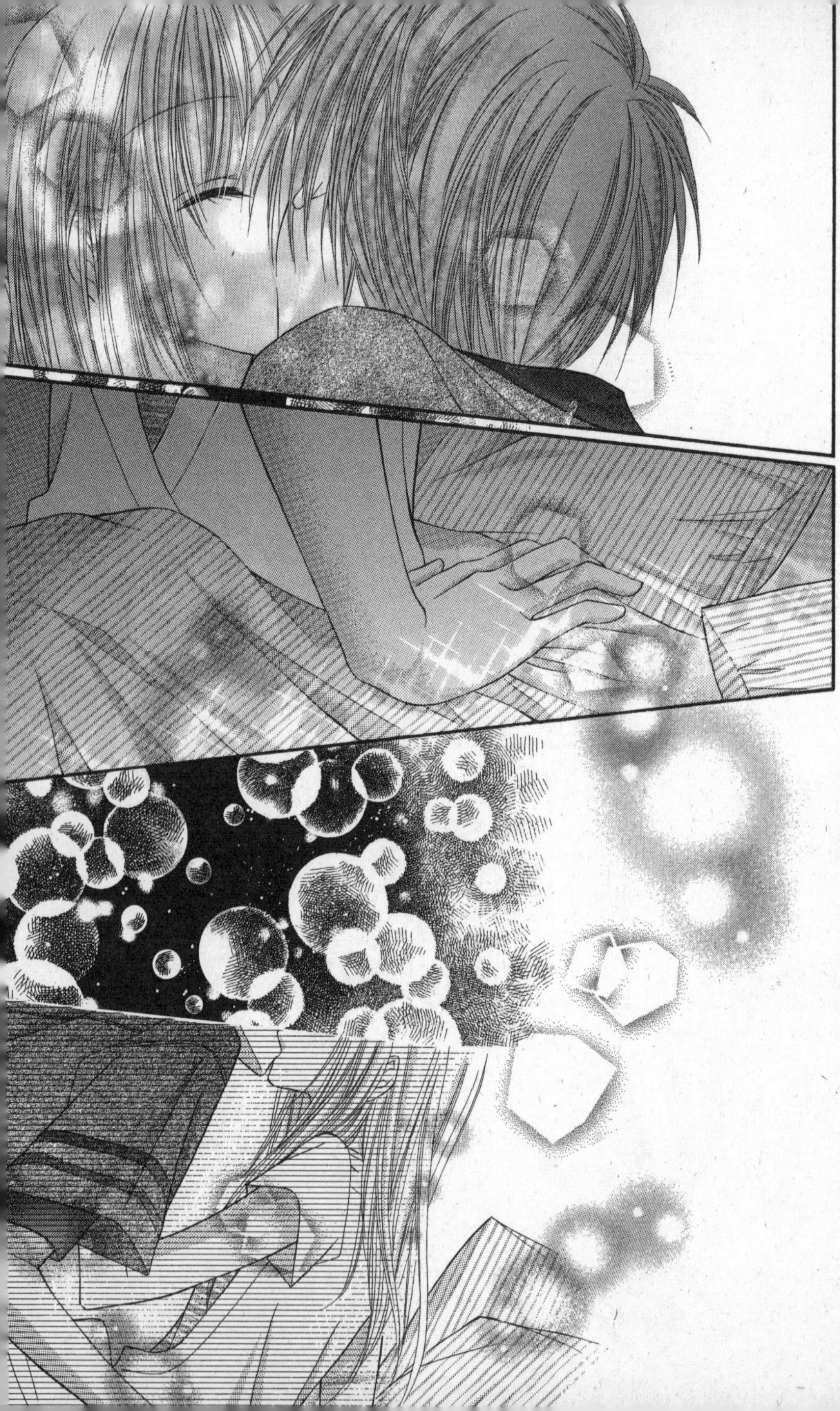

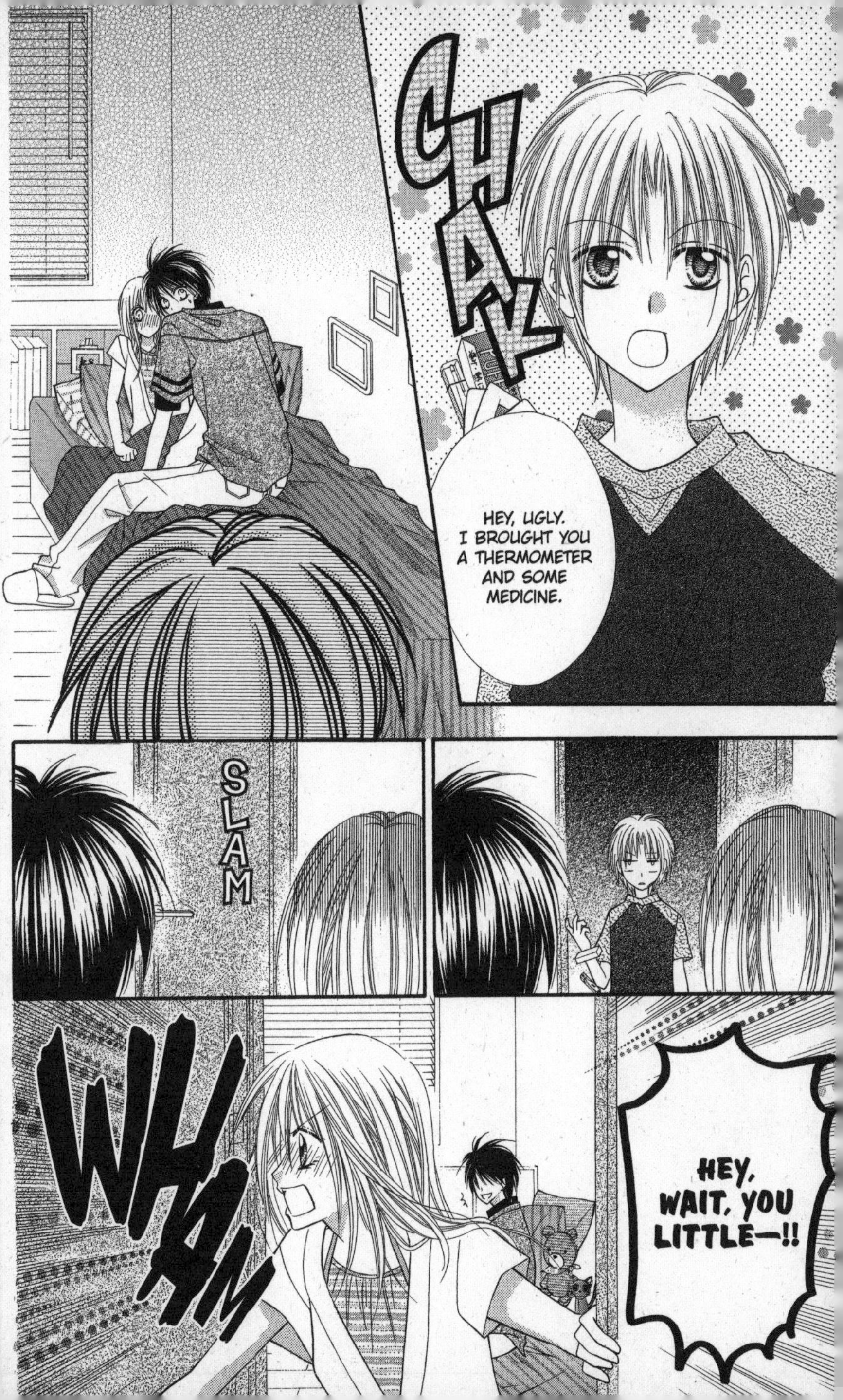
CHAK
HEY, UGLY. I BROUGHT YOU A THERMOMETER AND SOME MEDICINE.
SLAM
HEY, WAIT, YOU LITTLE—!!
WHAM

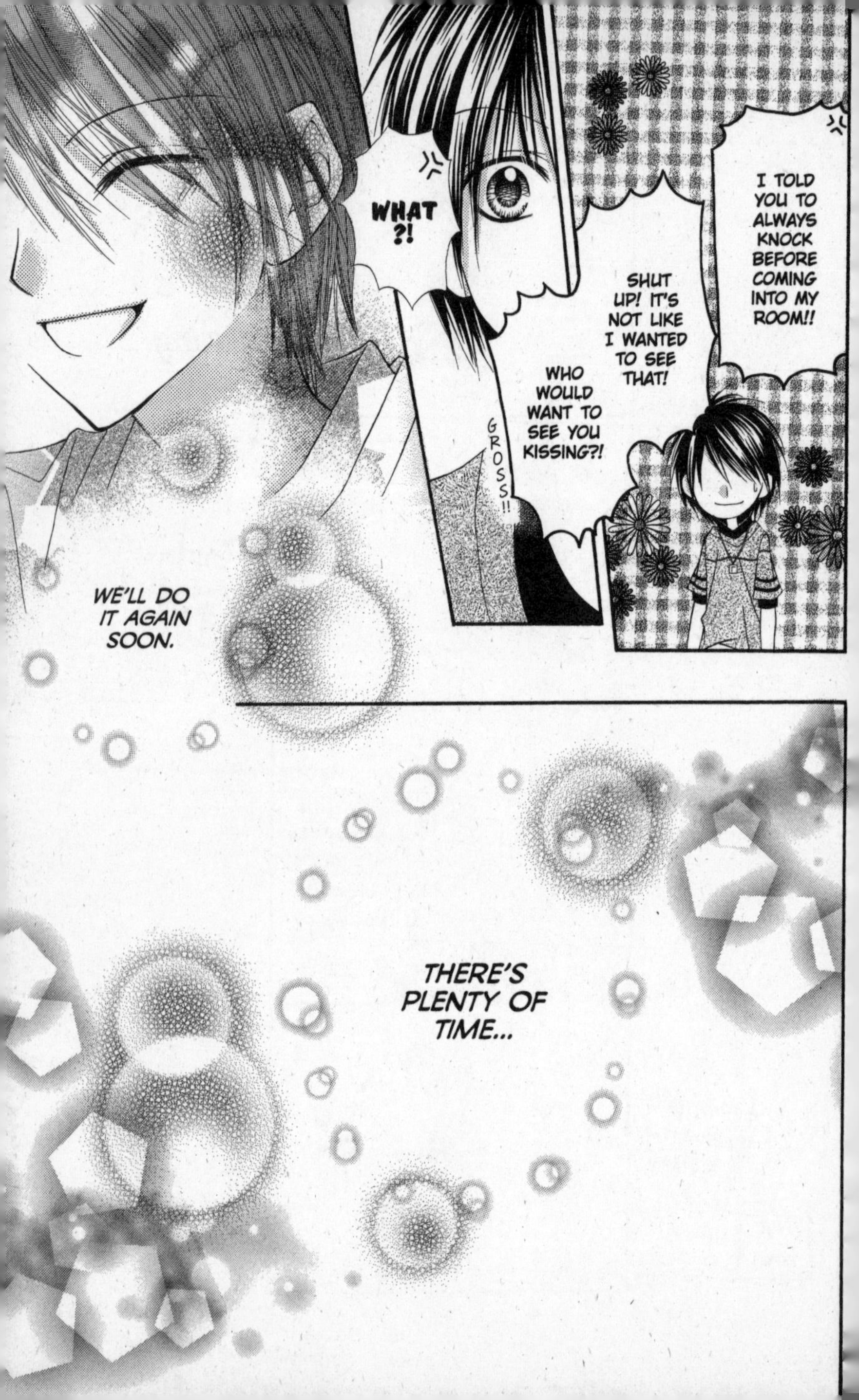
I TOLD YOU TO ALWAYS KNOCK BEFORE COMING INTO MY ROOM!!
SHUT UP! IT'S NOT LIKE I WANTED TO SEE THAT!
WHO WOULD WANT TO SEE YOU KISSING?!
GROSS!!
WHAT?!
WE'LL DO IT AGAIN SOON.
THERE'S PLENTY OF TIME...

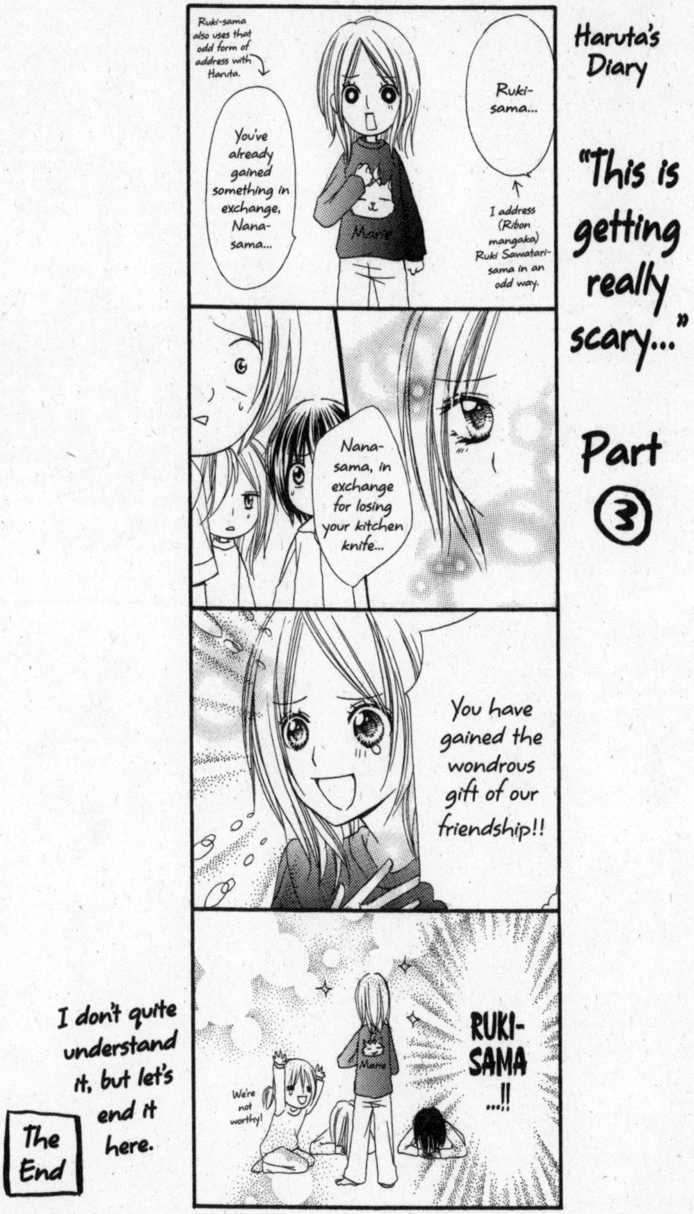
Haruta's Diary
"This is getting really scary..."
Part ③
Ruki-sama...
I address (Ribon mangaka) Ruki Sawatari-sama in an odd way.
You've already gained something in exchange, Nana-sama...
Ruki-sama also uses that odd form of address with Haruta.
Marie
Nana-sama, in exchange for losing your kitchen knife...
You have gained the wondrous gift of our friendship!!
RUKI-SAMA ...!!
Marie
We're not worthy!
I don't quite understand it, but let's end it here.
The End

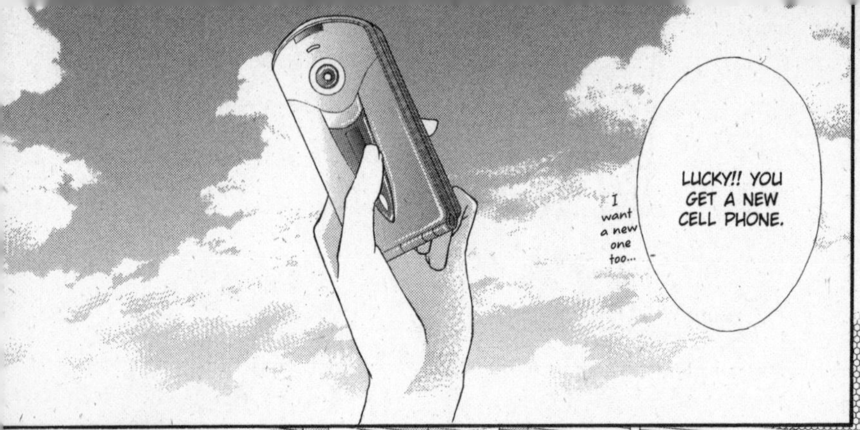
LUCKY!! YOU GET A NEW CELL PHONE.
I want a new one too...

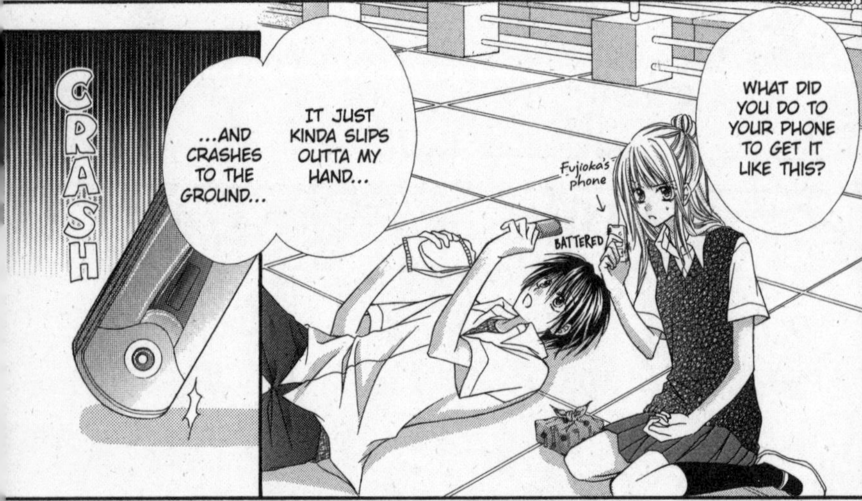
WHAT DID YOU DO TO YOUR PHONE TO GET IT LIKE THIS?
Fujioka's phone
BATTERED
IT JUST KINDA SLIPS OUTTA MY HAND...
...AND CRASHES TO THE GROUND...
CRASH

SMALL TALK ④

✿ Hee hee hee... I got one of my (very few) mangaka friends, Kaorin Hanzawa, to draw a Small Talk section for me. Thank you so much! I also got her to draw a bonus page at the end of the volume, so look forward to it! ♡ I'm hanging out at the Hanzawa home today!

And by the way, I'm not forcing my friends to do these! ♥

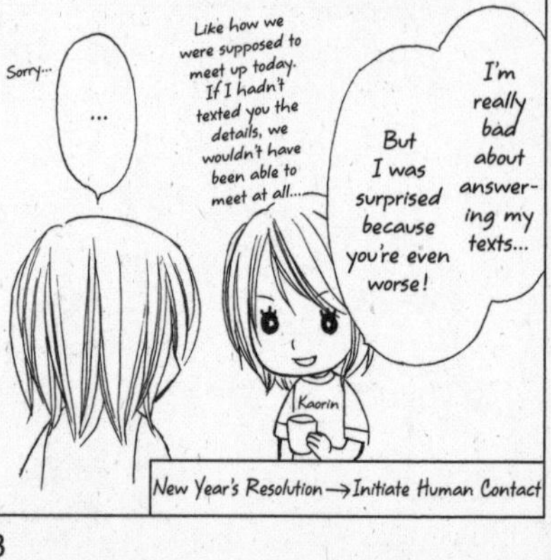
I'm really bad about answering my texts...
But I was surprised because you're even worse!
Like how we were supposed to meet up today. If I hadn't texted you the details, we wouldn't have been able to meet at all...
...
Sorry...
Kaorin
New Year's Resolution → Initiate Human Contact

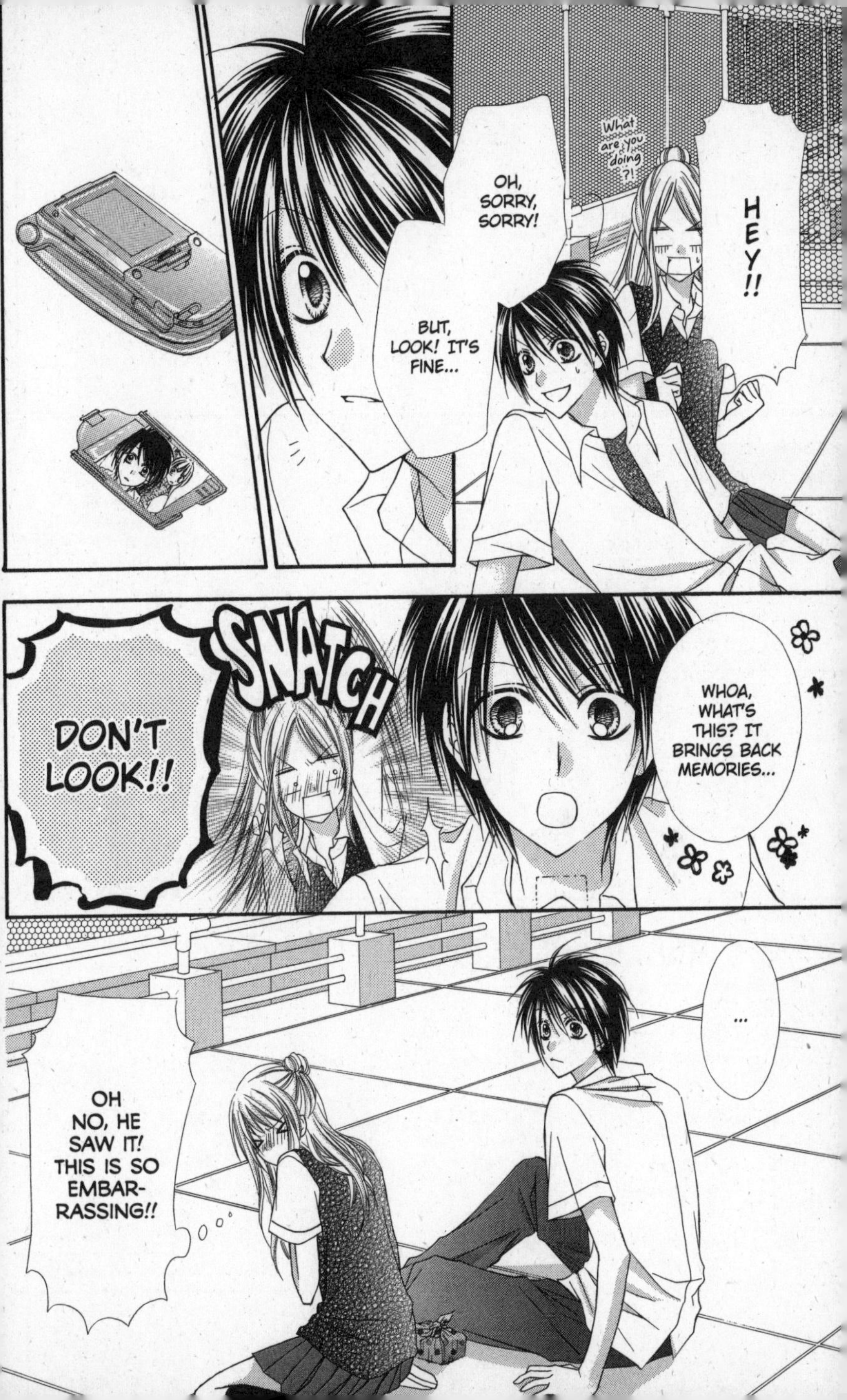
HEY!!
What are you doing?!
OH, SORRY, SORRY!
BUT, LOOK! IT'S FINE...
WHOA, WHAT'S THIS? IT BRINGS BACK MEMORIES...
SNATCH
DON'T LOOK!!
...
OH NO, HE SAW IT! THIS IS SO EMBAR-RASSING!!

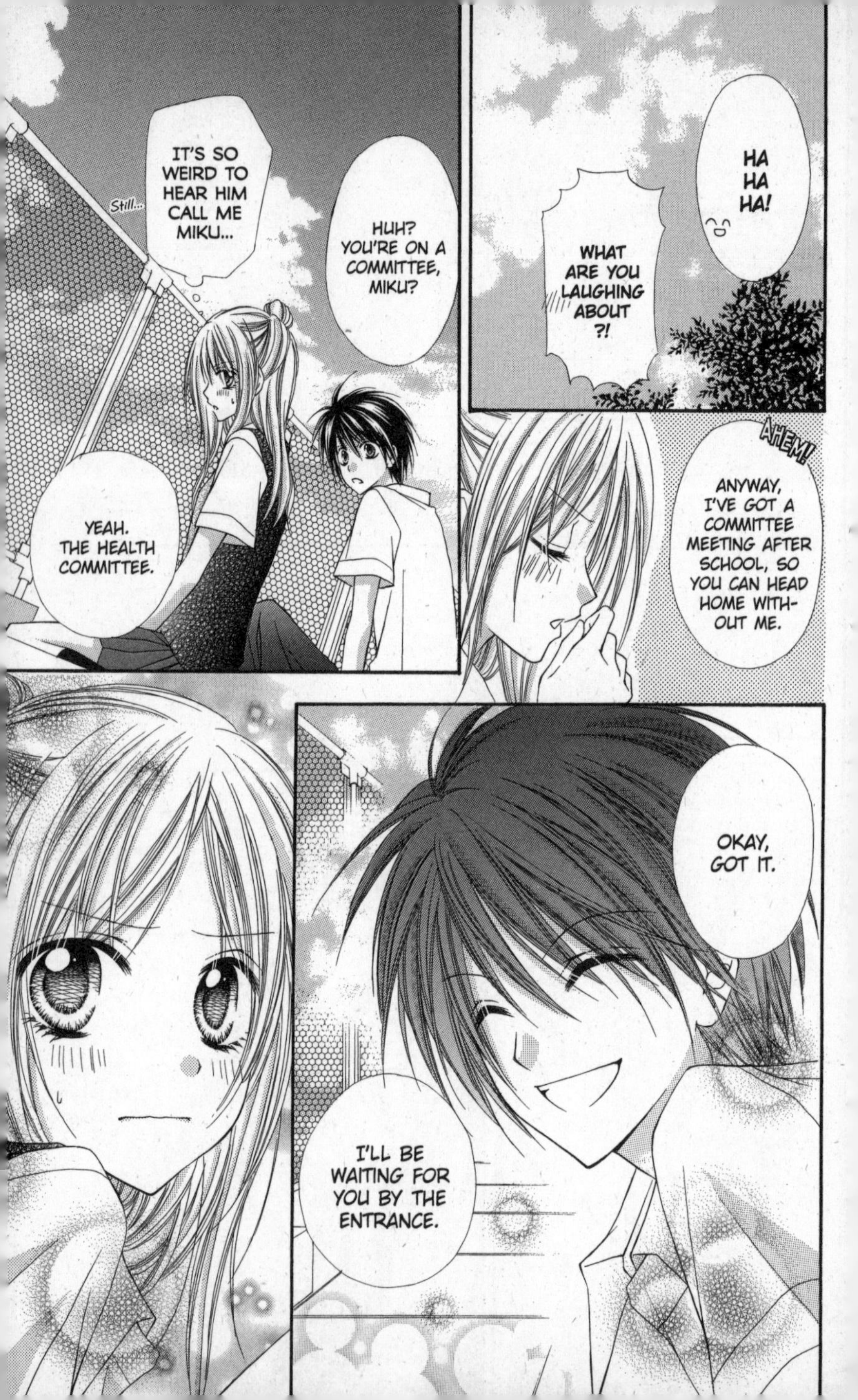
HA HA HA!
WHAT ARE YOU LAUGHING ABOUT?!
AHEM!
ANYWAY, I'VE GOT A COMMITTEE MEETING AFTER SCHOOL, SO YOU CAN HEAD HOME WITH-OUT ME.
HUH? YOU'RE ON A COMMITTEE, MIKU?
YEAH. THE HEALTH COMMITTEE.
Still...
IT'S SO WEIRD TO HEAR HIM CALL ME MIKU...
OKAY, GOT IT.
I'LL BE WAITING FOR YOU BY THE ENTRANCE.

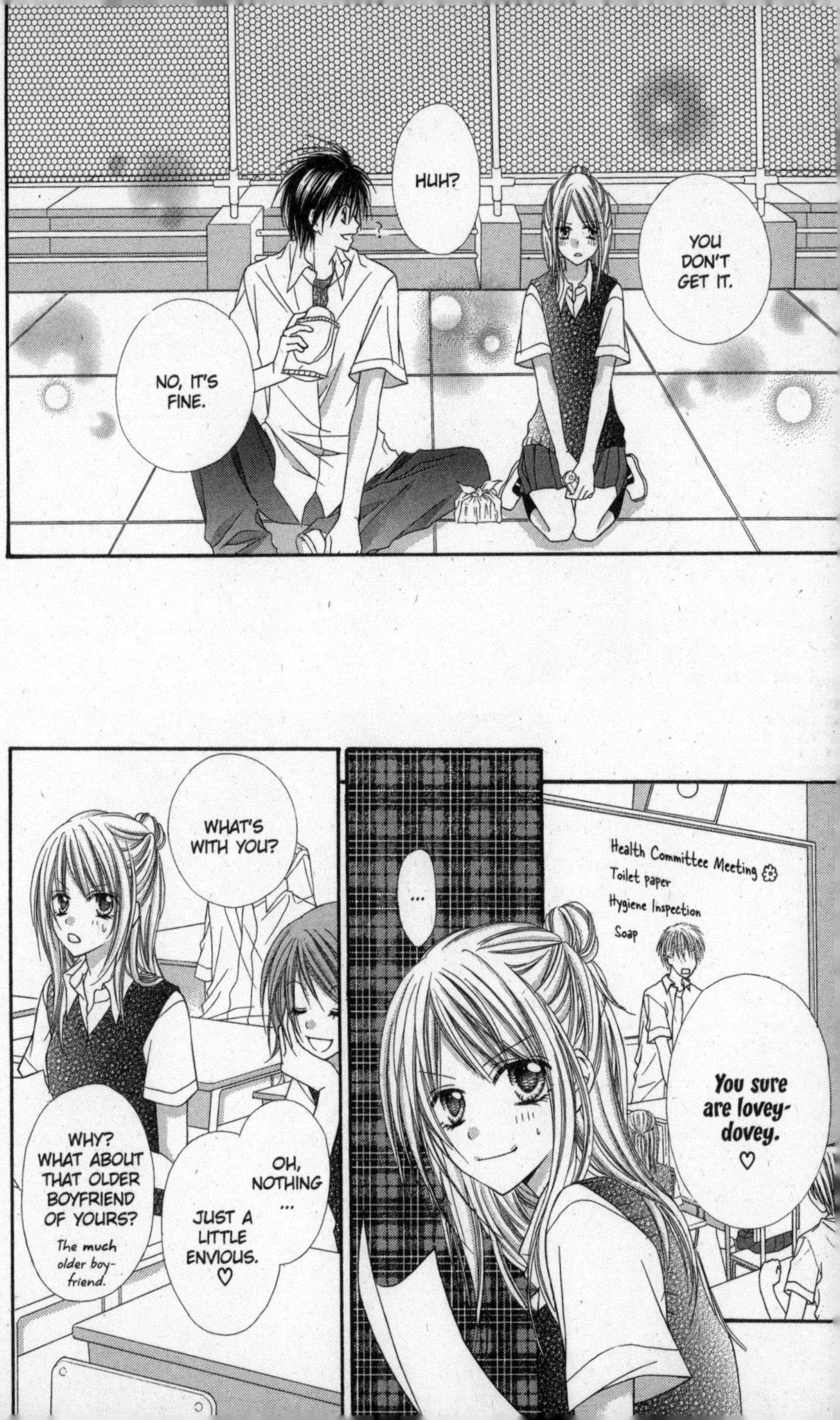
YOU DON'T GET IT.
HUH?
NO, IT'S FINE.
You sure are lovey-dovey. ♡
...
Health Committee Meeting
Toilet paper
Hygiene Inspection
Soap
WHAT'S WITH YOU?
OH, NOTHING...
JUST A LITTLE ENVIOUS. ♡
WHY? WHAT ABOUT THAT OLDER BOYFRIEND OF YOURS?
The much older boy-friend.

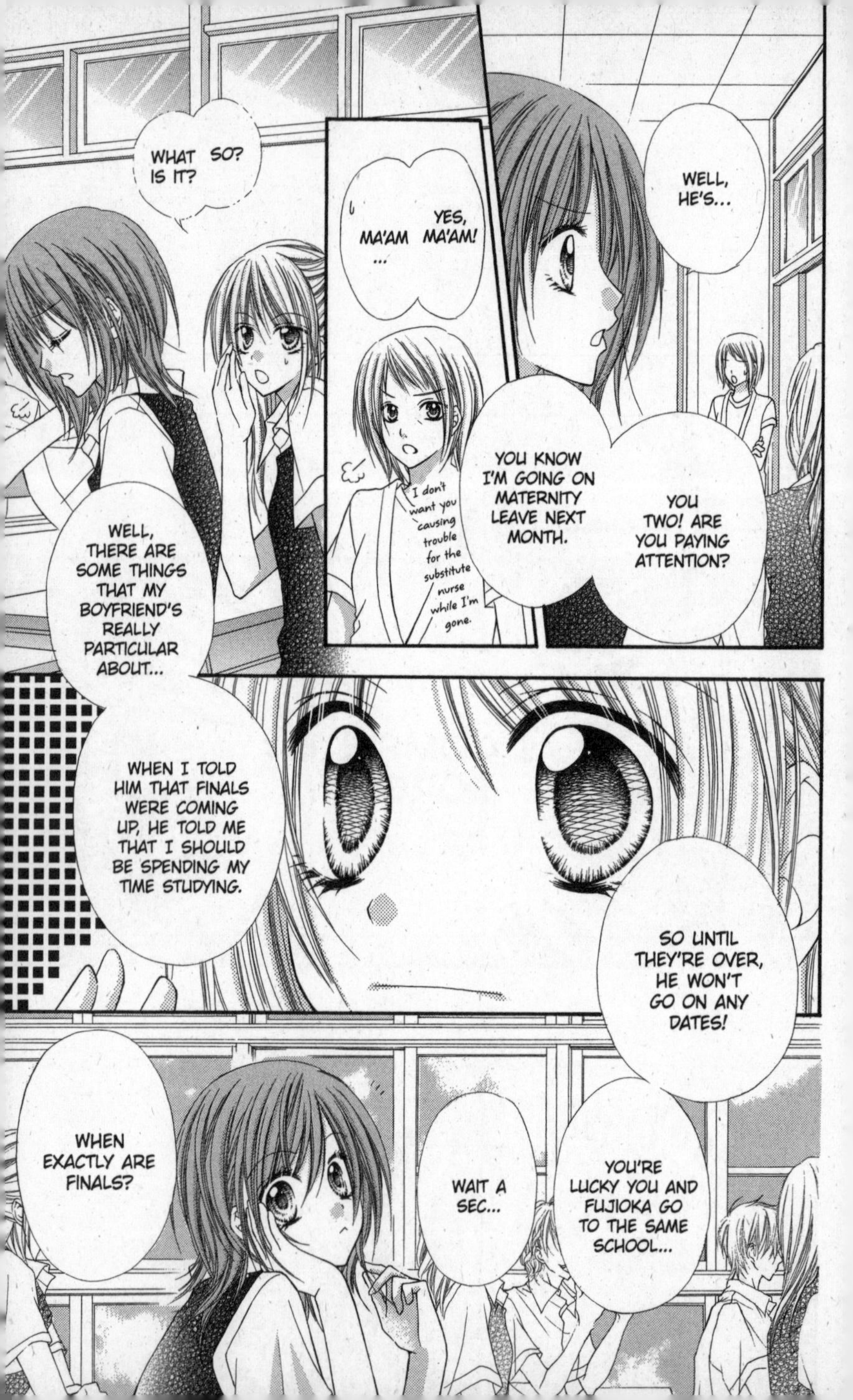
WELL, HE'S...
YOU TWO! ARE YOU PAYING ATTENTION?
YOU KNOW I'M GOING ON MATERNITY LEAVE NEXT MONTH.
I don't want you causing trouble for the substitute nurse while I'm gone.
YES, MA'AM! MA'AM ...
SO? WHAT IS IT?
WELL, THERE ARE SOME THINGS THAT MY BOYFRIEND'S REALLY PARTICULAR ABOUT...
WHEN I TOLD HIM THAT FINALS WERE COMING UP, HE TOLD ME THAT I SHOULD BE SPENDING MY TIME STUDYING.
SO UNTIL THEY'RE OVER, HE WON'T GO ON ANY DATES!
YOU'RE LUCKY YOU AND FUJIOKA GO TO THE SAME SCHOOL...
WAIT A SEC...
WHEN EXACTLY ARE FINALS?

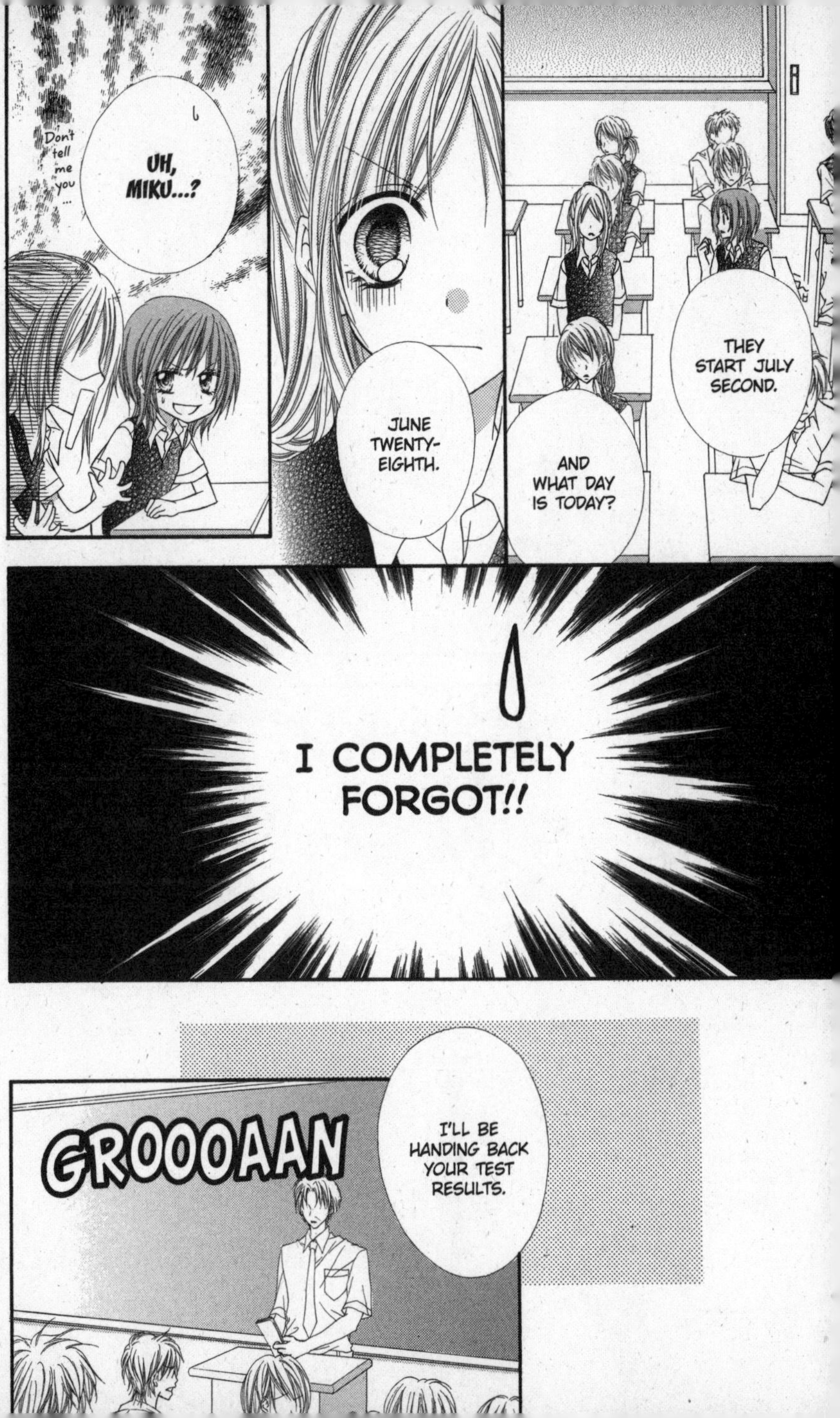
THEY START JULY SECOND.
AND WHAT DAY IS TODAY?
JUNE TWENTY-EIGHTH.
UH, MIKU...?
Don't tell me you ...
I COMPLETELY FORGOT!!
I'LL BE HANDING BACK YOUR TEST RESULTS.
GROOOAAN

10

I bought a Gameboy Advanced recently! I considered getting a Nintendo DS, but I don't really like the whole touchpad thing so I got the Gameboy instead. It's silver!

I only bought it because I really wanted to play *Kingdom Hearts: Chain of Memories!* It was the same when I bought my PS2—it was only because I wanted to play *Kingdom Hearts.* That's how much I love the *Kingdom Hearts* series out of all the games out there (though I only own about ten games or so...) More than anything, I love that the game is set in the different Disney worlds. It's so cute!! Especially *Alice in Wonderland's* "Wonderland," and *Nightmare Before Christmas's* "Halloween Town"! It is too cute!!☆

But to be honest, I haven't played much of *Chain of Memories.* I had heard that it followed up on *Kingdom Hearts 2* so I thought, "I have to play it!" But the card battling system is too much for me. I can only play the most simple, uncomplicated games. I did manage to finish *Final Fantasy VII* and *VIII*, but if I didn't have the strategy guides to help me, I would have never been able to finish them!! In fact, I had someone else play about half of *VII* for me... Ha ha ha!

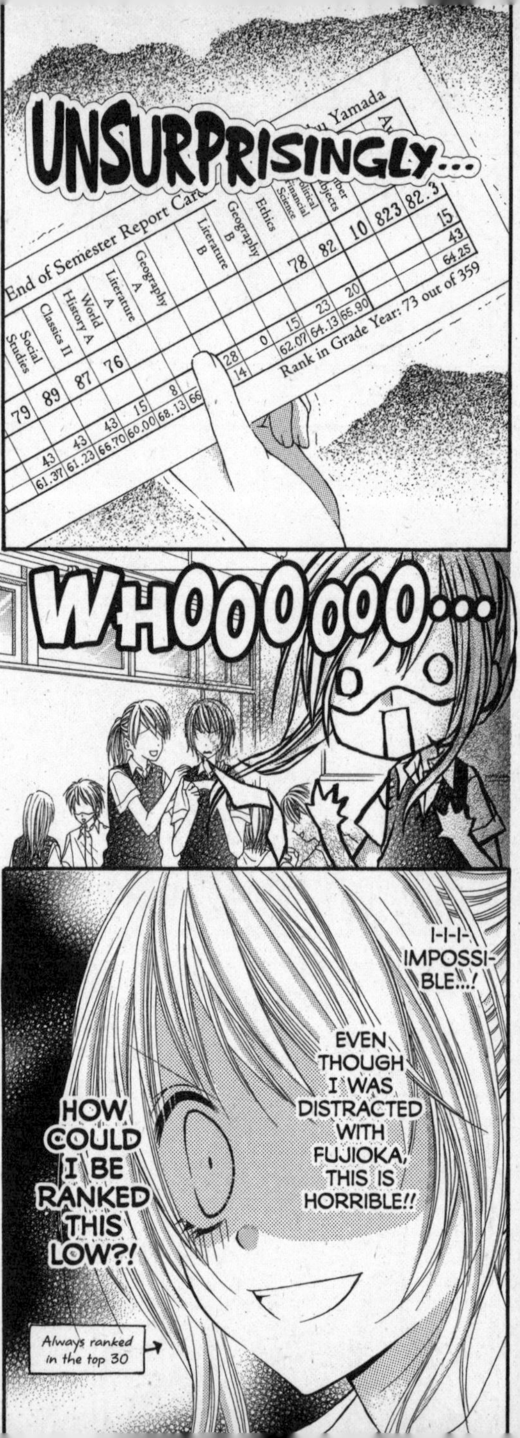
UNSURPRISINGLY...
End of Semester Report Card
Rank in Grade Year: 73 out of 359
WHOOOOOOO...
I-I-I-IMPOSSIBLE...!
EVEN THOUGH I WAS DISTRACTED WITH FUJIOKA, THIS IS HORRIBLE!!
HOW COULD I BE RANKED THIS LOW?!
Always ranked in the top 30

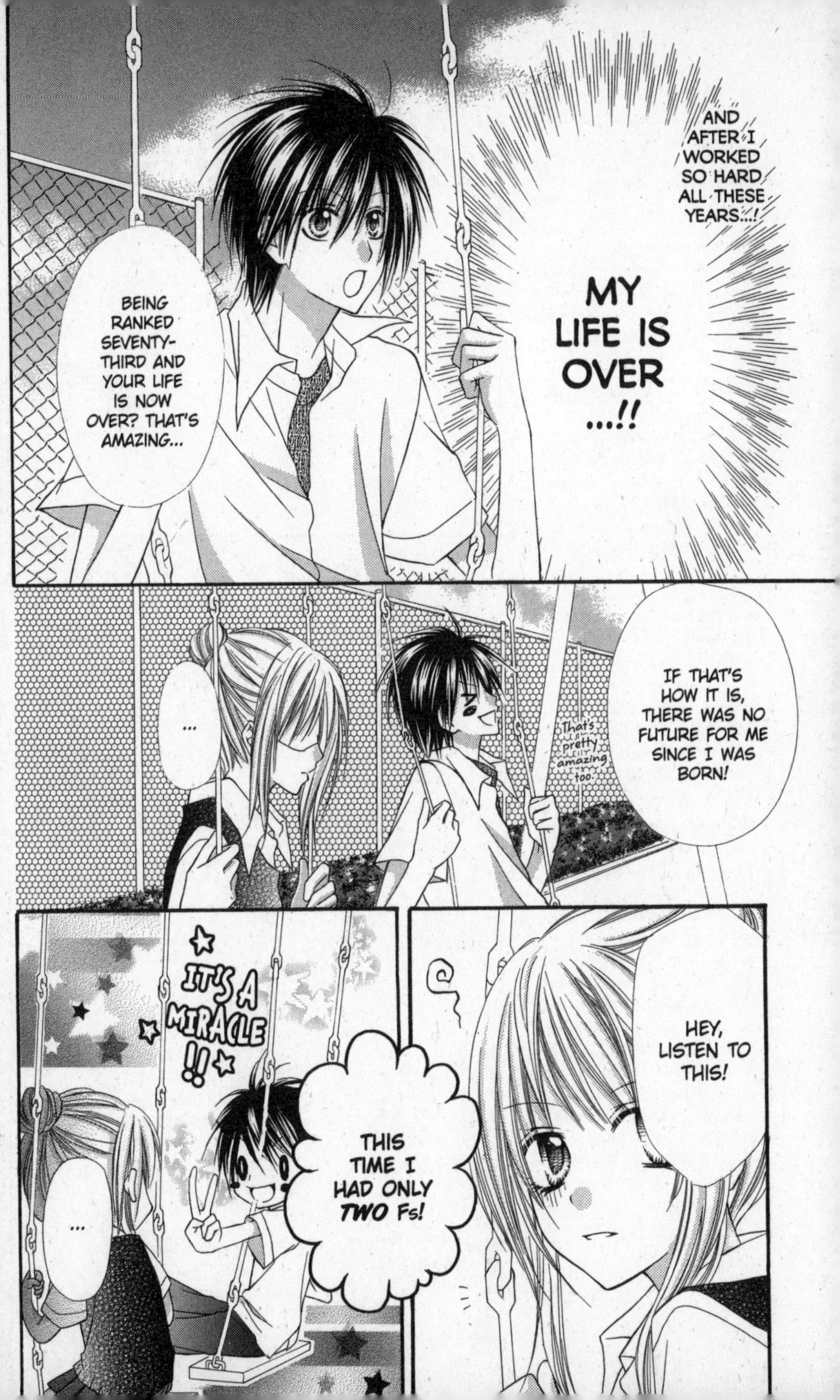
AND AFTER I WORKED SO HARD ALL THESE YEARS...!
MY LIFE IS OVER ...!!
BEING RANKED SEVENTY-THIRD AND YOUR LIFE IS NOW OVER? THAT'S AMAZING...
IF THAT'S HOW IT IS, THERE WAS NO FUTURE FOR ME SINCE I WAS BORN!
That's pretty amazing too.
...
HEY, LISTEN TO THIS!
THIS TIME I HAD ONLY TWO Fs!
IT'S A MIRACLE!!
...

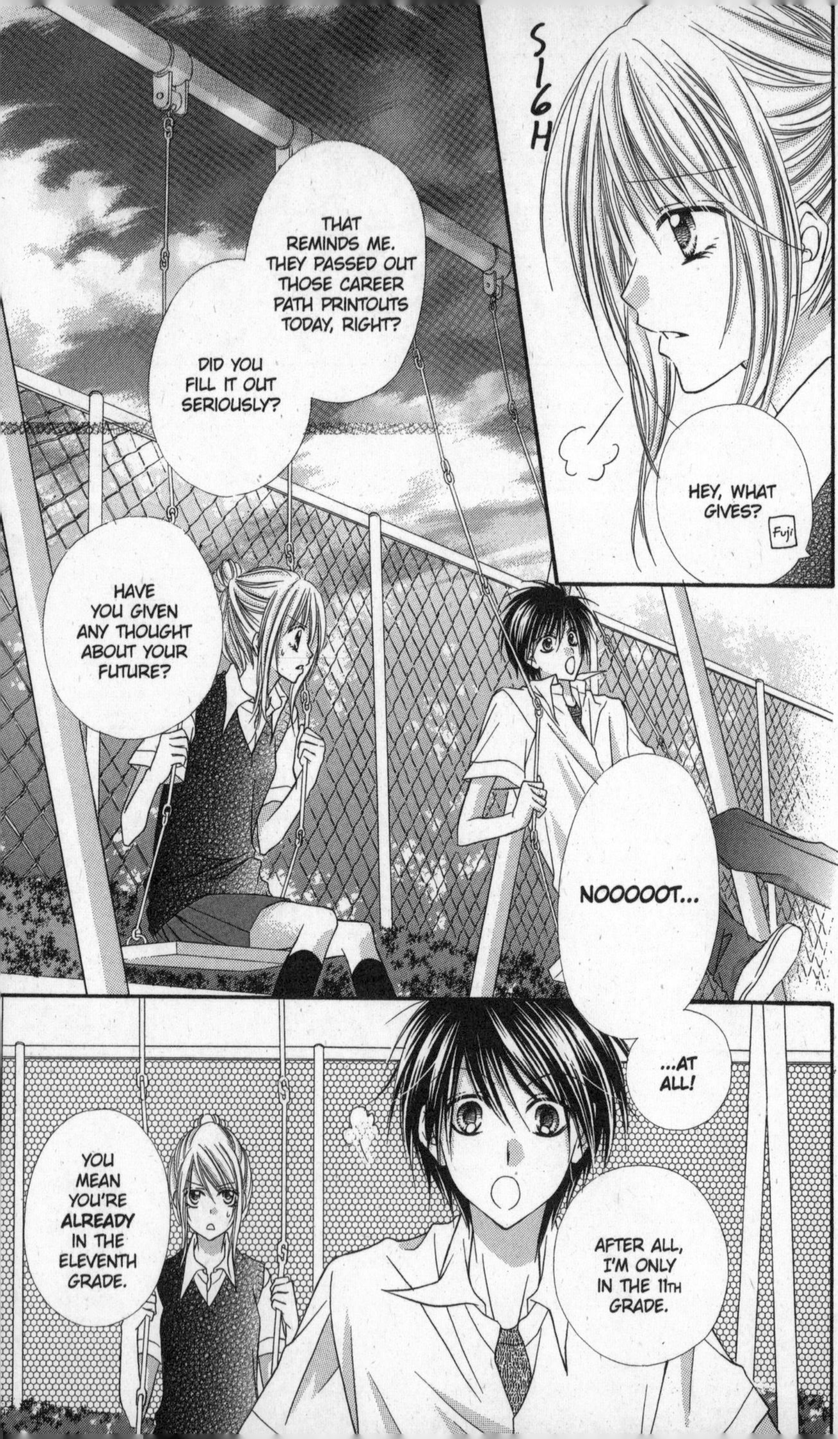
SIGH
HEY, WHAT GIVES?
Fuji
THAT REMINDS ME. THEY PASSED OUT THOSE CAREER PATH PRINTOUTS TODAY, RIGHT?
DID YOU FILL IT OUT SERIOUSLY?
HAVE YOU GIVEN ANY THOUGHT ABOUT YOUR FUTURE?
NOOOOOT...
...AT ALL!
AFTER ALL, I'M ONLY IN THE 11TH GRADE.
YOU MEAN YOU'RE ALREADY IN THE ELEVENTH GRADE.

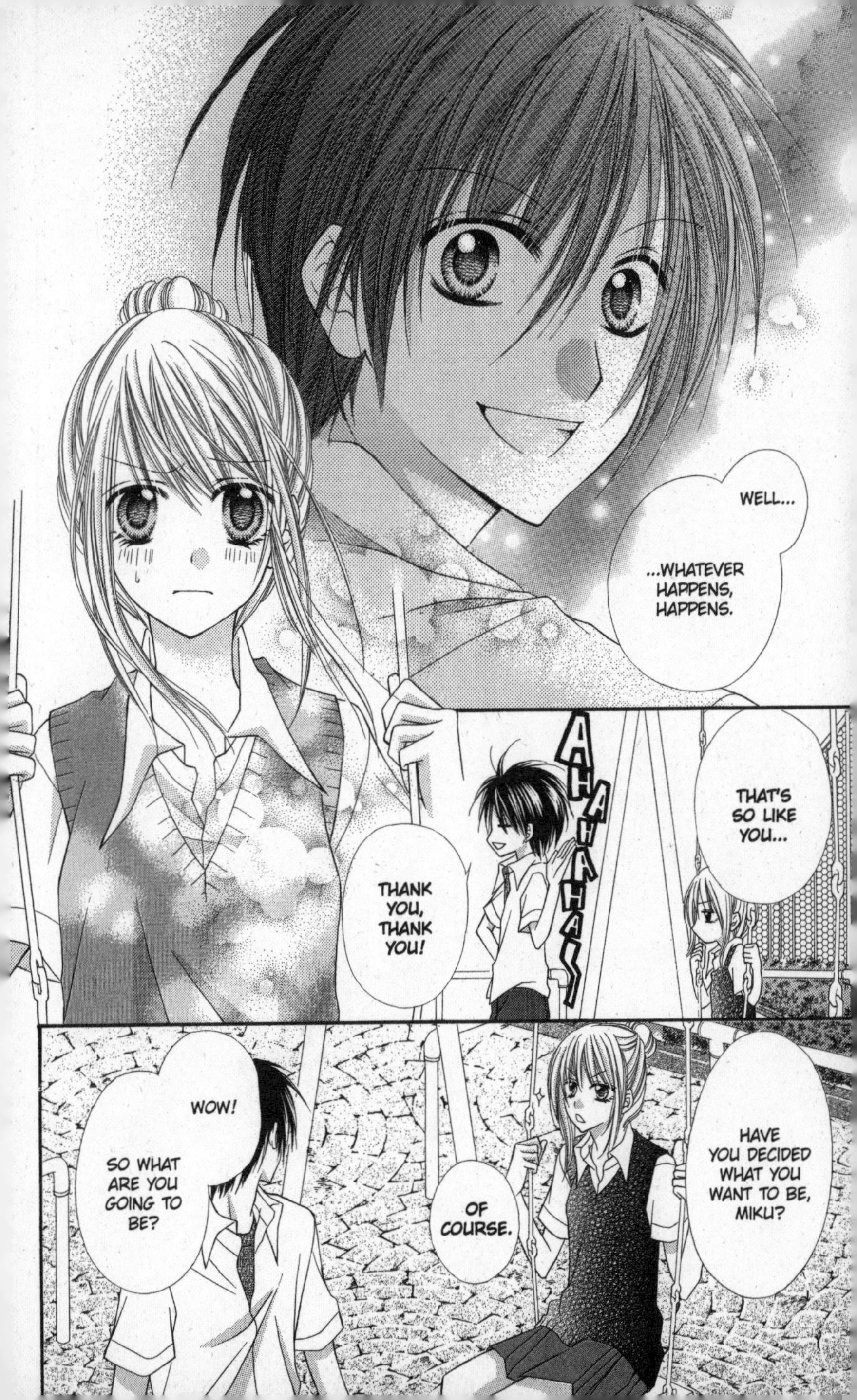
WELL...
...WHATEVER HAPPENS, HAPPENS.
THAT'S SO LIKE YOU...
AHAHAHAHA
THANK YOU, THANK YOU!
HAVE YOU DECIDED WHAT YOU WANT TO BE, MIKU?
OF COURSE.
WOW!
SO WHAT ARE YOU GOING TO BE?

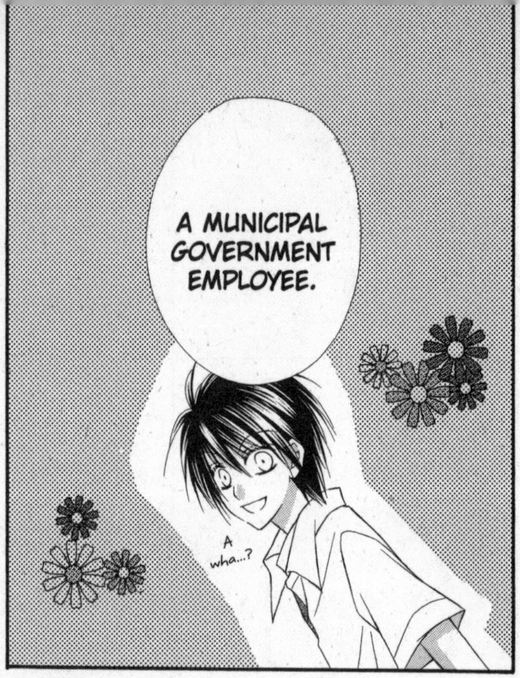
A MUNICIPAL GOVERNMENT EMPLOYEE.
A wha...?

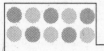

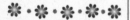

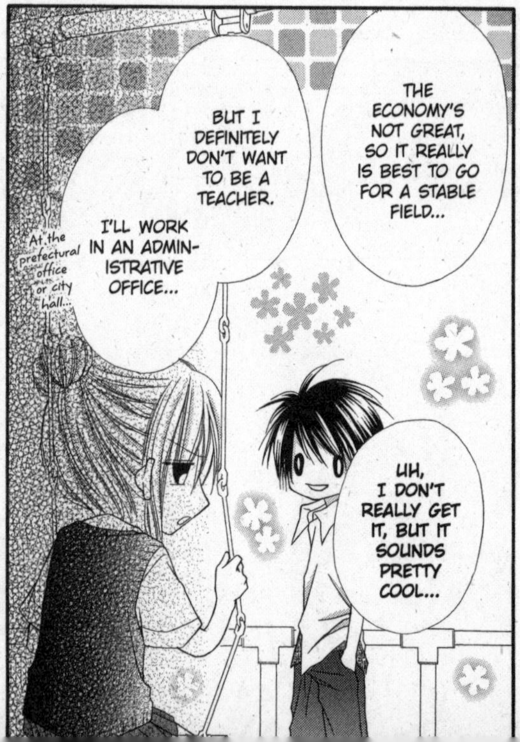
THE ECONOMY'S NOT GREAT, SO IT REALLY IS BEST TO GO FOR A STABLE FIELD...
BUT I DEFINITELY DON'T WANT TO BE A TEACHER.
I'LL WORK IN AN ADMIN-ISTRATIVE OFFICE...
At the prefectural office or city hall...
UH, I DON'T REALLY GET IT, BUT IT SOUNDS PRETTY COOL...

11

Just like *Chain of Memories*, I've got a whole bunch of other games that I've started because people recommended them to me, but haven't had the time to play. ♪ Like *Final Fantasy IX*—one of my assistants highly recommended it and lent it to me, but I haven't even played it once. ♪ Same with *FF10*—I bought it but I've only played an hour of it. Mayupon Sakai-sensei lent me the *Phoenix Wright: Ace Attorney* games but I haven't gotten to the third one yet (she lent me all three games and I'm still stuck on the second one). I have to finish them! ♪

Oh yeah—speaking of video games, I recently played an old one—*Tamagotchi*! It was really popular around the time I was in fifth grade...to the extent where they'd always be sold out and it was really hard to get your hands on one. But nowadays you can even find it as a cell phone app. In fact, I was playing it the other day on my cell phone. I was raising it while I was in the middle of drawing a manuscript (hey...) and took such good care of it (geez, do your work!), but it grew up to be one of the bad pets! I was shocked... One of my assistants, who was raising one at the same time I was got a Mimitchi (a good pet) and I got a Zukitchi!! Why?!

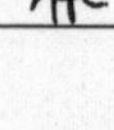
Zukitchi
Um..

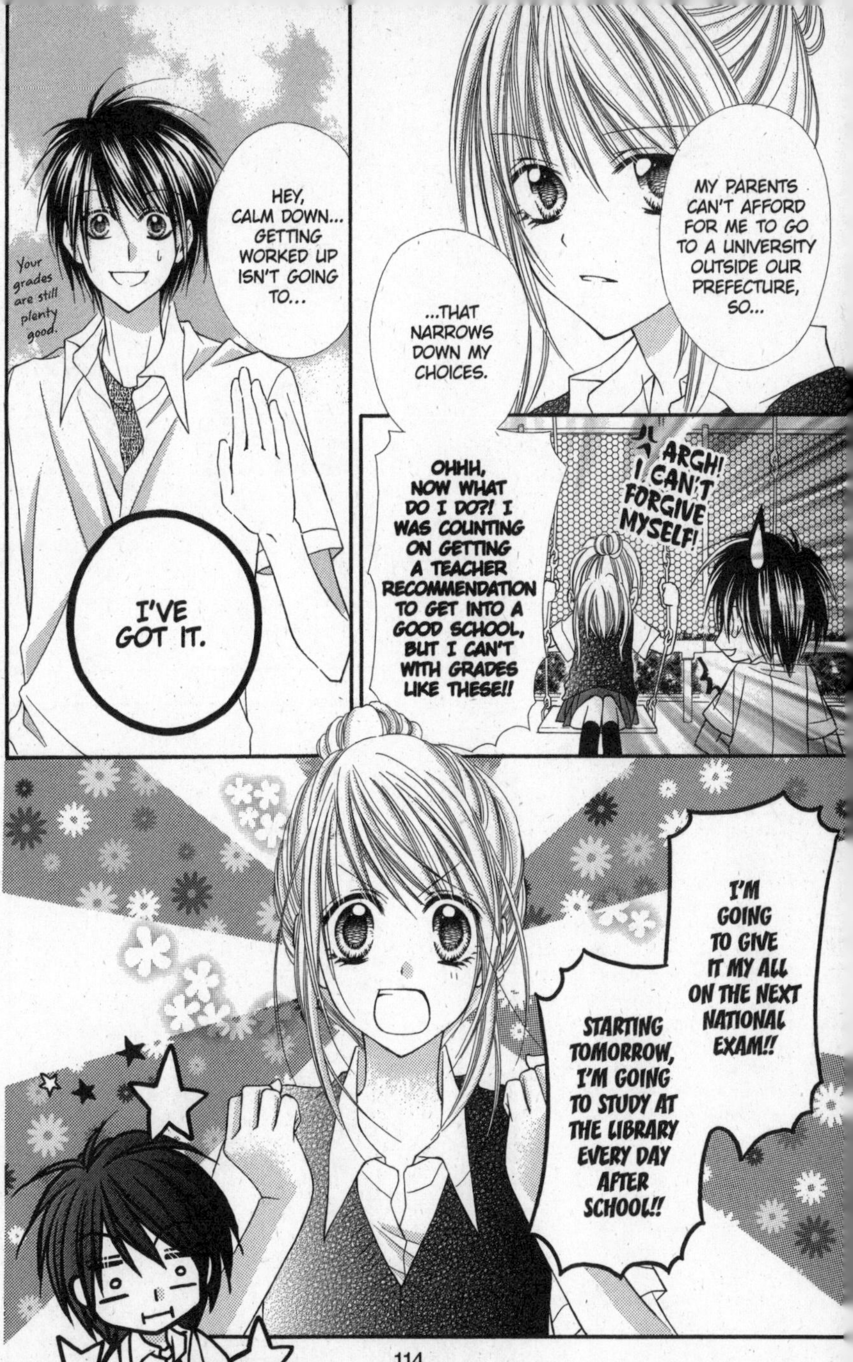
MY PARENTS CAN'T AFFORD FOR ME TO GO TO A UNIVERSITY OUTSIDE OUR PREFECTURE, SO...
...THAT NARROWS DOWN MY CHOICES.
ARGH! I CAN'T FORGIVE MYSELF!
OHHH, NOW WHAT DO I DO?! I WAS COUNTING ON GETTING A TEACHER RECOMMENDATION TO GET INTO A GOOD SCHOOL, BUT I CAN'T WITH GRADES LIKE THESE!!
HEY, CALM DOWN... GETTING WORKED UP ISN'T GOING TO...
Your grades are still plenty good.
I'VE GOT IT.
I'M GOING TO GIVE IT MY ALL ON THE NEXT NATIONAL EXAM!!
STARTING TOMORROW, I'M GOING TO STUDY AT THE LIBRARY EVERY DAY AFTER SCHOOL!!

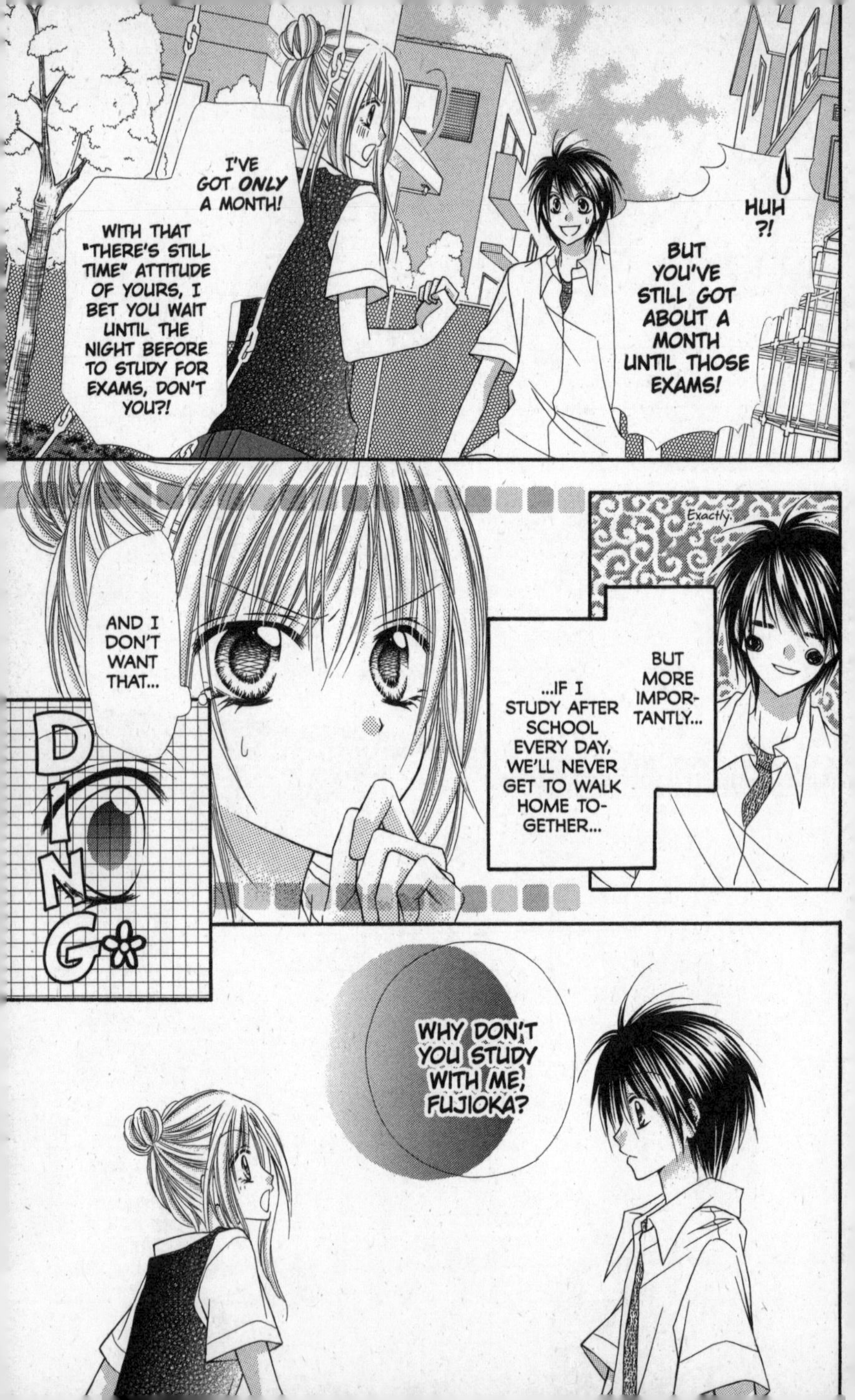
HUH ?!
BUT YOU'VE STILL GOT ABOUT A MONTH UNTIL THOSE EXAMS!
I'VE GOT *ONLY* A MONTH!
WITH THAT "THERE'S STILL TIME" ATTITUDE OF YOURS, I BET YOU WAIT UNTIL THE NIGHT BEFORE TO STUDY FOR EXAMS, DON'T YOU?!
Exactly.
BUT MORE IMPOR-TANTLY...
...IF I STUDY AFTER SCHOOL EVERY DAY, WE'LL NEVER GET TO WALK HOME TO-GETHER...
AND I DON'T WANT THAT...
DING
WHY DON'T YOU STUDY WITH ME, FUJIOKA?

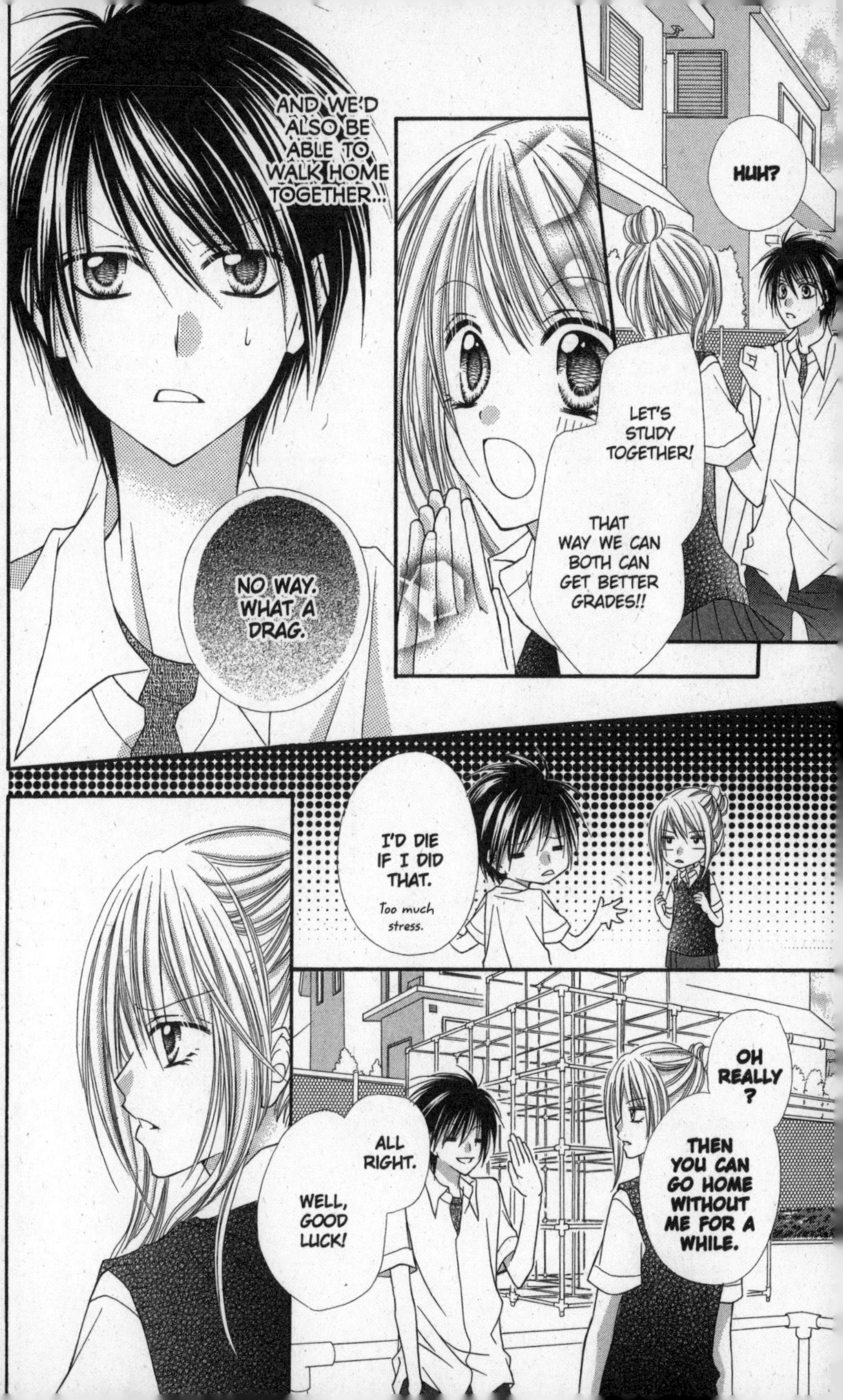
HUH?
LET'S STUDY TOGETHER!
THAT WAY WE CAN BOTH CAN GET BETTER GRADES!!
AND WE'D ALSO BE ABLE TO WALK HOME TOGETHER...!
NO WAY. WHAT A DRAG.
I'D DIE IF I DID THAT.
Too much stress.
OH REALLY?
THEN YOU CAN GO HOME WITHOUT ME FOR A WHILE.
ALL RIGHT.
WELL, GOOD LUCK!

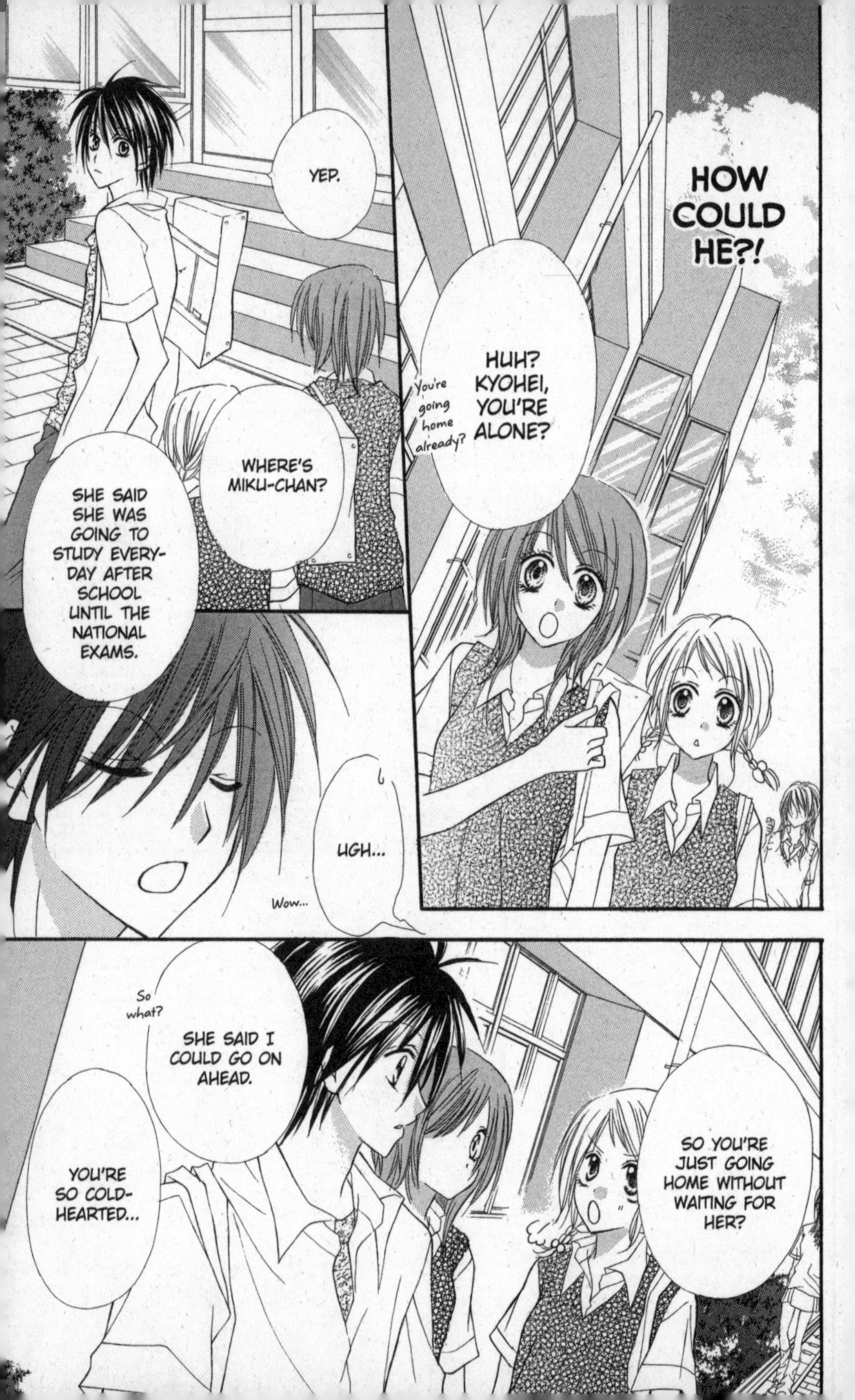

HOW COULD HE?!
HUH? KYOHEI, YOU'RE ALONE?
You're going home already?
YEP.
WHERE'S MIKU-CHAN?
SHE SAID SHE WAS GOING TO STUDY EVERY-DAY AFTER SCHOOL UNTIL THE NATIONAL EXAMS.
UGH...
Wow...
SO YOU'RE JUST GOING HOME WITHOUT WAITING FOR HER?
SHE SAID I COULD GO ON AHEAD.
So what?
YOU'RE SO COLD-HEARTED...

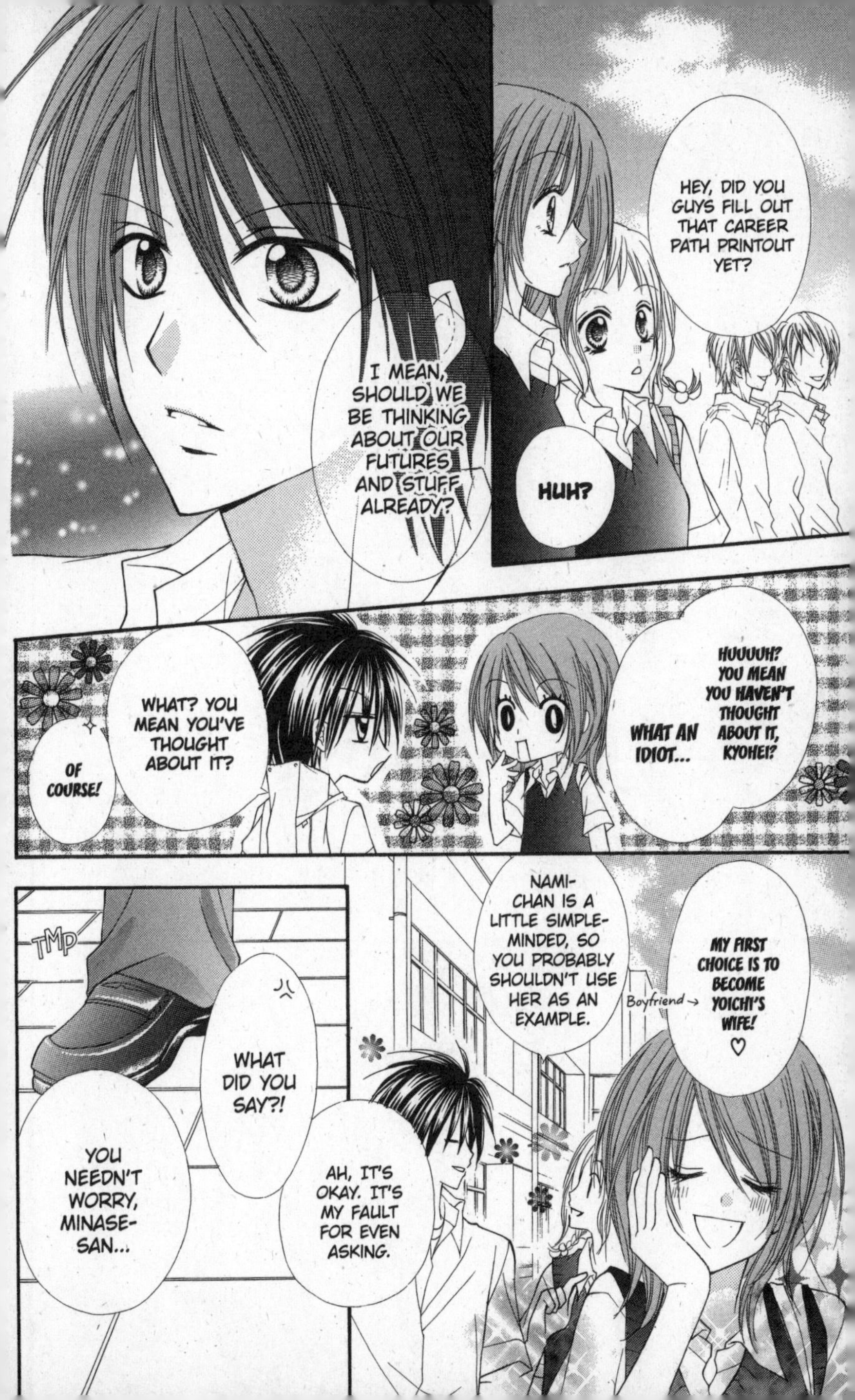
HEY, DID YOU GUYS FILL OUT THAT CAREER PATH PRINTOUT YET?
HUH?
I MEAN, SHOULD WE BE THINKING ABOUT OUR FUTURES AND STUFF ALREADY?
HUUUUH? YOU MEAN YOU HAVEN'T THOUGHT ABOUT IT, KYOHEI?
WHAT AN IDIOT...
WHAT? YOU MEAN YOU'VE THOUGHT ABOUT IT?
OF COURSE!
MY FIRST CHOICE IS TO BECOME YOICHI'S WIFE! ♡
Boyfriend →
NAMI-CHAN IS A LITTLE SIMPLE-MINDED, SO YOU PROBABLY SHOULDN'T USE HER AS AN EXAMPLE.
AH, IT'S OKAY. IT'S MY FAULT FOR EVEN ASKING.
WHAT DID YOU SAY?!
YOU NEEDN'T WORRY, MINASE-SAN...
TMP

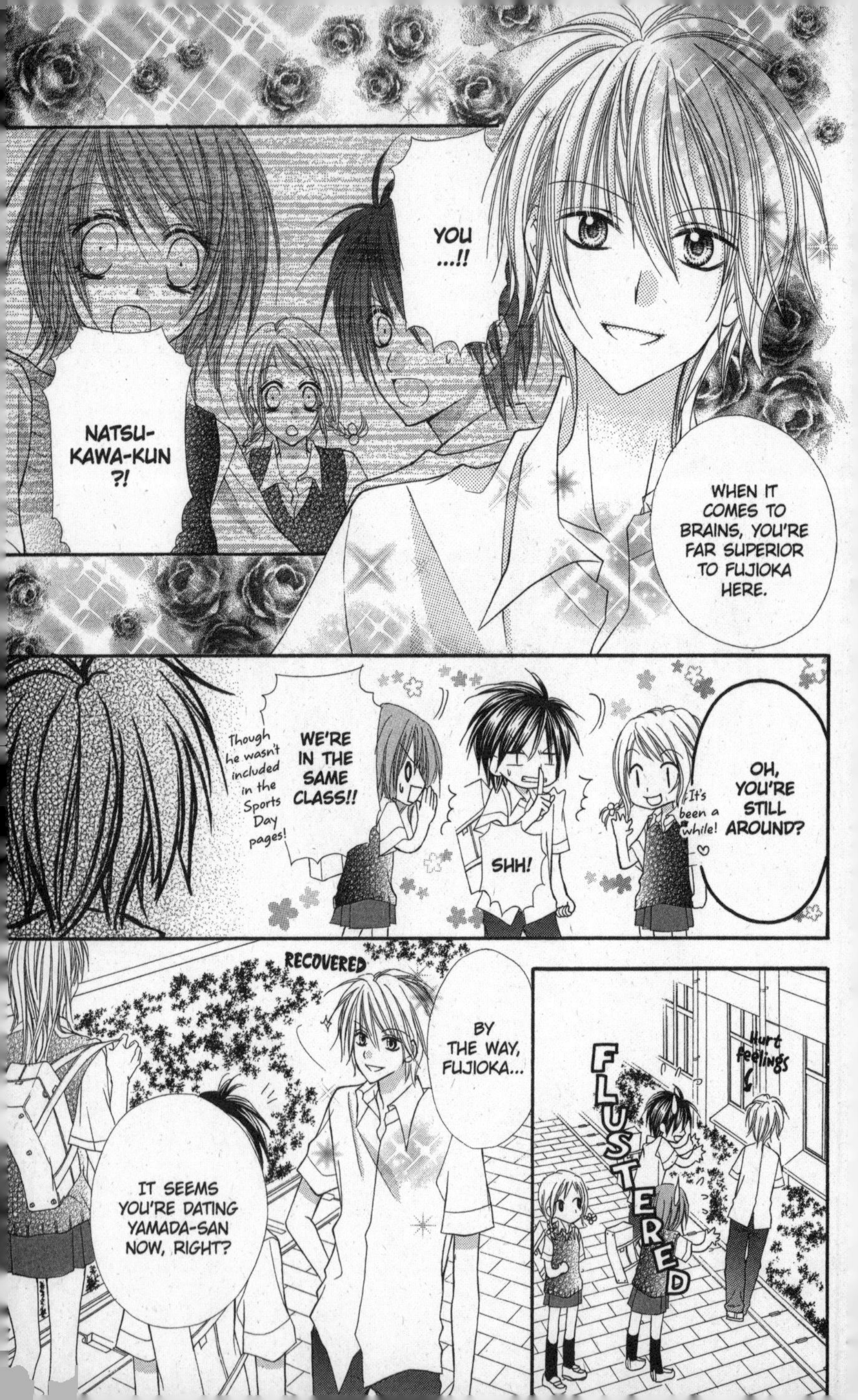
WHEN IT COMES TO BRAINS, YOU'RE FAR SUPERIOR TO FUJIOKA HERE.
YOU ...!!
NATSU-KAWA-KUN ?!
OH, YOU'RE STILL AROUND?
It's been a while! ♡
SHH!
WE'RE IN THE SAME CLASS!!
Though he wasn't included in the Sports Day pages!
Hurt feelings
FLUSTERED
RECOVERED
BY THE WAY, FUJIOKA...
IT SEEMS YOU'RE DATING YAMADA-SAN NOW, RIGHT?

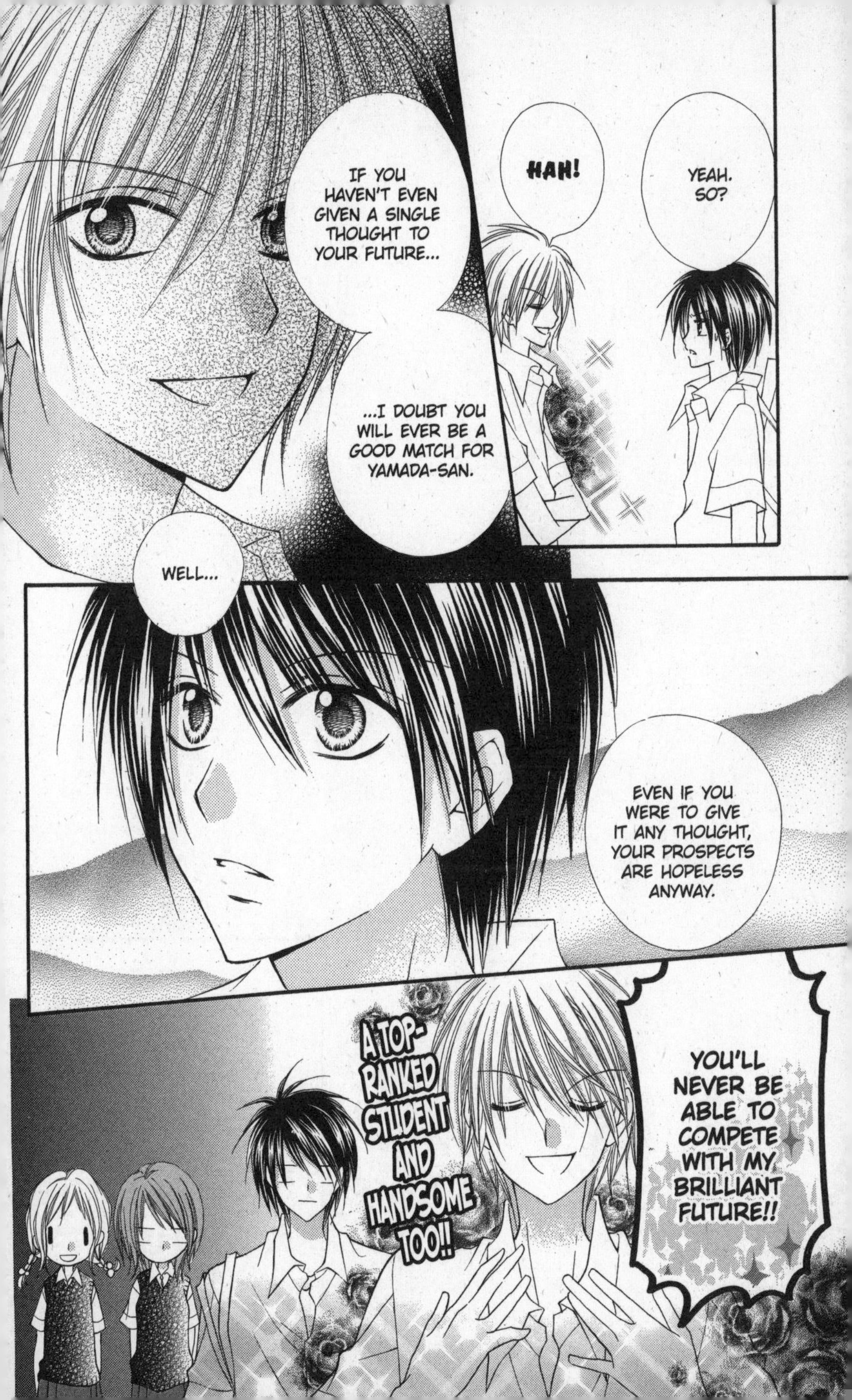
YEAH. SO?
HAH!
IF YOU HAVEN'T EVEN GIVEN A SINGLE THOUGHT TO YOUR FUTURE...
...I DOUBT YOU WILL EVER BE A GOOD MATCH FOR YAMADA-SAN.
WELL...
EVEN IF YOU WERE TO GIVE IT ANY THOUGHT, YOUR PROSPECTS ARE HOPELESS ANYWAY.
YOU'LL NEVER BE ABLE TO COMPETE WITH MY BRILLIANT FUTURE!!
A TOP-RANKED STUDENT AND HANDSOME TOO!!

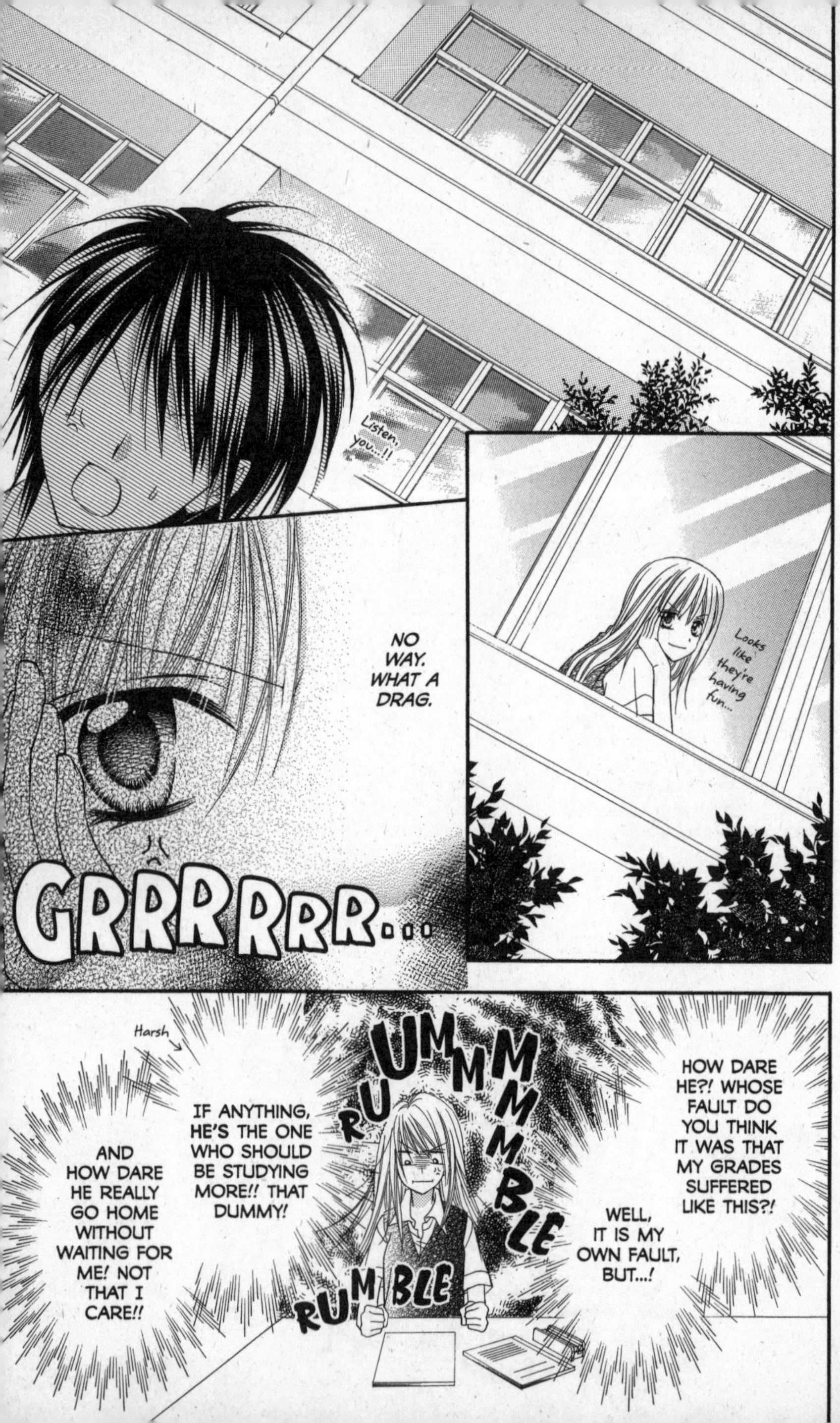
Listen, you...!!
Looks like they're having fun...
NO WAY. WHAT A DRAG.
GRRRRRR...
HOW DARE HE?! WHOSE FAULT DO YOU THINK IT WAS THAT MY GRADES SUFFERED LIKE THIS?!
WELL, IT IS MY OWN FAULT, BUT...!
RUMMMMMBLE
IF ANYTHING, HE'S THE ONE WHO SHOULD BE STUDYING MORE!! THAT DUMMY!
Harsh
AND HOW DARE HE REALLY GO HOME WITHOUT WAITING FOR ME! NOT THAT I CARE!!
RUMBLE

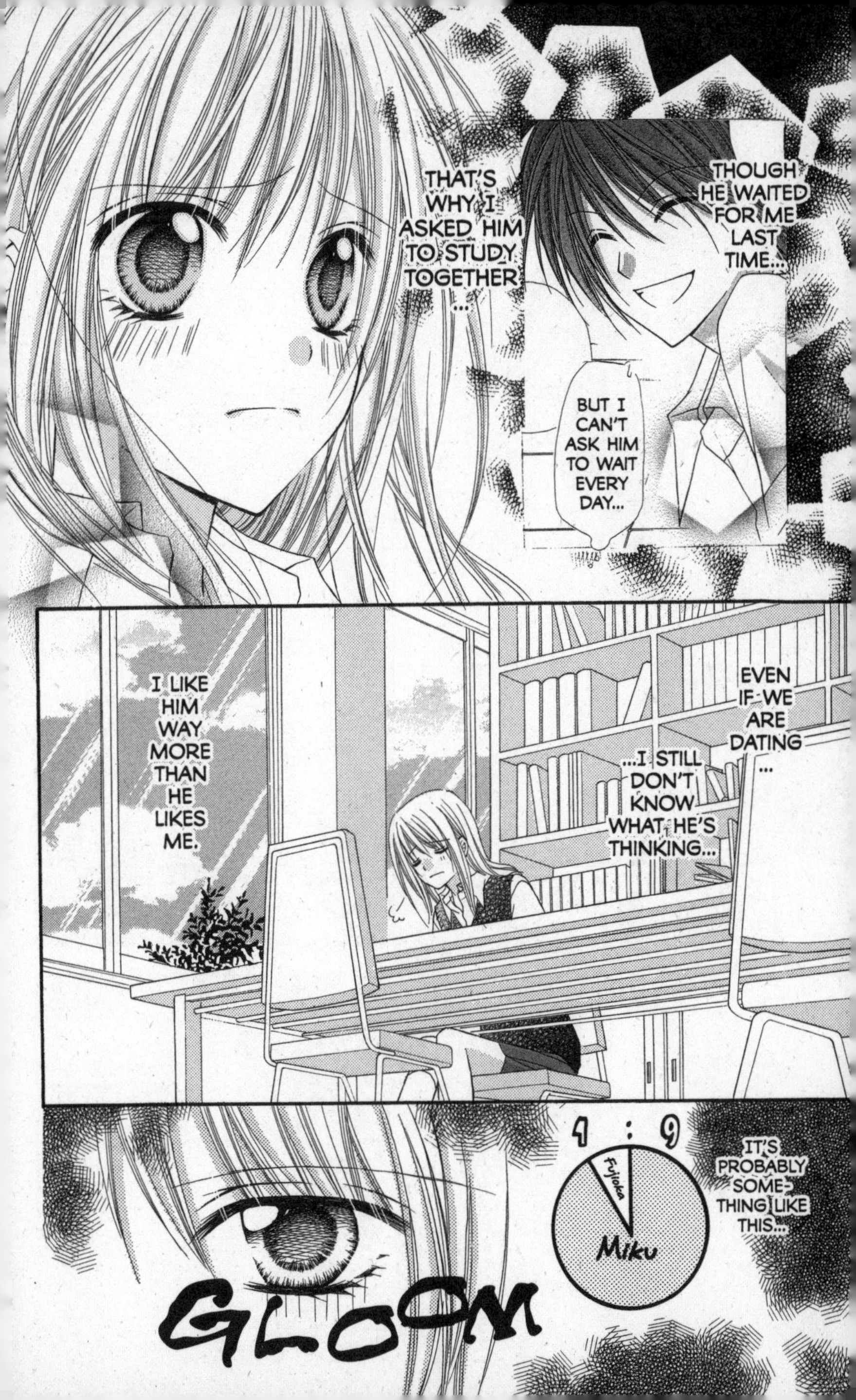
THOUGH HE WAITED FOR ME LAST TIME...
BUT I CAN'T ASK HIM TO WAIT EVERY DAY...
THAT'S WHY I ASKED HIM TO STUDY TOGETHER...
EVEN IF WE ARE DATING...
...I STILL DON'T KNOW WHAT HE'S THINKING...
I LIKE HIM WAY MORE THAN HE LIKES ME.
IT'S PROBABLY SOME-THING LIKE THIS...
1 : 9
Fujioka
Miku
GLOOM

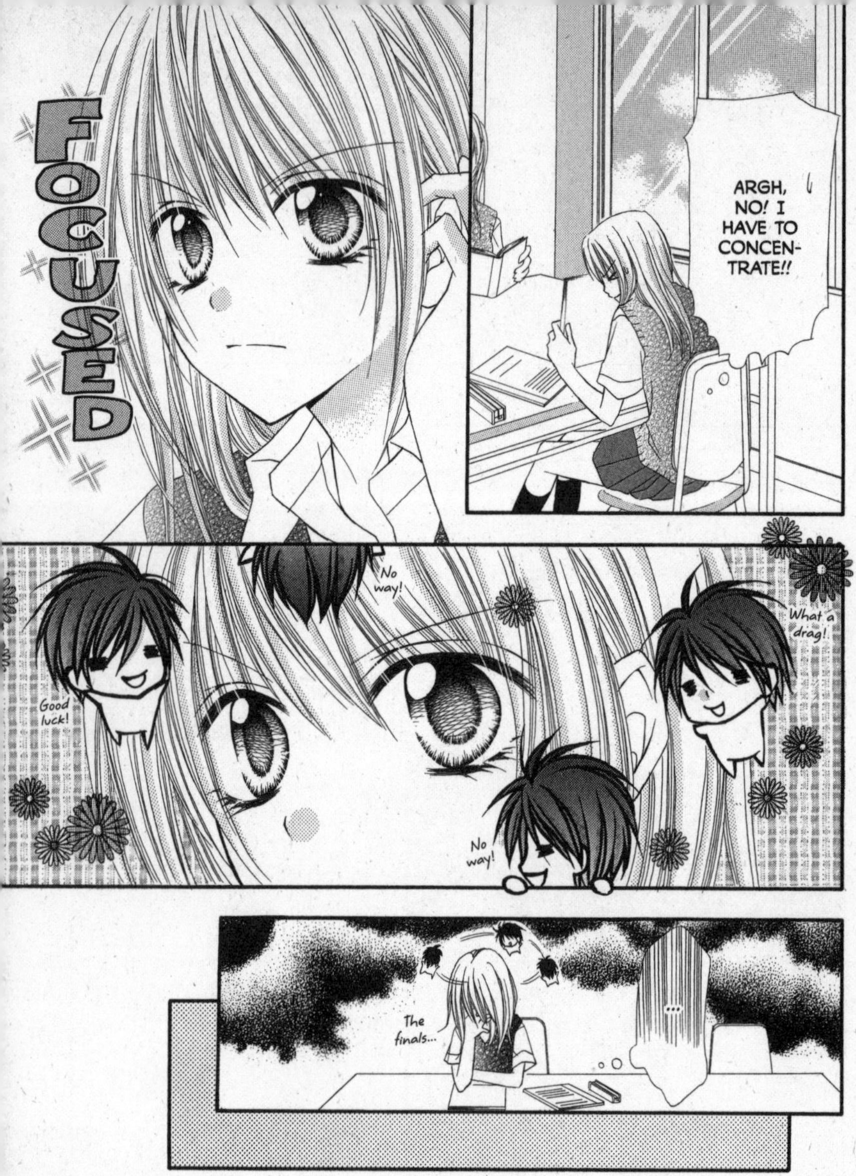
ARGH, NO! I HAVE TO CONCENTRATE!!
FOCUSED
What a drag!
No way!
No way!
Good luck!
...
The finals...

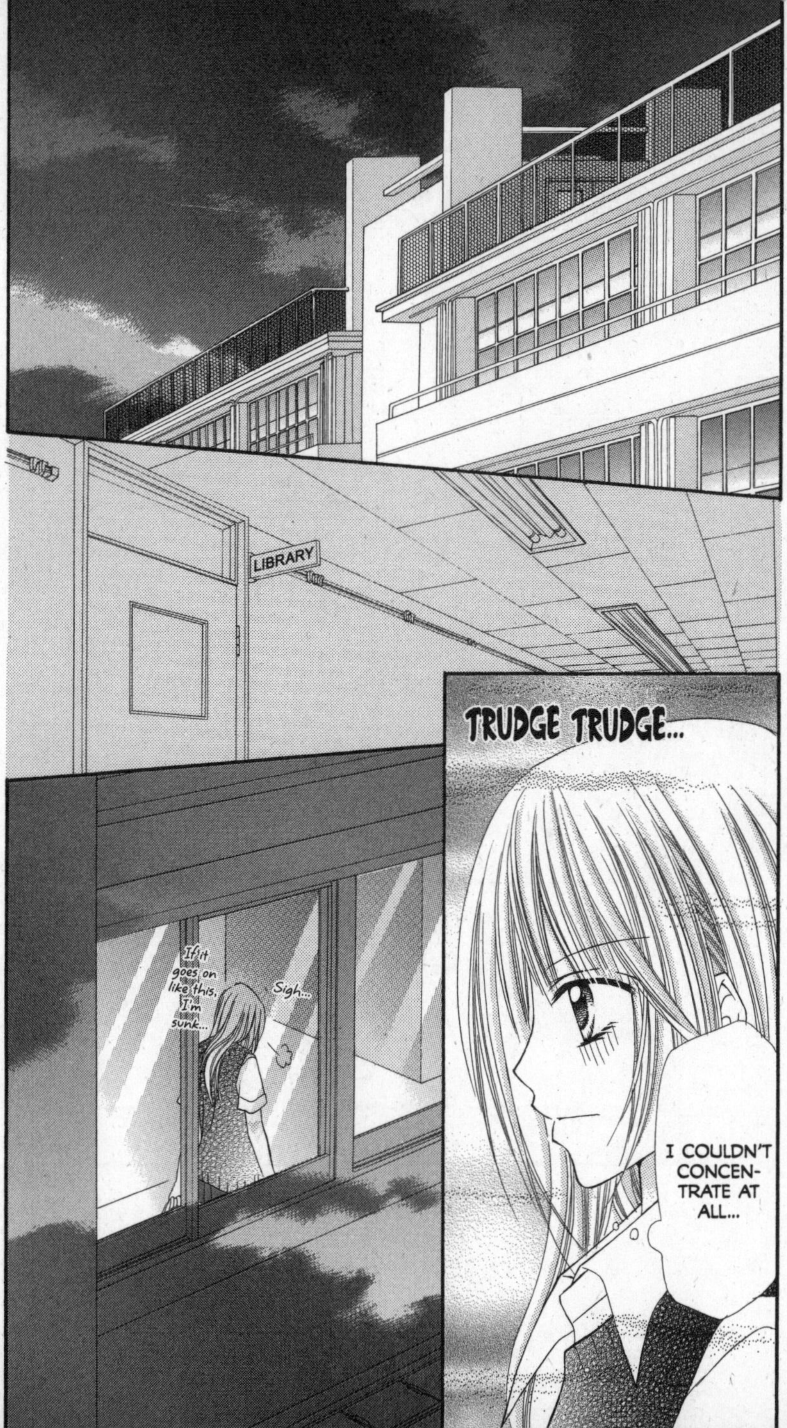
LIBRARY
TRUDGE TRUDGE...
I COULDN'T CONCENTRATE AT ALL...
Sigh...
If it goes on like this, I'm sunk...

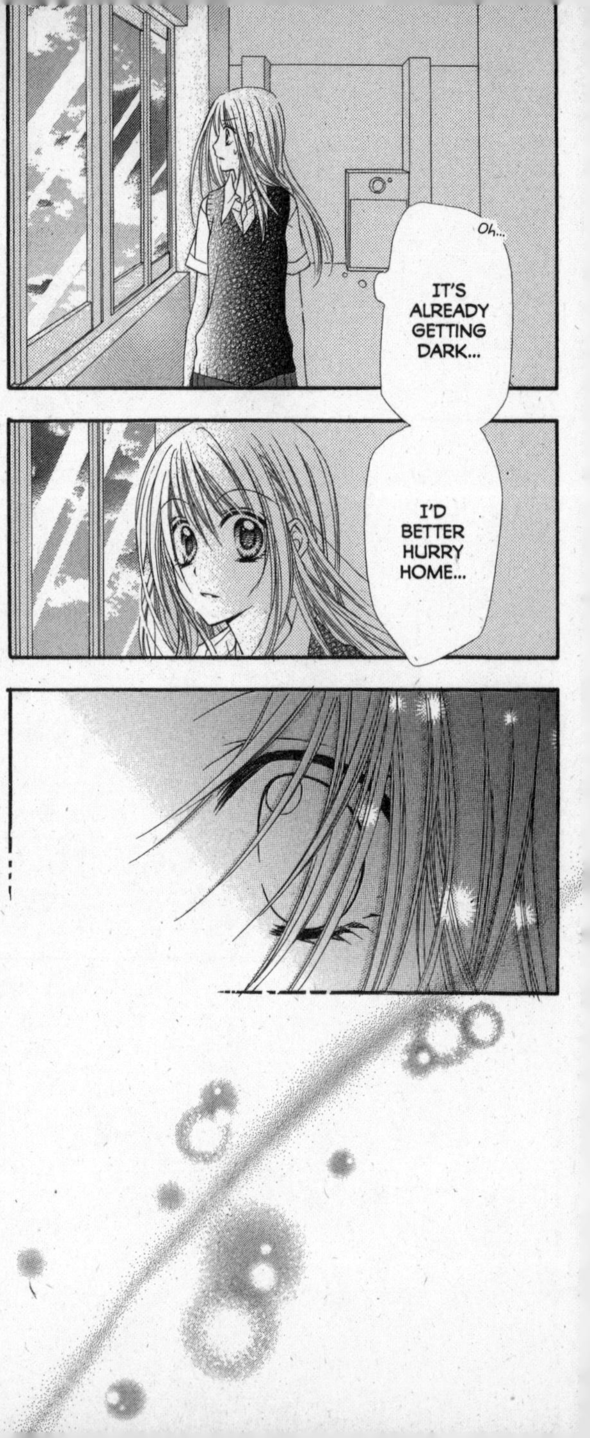
Oh...
IT'S ALREADY GETTING DARK...
I'D BETTER HURRY HOME...

12

Phew... We're already on the last column!! I managed to complete all of them this time, thank goodness. I'm not even gonna worry whether I made typos this time. Actually, I should worry.

Well, even though this is the last of the columns, there are some bonus pages in the back, so if you have a little time, please do take a look. I hope you'll like them!

If you want to send in any opinions or thoughts on the manga, you can send your letters to...
↓

Cactus's Secret Editor
c/o VIZ Media
P.O. Box 77010
San Francisco, CA 94107

Okay then, I look forward to seeing you all again in the final volume of Cactus's Secret vol. 4. Although Cactus's run is over, my new series is starting in the September 2005 issue of Ribon magazine, so please check that out too!

See you later!

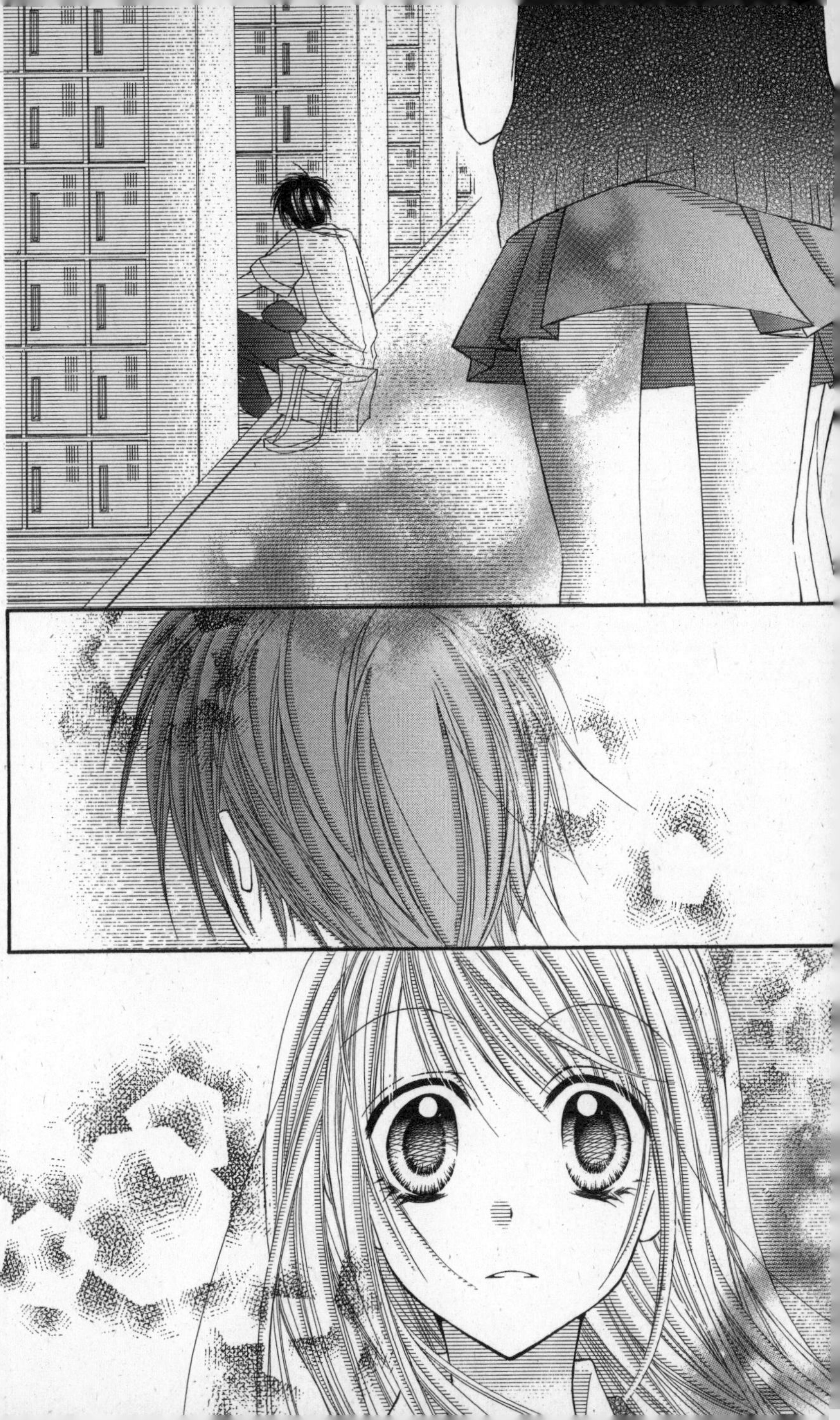

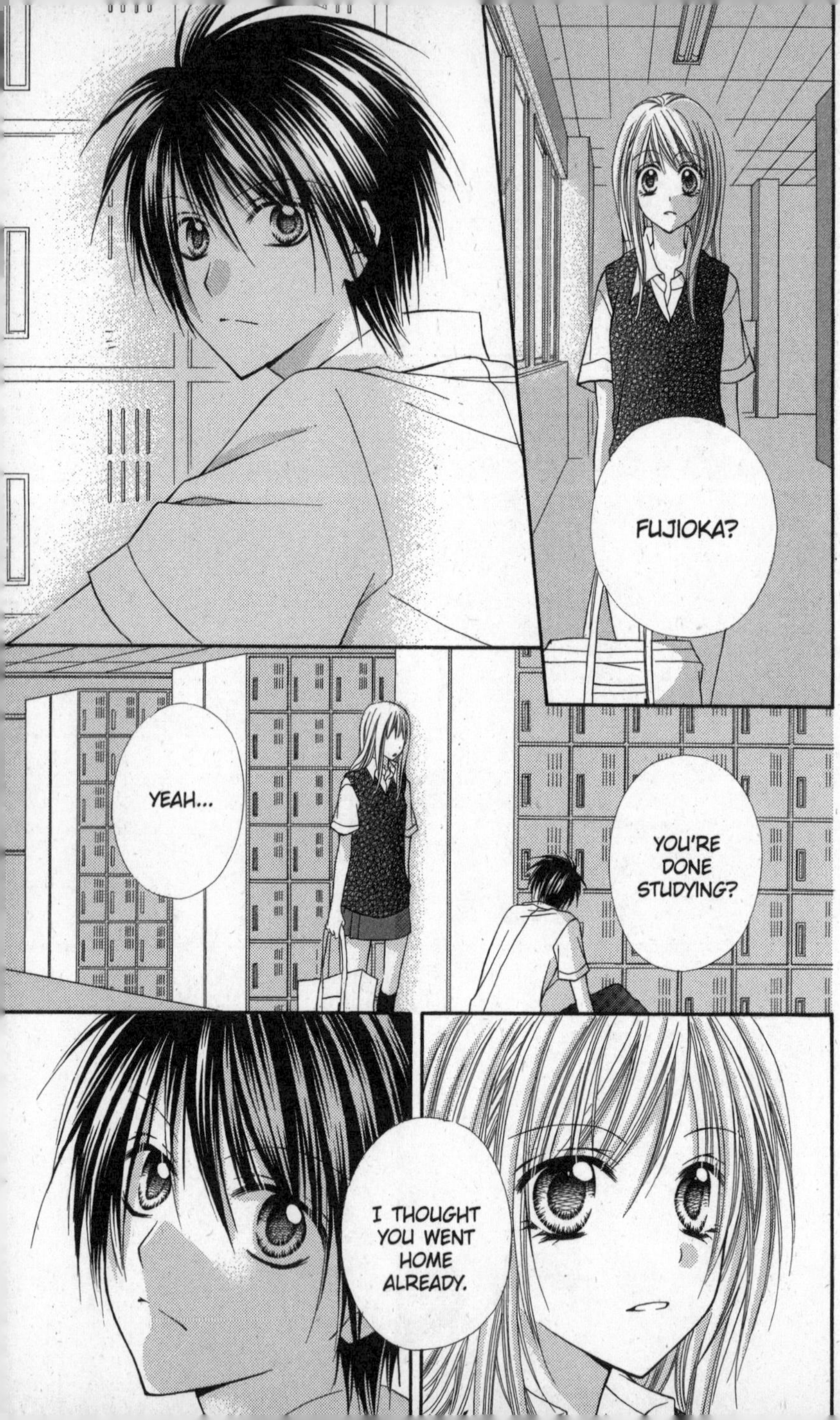
FUJIOKA?
YOU'RE DONE STUDYING?
YEAH...
I THOUGHT YOU WENT HOME ALREADY.

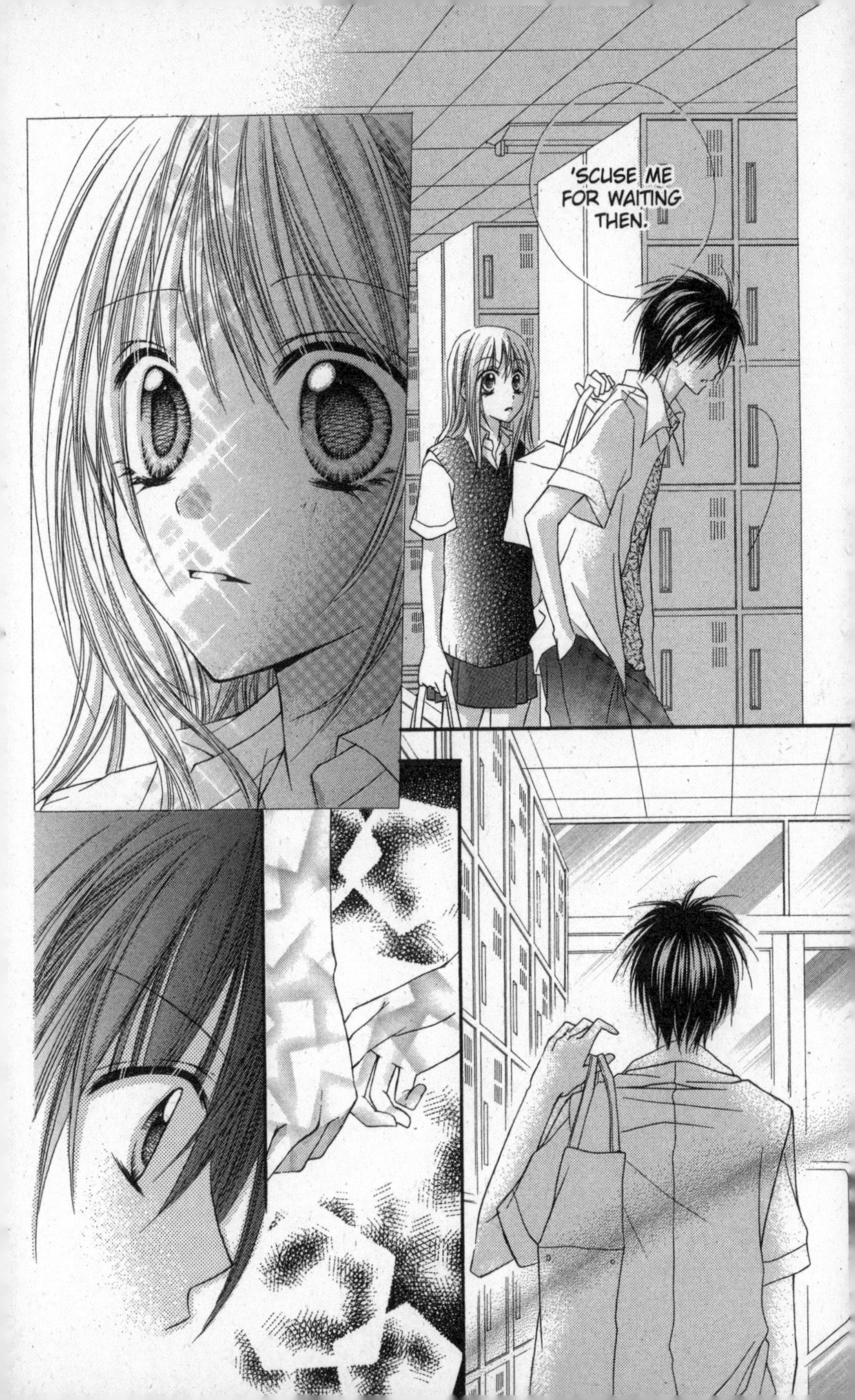
'SCUSE ME FOR WAITING THEN.

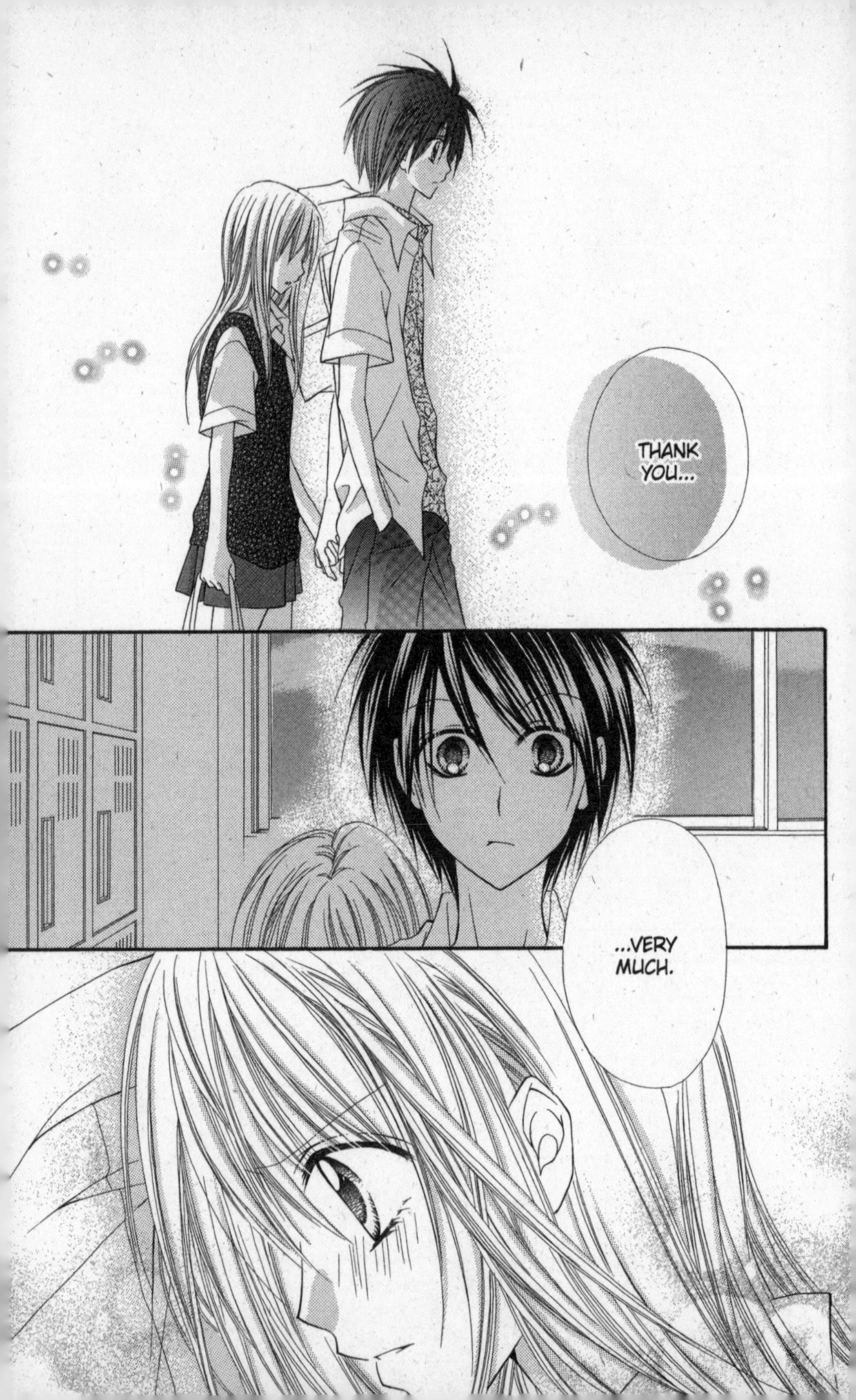
THANK YOU...
...VERY MUCH.

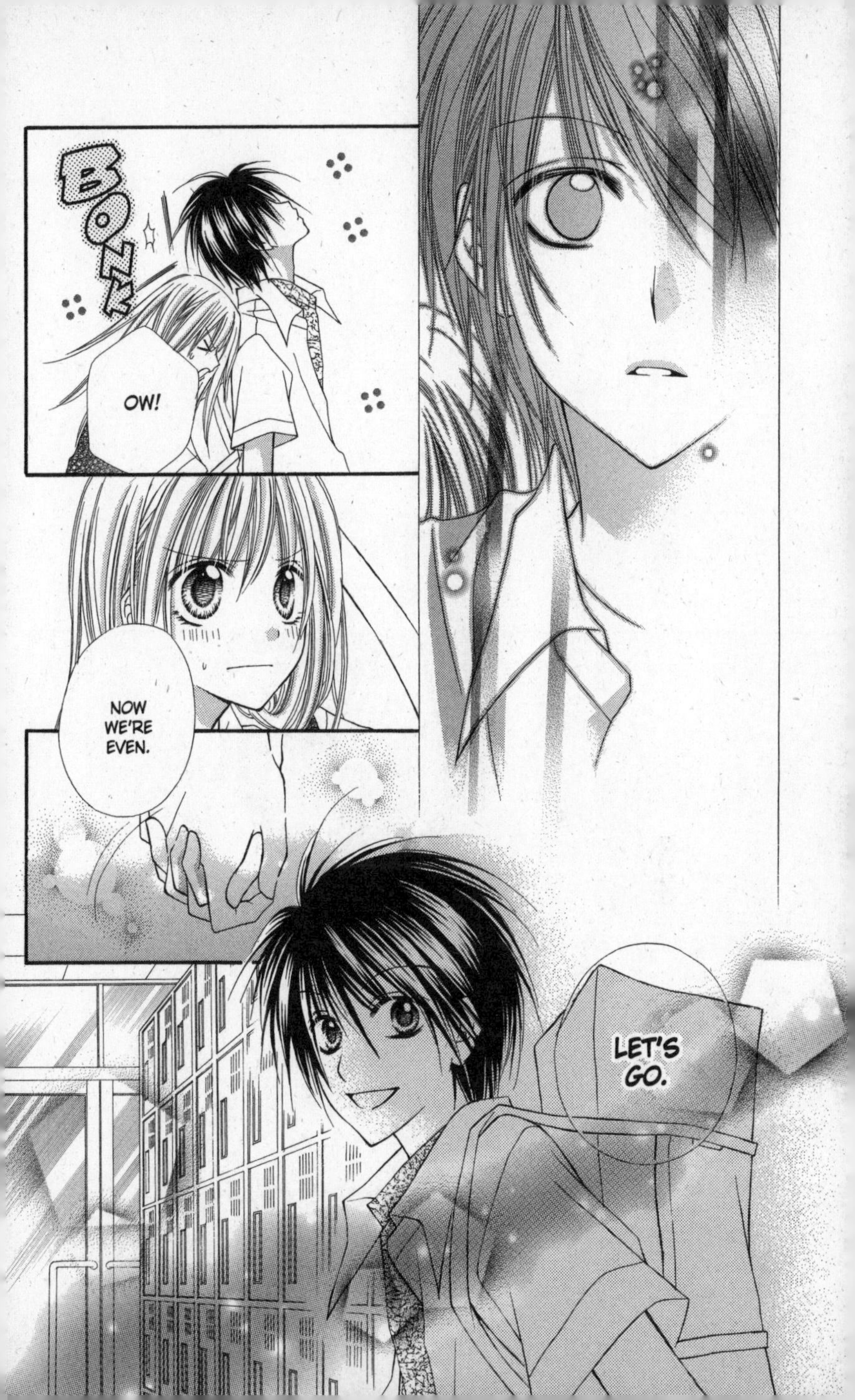
BONK
OW!
NOW WE'RE EVEN.
LET'S GO.

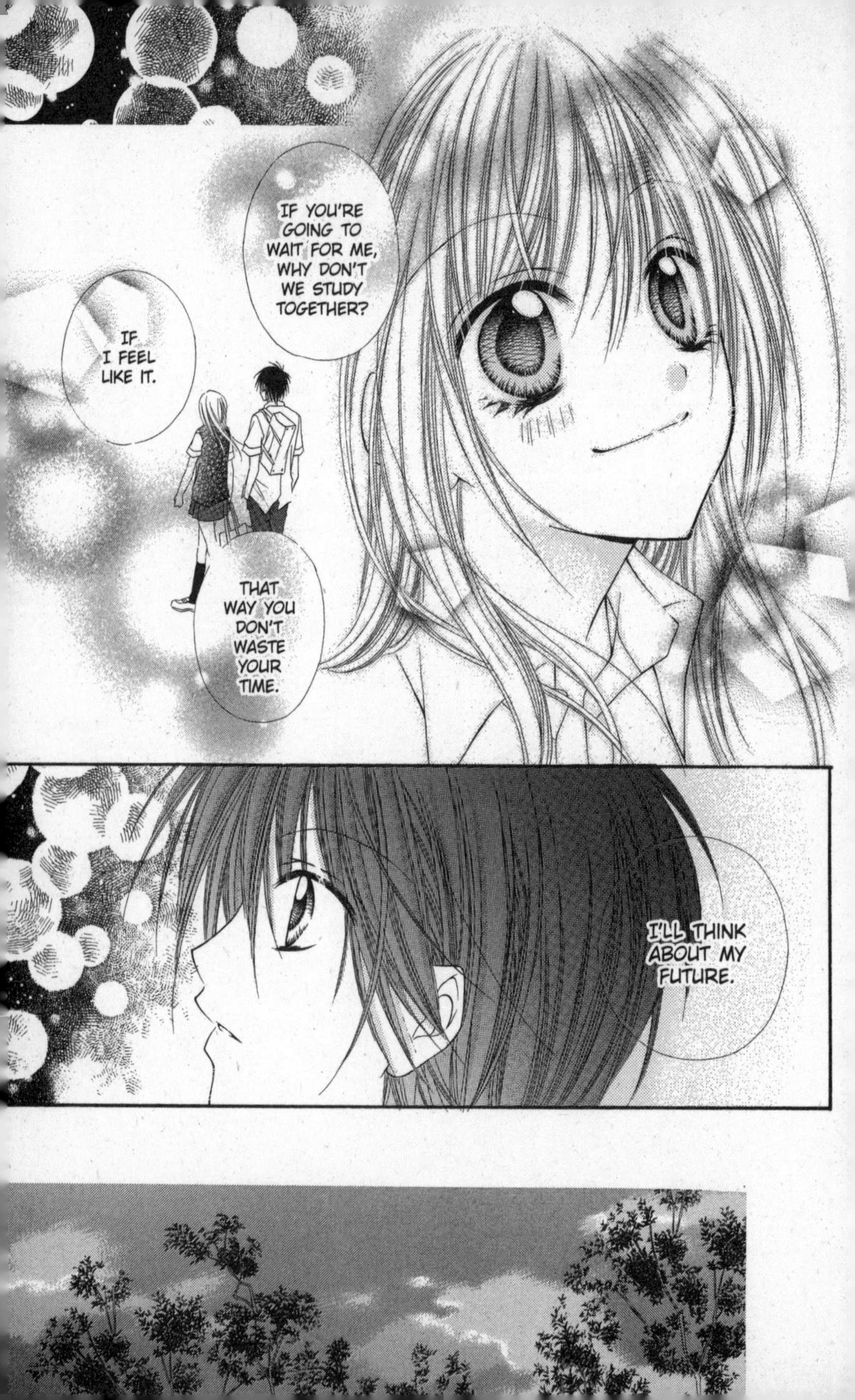
IF YOU'RE GOING TO WAIT FOR ME, WHY DON'T WE STUDY TOGETHER?
THAT WAY YOU DON'T WASTE YOUR TIME.
IF I FEEL LIKE IT.
I'LL THINK ABOUT MY FUTURE.

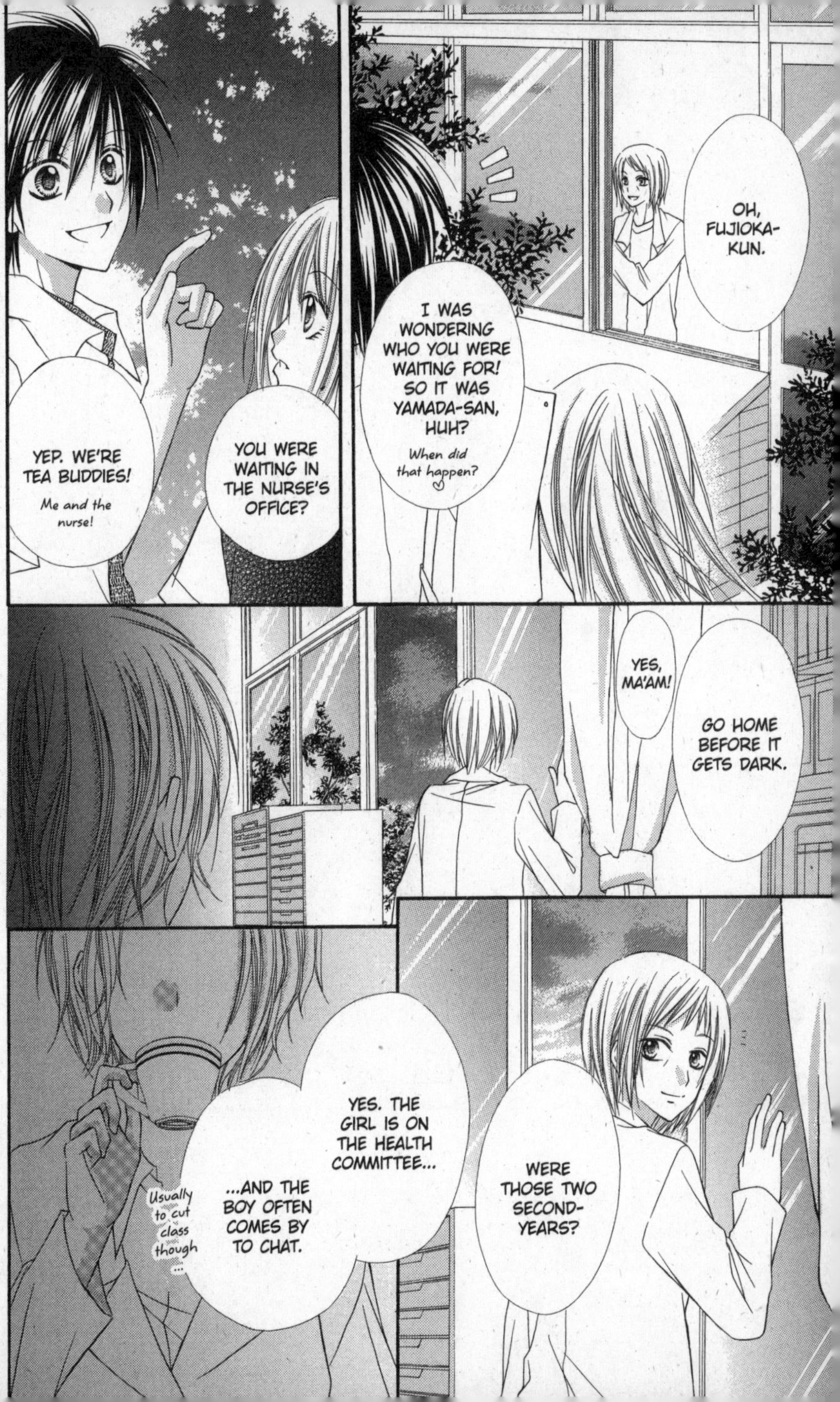
OH, FUJIOKA-KUN.
I WAS WONDERING WHO YOU WERE WAITING FOR! SO IT WAS YAMADA-SAN, HUH?
When did that happen?
YOU WERE WAITING IN THE NURSE'S OFFICE?
YEP. WE'RE TEA BUDDIES!
Me and the nurse!
GO HOME BEFORE IT GETS DARK.
YES, MA'AM!
WERE THOSE TWO SECOND-YEARS?
YES. THE GIRL IS ON THE HEALTH COMMITTEE...
...AND THE BOY OFTEN COMES BY TO CHAT.
Usually to cut class though...

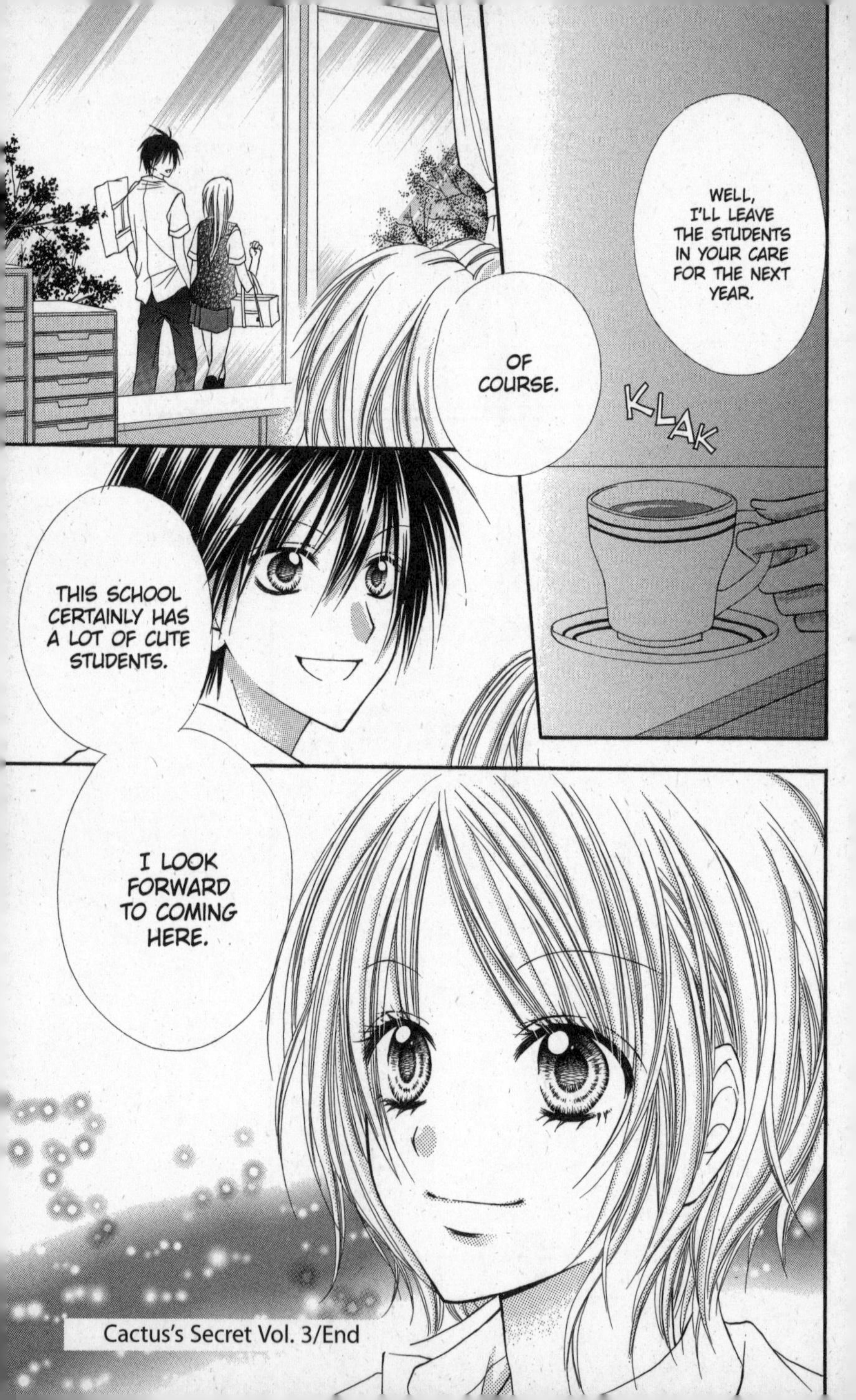
WELL, I'LL LEAVE THE STUDENTS IN YOUR CARE FOR THE NEXT YEAR.
OF COURSE.
KLAK
THIS SCHOOL CERTAINLY HAS A LOT OF CUTE STUDENTS.
I LOOK FORWARD TO COMING HERE.

Cactus's Secret Vol. 3/End

Haruta's Diary

"This is getting really scary..."

Bonus Comic

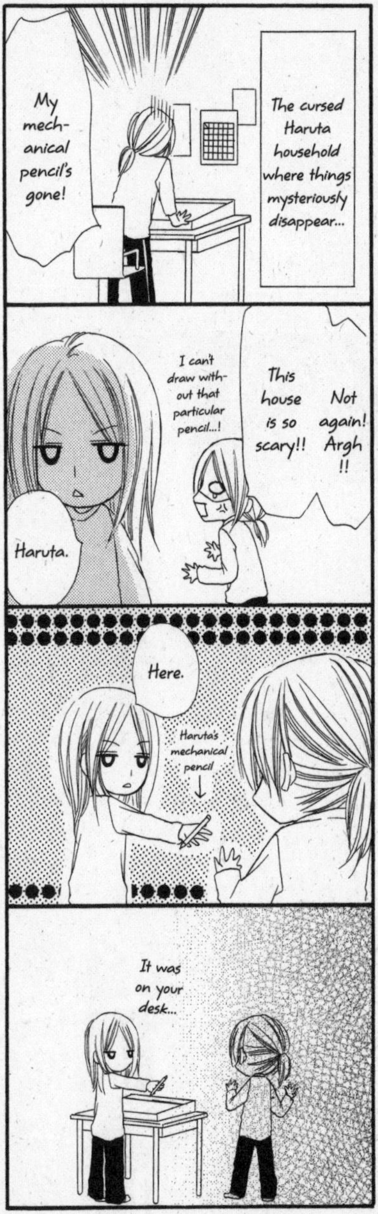
The cursed Haruta household where things mysteriously disappear...
My mechanical pencil's gone!
Not again! Argh!!
This house is so scary!!
I can't draw without that particular pencil...!
Haruta.
Here.
Haruta's mechanical pencil
It was on your desk...

My assistant Marinakko is such a master at finding the stuff I've lost! ♡

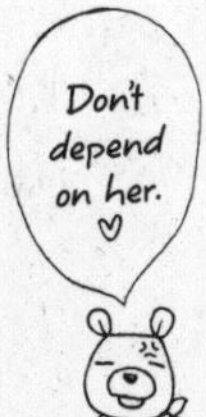
Don't depend on her. ♡

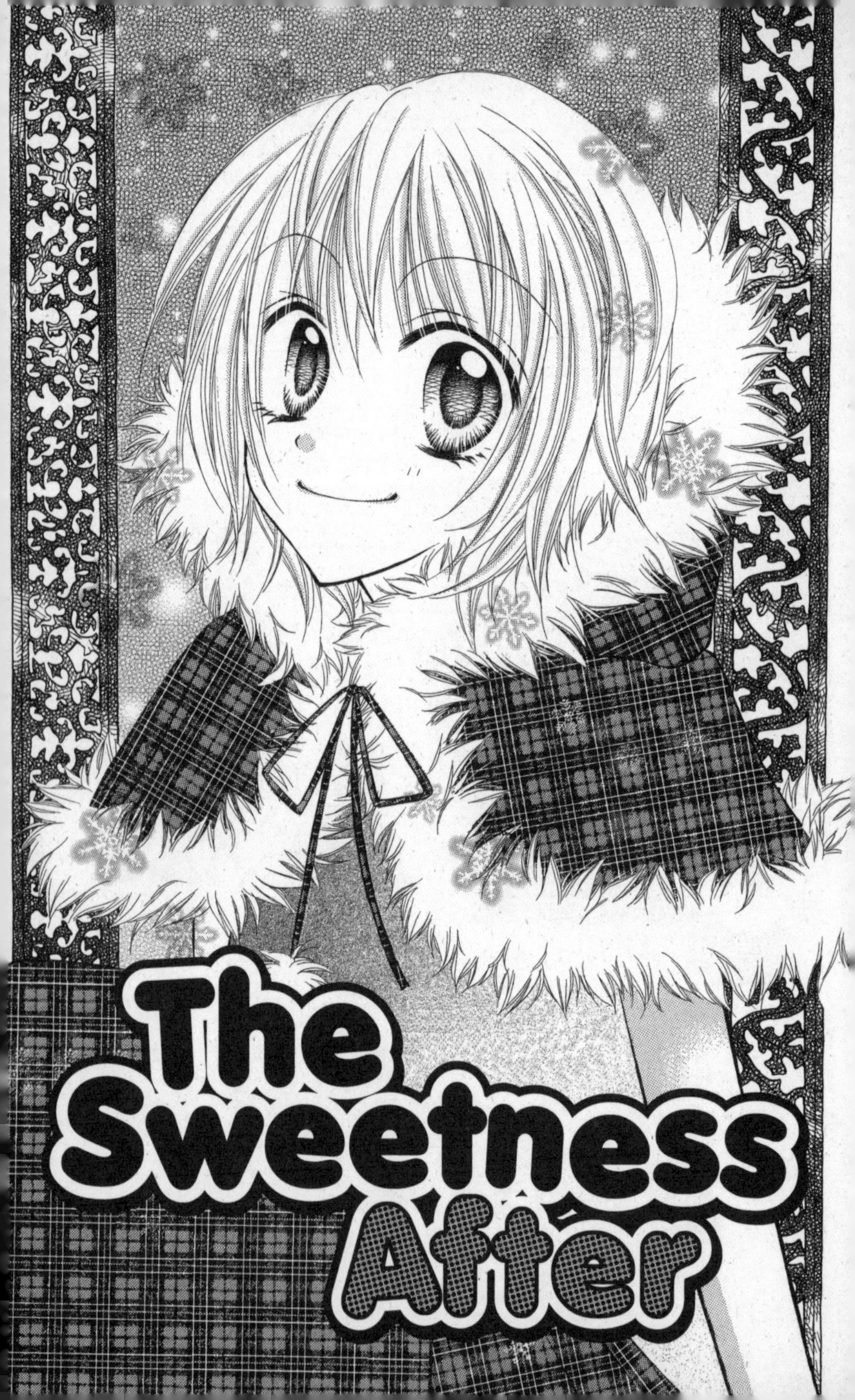
The Sweetness After

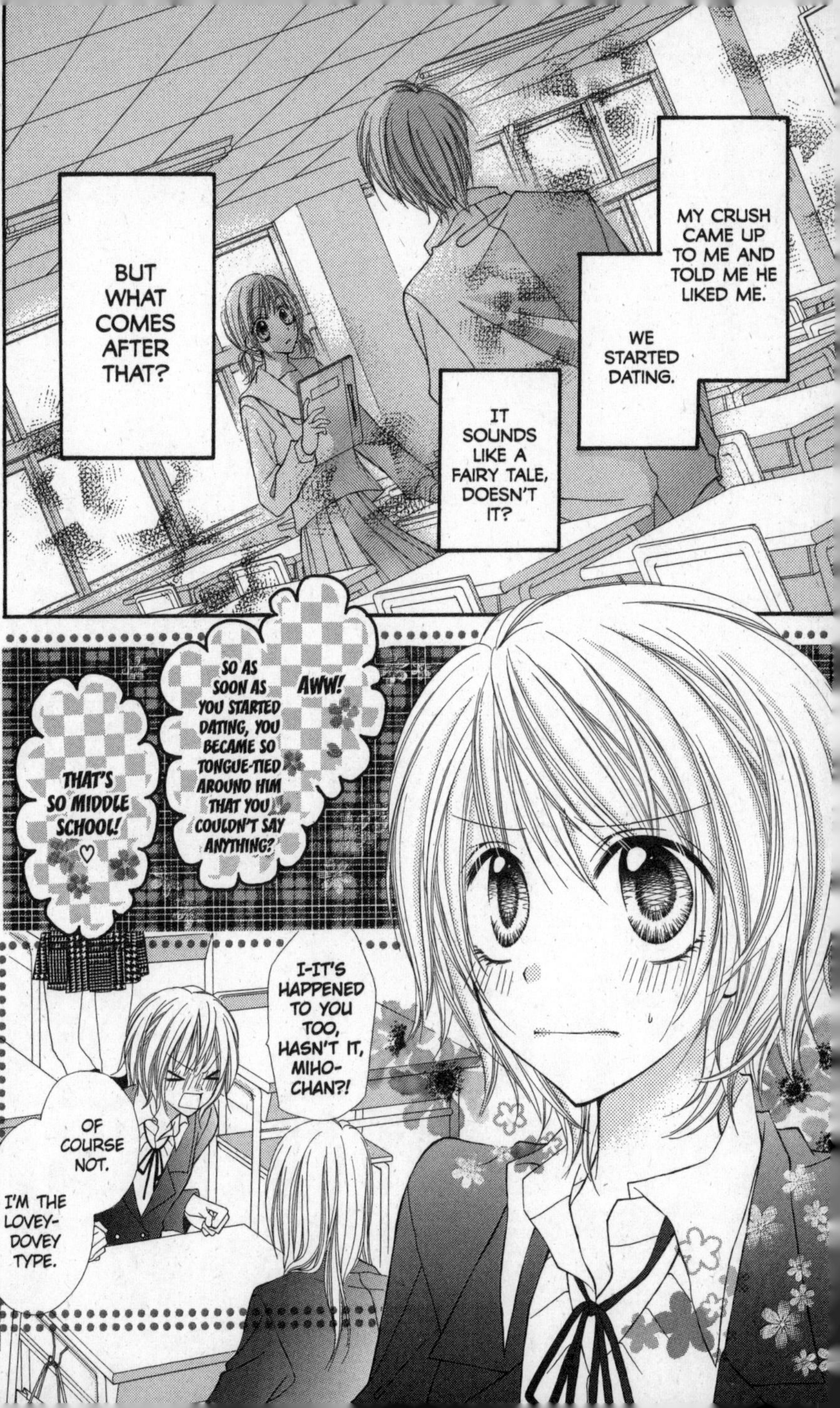
MY CRUSH CAME UP TO ME AND TOLD ME HE LIKED ME.
WE STARTED DATING.
IT SOUNDS LIKE A FAIRY TALE, DOESN'T IT?
BUT WHAT COMES AFTER THAT?
AWW!
SO AS SOON AS YOU STARTED DATING, YOU BECAME SO TONGUE-TIED AROUND HIM THAT YOU COULDN'T SAY ANYTHING?
THAT'S SO MIDDLE SCHOOL! ♡
I-IT'S HAPPENED TO YOU TOO, HASN'T IT, MIHO-CHAN?!
OF COURSE NOT.
I'M THE LOVEY-DOVEY TYPE.

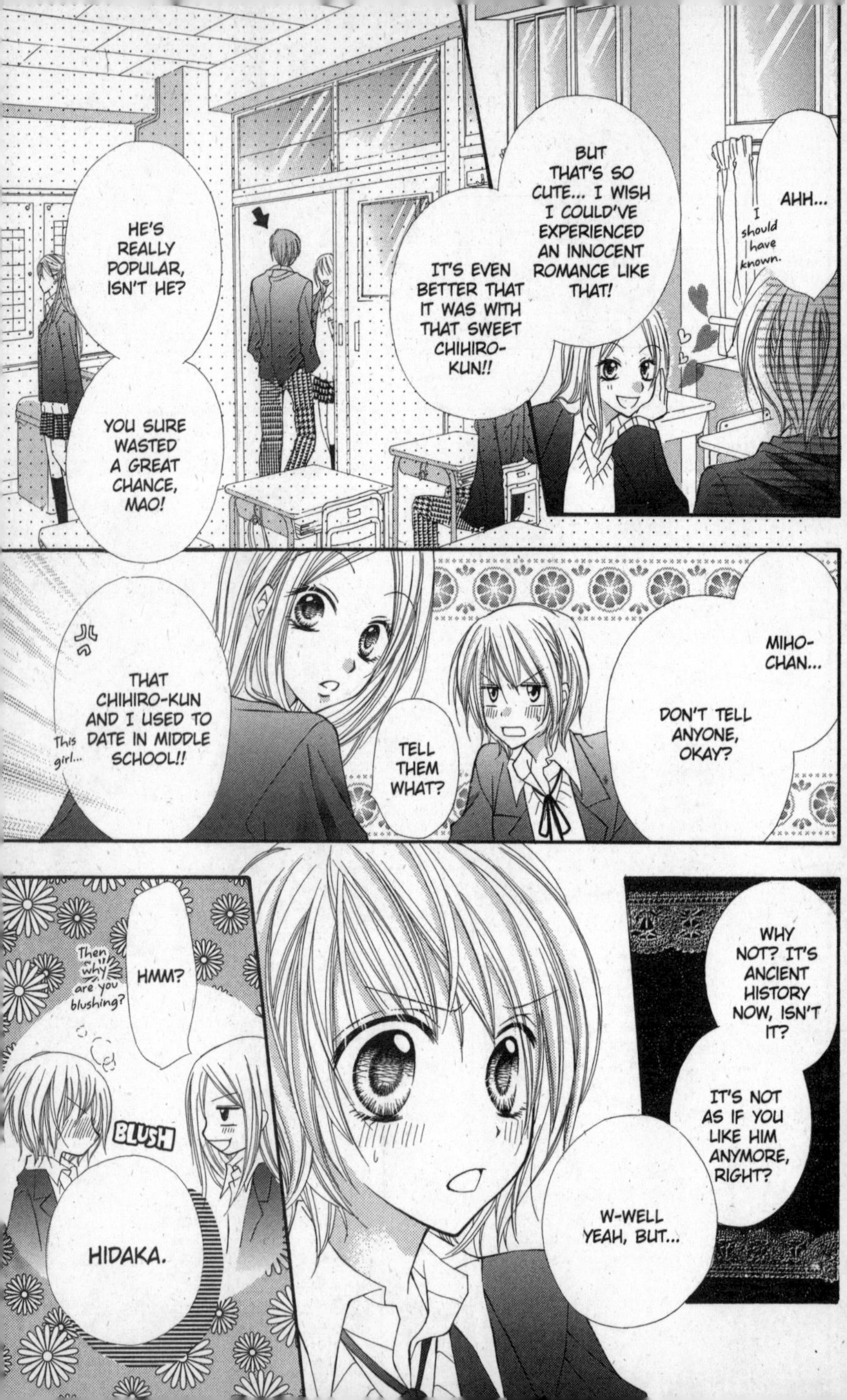
AHH...
I should have known.
BUT THAT'S SO CUTE... I WISH I COULD'VE EXPERIENCED AN INNOCENT ROMANCE LIKE THAT!
IT'S EVEN BETTER THAT IT WAS WITH THAT SWEET CHIHIRO-KUN!!
HE'S REALLY POPULAR, ISN'T HE?
YOU SURE WASTED A GREAT CHANCE, MAO!
MIHO-CHAN...
DON'T TELL ANYONE, OKAY?
TELL THEM WHAT?
THAT CHIHIRO-KUN AND I USED TO DATE IN MIDDLE SCHOOL!!
This girl...
WHY NOT? IT'S ANCIENT HISTORY NOW, ISN'T IT?
IT'S NOT AS IF YOU LIKE HIM ANYMORE, RIGHT?
W-WELL YEAH, BUT...
HMM?
Then why are you blushing?
BLUSH
HIDAKA.

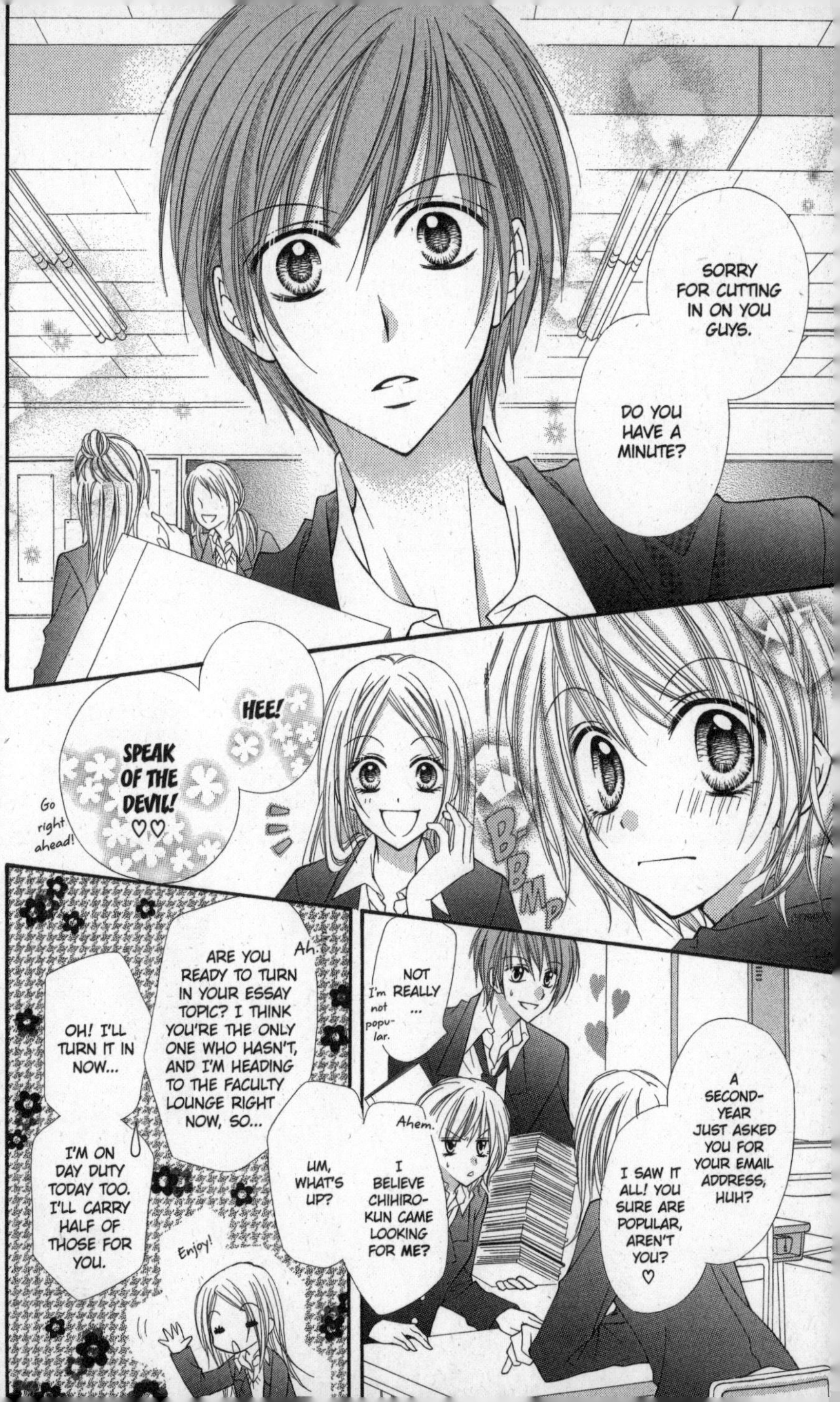
SORRY FOR CUTTING IN ON YOU GUYS.
DO YOU HAVE A MINUTE?
HEE!
SPEAK OF THE DEVIL! ♡♡
Go right ahead!
B-BUMP
A SECOND-YEAR JUST ASKED YOU FOR YOUR EMAIL ADDRESS, HUH?
I SAW IT ALL! YOU SURE ARE POPULAR, AREN'T YOU? ♡
NOT REALLY...
I'm not popular.
Ahem.
I BELIEVE CHIHIRO-KUN CAME LOOKING FOR ME?
UM, WHAT'S UP?
Ah.
ARE YOU READY TO TURN IN YOUR ESSAY TOPIC? I THINK YOU'RE THE ONLY ONE WHO HASN'T, AND I'M HEADING TO THE FACULTY LOUNGE RIGHT NOW, SO...
OH! I'LL TURN IT IN NOW...
I'M ON DAY DUTY TODAY TOO. I'LL CARRY HALF OF THOSE FOR YOU.
Enjoy!

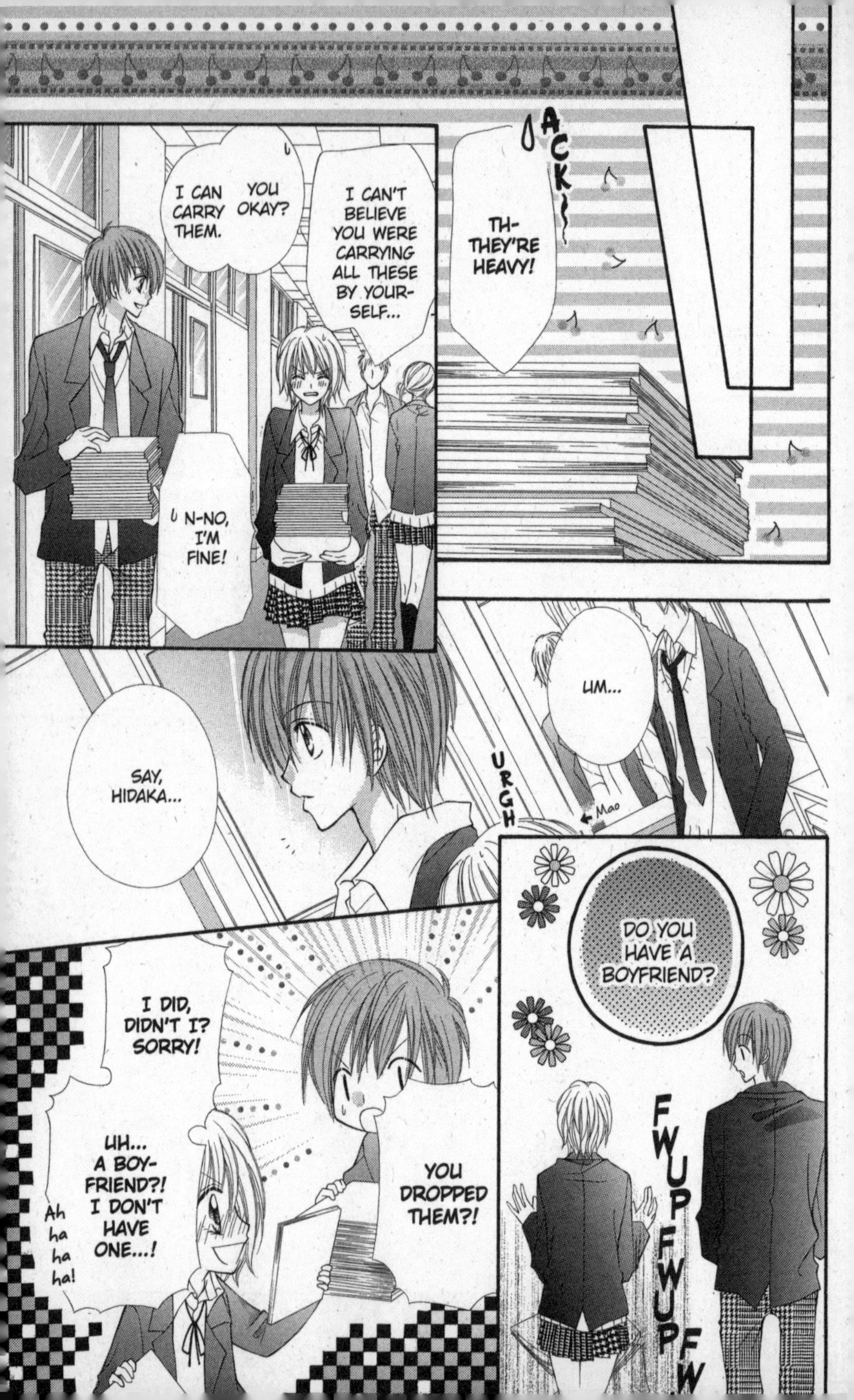
ACK~
TH-THEY'RE HEAVY!
I CAN'T BELIEVE YOU WERE CARRYING ALL THESE BY YOURSELF...
YOU OKAY? I CAN CARRY THEM.
N-NO, I'M FINE!
UM...
URGH
Mao
SAY, HIDAKA...
DO YOU HAVE A BOYFRIEND?
FWUP FWUP FW
YOU DROPPED THEM?!
I DID, DIDN'T I? SORRY!
UH... A BOY-FRIEND?! I DON'T HAVE ONE...!
Ah ha ha ha!

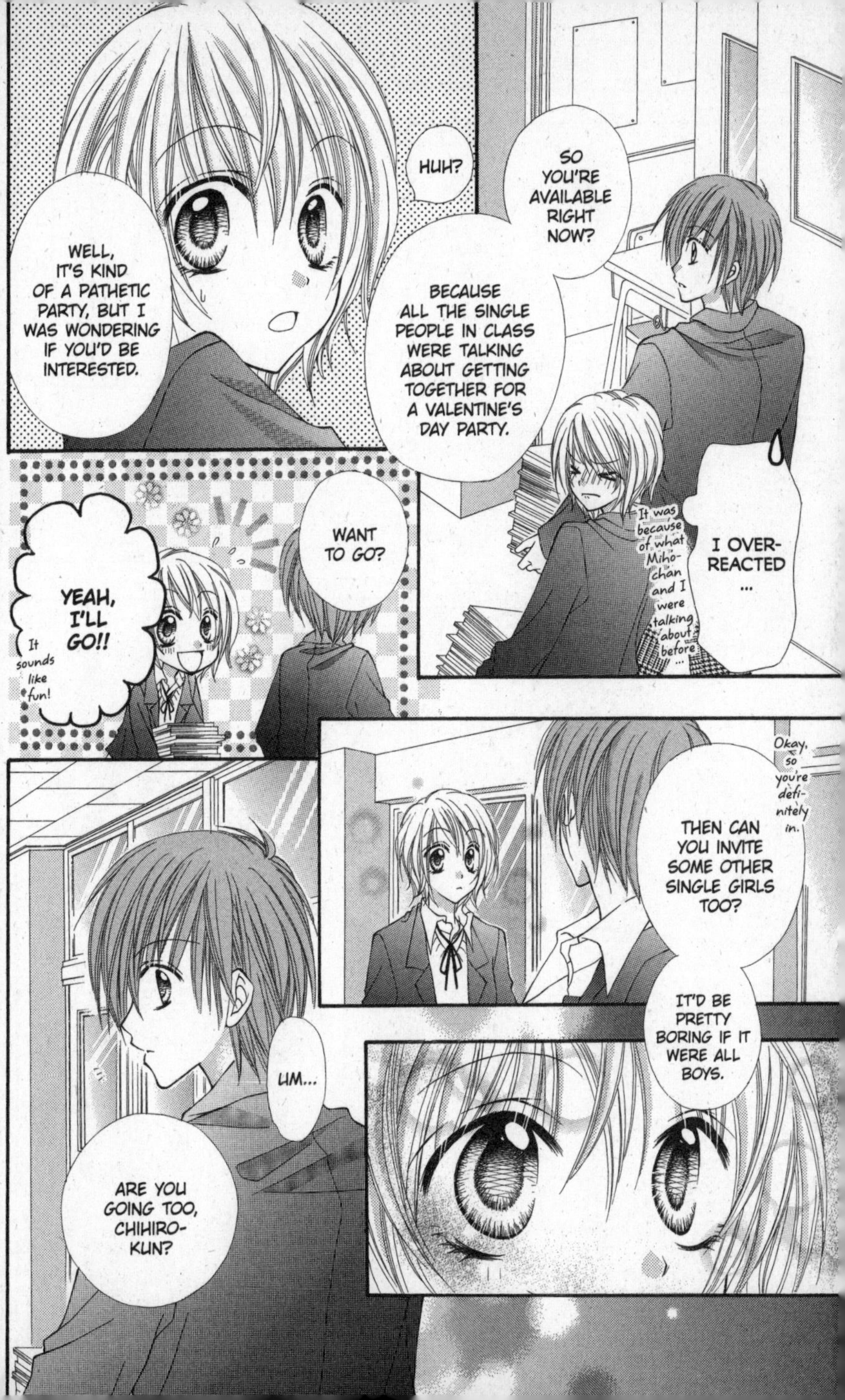
SO YOU'RE AVAILABLE RIGHT NOW?
I OVER-REACTED ...
It was because of what Miho-chan and I were talking about before ...
HUH?
BECAUSE ALL THE SINGLE PEOPLE IN CLASS WERE TALKING ABOUT GETTING TOGETHER FOR A VALENTINE'S DAY PARTY.
WELL, IT'S KIND OF A PATHETIC PARTY, BUT I WAS WONDERING IF YOU'D BE INTERESTED.
WANT TO GO?
YEAH, I'LL GO!!
It sounds like fun!
Okay, so you're definitely in.
THEN CAN YOU INVITE SOME OTHER SINGLE GIRLS TOO?
IT'D BE PRETTY BORING IF IT WERE ALL BOYS.
UM...
ARE YOU GOING TOO, CHIHIRO-KUN?

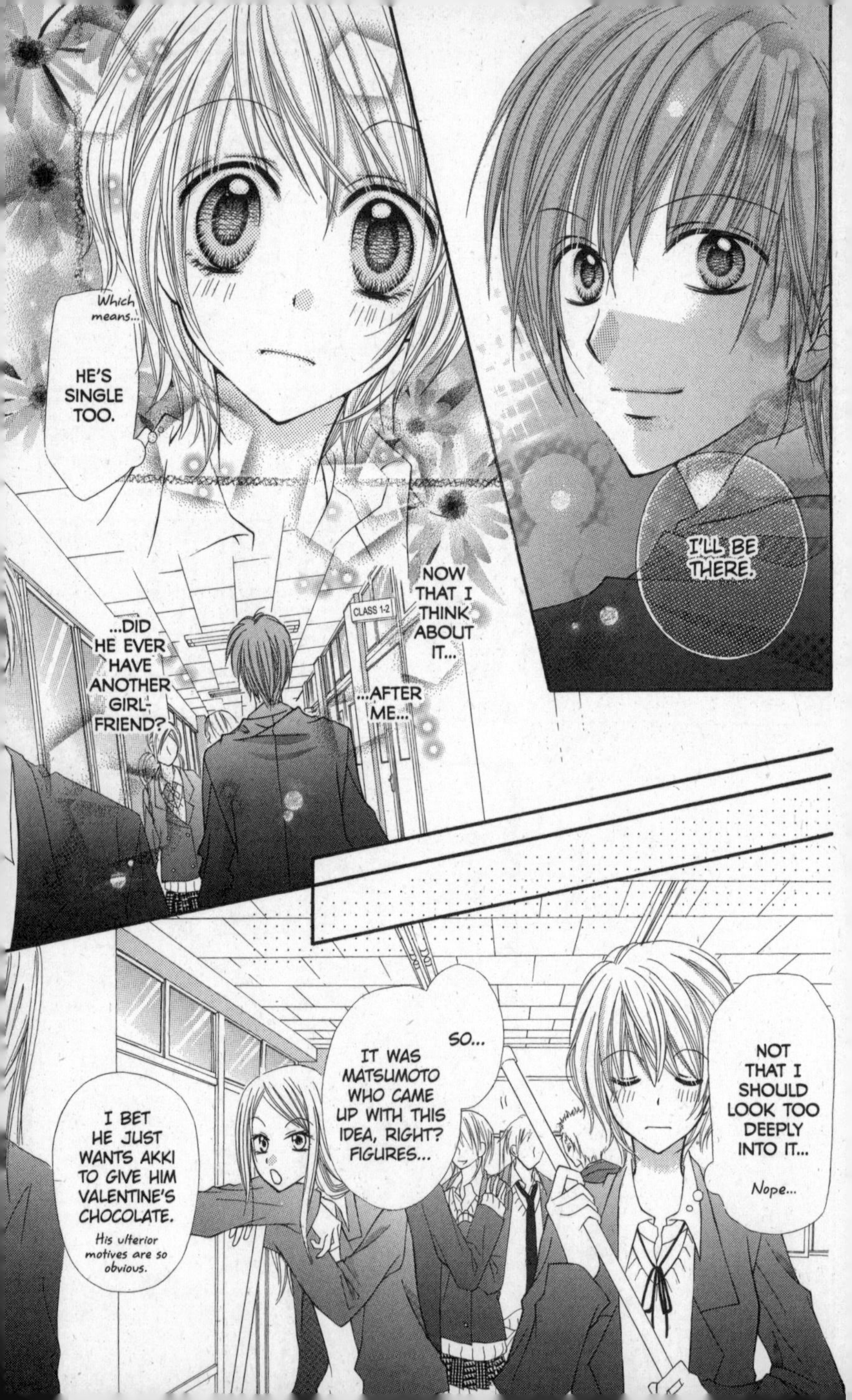
I'LL BE THERE.
Which means...
HE'S SINGLE TOO.
CLASS 1-2
NOW THAT I THINK ABOUT IT...
...AFTER ME...
...DID HE EVER HAVE ANOTHER GIRL-FRIEND?
NOT THAT I SHOULD LOOK TOO DEEPLY INTO IT...
Nope...
SO...
IT WAS MATSUMOTO WHO CAME UP WITH THIS IDEA, RIGHT? FIGURES...
I BET HE JUST WANTS AKKI TO GIVE HIM VALENTINE'S CHOCOLATE.
His ulterior motives are so obvious.

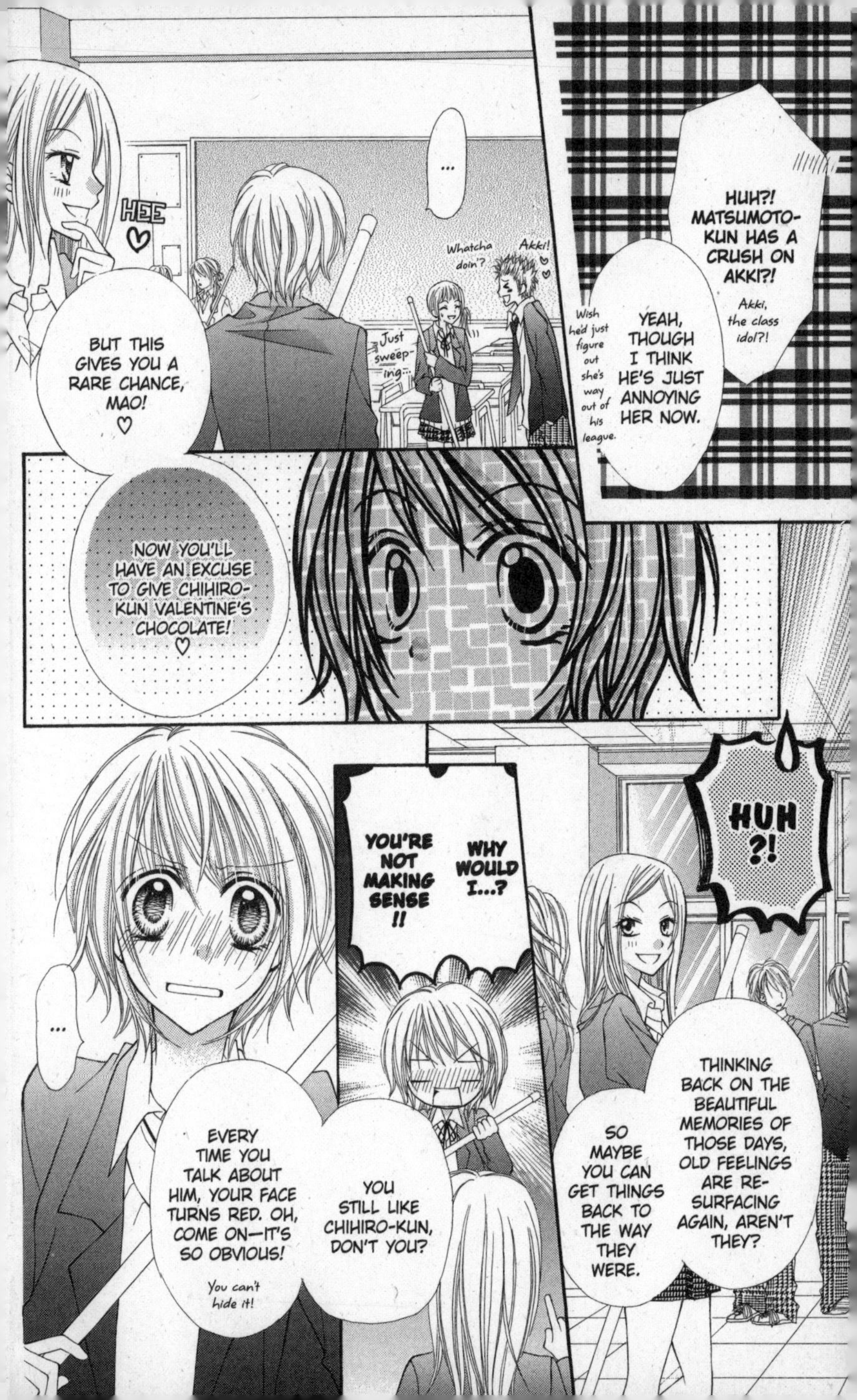
HUH?! MATSUMOTO-KUN HAS A CRUSH ON AKKI?!
Akki, the class idol?!
YEAH, THOUGH I THINK HE'S JUST ANNOYING HER NOW.
Wish he'd just figure out she's way out of his league.
...
Akki! ♡
Whatcha doin'?
Just sweeping...
HEE ♡
BUT THIS GIVES YOU A RARE CHANCE, MAO! ♡
NOW YOU'LL HAVE AN EXCUSE TO GIVE CHIHIRO-KUN VALENTINE'S CHOCOLATE! ♡
HUH ?!
THINKING BACK ON THE BEAUTIFUL MEMORIES OF THOSE DAYS, OLD FEELINGS ARE RE-SURFACING AGAIN, AREN'T THEY?
SO MAYBE YOU CAN GET THINGS BACK TO THE WAY THEY WERE.
WHY WOULD I...?
YOU'RE NOT MAKING SENSE !!
YOU STILL LIKE CHIHIRO-KUN, DON'T YOU?
EVERY TIME YOU TALK ABOUT HIM, YOUR FACE TURNS RED. OH, COME ON—IT'S SO OBVIOUS!
You can't hide it!
...

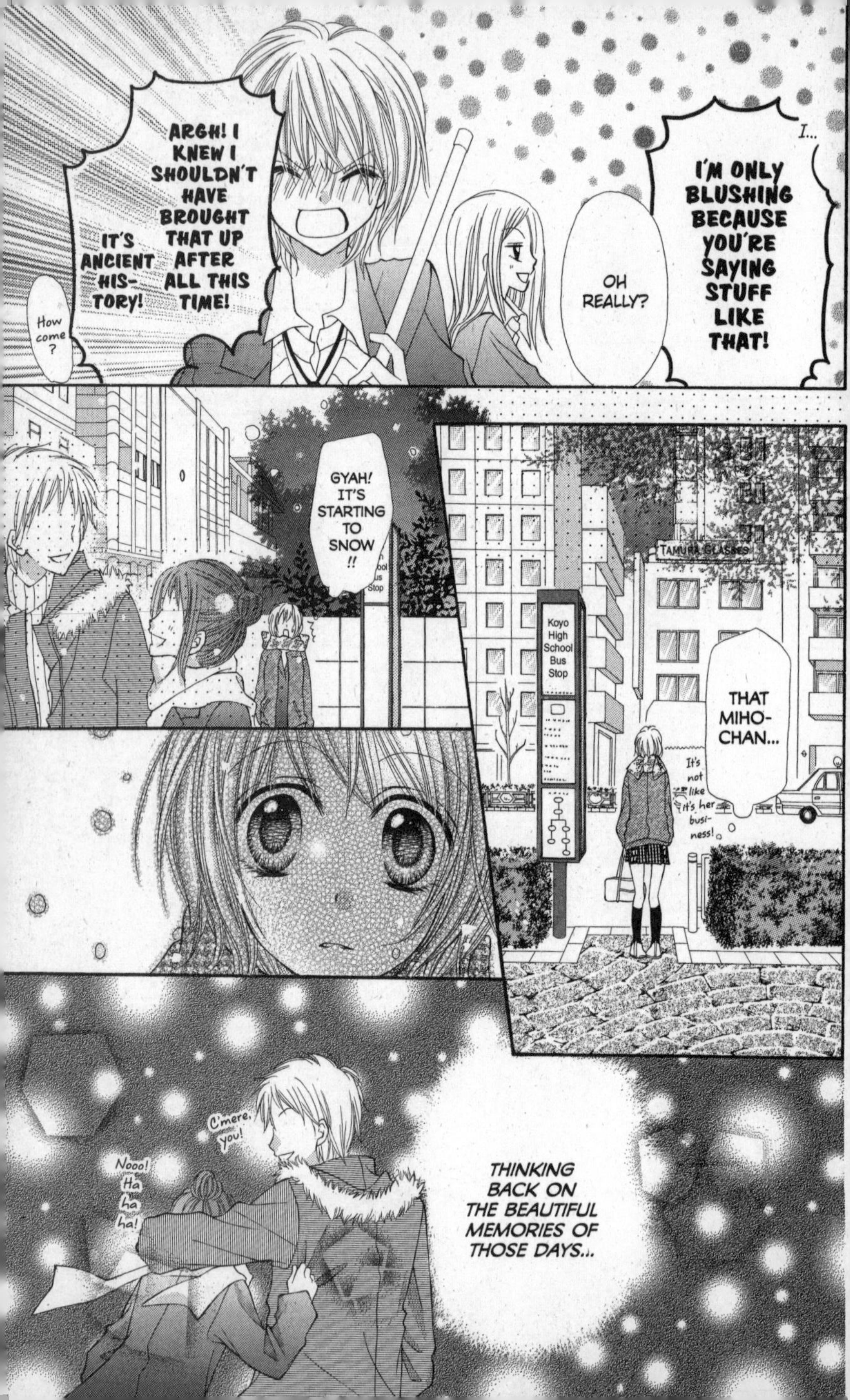
I...
I'M ONLY BLUSHING BECAUSE YOU'RE SAYING STUFF LIKE THAT!
OH REALLY?
ARGH! I KNEW I SHOULDN'T HAVE BROUGHT THAT UP AFTER ALL THIS TIME!
IT'S ANCIENT HIS-TORY!
How come?
TAMURA GLASSES
Koyo High School Bus Stop
THAT MIHO-CHAN...
It's not like it's her busi-ness!
GYAH! IT'S STARTING TO SNOW!!
C'mere, you!
Nooo! Ha ha ha!
THINKING BACK ON THE BEAUTIFUL MEMORIES OF THOSE DAYS...

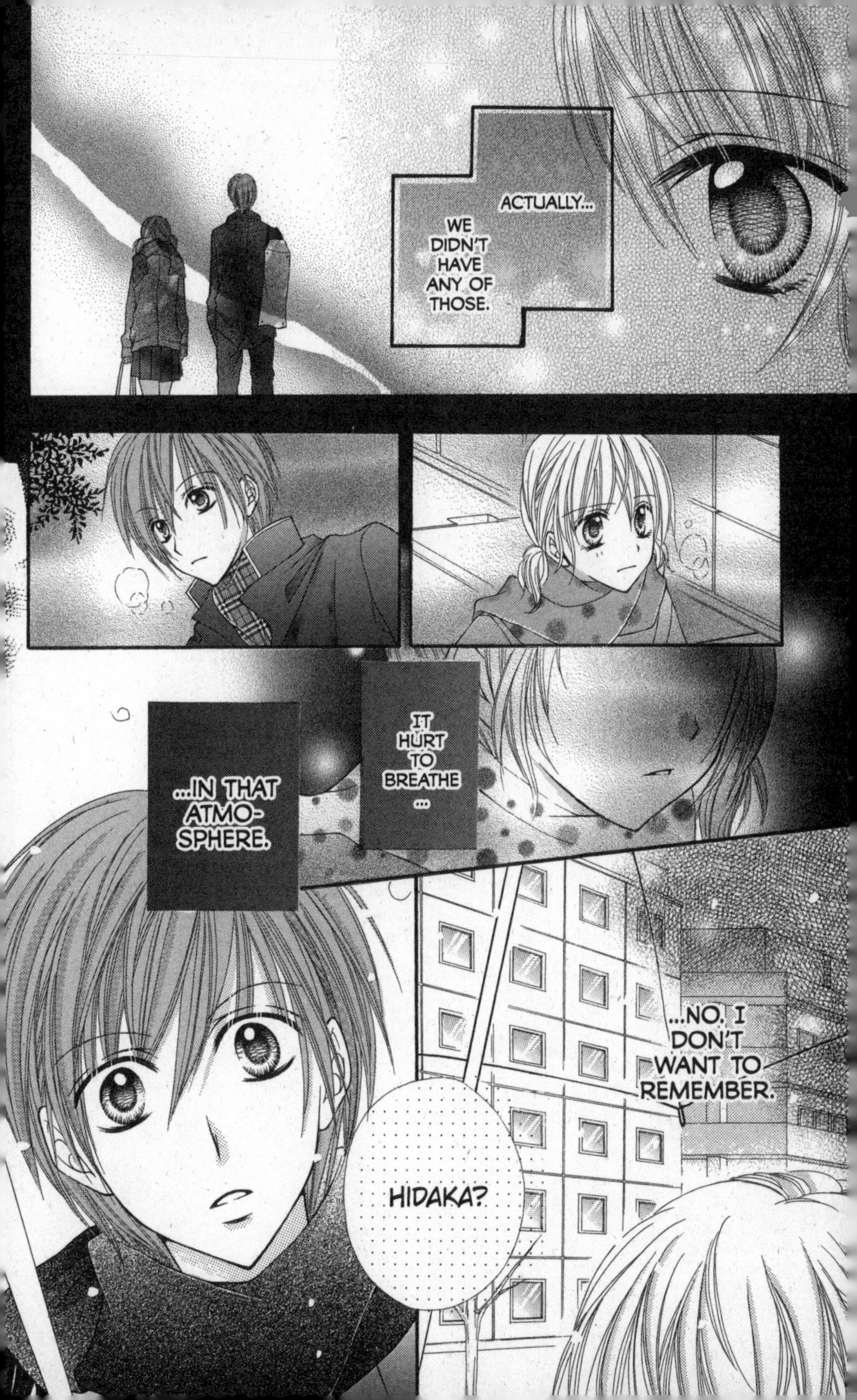
ACTUALLY...
WE DIDN'T HAVE ANY OF THOSE.
IT HURT TO BREATHE ...
...IN THAT ATMO-SPHERE.
...NO. I DON'T WANT TO REMEMBER.
HIDAKA?

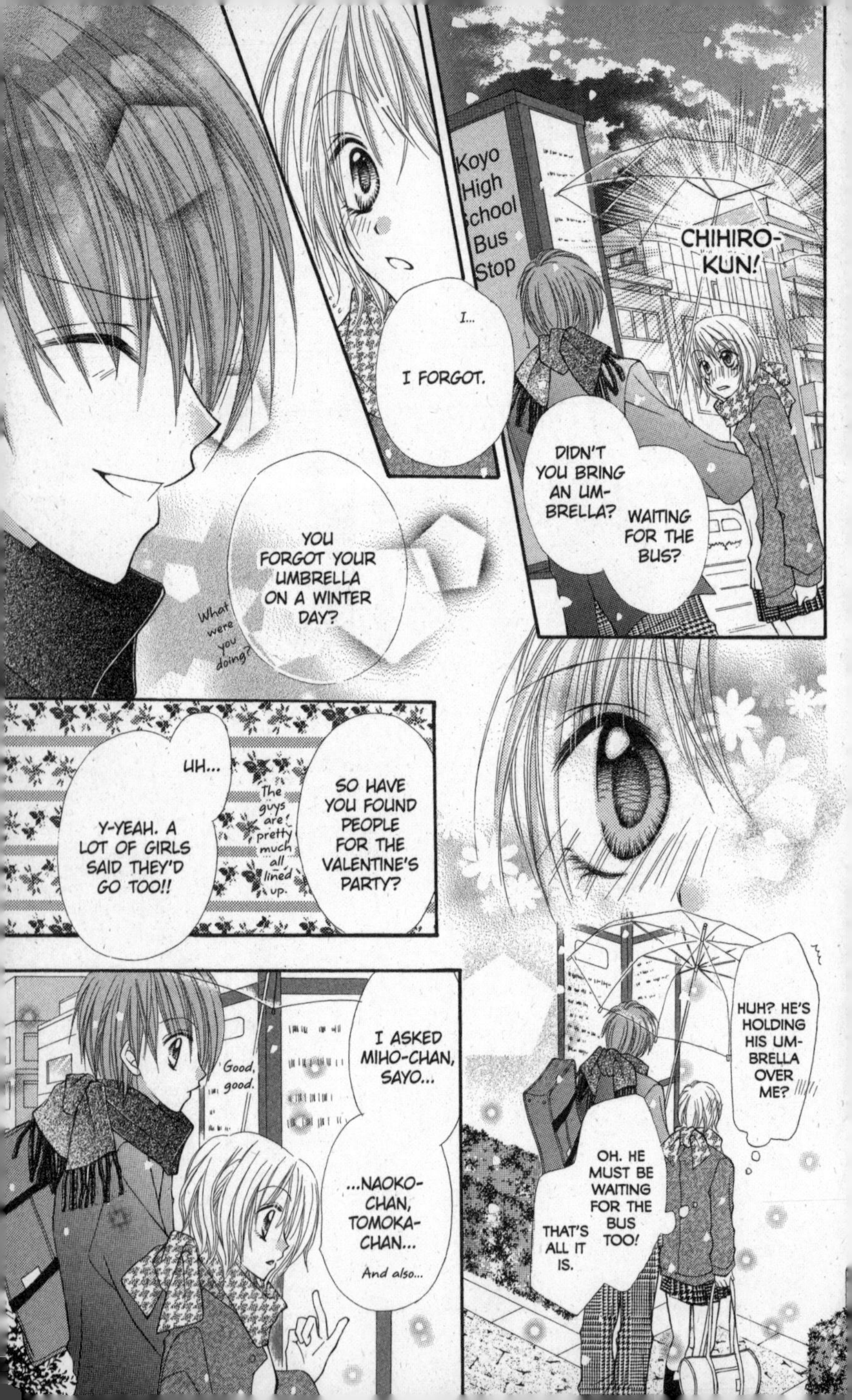
CHIHIRO-KUN!
Koyo High School Bus Stop
WAITING FOR THE BUS?
DIDN'T YOU BRING AN UM-BRELLA?
I...
I FORGOT.
YOU FORGOT YOUR UMBRELLA ON A WINTER DAY?
What were you doing?
SO HAVE YOU FOUND PEOPLE FOR THE VALENTINE'S PARTY?
The guys are pretty much all lined up.
UH...
Y-YEAH. A LOT OF GIRLS SAID THEY'D GO TOO!!
HUH? HE'S HOLDING HIS UM-BRELLA OVER ME?
OH. HE MUST BE WAITING FOR THE BUS TOO!
THAT'S ALL IT IS.
I ASKED MIHO-CHAN, SAYO...
...NAOKO-CHAN, TOMOKA-CHAN...
And also...
Good, good.

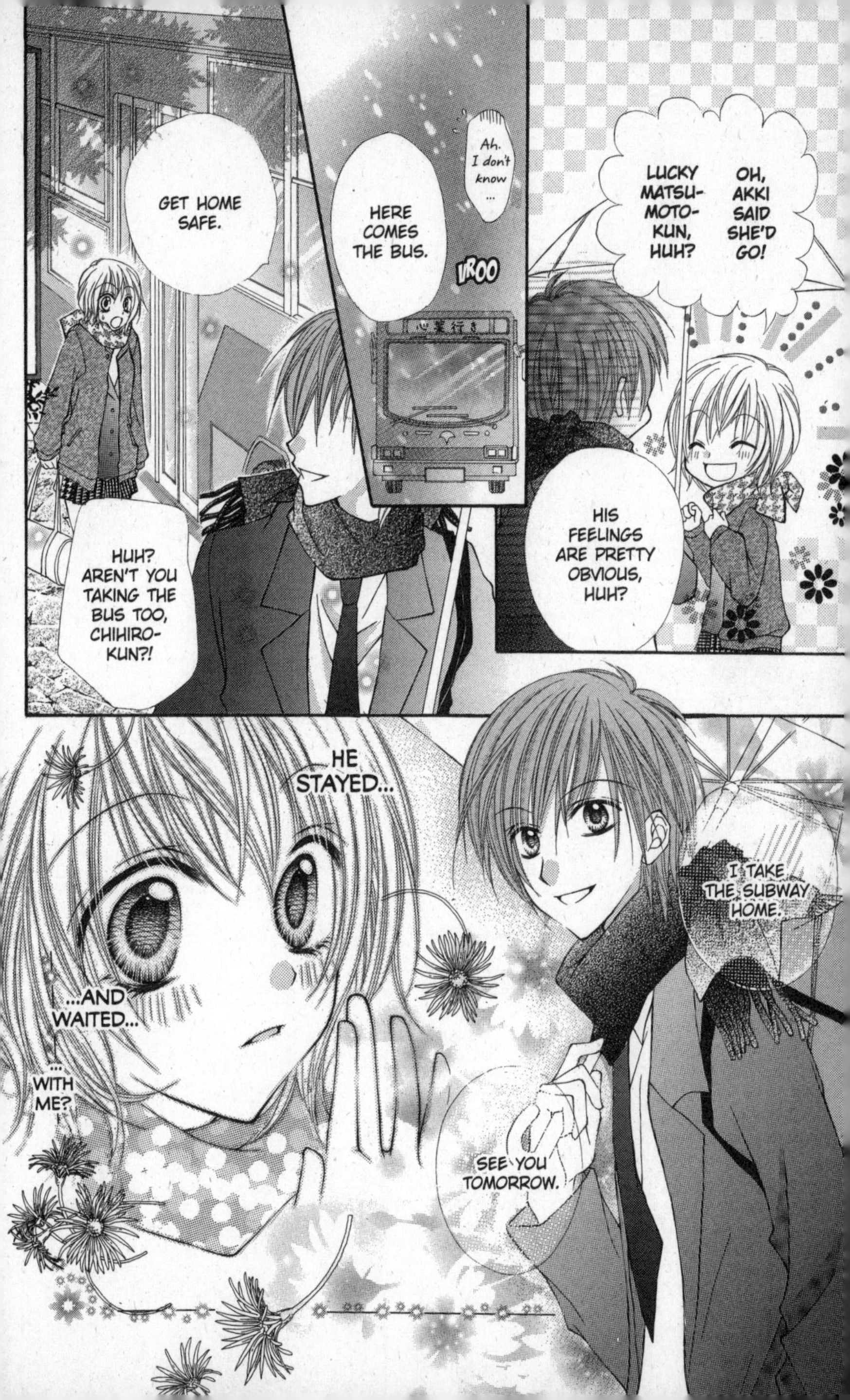
OH, AKKI SAID SHE'D GO!
LUCKY MATSU-MOTO-KUN, HUH?
HIS FEELINGS ARE PRETTY OBVIOUS, HUH?
Ah. I don't know ...
HERE COMES THE BUS.
VROO
GET HOME SAFE.
HUH? AREN'T YOU TAKING THE BUS TOO, CHIHIRO-KUN?!
I TAKE THE SUBWAY HOME.
SEE YOU TOMORROW.
HE STAYED...
...AND WAITED...
... WITH ME?

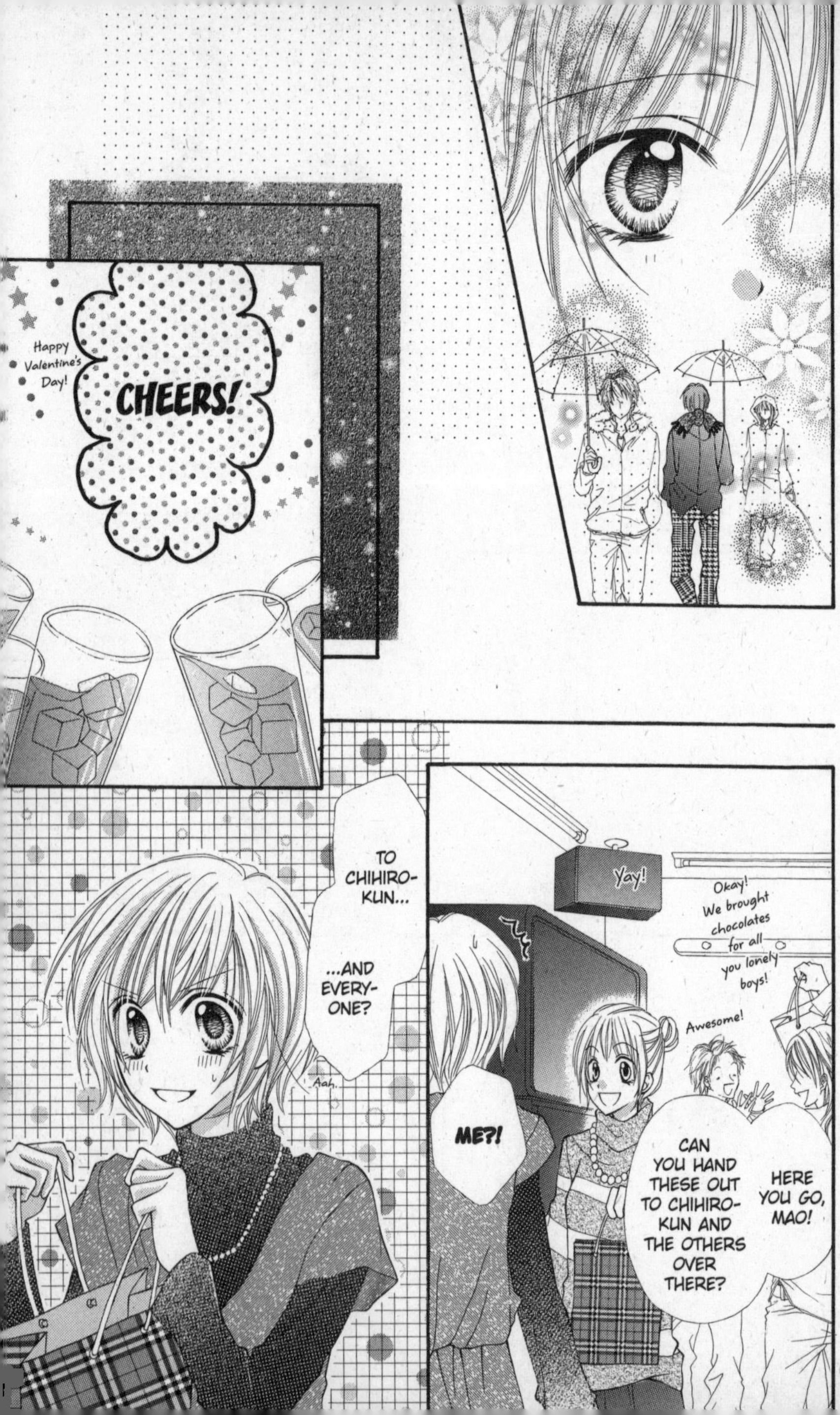

Happy Valentine's Day!
CHEERS!
Yay!
Okay! We brought chocolates for all you lonely boys!
Awesome!
HERE YOU GO, MAO!
CAN YOU HAND THESE OUT TO CHIHIRO-KUN AND THE OTHERS OVER THERE?
ME?!
TO CHIHIRO-KUN...
...AND EVERY-ONE?
Aah.

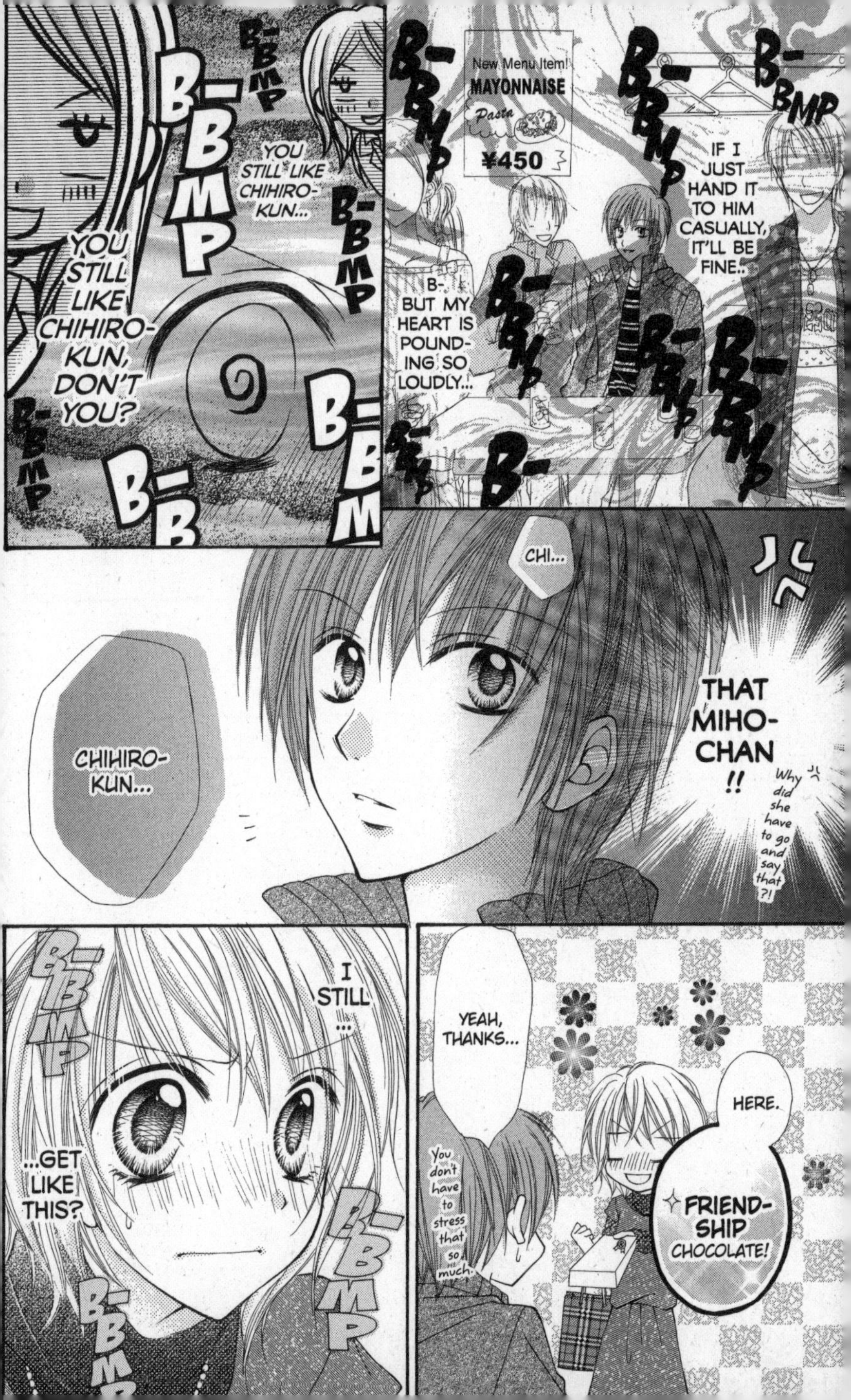
B-BMP
New Menu Item!
MAYONNAISE
Pasta
¥450
IF I JUST HAND IT TO HIM CASUALLY, IT'LL BE FINE..
B-BUT MY HEART IS POUNDING SO LOUDLY...
B-
B-BMP
YOU STILL LIKE CHIHIRO-KUN...
B-BMP
YOU STILL LIKE CHIHIRO-KUN, DON'T YOU?
B-BMP
B-BMP
B-B
B-BM
CHI...
THAT MIHO-CHAN!!
Why did she have to go and say that?!
CHIHIRO-KUN...
HERE.
FRIENDSHIP CHOCOLATE!
YEAH, THANKS...
You don't have to stress that so much.
I STILL ...
...GET LIKE THIS?
B-BMP
B-BMP
B-BMP

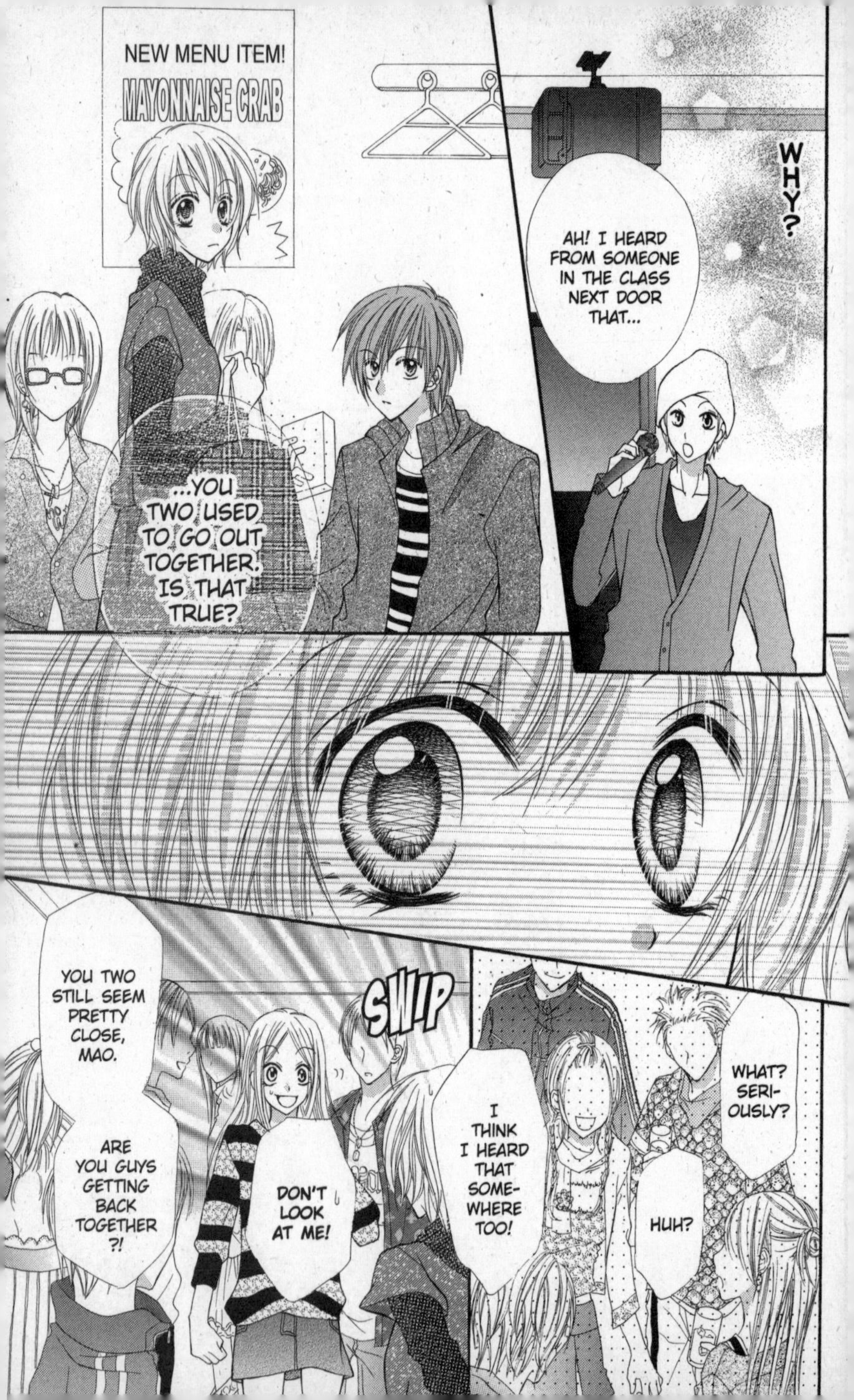
WHY?
AH! I HEARD FROM SOMEONE IN THE CLASS NEXT DOOR THAT...
NEW MENU ITEM!
MAYONNAISE CRAB
...YOU TWO USED TO GO OUT TOGETHER. IS THAT TRUE?
WHAT? SERI-OUSLY?
HUH?
I THINK I HEARD THAT SOME-WHERE TOO!
SWIP
DON'T LOOK AT ME!
YOU TWO STILL SEEM PRETTY CLOSE, MAO.
ARE YOU GUYS GETTING BACK TOGETHER?!

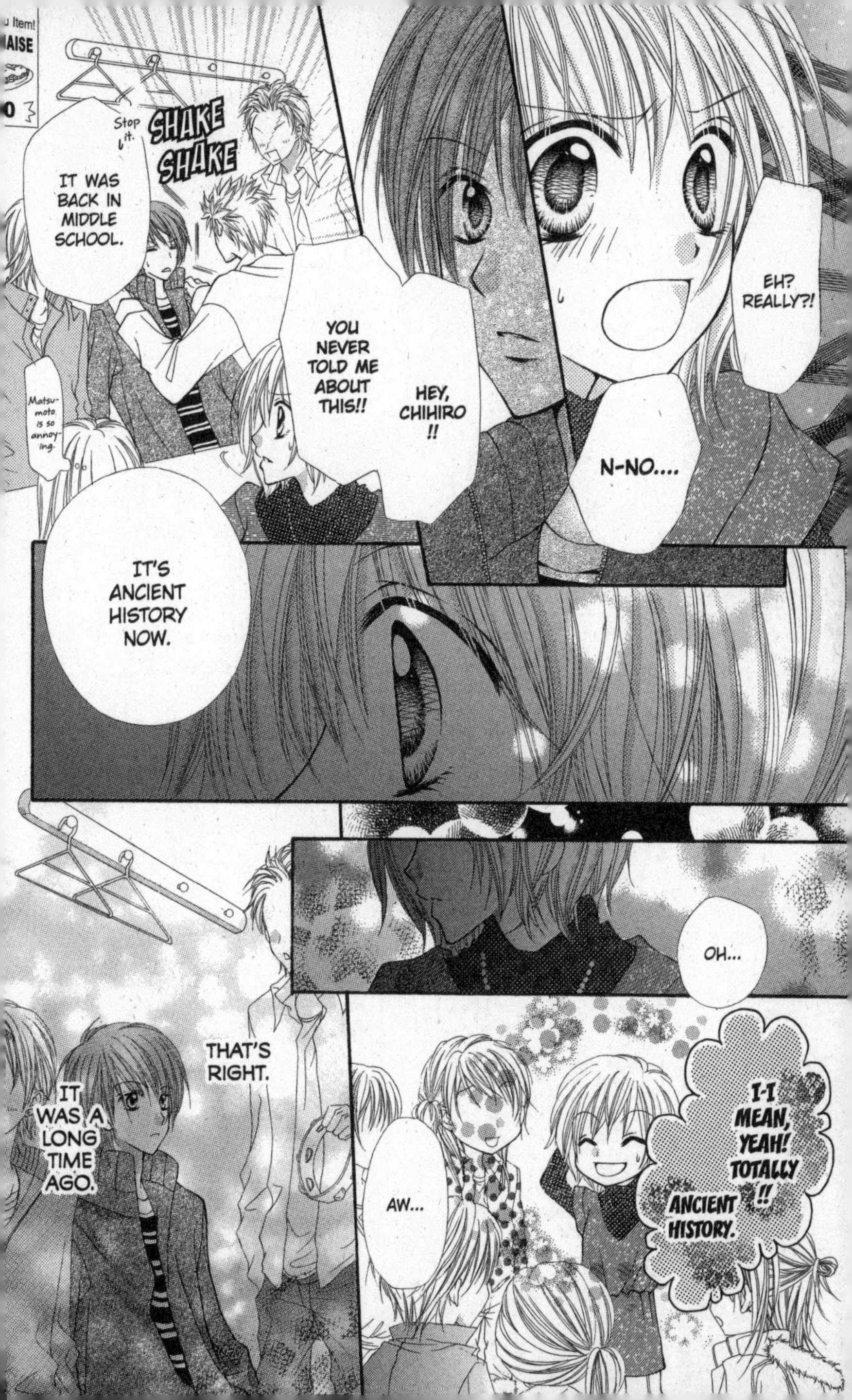
EH? REALLY?!
N-NO....
HEY, CHIHIRO!!
YOU NEVER TOLD ME ABOUT THIS!!
IT WAS BACK IN MIDDLE SCHOOL.
SHAKE SHAKE
Stop it.
Matsu-moto is so annoy-ing.
IT'S ANCIENT HISTORY NOW.
OH...
I-I MEAN, YEAH! TOTALLY!!
ANCIENT HISTORY.
AW...
THAT'S RIGHT.
IT WAS A LONG TIME AGO.

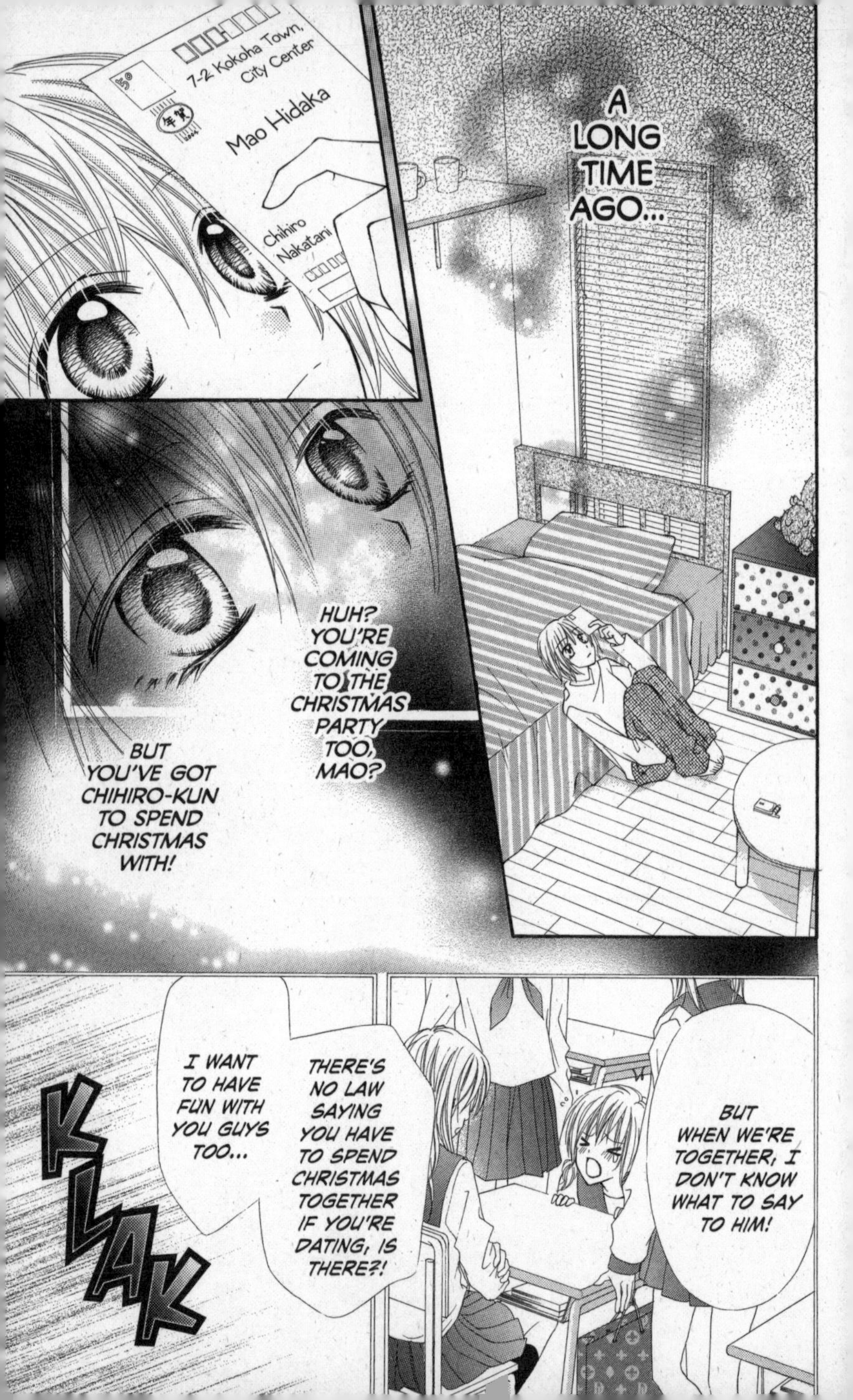
A LONG TIME AGO...
7-2 Kokoha Town, City Center
Mao Hidaka
Chihiro Nakatani
HUH? YOU'RE COMING TO THE CHRISTMAS PARTY TOO, MAO?
BUT YOU'VE GOT CHIHIRO-KUN TO SPEND CHRISTMAS WITH!
BUT WHEN WE'RE TOGETHER, I DON'T KNOW WHAT TO SAY TO HIM!
THERE'S NO LAW SAYING YOU HAVE TO SPEND CHRISTMAS TOGETHER IF YOU'RE DATING, IS THERE?!
I WANT TO HAVE FUN WITH YOU GUYS TOO...
KLAK

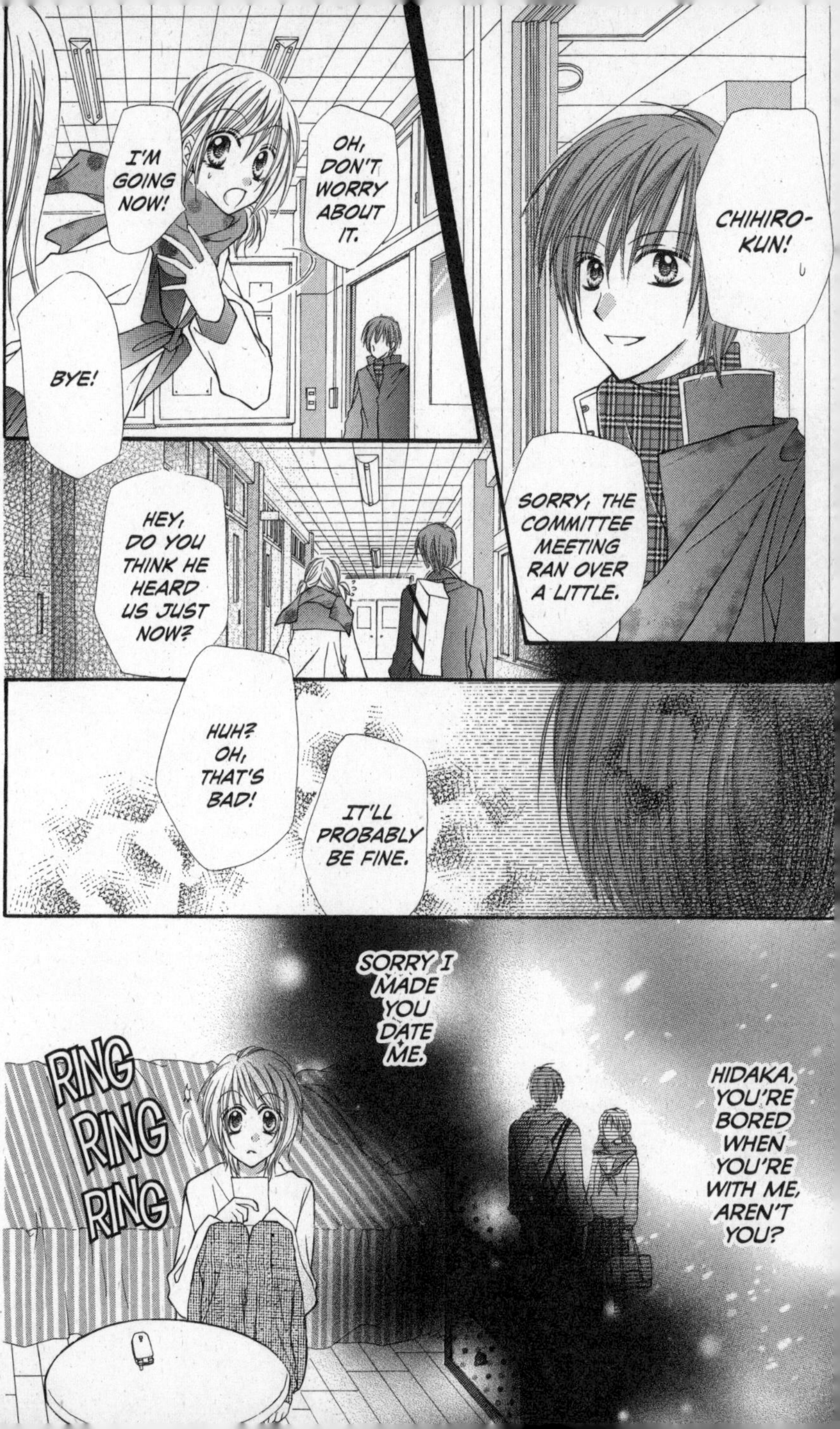
CHIHIRO-KUN!
SORRY, THE COMMITTEE MEETING RAN OVER A LITTLE.
OH, DON'T WORRY ABOUT IT.
I'M GOING NOW!
BYE!
HEY, DO YOU THINK HE HEARD US JUST NOW?
HUH? OH, THAT'S BAD!
IT'LL PROBABLY BE FINE.
HIDAKA, YOU'RE BORED WHEN YOU'RE WITH ME, AREN'T YOU?
SORRY I MADE YOU DATE ME.
RING RING RING

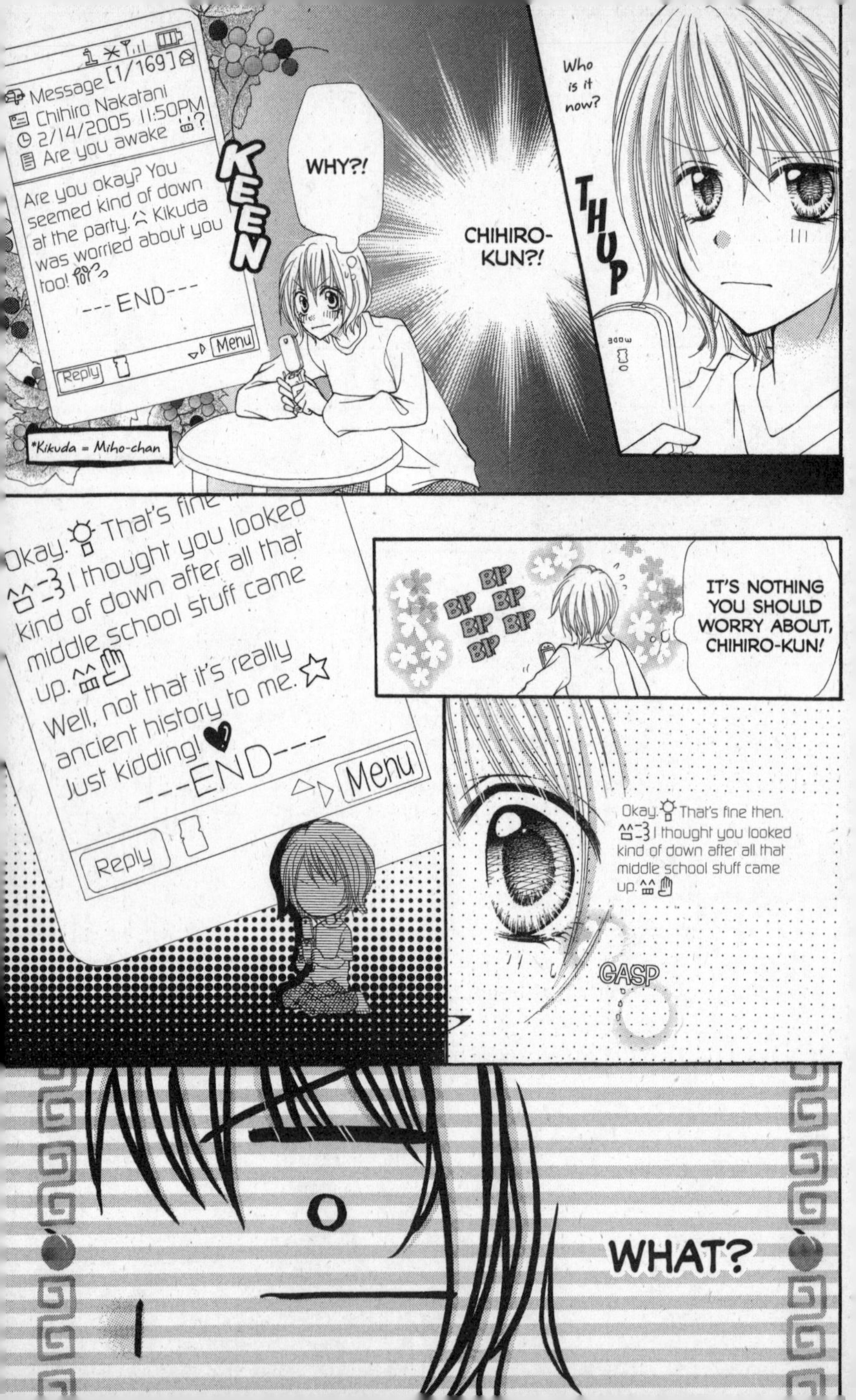

Who is it now?
THUP
CHIHIRO-KUN?!
WHY?!
KEEN
Message [1/169]
Chihiro Nakatani
2/14/2005 11:50PM
Are you awake
Are you okay? You seemed kind of down at the party. Kikuda was worried about you too!
---END---
Menu
Reply
*Kikuda = Miho-chan
IT'S NOTHING YOU SHOULD WORRY ABOUT, CHIHIRO-KUN!
BIP BIP BIP BIP BIP BIP BIP
Okay. That's fine then. I thought you looked kind of down after all that middle school stuff came up.
GASP
Okay. That's fine then. I thought you looked kind of down after all that middle school stuff came up. Well, not that it's really ancient history to me. Just kidding!
---END---
Menu
Reply
WHAT?

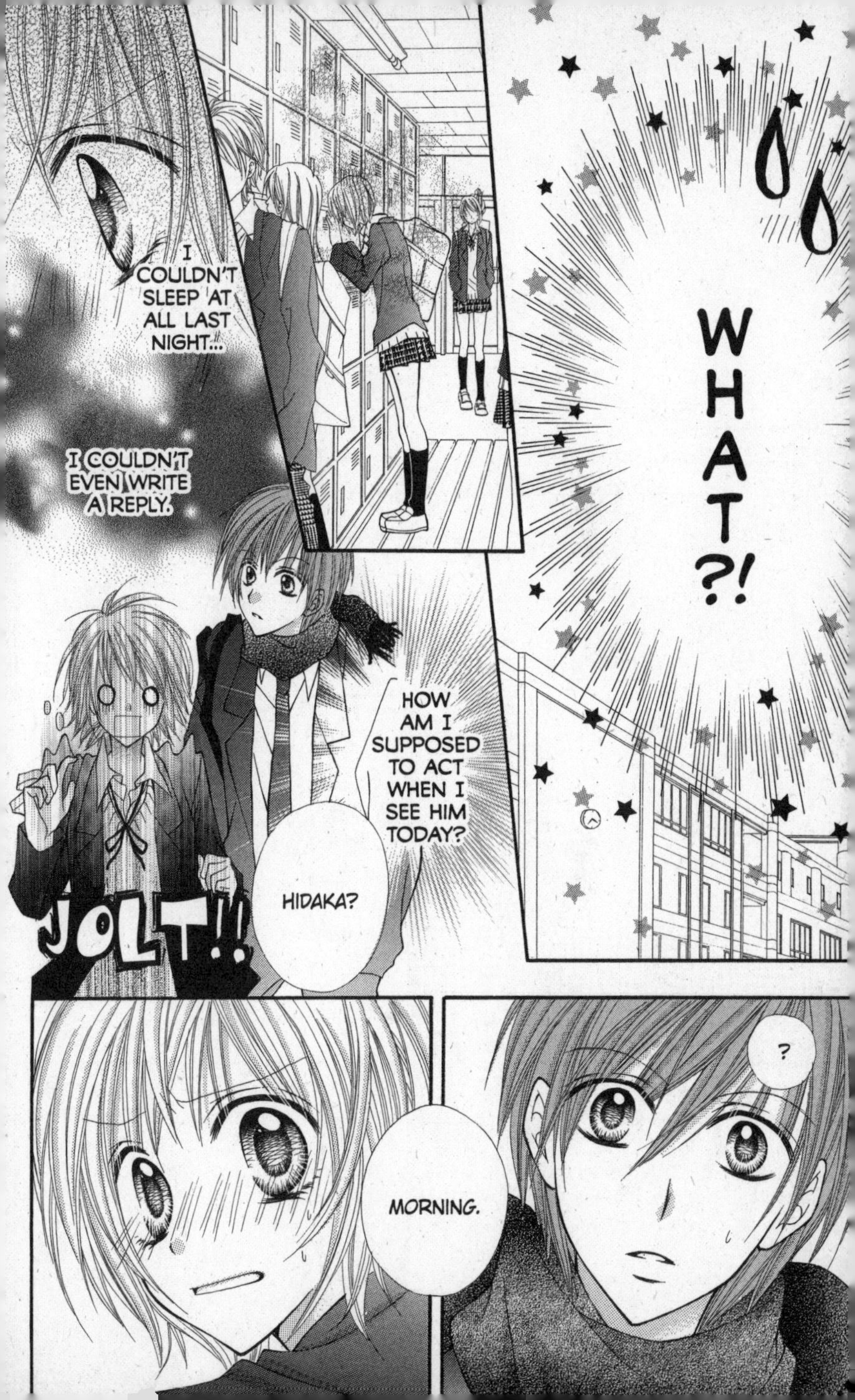
WHAT?!
I COULDN'T SLEEP AT ALL LAST NIGHT...
I COULDN'T EVEN WRITE A REPLY.
HOW AM I SUPPOSED TO ACT WHEN I SEE HIM TODAY?
HIDAKA?
JOLT!!
?
MORNING.

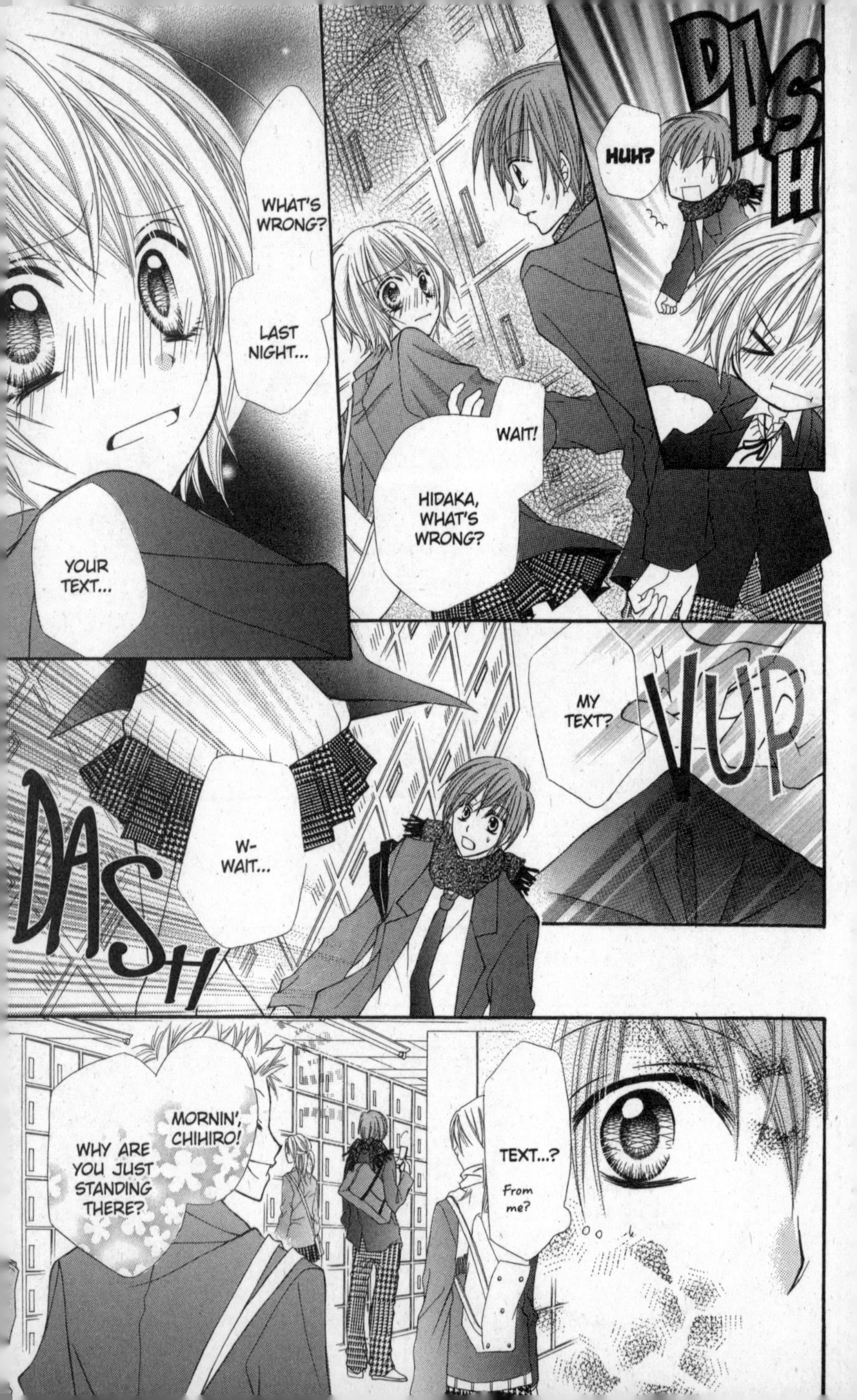
DASH
HUH?
WAIT!
HIDAKA, WHAT'S WRONG?
WHAT'S WRONG?
LAST NIGHT...
YOUR TEXT...
VUP
MY TEXT?
W-WAIT...
DASH
TEXT...?
From me?
MORNIN', CHIHIRO!
WHY ARE YOU JUST STANDING THERE?

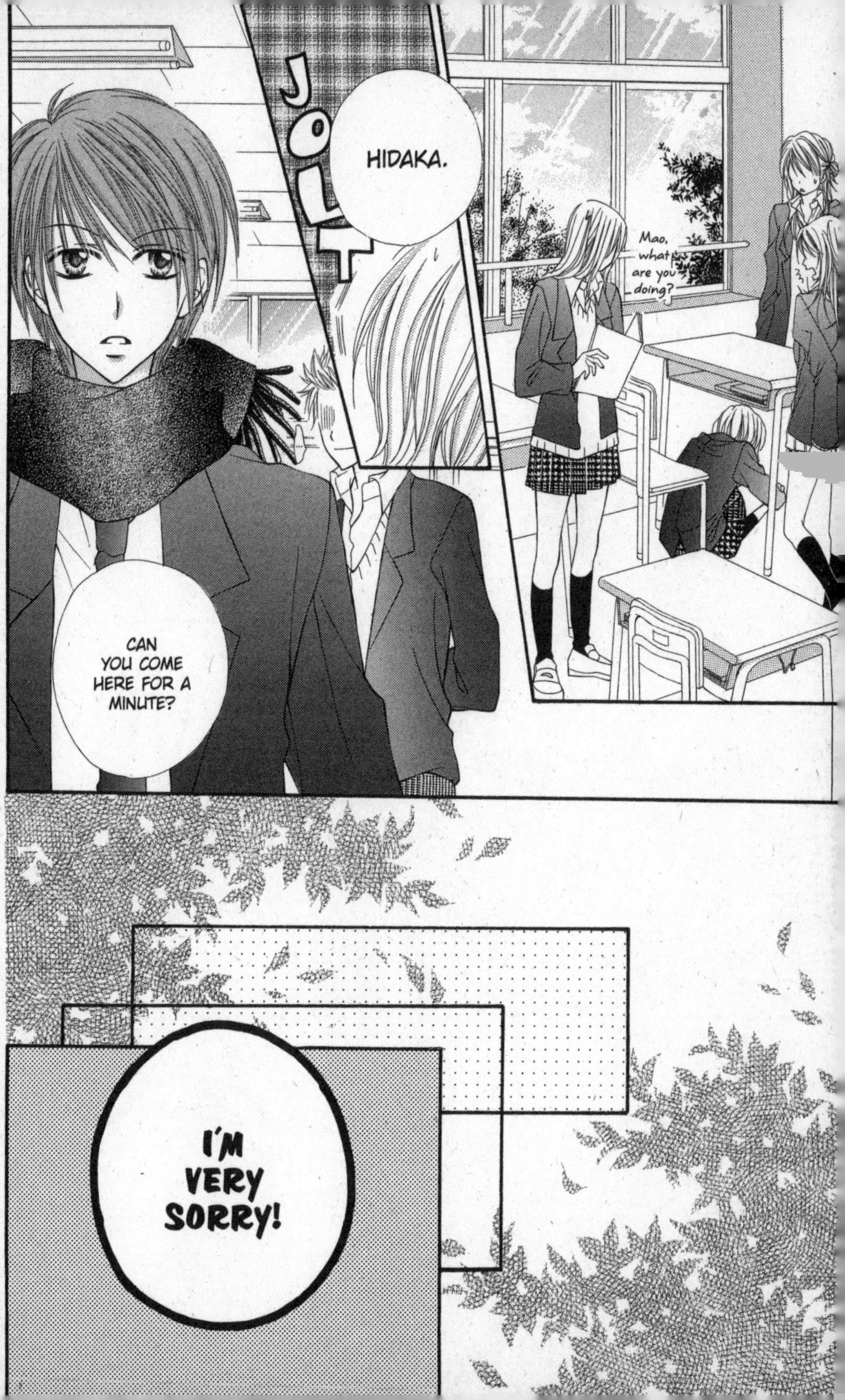
Mao, what are you doing?
JOLT
HIDAKA.
CAN YOU COME HERE FOR A MINUTE?
I'M VERY SORRY!

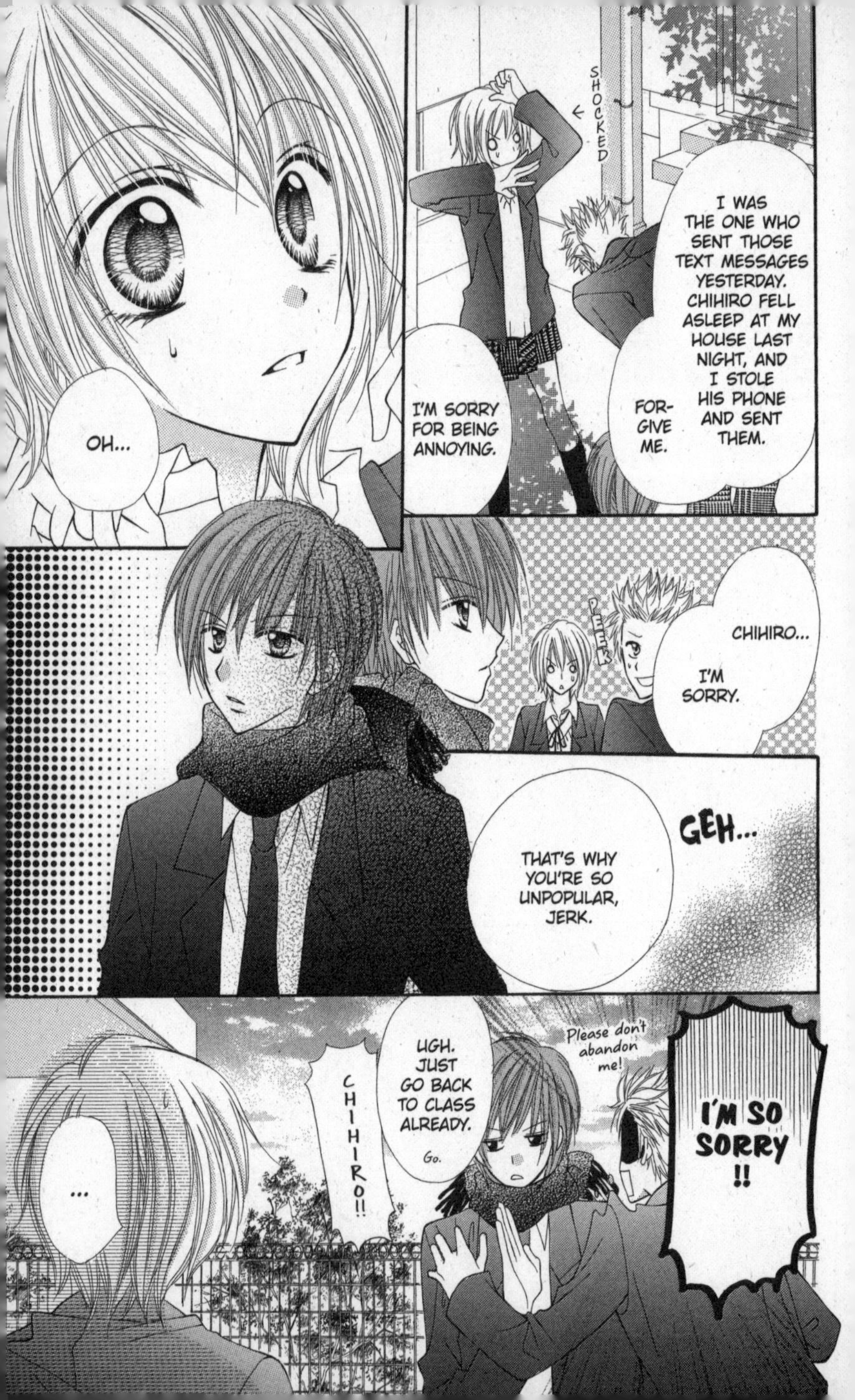
SHOCKED
I WAS THE ONE WHO SENT THOSE TEXT MESSAGES YESTERDAY. CHIHIRO FELL ASLEEP AT MY HOUSE LAST NIGHT, AND I STOLE HIS PHONE AND SENT THEM.
FOR-GIVE ME.
I'M SORRY FOR BEING ANNOYING.
OH...
PEEK
CHIHIRO...
I'M SORRY.
GEH...
THAT'S WHY YOU'RE SO UNPOPULAR, JERK.
I'M SO SORRY!!
Please don't abandon me!
UGH. JUST GO BACK TO CLASS ALREADY.
Go.
CHIHIRO!!
...

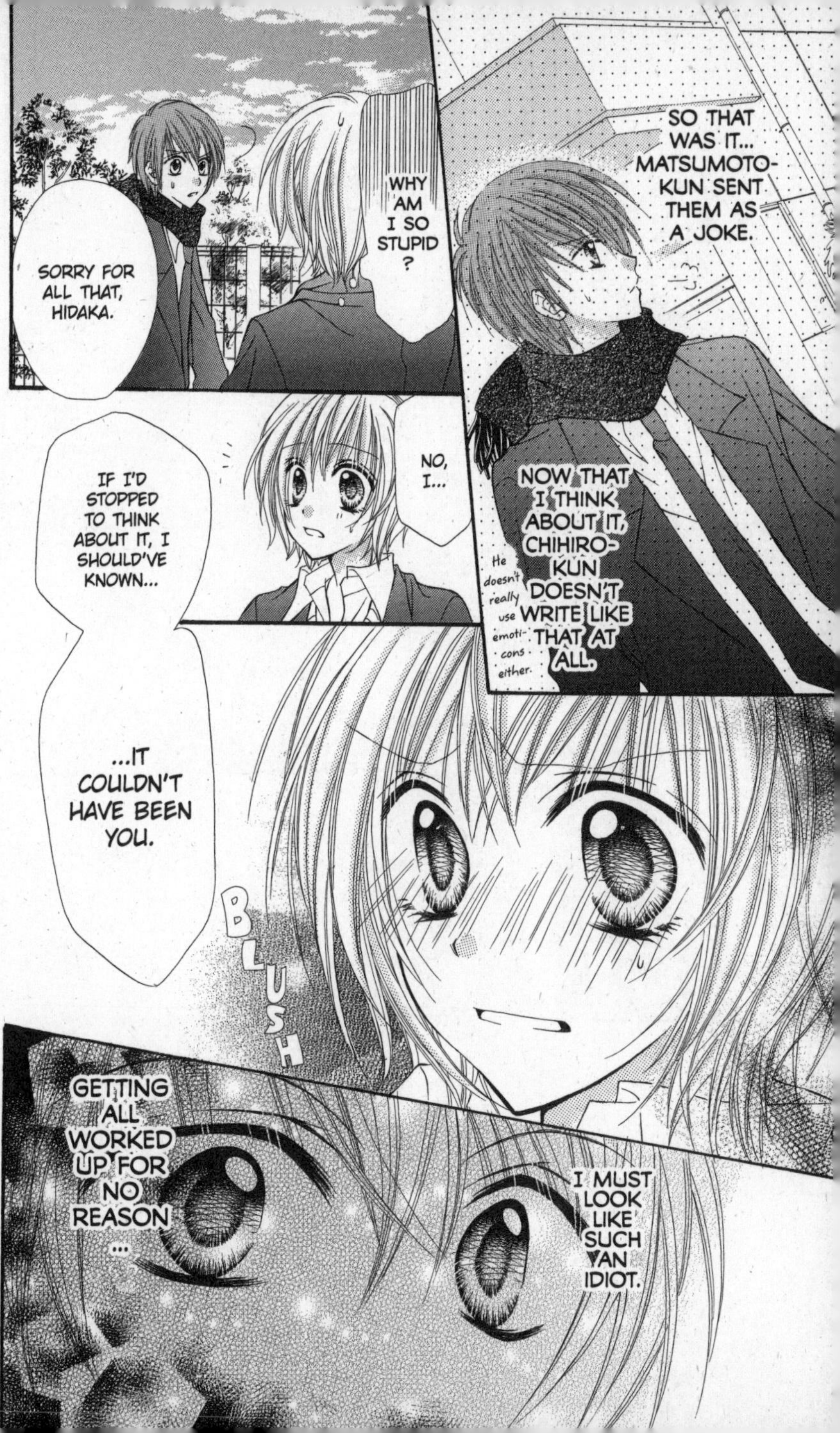
SO THAT WAS IT... MATSUMOTO-KUN SENT THEM AS A JOKE.
NOW THAT I THINK ABOUT IT, CHIHIRO-KUN DOESN'T WRITE LIKE THAT AT ALL.
He doesn't really use emoticons either.
WHY AM I SO STUPID?
SORRY FOR ALL THAT, HIDAKA.
NO, I...
IF I'D STOPPED TO THINK ABOUT IT, I SHOULD'VE KNOWN...
...IT COULDN'T HAVE BEEN YOU.
BLUSH
I MUST LOOK LIKE SUCH AN IDIOT.
GETTING ALL WORKED UP FOR NO REASON...

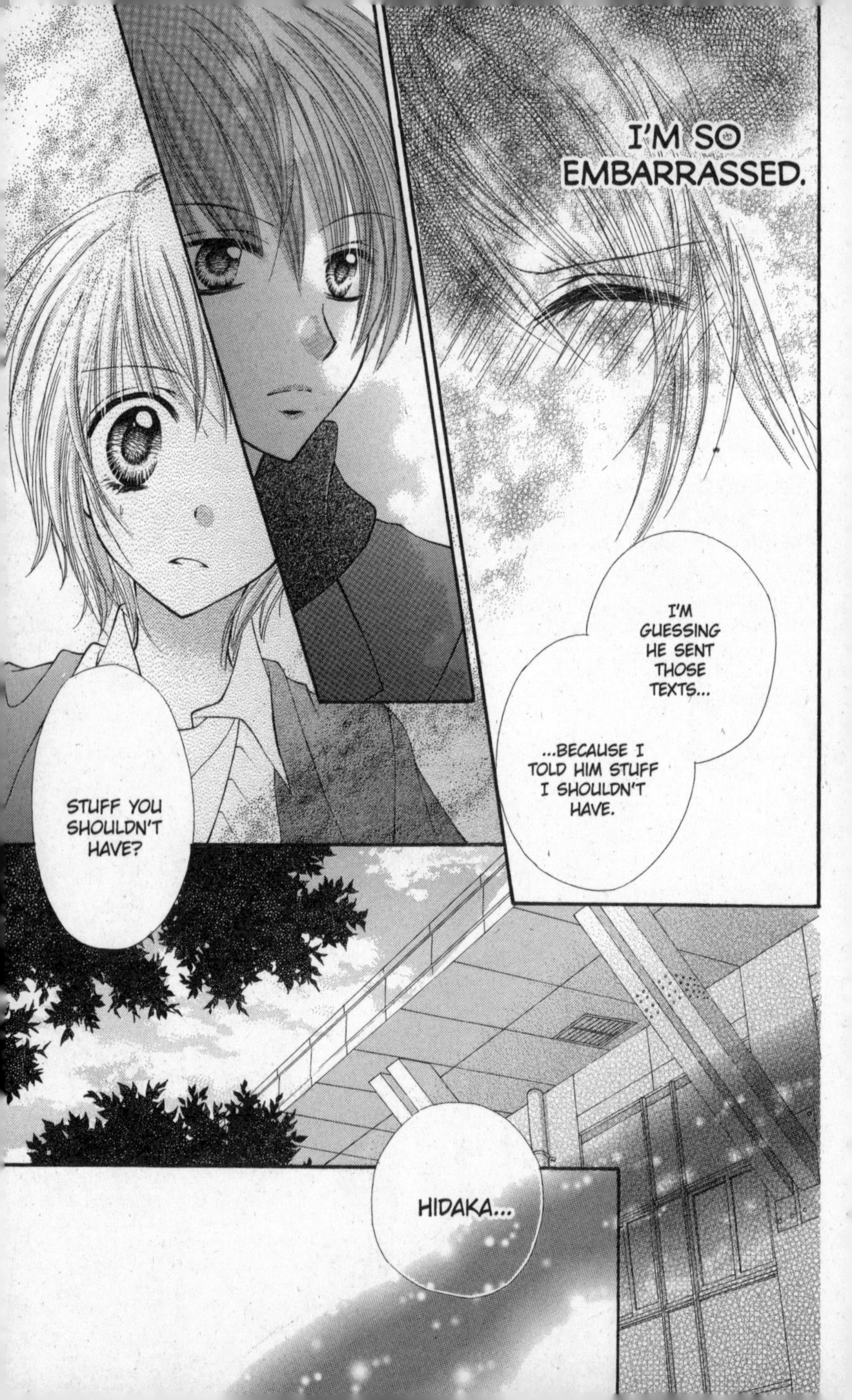
I'M SO EMBARRASSED.
I'M GUESSING HE SENT THOSE TEXTS...
...BECAUSE I TOLD HIM STUFF I SHOULDN'T HAVE.
STUFF YOU SHOULDN'T HAVE?
HIDAKA...

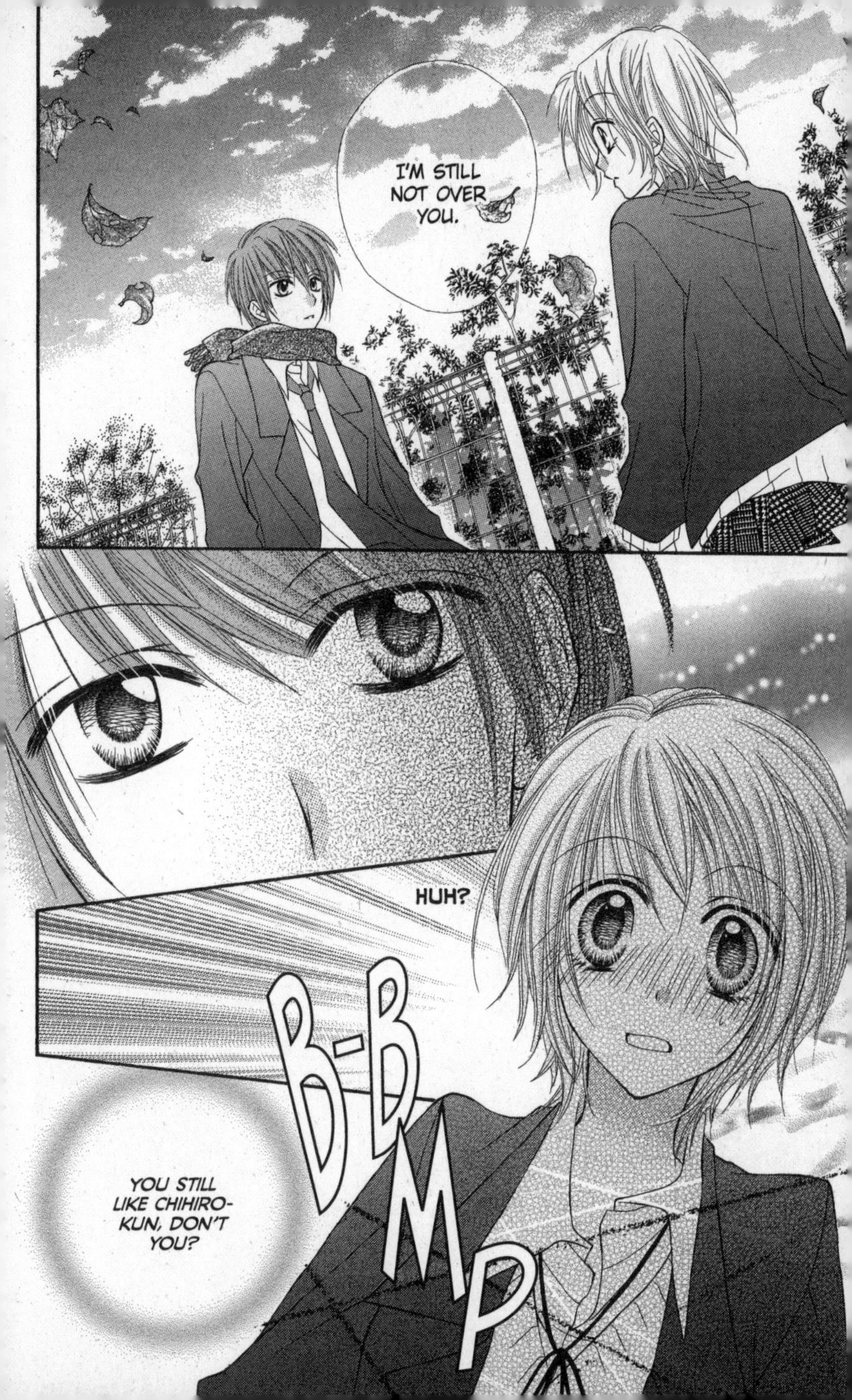
I'M STILL NOT OVER YOU.
HUH?
B-BMP
YOU STILL LIKE CHIHIRO-KUN, DON'T YOU?

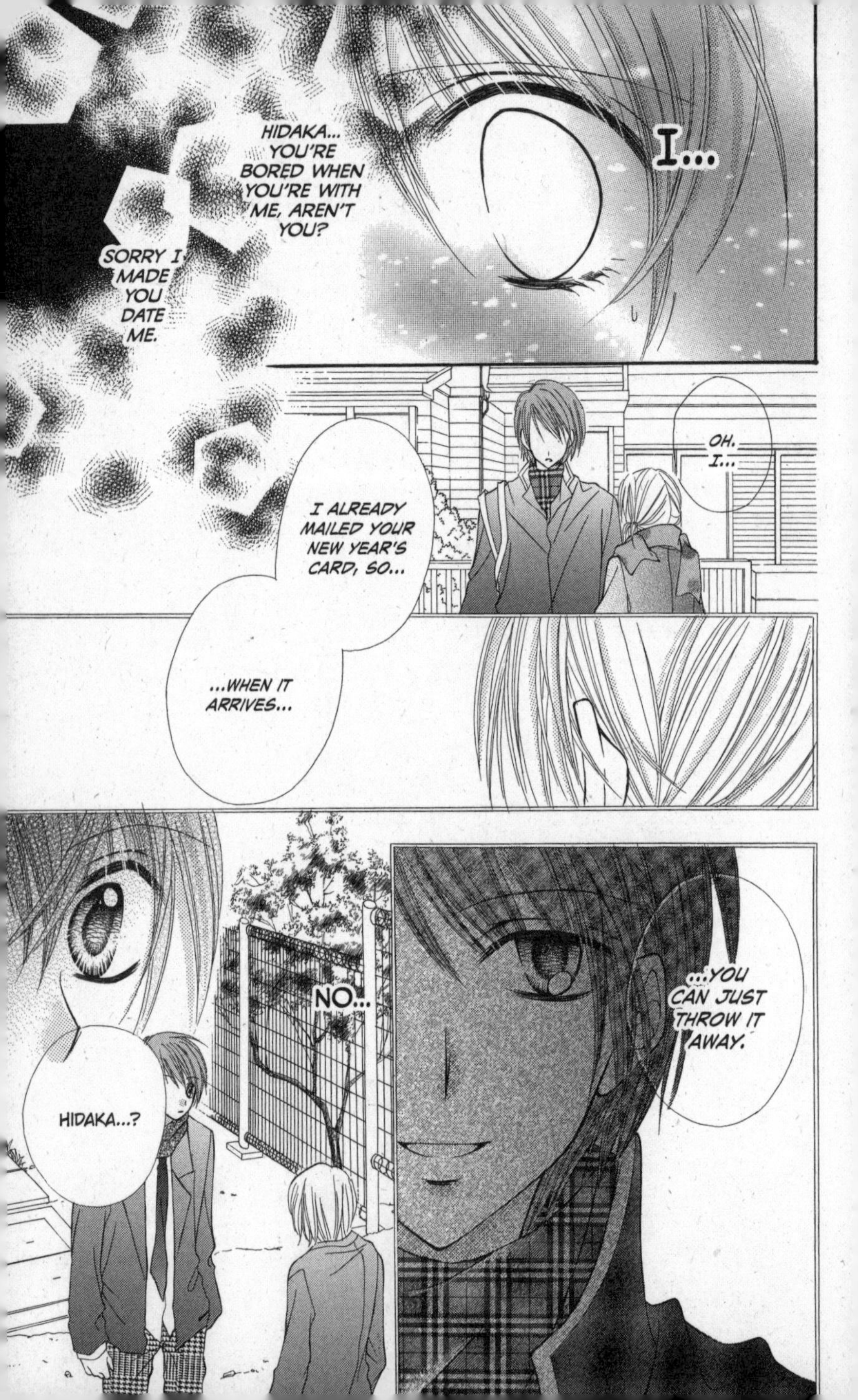
I...
HIDAKA... YOU'RE BORED WHEN YOU'RE WITH ME, AREN'T YOU?
SORRY I MADE YOU DATE ME.
OH. I...
I ALREADY MAILED YOUR NEW YEAR'S CARD, SO...
...WHEN IT ARRIVES...
...YOU CAN JUST THROW IT AWAY.
NO...
HIDAKA...?

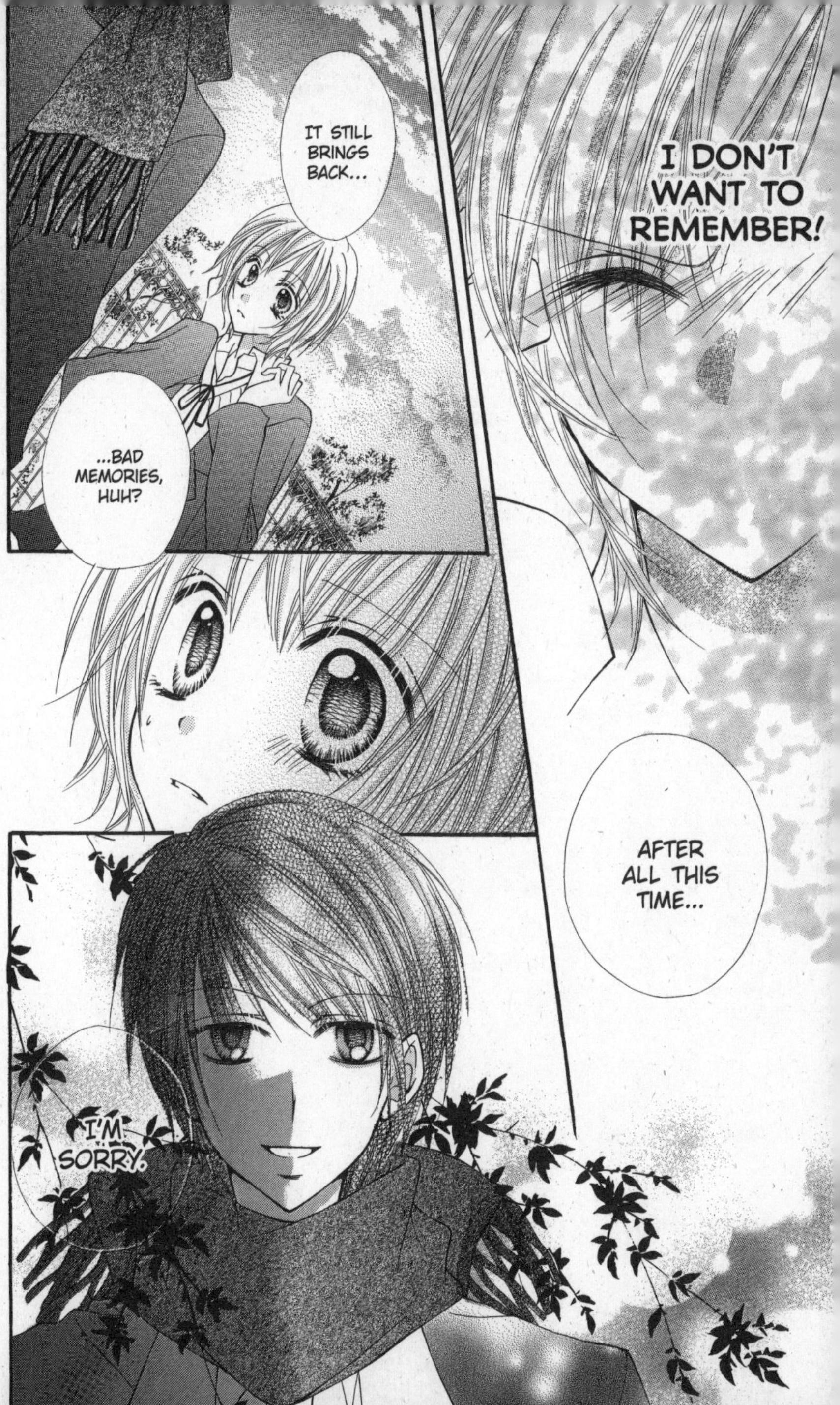
I DON'T WANT TO REMEMBER!
AFTER ALL THIS TIME...
IT STILL BRINGS BACK...
...BAD MEMORIES, HUH?
I'M SORRY.

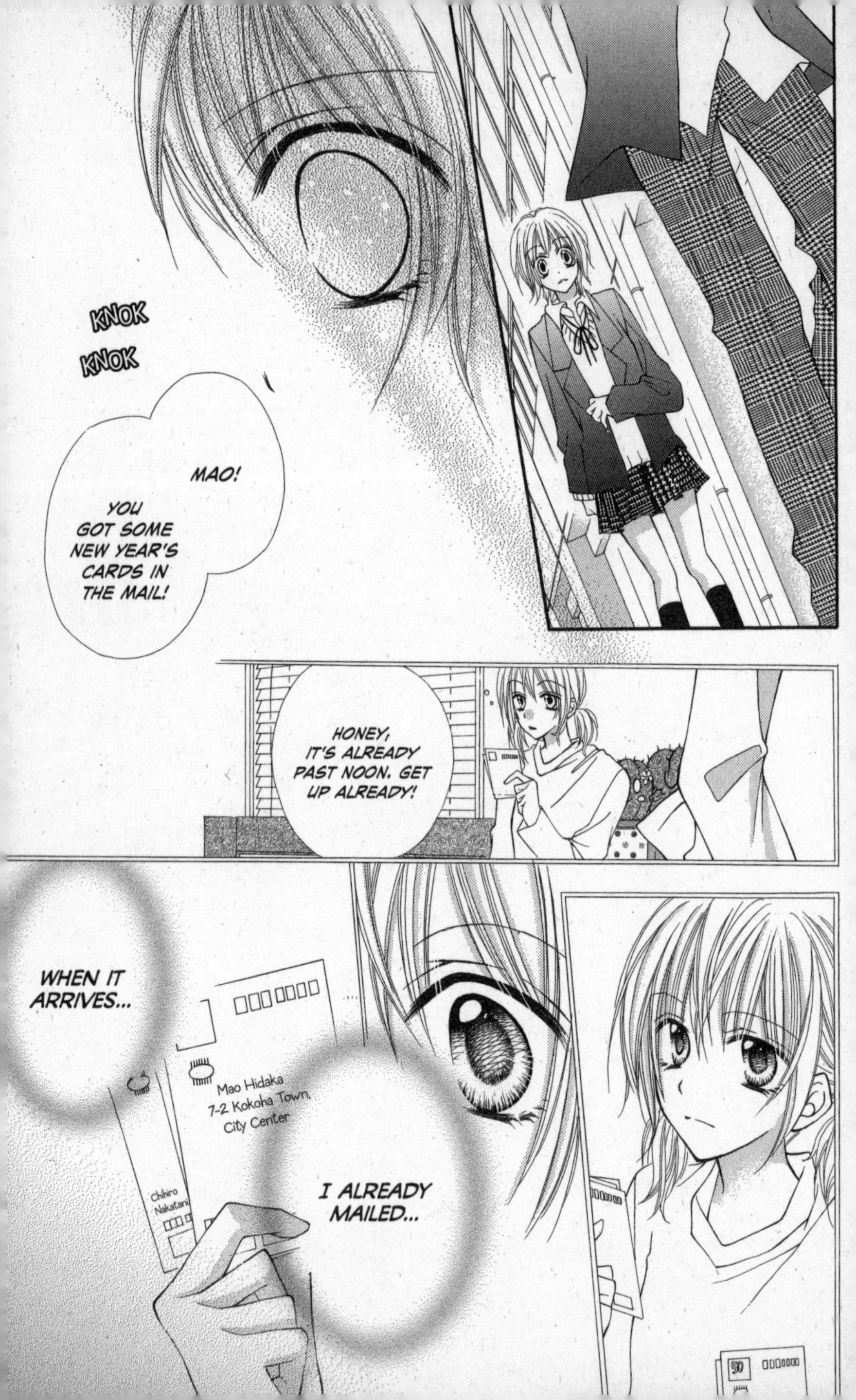
KNOK
KNOK
MAO!
YOU GOT SOME NEW YEAR'S CARDS IN THE MAIL!
HONEY, IT'S ALREADY PAST NOON. GET UP ALREADY!
...
WHEN IT ARRIVES...
Mao Hidaka
7-2 Kokoha Town,
City Center
Chihiro
Nakatani
I ALREADY MAILED...

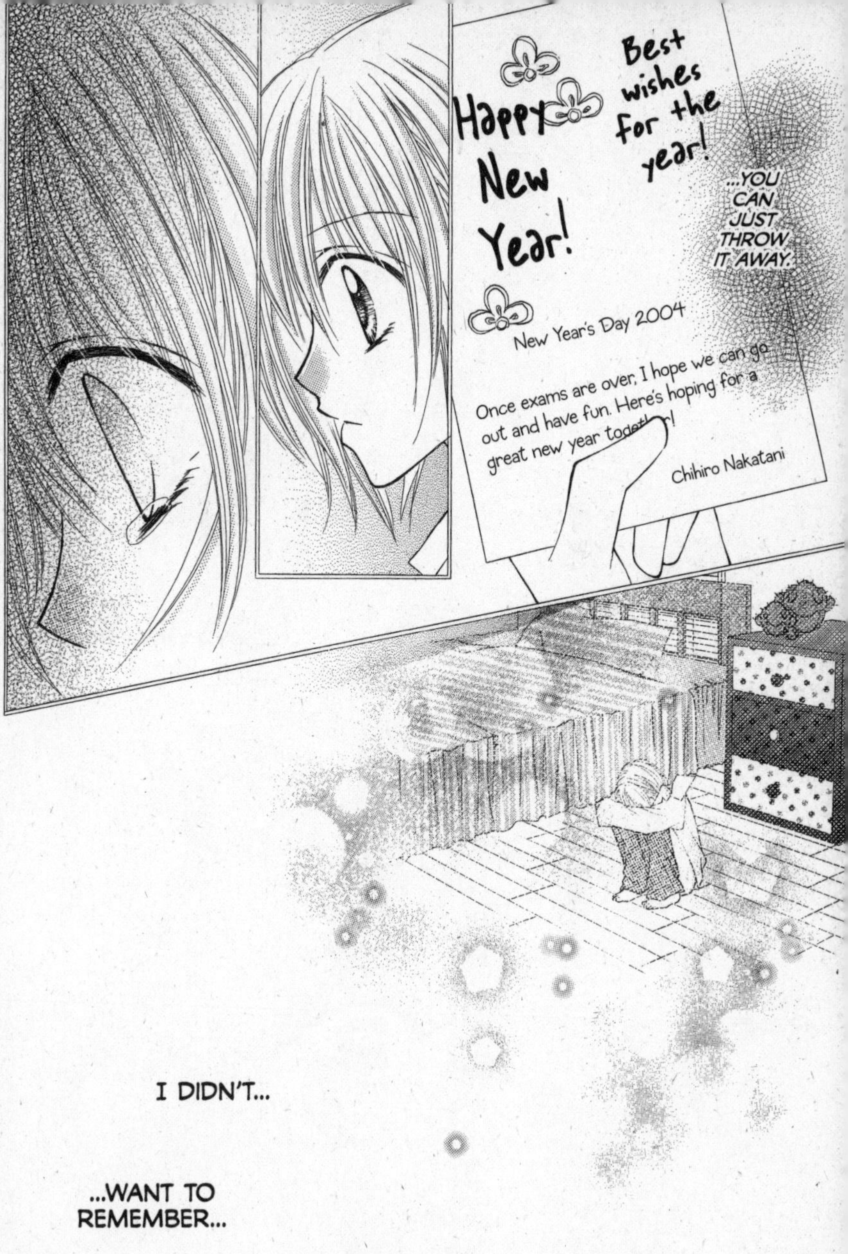
Happy New Year!
Best wishes for the year!
New Year's Day 2004
Once exams are over, I hope we can go out and have fun. Here's hoping for a great new year toget r!
Chihiro Nakatani
...YOU CAN JUST THROW IT AWAY.
I DIDN'T...
...WANT TO REMEMBER...

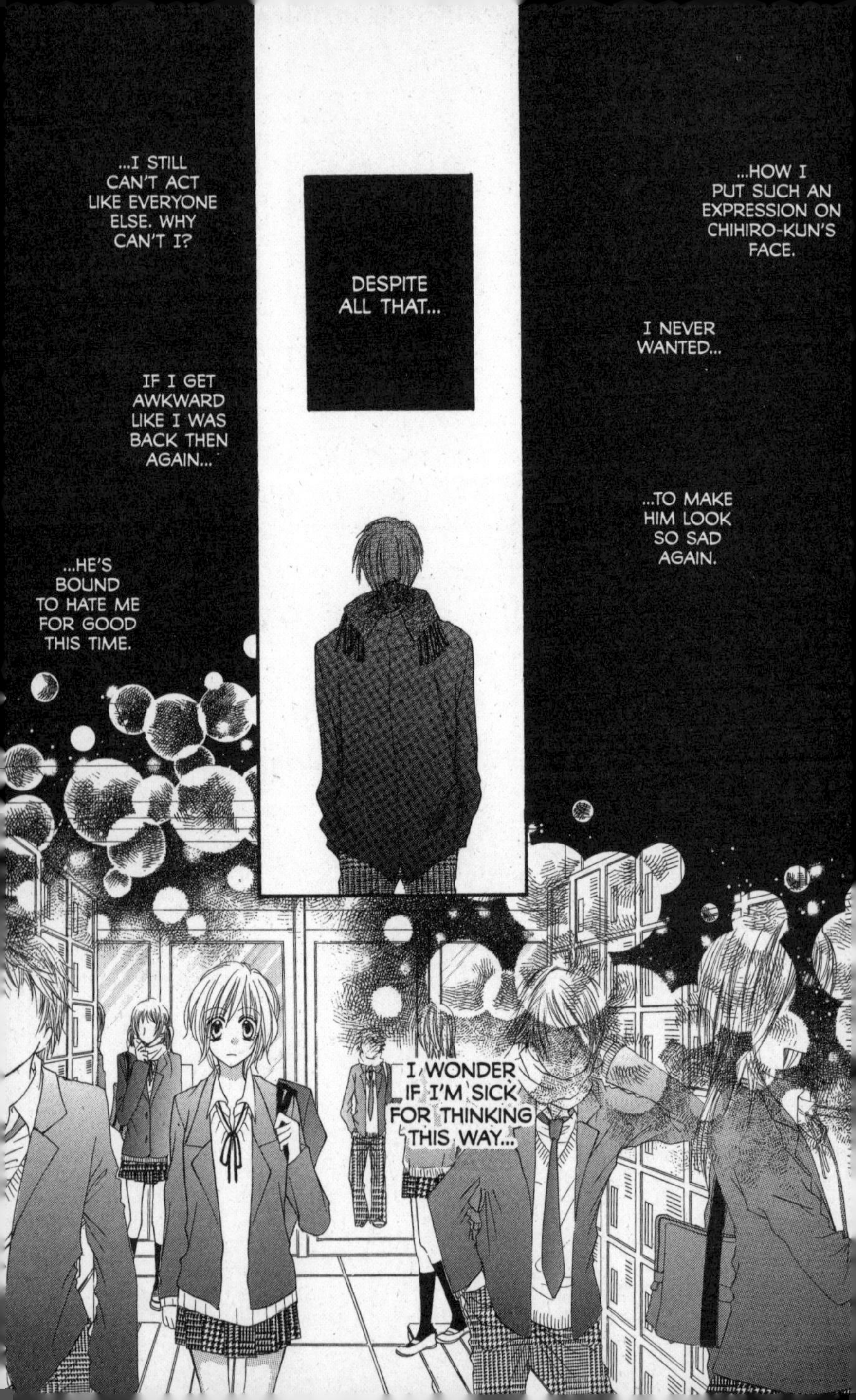
...HOW I PUT SUCH AN EXPRESSION ON CHIHIRO-KUN'S FACE.
I NEVER WANTED...
...TO MAKE HIM LOOK SO SAD AGAIN.
DESPITE ALL THAT...
...I STILL CAN'T ACT LIKE EVERYONE ELSE. WHY CAN'T I?
IF I GET AWKWARD LIKE I WAS BACK THEN AGAIN...
...HE'S BOUND TO HATE ME FOR GOOD THIS TIME.
I WONDER IF I'M SICK FOR THINKING THIS WAY...

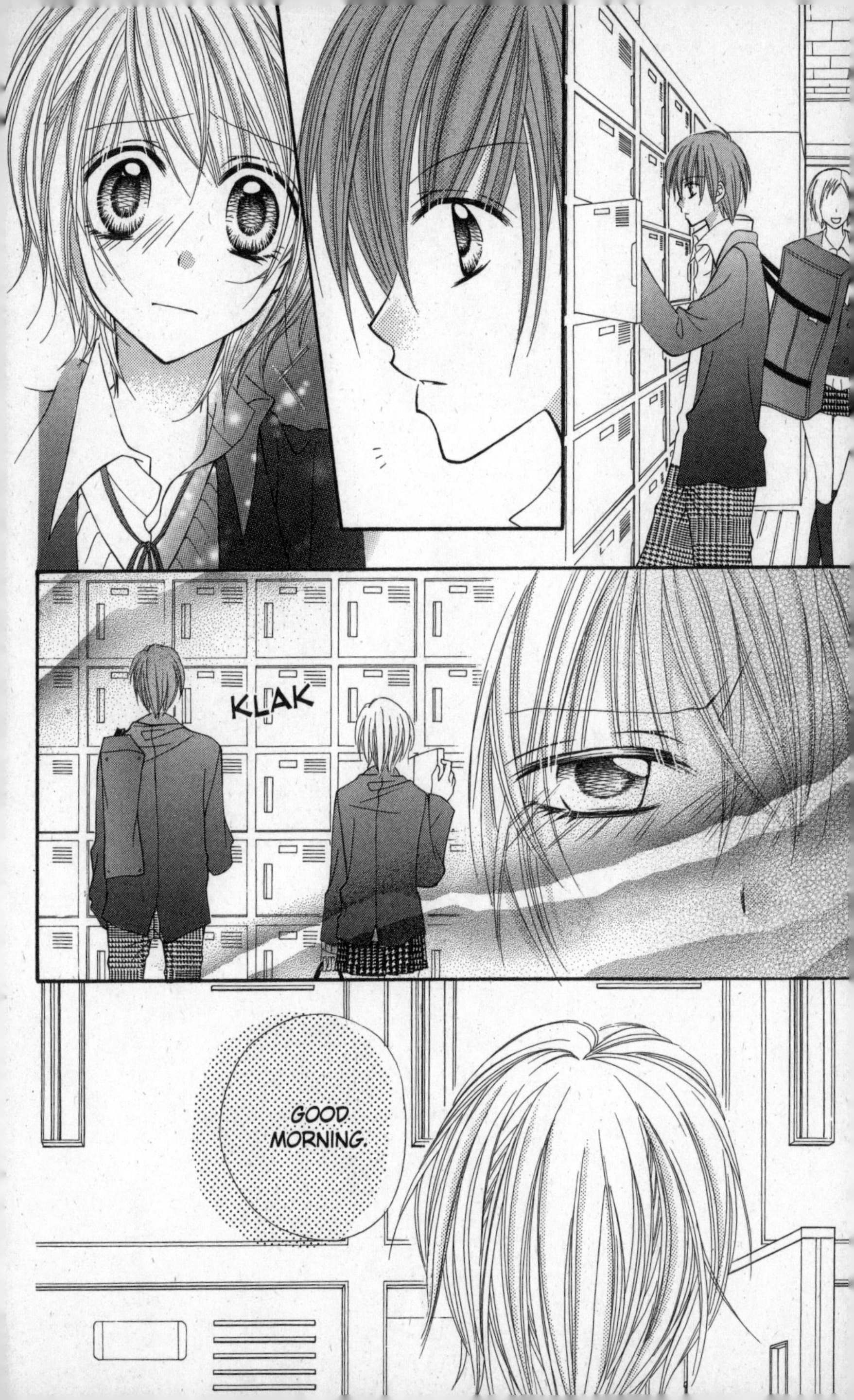
KLAK
GOOD MORNING.

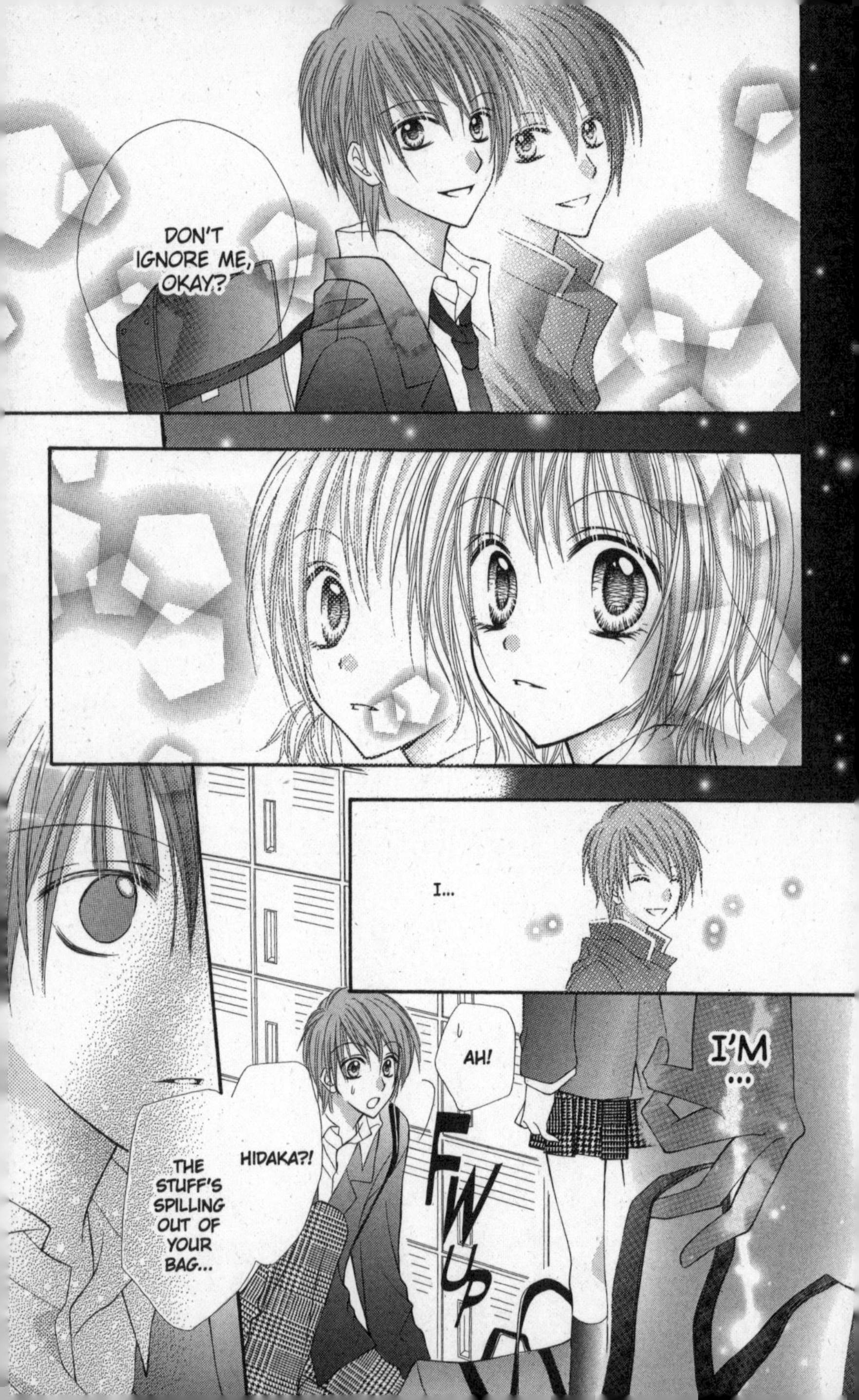
DON'T IGNORE ME, OKAY?
I...
I'M ...
AH!
FWUP
HIDAKA?!
THE STUFF'S SPILLING OUT OF YOUR BAG...

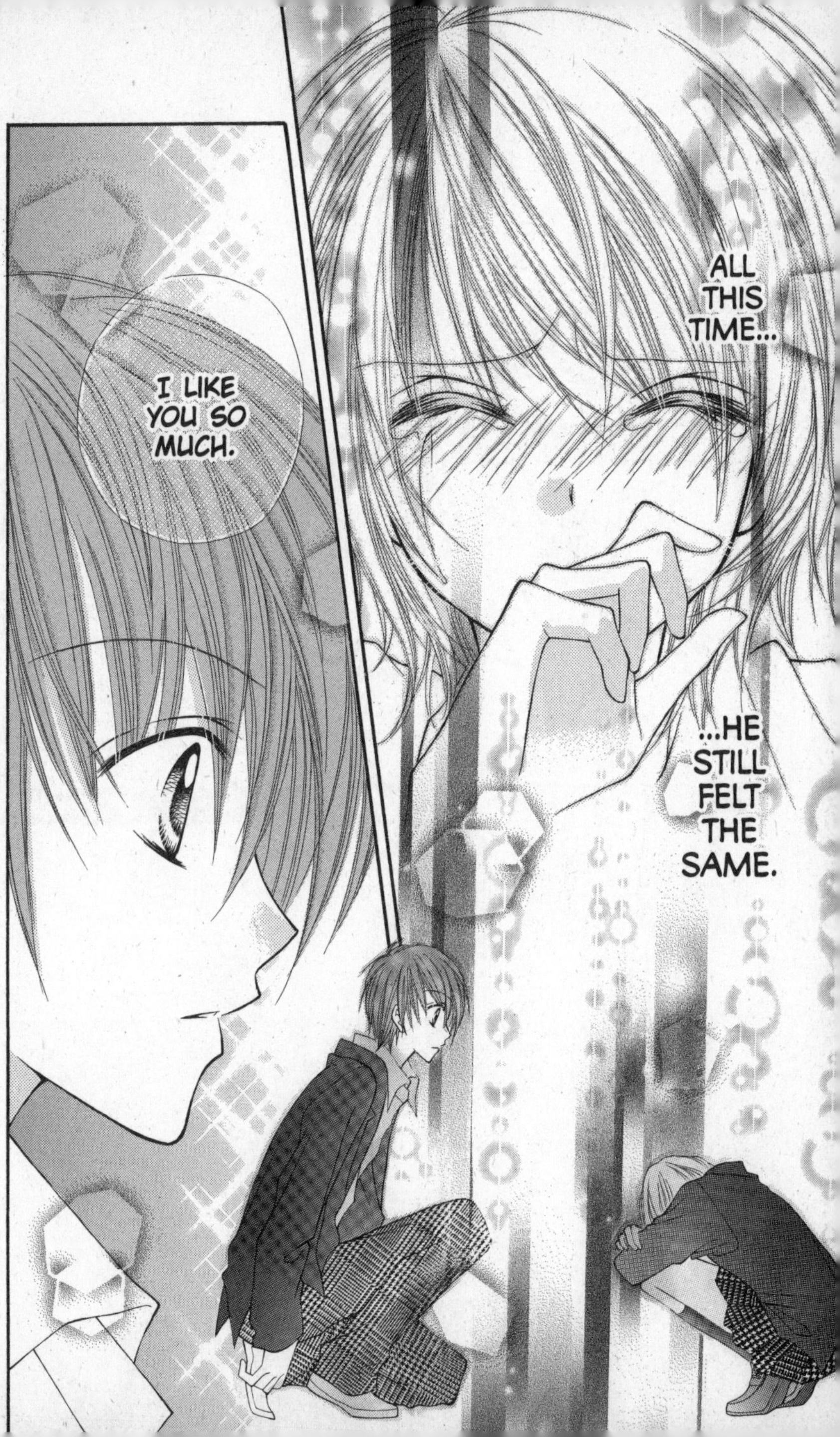
ALL THIS TIME...
...HE STILL FELT THE SAME.
I LIKE YOU SO MUCH.

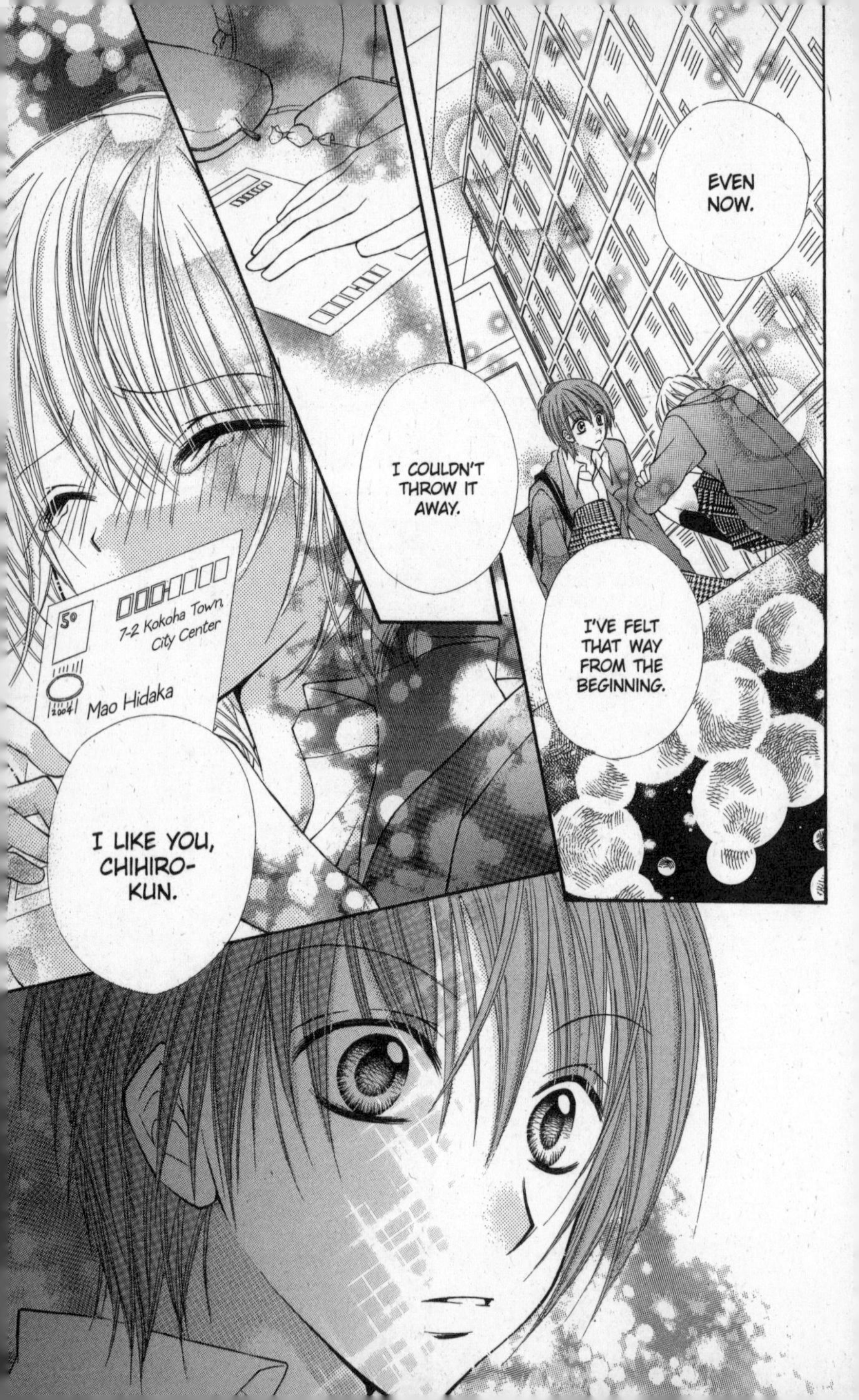
EVEN NOW.
I COULDN'T THROW IT AWAY.
I'VE FELT THAT WAY FROM THE BEGINNING.
5¢
7-2 Kokoha Town, City Center
Mao Hidaka
2004
I LIKE YOU, CHIHIRO-KUN.

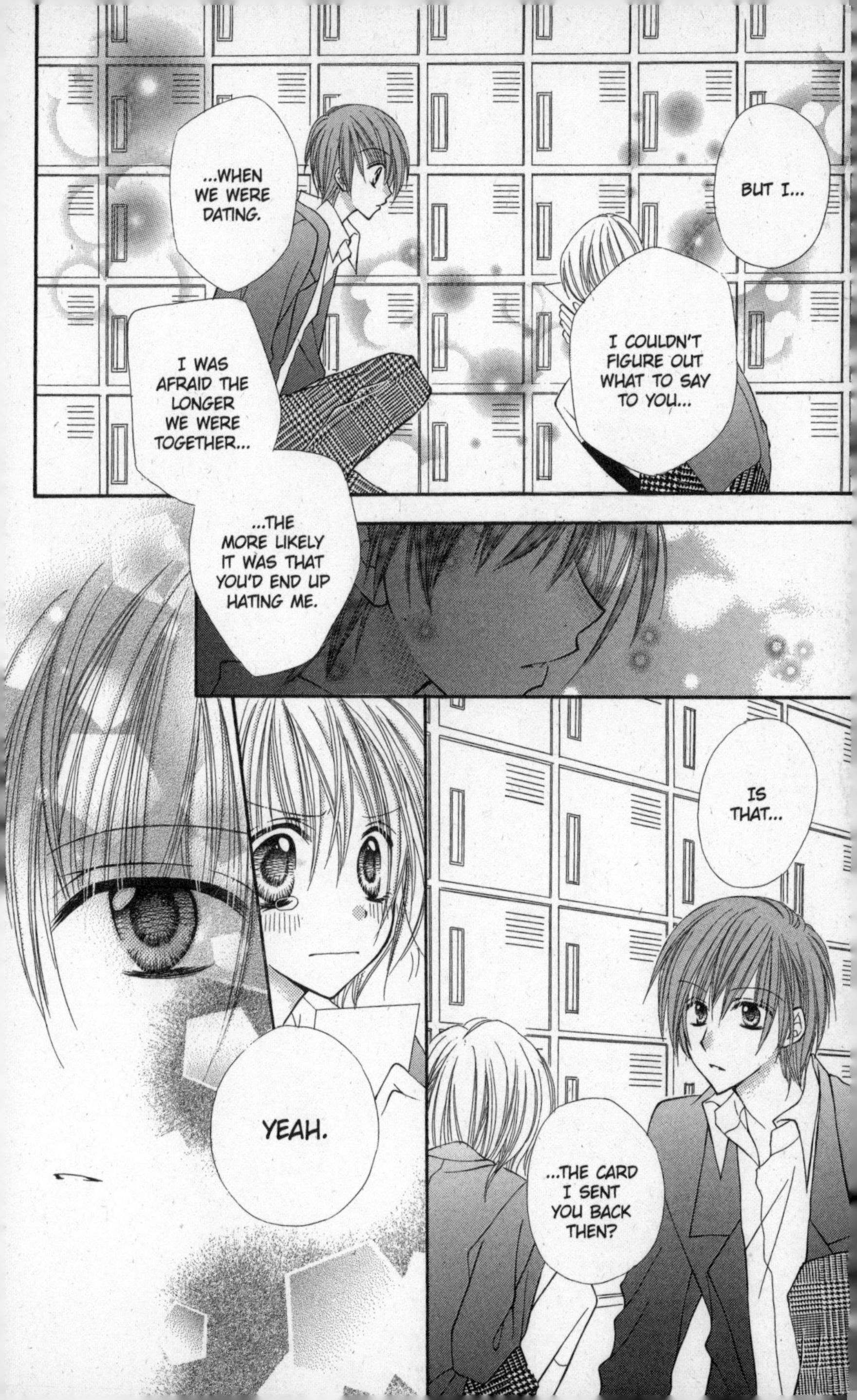
BUT I...
I COULDN'T FIGURE OUT WHAT TO SAY TO YOU...
...WHEN WE WERE DATING.
I WAS AFRAID THE LONGER WE WERE TOGETHER...
...THE MORE LIKELY IT WAS THAT YOU'D END UP HATING ME.
IS THAT...
...THE CARD I SENT YOU BACK THEN?
YEAH.

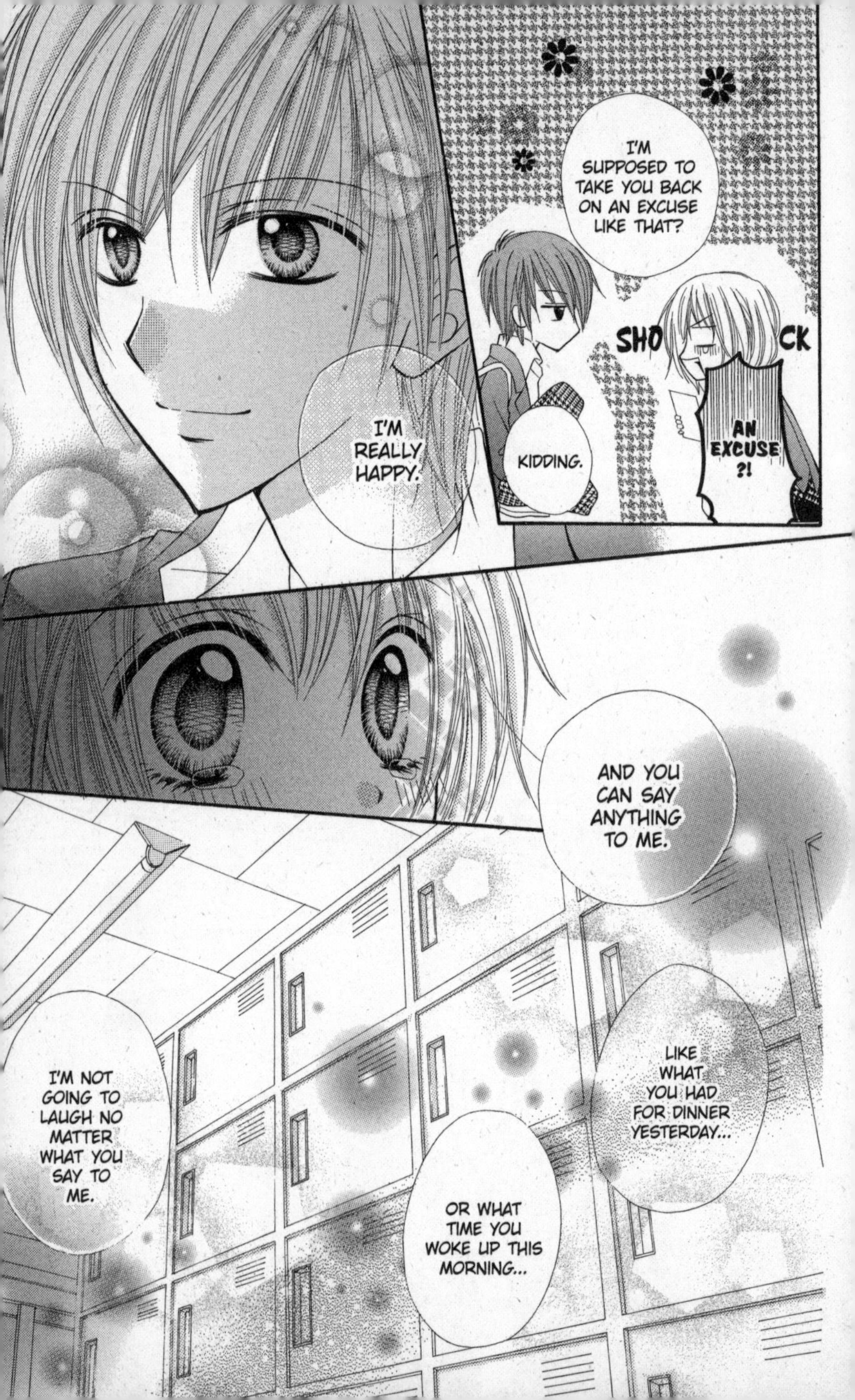
I'M SUPPOSED TO TAKE YOU BACK ON AN EXCUSE LIKE THAT?
SHOCK
AN EXCUSE ?!
KIDDING.
I'M REALLY HAPPY.
AND YOU CAN SAY ANYTHING TO ME.
LIKE WHAT YOU HAD FOR DINNER YESTERDAY...
OR WHAT TIME YOU WOKE UP THIS MORNING...
I'M NOT GOING TO LAUGH NO MATTER WHAT YOU SAY TO ME.

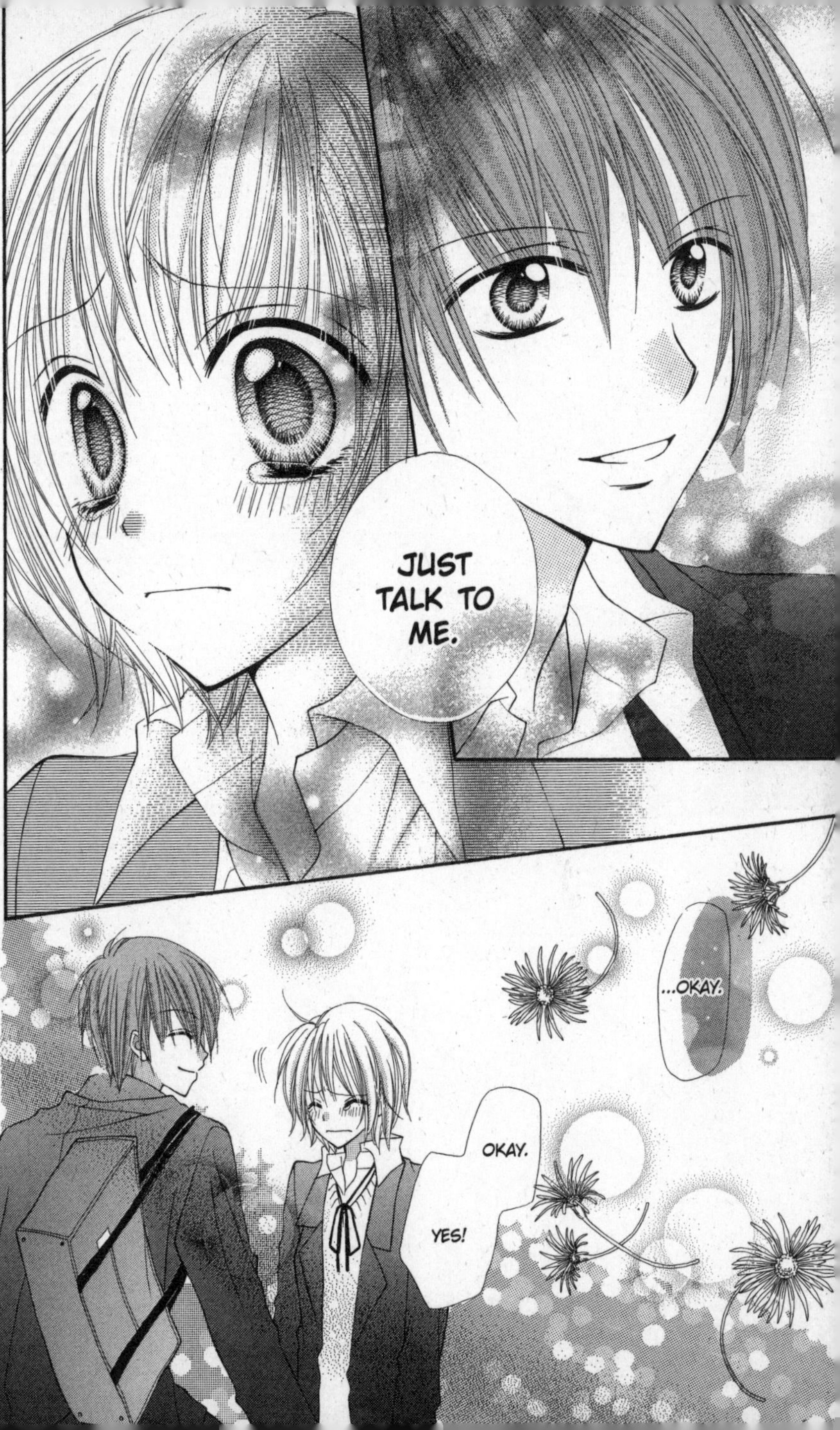
JUST TALK TO ME.
...OKAY.
OKAY.
YES!

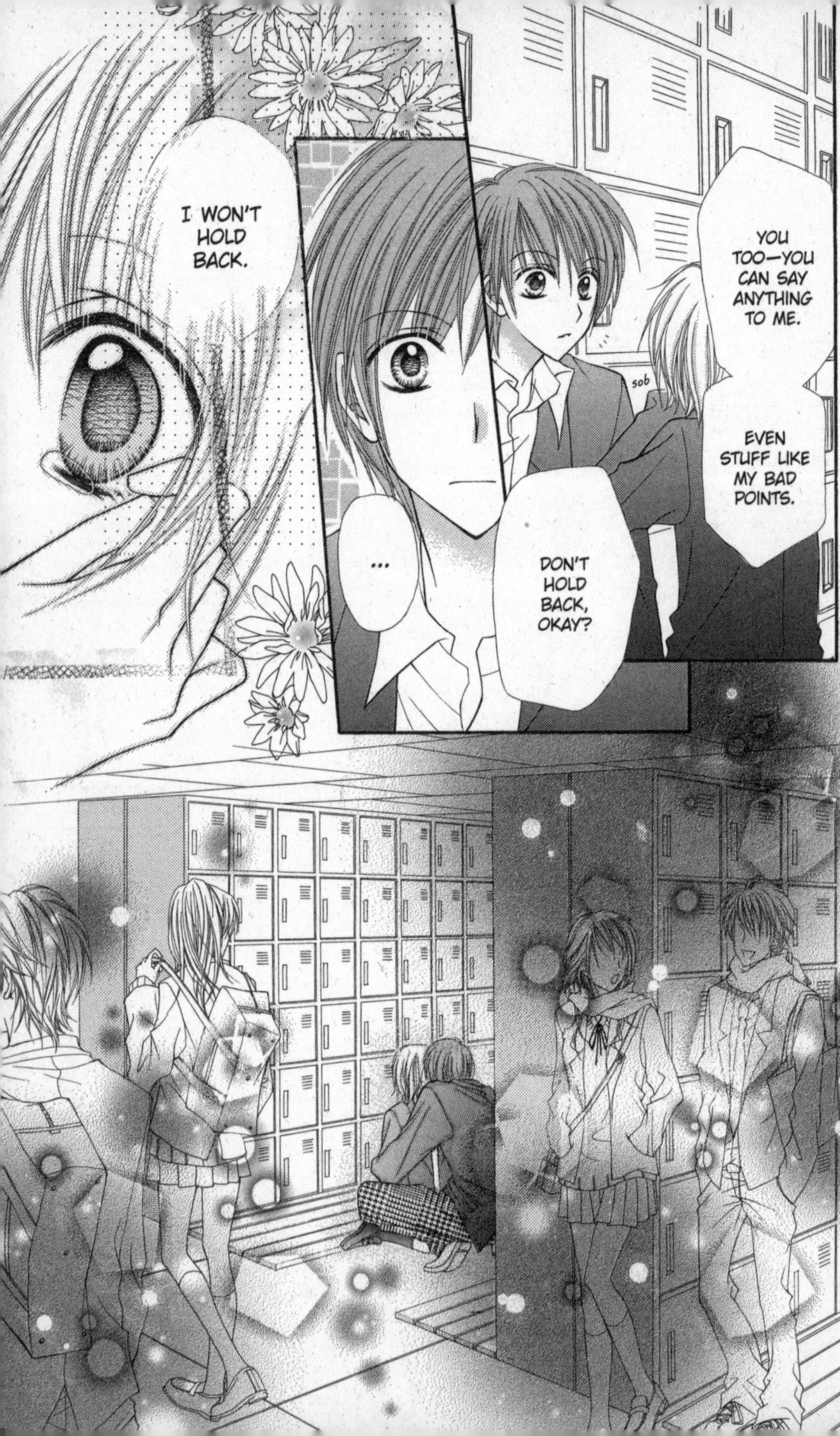
YOU TOO—YOU CAN SAY ANYTHING TO ME.
sob
EVEN STUFF LIKE MY BAD POINTS.
DON'T HOLD BACK, OKAY?
...
I WON'T HOLD BACK.

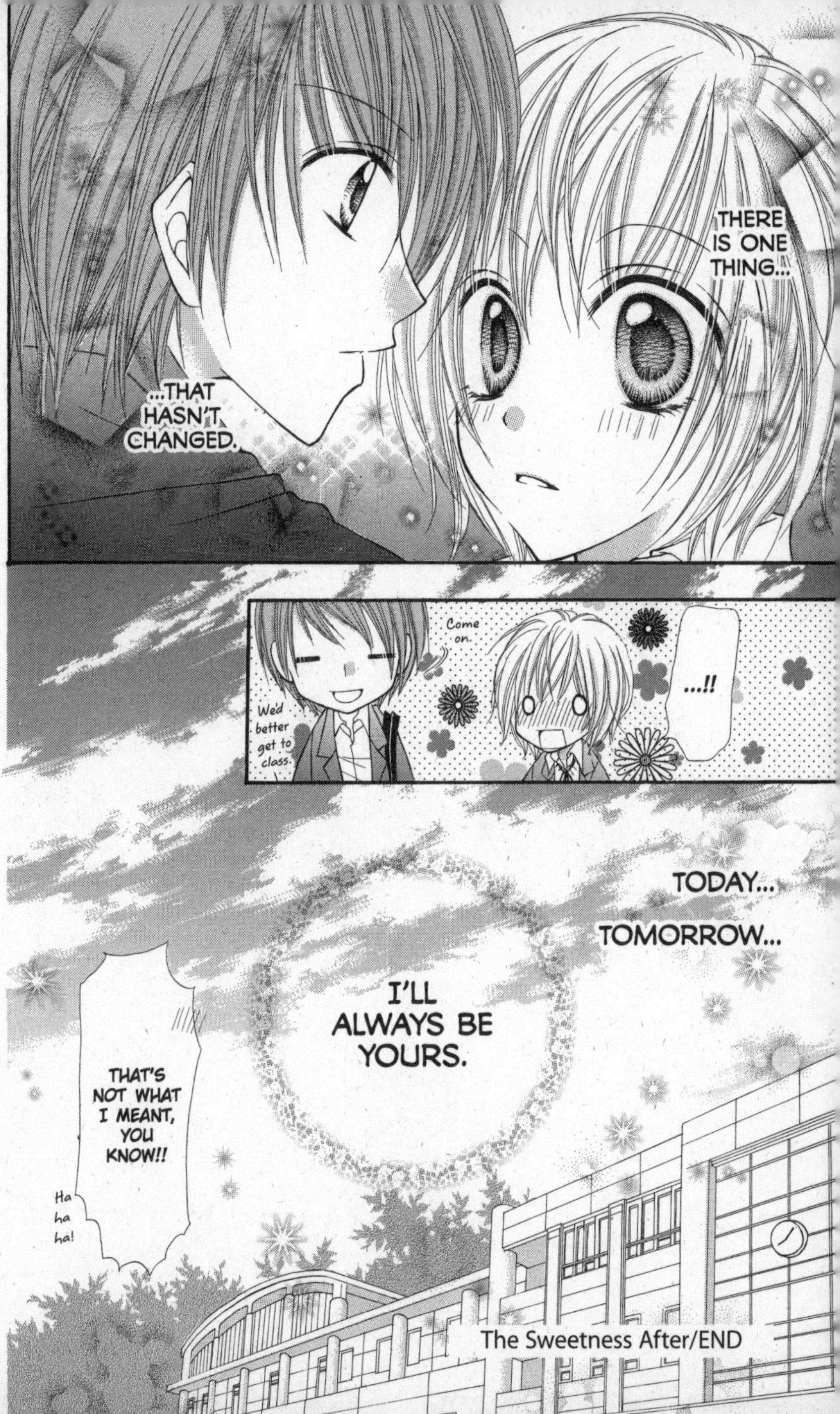
THERE IS ONE THING...
...THAT HASN'T CHANGED.
...!!
Come on.
We'd better get to class.
TODAY...
TOMORROW...
I'LL ALWAYS BE YOURS.
THAT'S NOT WHAT I MEANT, YOU KNOW!!
Ha ha ha!
The Sweetness After/END

BONUS SEC-TION

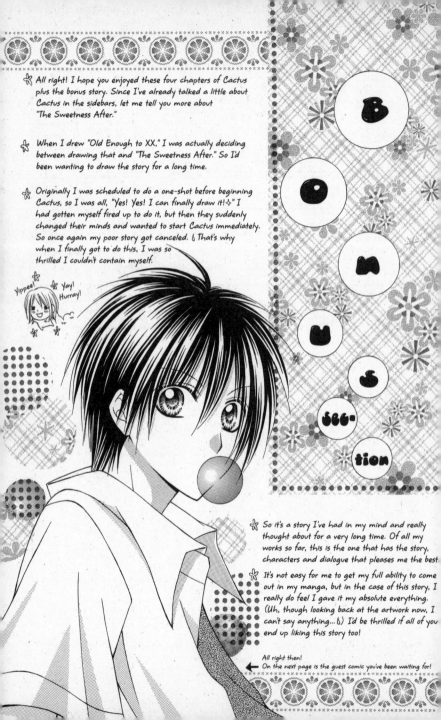

✿ All right! I hope you enjoyed these four chapters of *Cactus* plus the bonus story. Since I've already talked a little about *Cactus* in the sidebars, let me tell you more about "The Sweetness After."

✿ When I drew "Old Enough to XX," I was actually deciding between drawing that and "The Sweetness After." So I'd been wanting to draw the story for a long time.

✿ Originally I was scheduled to do a one-shot before beginning *Cactus*, so I was all, "Yes! Yes! I can finally draw it!✧" I had gotten myself fired up to do it, but then they suddenly changed their minds and wanted to start *Cactus* immediately. So once again my poor story got canceled. That's why when I finally got to do this, I was so thrilled I couldn't contain myself.

Yippee!
Yay! Hurray!

✿ So it's a story I've had in my mind and really thought about for a very long time. Of all my works so far, this is the one that has the story, characters and dialogue that pleases me the best.

✿ It's not easy for me to get my full ability to come out in my manga, but in the case of this story, I really do feel I gave it my absolute everything. (Uh, though looking back at the artwork now, I can't say anything...) I'd be thrilled if all of you end up liking this story too!

All right then!
← On the next page is the guest comic you've been waiting for!

Greetings from someone who owes Haruta-san a lot.

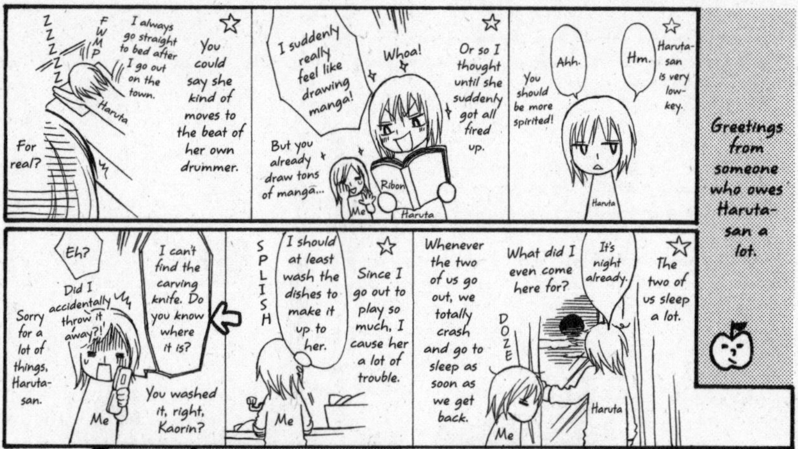
Haruta-san is very low-key.
Hm.
Ahh.
You should be more spirited!
Haruta
Or so I thought until she suddenly got all fired up.
Whoa!
I suddenly really feel like drawing manga!
But you already draw tons of manga...
Ribon
Haruta
Me
You could say she kind of moves to the beat of her own drummer.
I always go straight to bed after I go out on the town.
F W M P
Z Z Z Z Z
Haruta
For real?
The two of us sleep a lot.
It's night already.
What did I even come here for?
DOZE
Haruta
Me
Whenever the two of us go out, we totally crash and go to sleep as soon as we get back.
Since I go out to play so much, I cause her a lot of trouble.
I should at least wash the dishes to make it up to her.
SPLISH
Me
I can't find the carving knife. Do you know where it is?
You washed it, right, Kaorin?
Eh?
Did I accidentally throw it away?!
Sorry for a lot of things, Haruta-san.
Me

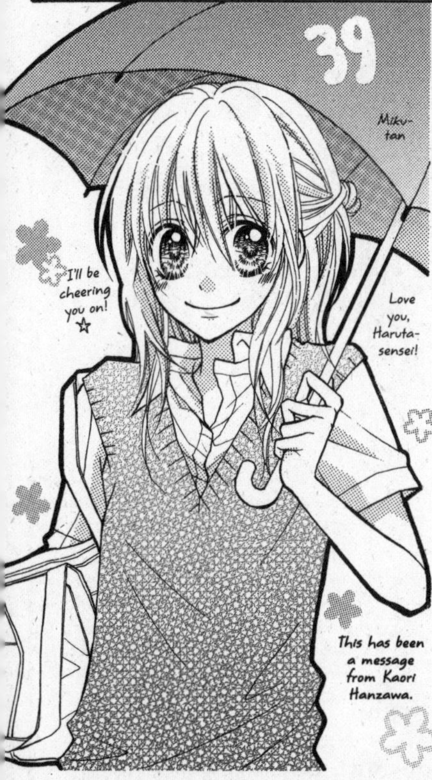
39
Miku-tan
I'll be cheering you on!
Love you, Haruta-sensei!
This has been a message from Kaori Hanzawa.

Today Haruta-san is visiting me at my place!

Our underlying goal for the visit was supposed to be for Haruta-san to teach me ways to improve my cooking, but before I knew it, I was doing all the cooking myself...

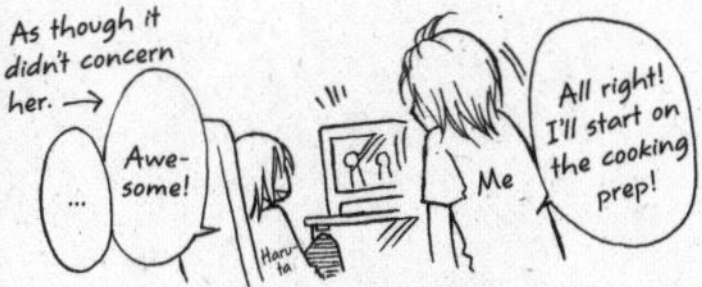
As though it didn't concern her. →
...
Awe-some!
Haruta
Me
All right! I'll start on the cooking prep!

You're no help at all!! (sob)

The two of us watched Yukorin's DVD just now. We were utterly captivated.

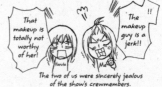

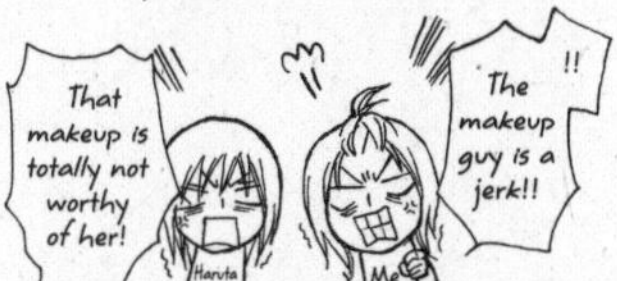
That makeup is totally not worthy of her!
Haruta
Me
The makeup guy is a jerk!!
!!

The two of us were sincerely jealous of the show's crewmembers.

Haruta-san and I are crazy about this girl. Ayaya is also like a master of cuteness too.

We were so fired up we tried doing some collaborative artwork of a "Yukorin-like character," but in the end we were like, "who is this?" (¯o¯;)

Still, the girl Haruta-san drew was insanely cute too. ♥♥♥

✿ That was by Kaori Hanzawa-san! Thank you so much!!

✿ But she drew me like a total airhead... Uh, though everything she said was pure fact. (laugh) But I really can't cook. Hanzawa-san prepared all the toppings for our okonomiyaki and then said, "At least do the grilling or something!" So I did, and for some reason, only mine came out undercooked.

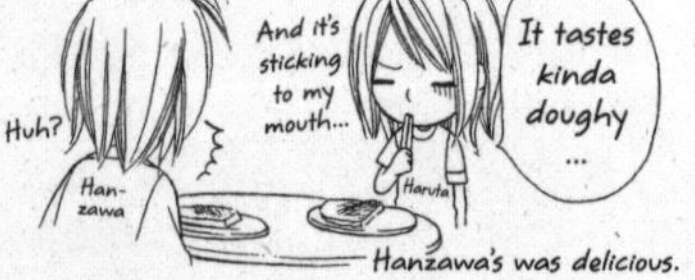
It tastes kinda doughy ...
And it's sticking to my mouth...
Huh?
Haruta
Hanzawa
Hanzawa's was delicious.

Even then I made her do too much for me, didn't I? Sorry about that! And thank you in advance for everything else you'll end up doing for me! ☆

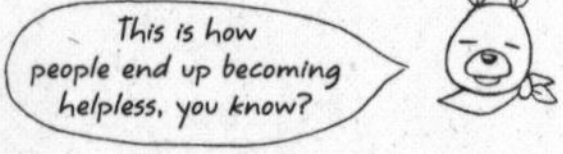
This is how people end up becoming helpless, you know?

✿ About this Yukorin DVD—I was at the store the previous day debating whether or not to buy it. I ended up not buying it so I was totally surprised when I got to Hanzawa-san's the next day and saw it there.

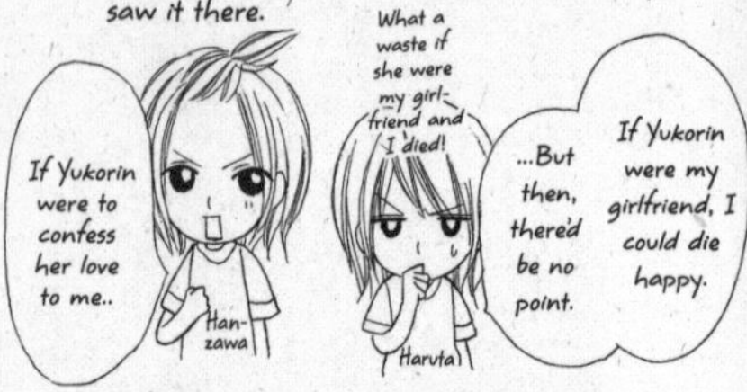
If Yukorin were my girlfriend, I could die happy.
...But then, there'd be no point.
What a waste if she were my girlfriend and I died!
If Yukorin were to confess her love to me..
Haruta
Hanzawa

We watched the whole DVD having very serious, "dangerous" discussions about virtual fantasies like that. Although it was all under the premise of "if we were guys," of course. (Like I said, completely virtual.) We're so bad!

✿ But sorry I'm a very low-spirited woman normally. And I'll make an announcement if we ever find that carving knife. Here's to hoping!

✿ With that, I'd like to end volume 3 of Cactus's Secret! Until we meet again!!

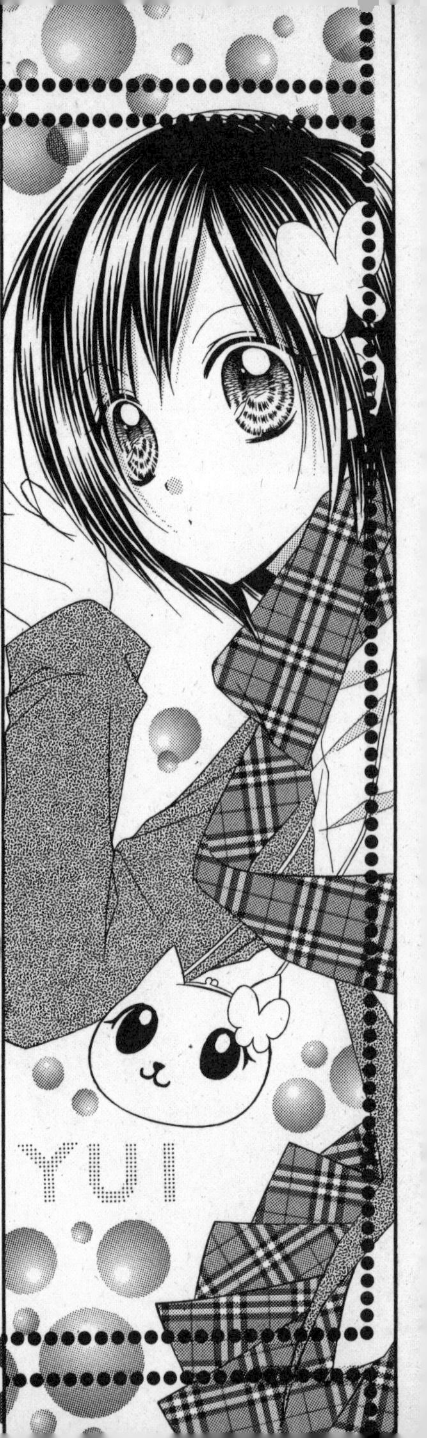
YUI

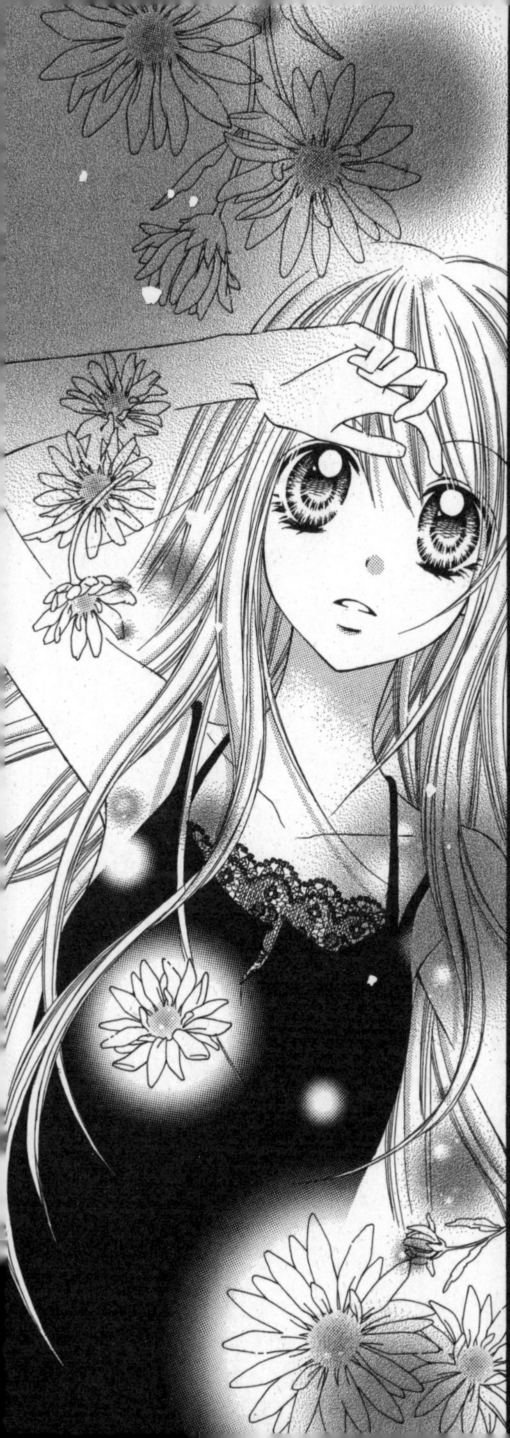

Special Thanks

M. Shinano
M. Umezawa
A. Ryui
S. Nakano
M. Yukimaru
R. Sawatari
R. Hayase
R. Outa
H. Nozaki
H. Moriwake
K. Hanzawa

and You!

Thank you for reading.

2005.5
Nana. Haruta

Notes

Honorifics

In Japan, people are usually addressed by their name plus a suffix. The suffix shows familiarity or respect, depending on the relationship.

MALE (familiar): first or last name + kun

FEMALE (familiar): first or last name + chan

ADULT (polite): last name + san

UPPERCLASSMAN (polite): last name + senpai

TEACHER or PROFESSIONAL: last name + sensei

CLOSE FRIENDS or LOVERS: first name only, no suffix

Terms

"Cavalry Battle" or *kibasen* is a battle where one person (the rider) is held up by three others (the horse) and tries to knock off riders on the opposing teams or steal the other riders' hats. Versions vary among schools.

Antonio Inoki is a popular Japanese wrestler known for his familiar battle cry.

The Kanto area is the region around Tokyo (central Honshu).

Niigata (where Haruta is from) is in northern Honshu.

"Yukorin" is a nickname for Yuko Ogura, a pinup model and idol.

Okonomiyaki is a Japanese dish resembling a thick pancake that has any variety of vegetables, meat, seafood or noodles mixed in.

The age of adulthood (when you can legally drink, smoke and vote) in Japan is 20.

Wasabi (horseradish) is a condiment for sushi.

In June of this year (2005), I will reach the age that many consider the beginning of adulthood, so I have decided to start behaving like an adult. First up, I'll have to learn to like wasabi. I don't think I can...

    -NANA HARUTA

Nana Haruta debuted in 2000 with *Ai no ♥ Ai no Shirushi* (Love's ♥, Love's Symbol) in *Ribon Original* magazine. She was born in Niigata Prefecture and likes reading manga and taking baths. Her other works include *Love Berrish!* and *Chocolate Cosmos*. Her current series, *Stardust ★ Wink*, is serialized in *Ribon* magazine.